EDITH WHARTON'S PRISONERS OF SHAME

Also by Lev Raphael

DANCING ON TISHA B'AV
THE DYNAMICS OF POWER (*co-author*)
STICK UP FOR YOURSELF! (*co-author*)

Edith Wharton's Prisoners of Shame

A New Perspective on Her Neglected Fiction

Lev Raphael

St. Martin's Press   New York

First published in the United States of America in 1991

Printed in Hong Kong

ISBN 0–312–05557–9

Library of Congress Cataloging-in-Publication Data
Raphael, Lev.
Edith Wharton's prisoners of shame : a new perspective on her
neglected fiction / Lev Raphael.
    p.   cm.
Includes bibliographical references and index.
ISBN 0–312–05557–9
1. Wharton, Edith, 1862–1937—Criticism and interpretation.
I. Title.
PS3545.H16Z87 1991
813′.52—dc20   90–21945
                                                          CIP

For Kris Lauer

'. . . beside him was that other consciousness which seemed an extension of his own, in which every inspiration, as it came, instantly rooted and flowered, and every mistake withered and dropped out of sight.'

Hudson River Bracketed

'. . . in the innermost room. . . the soul sits alone and waits for a footstep that never comes.'

'The Fullness of Life', 1891

'. . . the change and movement carry me along, help to form an outer surface. But the mortal desolation is there, will always be there.'

Edith Wharton to Sara Norton, 18 November 1908

'We're all imprisoned, of course – '

'Autre Temps. . .', 1913

Contents

Preface

With the explosion of Wharton criticism over the last fifteen years, Wharton has at last, one hopes, emerged from the shadow of Henry James as a major American writer who deserves critical attention in her own right for unique social and psychological insights. But critics are still limiting their work to a small range of books and issues,[1] continuing the decades-long neglect of novels and novellas that have been almost abandoned by scholars. Her novels after 1920, for example, are still generally held to be melodramatic, shrill, unrealistic, shallow, sentimental – judgments made during her lifetime but not adequately challenged in recent years except by Margaret McDowell and Carol Wershoven. Among those later books are at least two of her strongest, I contend.

In studying Wharton's work and life, critics have completely neglected the impact of the affect of shame as a source of defeat, indignity and transgression. What is offered here is an entirely new perspective on a body of Wharton's fiction that has been seriously undervalued and neglected. This study draws on recent discoveries in the psychology of emotion, most notably Dr Silvan Tomkins' affect theory, to examine Wharton's fiction from a fresh angle. It is only through the application of affect theory that we can both appreciate Wharton's neglected fiction as generally far superior than previous critics have acknowledged, and fully comprehend decisions of her characters that have been misinterpreted, or dismissed as artistically unconvincing and flawed.

Affect theory has a markedly different view of human motivation than psychoanalytic thought, which has shaped literary criticism in general, and the psychological criticism of Wharton in particular. Tomkins considers *affect* to be the primary innate biological motivating mechanism, more urgent than drive deprivation and more urgent than even pain. This revolutionary idea, already transforming psychological theory, holds great possibilities for new insight into Wharton's fiction.

One of the major themes in her work that has received consistent exploration is, in Blake Nevius' phrase, that of 'wasteful submission': a noble spirit subjecting itself to a meaner one.[2] The causes of Wharton's characters' defeat in this way have almost uniformly been theorized as *exterior* to them – in egotistical men, a repressive and sexist society, or in irrational fate.[3] Shame is a key to those defeats, and one finds it playing an important role in Wharton's fiction from her earliest short stories and novellas onward.

Exploring the role of shame explains works that have been widely considered to be 'fragmentary' or 'melodramatic' – like *Sanctuary* and *The Mother's Recompense* – and offers a much needed reassessment of the universally and rather unfairly derided *The Glimpses of the Moon*. Examining shame, and its most intense form, humiliation, brings new light to those characters of Wharton's who have been too easily classified and thus dismissed – Stephen Glennard in *The Touchstone*, George Darrow in *The Reef*, Martin Boyne in *The Children*. While the neglected works under examination here vary in quality – *The Marne* is certainly a weaker work than *A Son at the Front* (but both deserve more attention than they have received) – all have suffered from a lack of appreciation or insight because critics have not seen that so many of Wharton's characters were, as she was, imprisoned by shame.

The theory offered here is by no means a global one. My aim is not to prove that shame is central to every single piece of fiction Wharton wrote, but rather to demonstrate that in certain cases the failure to recognize the centrality of shame has led to inappropriate evaluations and mistaken interpretations of a number of Wharton's novels and novellas. Shame is also an important, little understood dynamic of her personality, and as such, deserves attention for that reason alone. An understanding of the dynamics and impact of shame can also deepen our appreciation of Wharton's classics: *The House of Mirth, Ethan Frome, Summer, The Custom of the Country,* and *The Age of Innocence*.

This study is offered at a time when shame is receiving growing national attention. The American Psychiatric Association presented seminars on shame in 1987 and 1988, and several new books on shame have recently been published. There is a spreading sense among psychologists that shame has been a missing link in our understanding of many psychological phenomena, leading some researchers to suggest that shame may be 'the most frequent and possibly the most important of emotions. . .'[4] The first international conference on shame was held in California in December, 1988, and an information network of scholars in the humanities and social sciences who are studying shame has recently been established.

I owe my own understanding of the impact and phenomenology of shame to Gershen Kaufman of Michigan State University, whose books I have found professionally and personally enlightening. He has also deepened and clarified my understanding of Tomkins' seminal work, and has been remarkably generous with his time in reading various drafts of my previously published work on Wharton, and all versions of this study. His careful reading and his warm encouragement have made writing this book consistently enjoyable.

I had the great good fortune to study Wharton with Cynthia Griffin Wolff at the University of Massachusetts at Amherst, just before her brilliant *A Feast of Words* was published. Dr Wolff was the ideal professor: probing, provocative, mesmerizing, good-humored and unfailingly witty and human. The students in her graduate Wharton seminar glowed after each class and talked excitedly about it for days. *A Feast of Words*, which demonstrates so profound an understanding and love of Wharton's fiction, is indispensible for students of Wharton.

Kristin Olson Lauer, my mentor at Fordham University, and co-author of Garland Press's Wharton bibliography, has been a consistent source of inspiration, information, and common sense at every point in this project. A true Wharton scholar, she has frequently directed my attention to articles and reviews I might otherwise have missed, and our discussions of Wharton and shame have been enormously helpful and stimulating. Her critical insights have helped shape all my published work on Wharton, and she and Gershen Kaufman have been my enthusiastic but always demanding first audience. Their input has been invaluable in helping me sharpen and clarify my ideas.

Sections of Chapters 1, 2, 3, 5 and the Appendix originally appeared in *The Journal of Evolutionary Psychology, Massachusetts Studies in English, The University of Mississippi Studies in English Studies in the Humanities,* and *American Imago* and are reprinted with the permission of the editors, and Wayne State University Press. Quotations from Edith Wharton's 'Life and I' and the 'Beatrice Palmato' fragment appear with the permission of William Royall Tyler.

Introduction

The last decade and a half has witnessed an extraordinary revival of interest in Edith Wharton's life and work: R. W. B. Lewis's Pulitzer Prize-winning biography, *Edith Wharton* (1975), surely began this resurgence of attention by discussing the sexual frigidity of the Whartons' marriage and even more, perhaps, by exploring the liberating impact upon her of a passionate love affair that began in her mid-forties. My own book, *A Feast of Words: The Triumph of Edith Wharton* (1976), explored the impact of early emotional impoverishment upon her writing and introduced an extensive investigation of the specific dilemmas that Edith Jones Wharton encountered as an American girl – and woman – who was determined to become a major novelist. Both Lewis's work and my own drew heavily upon the standard theory of ego development, and this Eriksonian model permitted a suggestive understanding of the persistent, shaping legacies of Edith Wharton's earliest life – a lack of basic trust and a stifling sense of guilt. Yet the Eriksonian model is essentially neutral with regard to both gender and class: it does not allow for certain kinds of generalization. Thus one cannot extract from the Eriksonian model any prediction that all *females* will be at greater 'hazard' than males in developing a 'healthy' adult identity – or that in some surroundings, the very social mores that serve to 'define' adulthood might also be psychologically 'crippling' in one way or another to a healthy adult identity. It is not that such observations were impossible before (indeed, they have been made) – and not that, to some extent, they were not intuitively obvious; it is, however, the case that standard ego-psychology does not offer a model that could be employed to analyze or explain such phenomena. Thus, useful as this model might be, the inferences that one can draw from it have been necessarily limited.

This study of Wharton's fiction by Lev Raphael is provocative in many ways; however, perhaps its most significant contribution to our understanding of this author and her work is announced in the title: it offers the reader a *'New Perspective'*. Using the insights of a recently-developed school of emotional investigation, 'the psychology of *shame'*, Lev Raphael suggests an entirely new model –

one that is not inconsistent with the earlier, Eriksonian model, but which permits of broader and richer inferences.

Shame is essentially interpersonal: it is the effect of emotional injury, defeat, humiliation, and derisive isolation when one or more of these experiences has become internalized. Thus a person will experience *shame* whenever convinced that she or he has *been seen* in a painfully diminished way. If embarrassment is an essentially public and social experience, shame is its emotional equivalent; an individual who experiences shame feels intolerably exposed to the derisive criticism of others. It is true, as Raphael demonstrates in any number of painstakingly careful analyses of character, that an adult is capable of experiencing shame even when entirely alone, for the self is capable of anticipating the ridicule of others and cringing at this expectation itself. However, even the isolated experience has its interpersonal component; for we 'see' ourselves as we suppose others would 'see' us if they were present, and it is this sense of being (inescapably) both observed and severely censured that combine to forge the intolerable shackles of shame.

The most usual response is predictably social: we flush; we avert our gaze. Most of all, we seek to hide – either by withdrawing or by employing any number of inventive modes of camouflage.

Using insights from the psychology of shame, Lev Raphael is able to throw a brilliant new light on Edith Wharton and her fictions. His readings of *The Touchstone* and *The Children* are richly illuminating, and his analysis of *The Reef* suggests important new ways to read that much-examined and widely-admired work (allowing us for the first time, perhaps, to understand the reasons for Edith Wharton's own deeply ambivalent attitude toward the novel). Equally compelling is Raphael's introduction of new issues into Wharton's scholarship: for example, Wharton's tendency to write about 'artists who have failed' (a puzzling feature of the work given Edith Wharton's own early and abundant success) becomes an interesting and comprehensible element of the fiction under Raphael's skillful analysis.

Yet the implications of this book go well beyond any isolated observation or single reading. Because this mode of psychology allows the reader to examine the consequences of introjecting *social interactions*, it introduces us to methods that can be used to address a wide range of issues. Why might *the progress of* writing and publishing itself be more difficult for women than for men (that is, why might potential issues of shame be gender-linked)? What effect might Wharton's social standing have had upon her depiction of romantic relationships (that is, why might issues of shame, especially those related to sexuality, be *class-linked*)?

Readers who have completed *Edith Wharton's Prisoners of Shame* may find it difficult to decide whether they chiefly admire Raphael's fine study for its many excellent particular insights or for his demonstration of this superb new model for criticism. In an age of multiplying theoretical modes, only a critical study of real value could be the cause of such a pleasant dilemma.

Cynthia Griffin Wolff
Belmont, Massachusetts

1

Edith Wharton's Touchstone

'It's the woman's soul, absolutely torn up by the roots – her whole self laid bare; and to a man who evidently didn't care; who couldn't have cared. I don't mean to read another line: it's too much like listening at a keyhole.'[1]

That is not the voice of a reviewer describing Edith Wharton's letters to Morton Fullerton, though it certainly could be. After all, when Allen Gribben edited twenty-six of these letters for a University of Texas monograph in 1985, he confessed to a certain embarrassment. Though Wharton had been dead for almost fifty years, he thought readers would 'wince' at the letters' intimate revelations.[2]

With the availability of R. W. B. and Nancy Lewis's carefully edited edition of Wharton's letters, there is now much to make even an insensitive reader wince. A terrible pall of futility hangs over Wharton's correspondence with Fullerton, so much of which Wharton felt was 'cast into the void.'[3] Her early rejoicing over the intellectual and physical communion with Fullerton is gradually overshadowed by 'recurring expressions of subservience.'[4] The dominant notes are her sense of unworthiness and being left to feel like 'a course served & cleared away!'[5] The letters painfully reveal a growing 'sense of passive helplessness,' as Wharton watches 'eagerly for [Fullerton's] letters. . . [waits] for him to resume their meetings, postpone them further, or cease them altogether.' Wharton's 'awesome writing skills were completely ineffectual at gaining what she most wanted: a rekindling of the delirious passion of those precious first months of mutual desire.'[6]

Wharton's correspondence with Fullerton is certainly the most compelling in the Lewises' edition of her letters, and its publication has signaled changes in Wharton criticism. One such change is the attention suddenly being paid to Wharton's first published novella, *The Touchstone*, from which the opening passage is quoted above. This book has never been highly esteemed by her critics,

1

and has not received a great deal of attention despite the Wharton revival of the last fifteen years. Critics have tended to 'place' it as setting up themes Wharton would later develop with far more depth and range: the influence of the dead on the living; the role of the intruder freeing a conventional man; the male character revealed to be inferior and shabby; the value of the social scheme.[7]

This novella, a story of a man who failed to love a brilliant woman novelist, and suffers after selling her love letters to him, now seems in some ways uncannily predictive of her subsequent affair with Fullerton. It was very much in the air at a recent Wharton Society meeting (Fall 1988), but its importance transcends the most obvious correlation with Wharton's mid-life affair which began some seven years after the novella was published.

The dynamic center of this novella is the 'affect' of shame and its most intense form, humiliation. Shame had appeared in various ways in Wharton's first published stories, in her first collection, *The Greater Inclination*, and in *Bunner Sisters* (written in 1892, published in 1916), but receives its most significant early treatment in *The Touchstone*. This novella is a key to understanding Wharton's neglected fiction, just as shame is a touchstone for understanding Wharton herself.

Stephen Glennard, the novella's protagonist, is driven by shame – he feels himself to be a lifelong failure, and when he tries to overcome those feelings, he plunges into a long nightmare of humiliation that almost destroys his marriage and his life. To afford marrying Alexa Trent, Glennard sells the love letters he received from the novelist, Margaret Aubyn – now dead – a woman he couldn't love and felt inferior to. He hopes that selling the letters will help him become a success and *feel* like one, but the sale only partially fulfills his expectations. Published, Aubyn's letters become wildly popular, and as the unknown recipient, Glennard is excoriated for being unfeeling: he didn't love her; he sold the letters. He is unable to tell his wife he was the man unable to love the brilliant and sensitive Aubyn, because she too pities and criticizes Aubyn's correspondent. Glennard's torment grows as he feels more and more distant from his wife, and paradoxically comes to realize how great his loss was in not having been able to love Aubyn. Glennard's private failings become agonizingly public, and his prior sense of shame is deepened and magnified into pervasive and continuing humiliation. He becomes consumed by shame, attempts to fight it, and we are meant to feel at the end that Aubyn's influence has made him a better man, and deepened his relationship with his wife.

To fully understand the role of shame and *The Touchstone's* importance in Wharton's canon, we first need to start from an entirely new perspective. Previous psychological discussions of Wharton's work, however brilliant and provocative, have consistently overlooked shame. That is not suprising, since psychologists are only now beginning to recognize that shame plays a vital and often dominant role in personality and interpersonal relations. It is indeed currently being referred to as the 'keystone' or 'master' affect,[8] but shame's very ubiquity has made it difficult to recognize that so common a feeling can profoundly affect our lives.[9]

Silvan Tomkins is the pioneer in understanding the importance of shame in human motivation, and his affect theory is the foundation of all contemporary research on emotion.[10] Unlike psychoanalytic theory, which organizes human experience around innately unfolding primordial drives, affect theory organizes human behavior and development around an entirely different though related motivational system: the affect system. Tomkins does not view human beings as a battleground for imperious drives that urge them blindly on to pleasure and violence, contained only by a repressive society and its internalizations – the ego and super-ego. For Tomkins, *affect* is the primary innate biological motivating mechanism; 'without its amplification, nothing else matters, and with its amplification, anything else can matter. It thus combines urgency and generality. It lends its power to memory, to perception, to thought, and to action no less than to the drives.'[11] Tomkins defines 'affects' as

> sets of muscular, glandular, and skin receptor responses located in the face (and also widely distributed throughout the body) that generate sensory feedback to a system that finds them inherently 'acceptable' or 'unacceptable.' These organized sets of responses are triggered at subcortical centers where specific 'programs' are stored, programs that are innately endowed and have been genetically inherited.

When activated, these programs can simultaneously capture 'the face, the heart, and the endocrine glands and [impose] on them a specific pattern of correlated responses.'[12]

According to Tomkins, affect is more urgent than drive deprivation or even pain. Such a conclusion is not obvious when one considers the urgency of drives like hunger, or the need to breathe, or the importunities of sexual desire. Deprived of air, for example, one becomes terrified, but Tomkins explains that 'this terror is in no way part of the drive mechanism.'[13] One can become equally terrified by the fear of being caught in a fire or of contracting a fatal disease. In Tomkins' view, affects provide 'the primary blueprints for cognition, decision and action':

> Humans are responsive to whatever circumstances activate the varieties of positive and negative affects. Some of these circumstances innately activate the affects. At the same time the affect system is also capable of being instigated by learned stimuli and responses. The human being is thus urged by nature and by nurture to explore and to attempt to control the circumstances that evoke. . . positive and negative affective responses.[14]

Of the nine affects that Tomkins has identified, 'shame strikes deepest into the heart.'[15] An innate response to any perceived barrier to positive affect, shame is the affect of indignity, defeat, transgression and alienation. Shame is innately activated by the partial reduction of the positive affects (for example, joy); whenever an individual's expectations and needs are disappointed, shame is activated. Whether an individual has been shamed by self-mockery or the derisive laughter of others, that person feels naked and 'lacking in dignity or worth.'[16] Feeling shame, one immediately reduces communication with others by lowering one's eyes, face and neck, 'producing a head hung in shame.'[17]

Tomkins makes the important observation that shame, discouragement, shyness, embarrassment and guilt are *phenomenologically* the identical affect. It is because their causes and consequences differ that they result in different overall experiences. What we typically call guilt, for instance, is actually shame over a moral transgression, shyness is shame in the presence of strangers, and guilt is immorality shame. Psychologists have not grasped that underlying biological unity, with this result: 'The importance of the individual's struggles with his shame, the incessant effort to vanquish or come to terms with the alienating affect, his surrenders, transient or chronic, have too often been disregarded.'[18]

The underlying connection between shame and guilt is an important one and especially relevant in discussing Wharton's fiction. Critics sometimes mention her characters' 'guilt', but not in ways that yield much insight. Marilyn French, for instance, describes Kate Clephane's renunciation of happiness in *The Mother's Recompense*[19] as caused by guilt, when the emotional realities in that novel are far more complex, as will be discussed in Chapter 2. French uses the term 'guilt' as if every reader will know exactly what she means. Tomkins offers a much richer language for differentiating inner events at the more fundamental level of affect, whereas most psychologists have remained stuck in distinguishing guilt *from* shame. Guilt also has been used to refer ambiguously to many different experiences, which Tomkins is able to differentiate because working from the perspective of the affect system partitions inner events precisely. These ambiguous 'guilt states' include shame about moral matters, self-disgust for moral infractions, anger, distress or fear for moral infractions, any combination of these affects and judgments against the self by the self, or any of these negative affects and judgments experienced as coming from an 'internalized other' toward the self.

For our purposes here, it is important to keep in mind that the guilt Wharton's characters experience is rooted primarily in shame, and is not so very different, *at the level of affect*. When Wharton's heroes and heroines transgress or violate an accepted moral code, for instance, the affect experienced, expressed and described is invariably that of shame. When Wharton's characters are struggling with guilt, embarrassment, shyness, or failure, they are experiencing the affect of shame in a particular and distinctive context. While the meaning of the overall experience is somewhat different, the core affect present is nonetheless the same. The language of shame will be far more present in her fiction than specific references to guilt, and that language will be matched by facial and bodily responses, as we will see in discussing the novels, novellas and stories included here.

It is appropriate at this point to bring up the question of 'shame cultures' versus 'guilt cultures', a much-discussed distinction. As far back as 1953, the anthropologist Milton B. Singer pointed out that in 'comparative study of cultures it has become practically axiomatic to classify them into shame cultures and guilt cultures.'[20] Singer however found the distinction far less meaningful than it was generally considered, for a number of reasons. He observed that though the 'prevailing criterion for distinguishing shame and guilt cultures has been the distinction between external and internal sanctions' the distinction was confusing, in part because 'there are "inner" forms of shame paralleling almost exactly the forms of guilt.'[21] Psychometric data used to prove the distinction, he wrote, were plagued by the problems of cross-cultural differences. Singer also found that characterizing cultures psychologically produced comparisons 'of low validity because [such comparisons] seek to isolate "pure" psychological categories.' Singer additionally observed that there was insufficient evidence for the prevailing views of guilt cultures as more advanced than shame cultures: 'What evidence there is, tends to support the conclusion that the sense of guilt *and* the sense of shame are found in most cultures, and that the quantitative distribution of these sanctions has little to do with the "progressive" or "backward" character of a culture.'[22]

Gershen Kaufman's recent books (1985, 1989)[23] extend Tomkins' work by examining the developmental, interpersonal, intrapsychic and social dimensions of shame. Kaufman views shame along a continuum, and argues that in moderate doses, it has vital positive effects. 'The optimal development of conscience,' Kaufman observes, 'depends on adequate and appropriately graded doses of shame.' Shame also motivates 'the eventual correction of social indignities.'[24] When shame becomes magnified, however, it can dominate the personality and result in emotional crippling. Kaufman defines shame phenomenologically as feeling

> *seen* in a painfully diminished sense. Shame reveals the inner self, exposing it to view. The self feels exposed both to itself and to anyone else present. That exposure can be of the self *to* the self alone, or it can be of the self to others. Central to an understanding of the alienating affect is that shame can be an entirely *internal* experience. No one else need be present in order for shame to be felt, but when others are present shame is an impediment to further communication. . . Shame is felt as an interruption. . . In the midst of shame, the attention turns inward, thereby generating the torment of self-consciousness. *Sudden, unexpected exposure* coupled with *binding inner scrutiny* characterize the essential nature of the affect of shame [my emphasis]. Whether all eyes are upon us or only our own, we feel fundamentally deficient as individuals, diseased, defective.[25]

Though shame is innately activated by the incomplete reduction of positive affect, Kaufman sees the largest sources of activators as the learned and the interpersonal. The basic way in which shame is generated is when one significant person 'somehow breaks the interpersonal bridge with another.'[26] Originating between parent and child (and later linking any two individuals), this bridge is the emotional bond which enables the child to experience a sense of belonging and security. It can be severed through being disappointed, blamed, mistreated, ridiculed, disparaged, ignored.

The alienating and isolating effect of shame on the self is not enough 'to explain the significance of shame as a central motive in human development and interpersonal relations.' When shame is *internalized*, it 'becomes autonomous. . . and hence impervious to change.'[27] Kaufman observes that 'we internalize [through identification] not only what is said about us, but the ways in which we are treated by significant others.' We thus 'learn to treat ourselves according to the way we are treated by those significant to us, thereby continuing internally the very same pattern experienced externally.'[28]

> The internalization of shame is accomplished through imagery: scenes of shame [involving visual, auditory and kinesthetic dimensions] become a principal source of identity. These scenes become directly imprinted with shame when the expression of any affect, drive [like hunger], or interpersonal need[29] is followed by shaming. . . When the expression of any affect, drive or need becomes associated with shame, then later experiences of these affects, drives, or needs spontaneously activate shame by triggering the entire scene. Shame need no longer be directly activated. The particular affect, drive, or interpersonal need itself becomes bound by shame, its expression thereby constricted.[30]

Shame can have an almost paralyzing effect on the self, Kaufman observes: 'Sustained eye contact with others becomes intolerable. The head is hung. Spontaneous movement is interrupted. And speech is silenced. . . thereby causing shame to be almost incommunicable.'[31] Shame is of course not always so severe, and 'can occur in a wide range of intensity and depth, and in a variety of forms'[32] – like those Tomkins lists above, as well as inferiority, self-consciousness, and worthlessness. Shame leaves us feeling 'immobilized, trapped and alone.'[33] We feel impotent, as if there is no way to rectify or balance the situation – we have simply failed as human beings. Shame is the self's Achilles heel, its inescapable flaw.

In a general sense, internalized shame is 'experienced as a deep abiding sense of being defective, never quite good enough as a person.'[34] This central affect-belief gradually recedes from consciousness and becomes the unconscious core of the personality. We no longer have to suffer real defeats, rejections or failure, just *perceiving* events in these ways or even *anticipating* failure can confirm our sense of shame. Relating to oneself as an inherent failure absorbs, maintains and spreads shame further, leaving an individual with a precarious and vulnerable self, increasingly alienated from others and profoundly divided within.[35]

Stephen Glennard experiences shame in just this way, and it is hard to miss the prevalence of shame in *The Touchstone*. At the linguistic level, the words 'shame', 'ashamed', 'humiliation', 'humiliated' and various synonyms like 'abasement', 'dishonor', and 'baseness' appear with insistent frequency, sometimes twice in a paragraph. But more importantly, the felt experience of shame is communicated with depth and brilliance from the very beginning of the novella.

The Touchstone opens, fittingly enough, on a bleak and rainy day in a small, dingy men's club room, where Stephen Glennard feels himself to be very much a failure. He is steeped in futility; despite making ever more reductions in his living expenses in order to afford marrying Alexa Trent, there is really no hope of bringing himself 'appreciably nearer to such a conclusion.'[36] He seems caught in one of those nightmares in which we struggle towards a door down a corridor that only gets vertiginously longer. Annoyed and resentful, Glennard contemptuously eyes another club member whose wealth puts *him* beyond the need for any such shifts and privations. Contempt, Kaufman points out, is a strategy for defending against feelings of shame; its aim is to make one feel superior to the source of shame.[37] Glennard has momentarily reversed their situations by making himself feel superior to the man he criticized, and thus has salvaged his self-esteem. But the relief is only temporary, because there is a deeper source of shame in his life: Margaret Aubyn's great wealth of intellect and her inexhaustible 'alchemy of feeling' (13).

A newspaper notice by Aubyn's biographer, calling for letters and reminiscences of the late novelist, intrudes into Glennard's dismal privacy. The notice triggers all the bitterness he has come to feel about their relationship. He sees his failure not just in personal, private terms, but almost historically (which magnifies the failure):

he chafed at his own *inadequacy*, his stupid *inability* to rise to the height of her passion. . . To have been loved by the most brilliant woman of her day, and to have been *incapable* of loving her, seemed to him, in looking back, derisive evidence of his *limitations*; and his remorseful tenderness for her memory was complicated with a sense of irritation against her for her having given him once and for all the measure of his emotional capacity (5) [my emphases].

In short, she 'made him feel his inferiority' (11) both emotionally and intellectually; just thinking about her brings on 'flushes of humiliation' (15). Until this point, however, Glennard has been able to stave off the intensity of shame he experienced with Aubyn because she had become distant, depersonalized, a public 'monument.' 'In becoming a personage she so naturally ceased to be a person that Glennard could almost look back to his exploration of her spirit as on a visit to some famous shrine' (14). Ironically, it is her growing stature and notoriety in the wake of her letters appearing in print which will make Aubyn *more* personal to him and increase his sense of inferiority and failure. Late in the novella when she is at last 'revealed' to Glennard as womanly and desirable through a photograph he recognizes, he finally understands 'all that he had missed' (61).

Elizabeth Ammons observes that Wharton is unfair in asking us to criticize Glennard for not having risen to Aubyn's heights.[38] But criticism is not the point. We are, I believe, asked in the novella to *sympathize* with Glennard through his ordeal, however we may rightfully condemn his use of the letters. What Ammons seems to miss is the very real, deeply familiar and acutely embarrassing situation of a loved one quailing at the intensity of feeling he or she is simply unable to return. Any great gifts or accomplishments in the besieging lover further increase the distance, introducing another source of diminished self-esteem via shame. Such relationships are a trap for both participants, the one who loves too much and the one who loves too little. Wharton recognizes this; though Glennard was 'always tired of her' (14), he enjoyed exerting his power over Aubyn in such ways as he could.

Glennard's gloomy recollections of his feelings about Aubyn are consonant with further reminders in the opening chapter of his 'inability,' his 'depressing catalogue of lost opportunities' (6). Glennard is an outsider, suffering 'an accustomed twinge of humiliation' (7) while miserably hoping for a dinner invitation from a club member, like 'a beggar rummag[ing] for a crust in an ash-barrel[.]' – but it doesn't come (7). This fog of failure and depression will grow thicker and more menacing during the course of the novella. Everything will seem colored by his sense of defeat, which we learn has roots in his youthful acquaintance with Aubyn. Back in Hillbridge, where he met Aubyn, Glennard had felt himself 'cut out for a bigger place' (10) and eventually grew colder to Aubyn when she gained more fame as a writer. Tomkins notes that other people's successes can induce 'vicarious shame' when we invidiously compare ourselves to them.[39]

Glennard's beloved, Alexa Trent, is not at all tiresome – she is a very 'sanctuary' at which Glennard happily worships. But his inability to give Alexa the home and life she deserves (echoing his previous inability to return Aubyn's love) is a further source of shame and self-criticism: 'He saw himself sinking from depth to depth of sentimental cowardice in his reluctance to renounce his hold on her' (21). Glennard's role as her impoverished lover has been a shabby one, and when it seems that he will lose Alexa to a long European excursion with a wealthy relative, he feels trapped in 'dull resignation', in an 'endless labyrinth' (21). Only selling Aubyn's letters can rescue Alexa for him, yet that sale is not easy. When he plies Flamel, his bibliophile acquaintance, with questions about their worth, he is humiliated by his own desperation: 'It seemed to him at that moment that it would be impossible for him ever to sink lower in his own estimation' (26). Even before this moment, however, Glennard has consistently treated himself with contempt and disgust; interpersonally, these responses communicate unambivalent rejection and are potent sources of shame.[40] Thus, the way Glennard relates to *himself*, as revealed in his internal musing, further perpetuates shame and undermines his self-esteem – a pattern readily observable in Wharton's fiction.

The super-charged letters have become the very symbol of his terrible ineptitude, inferiority, failure and desperation. Selling them is Glennard's last resort, an act he hopes will free him of financial struggles, and of all the sources of shame in his life. However, Glennard feels that selling the letters is wrong, a violation of privacy, and his shame is compounded by having to lie to Flamel about how he came to own the letters. Yet he seems to have no choice, and Flamel offers a soothing observation: Aubyn's letters are so important Glennard wouldn't be justified in 'keeping them back,' (27) and selling them would thus be a public service, in a way. Wouldn't the letters, through publication, then become no longer private, no longer Glennard's and so cease to be embarrassing? Glennard would thus be free, he imagines, and later he admits having asked Flamel because he hoped for just such reassurance. Glennard may feel that this interview with Flamel is his most humiliating experience, but he is mistaken; the novella will in fact chart his sinking into a veritable whirlpool of shame.

Is it right to publish these letters? Wharton does not quite resolve the issue, though the lines of response are clearly drawn. Flamel insists that 'Anything of Margaret Aubyn's is more or less public property by this time. She's too great for any one of us' (27). A friend of Flamel's holds that the publication is 'the penalty of greatness,' adding on a more practical (and cynical) note that 'A woman shouldn't write such letters if she doesn't mean them to be published. . .' (38).

While at most the men in the book pity anyone who could receive Aubyn's passionate letters and not respond in kind, the women react far more indignantly. Glennard has kept his name out of the whole business, but he has to endure hearing women call him a 'vulture,' and wonder how 'he could ever hold up his head again' (37) – that is, not be *ashamed*. The women here do not read Aubyn's extremely intimate letters as historical documents with literary value, but as 'unloved letters' (37) which are embarrassing to read and experience, because of their relentless self-exposure and Aubyn's inability to move her correspondent. Like all affects, shame is contagious.

Ironically, Aubyn's *Letters* become a best seller, and are read aloud by an actress to raise money for a Home for Friendless Women. Male acquaintances of the Glennards' are simply amused, while the women are indignant, but fascinated. The intensity of Aubyn's feeling is almost repellent. One woman says, 'it *was* horrid, it was disgraceful. . . we all ought to be ashamed of ourselves for going.' Yet, this same woman notes, 'the big ballroom was *packed*. . . and all the women were crying like idiots – it was the most harrowing thing' (52). Alexa's attitude echoes this ambivalence: before she knows that Glennard sold the letters, she says it's 'horrible and degrading. . . to read the secrets of a woman one might have known' (46). It seems the exposure might not be so awful for her if Aubyn were more distant and less personal; then she would not have to feel Aubyn's shame so intensely.

Aubyn becomes a sort of voluble martyr, as it were, in a curious echo of her early years at Hillbridge. After a dignified 'manifesto' of a divorce there, she had emerged as 'the spokeswoman of outraged wifehood' (10), permitted a freedom of speech unusual for someone in her position. Through her letters to Glennard she becomes the spokeswoman of the unloved, able to bare her soul and express the most painful human experience – shame. In that sense, her *Letters* are liberating, but hardly the 'sly triumph' or 'belated victory' Cynthia Griffin Wolff finds them.⁴¹ After all, Aubyn is dead and unable to enjoy their 'success' or use it to heal and resolve her shame.

Tomkins notes that there is a taboo in American culture against revealing one's own shame.⁴² Glennard quite naturally tells his wife nothing about his relationship to the *Letters*. In an atmosphere where the unspeakable becomes fervidly public, Glennard keeps silent as long as he can under excruciating pressure. When he first reads of the *Letters'* publication, he has just been revelling in the joy of marriage, his child, in his home and garden, in his glorious reversal of fortune. His financial situation has become so positive, the Glennards may even take a winter home in the city. Then comes the plunge:

> Life, a moment before, had been like their plot of ground, shut off, hedged in from importunities, impenetrably his and hers. Now it seemed to him that every maple leaf, every privet-bud, was a *relentless* human *gaze, pressing close* upon their privacy. It was as though they sat in a *brightly lit* room, *uncurtained* from a darkness full of *hostile watchers*. . . His wife still smiled; and her unconsciousness of changes seemed in some horrible way to put her beyond the reach of rescue (31) [my emphases].

Wharton's metaphor brilliantly captures the felt experience of shame and she will often use images of glaring light to create a sense of her characters' sudden vulnerability. This terrible sense of exposure, isolation and alienation, coming as a sharp drop from joy and contentment (positive affect, in Tomkins' terms) is the very heart of shame. For Glennard, the shock is compounded by his not having guessed that publication 'would be like this' (31).

Once again, Glennard imagines that he has 'sounded the depth of humiliation'; once again, he is wrong. Not only do acquaintances discuss and debate the *Letters*, the air itself seems full of Aubyn's name. Shop windows flash it back at him 'in endless iteration,' (40) magazine covers thrust it at him on his train ride home. His private shame has become agonizingly public, and Kaufman observes that public humiliation 'creates a far deeper wound than the very same action done entirely in private.'[43]

Not only is Glennard 'agrope among alien forces that his own act had set in motion' (40), he has become alienated from his wife by his secret shame. Alexa usually reads new books when they are 'already on the home stretch' (39), but she wants to read the *Letters* immediately. And in another sharp drop from happiness and satisfaction, Glennard finds himself waking up to the realization that Alexa is a stranger to him. He is incapable of forecasting her judgment; her 'simplicity of outline was more puzzling than a complex surface' (46). Tomkins writes that paradoxically

> there is shame about shame. It is much easier to admit one is happy or sad than one feels ashamed. In part this is because of the close association between shame and inferiority. . . It is a self-validating affect. . . insofar as one believes one should try to conceal feelings of shame. This is particularly amplified in a culture which values achievement and success.[44]

Until selling Aubyn's letters, professional and romantic success had eluded Glennard; to confess his shame to his wife woud be intolerable, plunging him back into the long night of failure and despair. And the possibility of confession to Alexa becomes more remote as she feels increasingly unknowable. The bridge between them crumbles and falls as Glennard unsuccessfully struggles to contain his feelings of humiliation, thrust as he is, 'into a garb of *dishonor* surely meant for a *meaner* figure' (49) [my emphases]. Tensions in their marriage increase.

To begin with, Glennard's natural anger in response to his shame leaks into his marriage. He grows sharp, irritable, cold, and angry with Alexa whenever the *Letters* come up in some way, and finds himself further trapped because he craves her pity and compassion, yet fears her response. He is angry at her, and at Flamel for his role in getting Aubyn's letters to press. In both cases Glennard tries a further strategy that Kaufman notes is also used to defend against shame.[45] Glennard attempts to remove the stigma of his act by transferring blame to Alexa. Didn't he sell the letters for *her*, and didn't she present him with something of an ultimatum that forced him to either act or renounce her? He also blames Flamel: 'In his worst moments of *self-abasement* he tried to find solace in the thought that Flamel had sanctioned his course' (49) [my emphases]. The shame and anger create great ambivalence, however; he is drawn to Flamel

> in fitful impulses of friendliness, from each of which there was a sharper reaction of distrust and aversion. When Flamel was not at the house, he missed the support of implicit connivance; when he was there, his presence seemed the assertion of an intolerable claim (50).

Flamel is one more embodiment of the haunting shame triggered by Glennard's 'sale of his self-esteem' (51).

Shame is a deeply ambivalent affect in that one is cut off, but longs for reunion. 'This ambivalence,' Tomkins writes, 'is nowhere clearer than in the child who covers his face in the presence of the stranger, but also peeks through his fingers so that he may look without being seen.'[46] Glennard is trapped with no chance of escape in just such ambivalence in relation to his wife as well as to Flamel. He wants to tell her, but without the agony of confession, and he is torn by the desire to give up the burden of his secret and avoid further exposure and humiliation (we will see the same conflict in *The Mother's Recompense*).

To resolve his conflict, Glennard decides not to yield to the 'insidious temptation to confess,' but to 'let her find out for herself, and watch the effect of discovery before speaking' (55). He lets Alexa sort a pile of correspondence that includes a letter and royalties check from the publisher of Aubyn's *Letters*, but Alexa's *own* shame keeps her from responding. Alexa's initial reaction is to avoid looking at him when they are first alone, and to flee his presence for a concert. She soon after begins to be more social, filling the house with people as if to keep a safe distance between herself and Glennard.

The attempt to share his shame without experiencing it is of course a dismal failure: 'He had tried to shift a portion of his burden to his wife's shoulders; and now that she had tacitly refused to carry it, he felt the load too heavy to be taken' (58). In his growing estrangement from Alexa, contempt emerges again as a defense against shame. Glennard finds her burgeoning charm and humor artificial, and this 'cheapening of his wife put[s] him at ease with himself' (60). Alexa does eventually try to bridge the gap between them by blushingly mentioning a review of the *Letters*. Tomkins notes that blushing is a facial response to the heightened self-consciousness inherent in shame. Shame calls attention to the face, thereby heightening its visibility and generating the torment of self-consciousness. The blushing in pivotal scenes in this novella and other works of Wharton's examined here is a signal of the shame that cannot be expressed, but is nonetheless a powerful presence.

Glennard's response when Alexa mentions the *Letters* is anger (Wharton recognizes it as a 'natural' consequence of his shame), and then he turns from her, pretending not to care. What he takes for her virtual indifference seems degrading, putting 'him on a level with his dishonor' (65), and of course, he feels despicable enough already. Indifference and shame are causally linked throughout the novella, and below we will examine the personal significance of this phenomenon for Wharton.

The crisis Glennard has suffered creates such paranoia that he imagines at first that the public reading of the *Letters* was planned to expose him in some way! In Kaufman's view, paranoia develops from the awareness of intolerable defect (shame), which then necessitates a strategy of transferring the blame for the defect away from the self. The misinterpretation of innocent events as malevolent and conspiratorial completes the paranoid posture.[47] Even more unreasonably than imagining that the reading was aimed against him, Glennard later suspects his wife of some 'abominable' relation with Flamel when he sees them talking on Riverside Drive. It is surely his shameful relationship with both that magnifies his surprise, anger and shame at finding them together. His paranoid response here is an unsuccessful effort to alleviate the burden of shame.

Glennard makes one last attempt to deal with his shame when he sends Flamel an insulting check for 'services rendered' in getting Aubyn's letters published. Glennard is obviously trying to start a fight with Flamel by taunting and humiliating him, as if begging to be beaten, whipped. The aim of such apparently masochistic behavior, Tomkins finds, is 'to increase negative affect to such a point that it produces an explosive overt eruption of affect which ultimately thereby reduces itself.'[48] Tomkins calls this self-defeating strategy 'reduction through magnification'.[49] The eruption doesn't come, however, because Flamel will not be bullied into fighting. Glennard had hoped to restore his self-respect, but 'Flamel's unwillingness to quarrel with him was the last stage of his abasement.' Once again, he feels he has found his 'final humiliation' (70).

Ultimately Glennard breaks down and confesses to Alexa, but only after attacking her about being seen in public with Flamel, and in an atmosphere of tension, resentment, and challenge. He hurls his confession at her, as if cloaking the shamefulness in rage, and putting her in the wrong first. In the course of this confrontation, they avert their eyes at several points, hang their heads and blush in response to the unbearable intimacy of Glennard's revelation. Both husband and wife are 'driven together down the same fierce blast of shame' (75). Alexa's first thought when she recovers from the shock is to return the money earned from the *Letters*, which would ease her guilt by association (Kate Orme in *Sanctuary* reacts somewhat similarly in a situation where money has been shamefully earned). Glennard doubts, however, that this aim of Alexa's will be more than a temporary 'refuge.'

Until this point, we have watched in fascination as Glennard's shame grows to inordinate proportions in the shadow of Margaret Aubyn's own shame, which has become monstrously ubiquitous. Wharton's case study is rivetting in its acuity and drama, and the book is anything but 'sluggish and long drawn out'[50] when one recognizes the centrality of shame, which Wharton (consciously or not) hammers home by repeating the words 'shame', 'humiliation' and 'abasement.' Wharton also makes it clear that shame is the key element of many turning points of the story, both in dialogue, narration, and phenomenologically, in the blushing and flushing, the averted eyes, the hung heads, the turning away.

I think that readers and scholars may have found this work unsatisfying or incomplete because they have been made to feel uncomfortable by Glennard's shame, which is never really actually resolved in a way that feels emotionally authentic. At one point, when Glennard finally seems to understand what he missed in not loving Aubyn, Wharton offers what at first appears to be an epiphany:

> . . . a sense of shame rushed over him. Face to face with [Aubyn's picture], he felt himself laid bare to the inmost fold of consciousness. The shame was deep, but it was a renovating anguish: he was like a man whom intolerable pain has roused from the creeping lethargy of death (61).

Yet it is soon after this experience that Glennard tries to humiliate Flamel into a fight, so he has clearly not been released from the burden of his shame, only reached a deeper level of torment in that moment gazing at Aubyn's picture. The novella ends with Glennard learning from Alexa that he has at last (in her eyes) become worthy of Aubyn's devotion, through his suffering. It is a factitious conclusion (and *Sanctuary* suffers a similar flaw, as discussed in Chapter 2). For shame to be truly healed, insight – like Glennard realizing what he missed in not loving Aubyn – and confession are not sufficient in themselves. There needs to be a *mutual* unburdening: 'Confession and open avowal of humiliation in the presence of a sympathetic other not only presupposes intimacy but also deepens it. The mutual avowal of past humiliations can produce a tie that binds.'[51] If Alexa had, for instance, revealed to her husband that she knew all along about the *Letters*, approved and was ashamed of herself for doing so, they would then be reunited as equals. However, Alexa is superior to him, having apparently waited for Glennard to confess, to grow as a moral being and understand the meaning of his act, as *she* did. Glennard thus in some measure becomes to his wife what Aubyn was to him: longing, subservient, crushed. It is the development of this deep emotional connection between Glennard and Margaret Aubyn, the shame they ironically come to share, that in part fuels the novella and draws Wharton's sympathy and intelligence.

That there is no mutuality between Glennard and his wife at the end of *The Touchstone* is not due to Wharton's inability to create a real woman in Alexa Trent.[52] There is a deeper cause. In Wharton's emotional universe, as we shall see in the following chapters, a complete healing of shame is generally impossible. Even in later novels when few would argue that the heroines are real women, there is a terrible sense of confessions gone awry, words lost in silence, chances missed, gaps never bridged. There is great irony in Charles Du Bos' anecdote of sitting in what *he* saw as harmonious silence, with 'the angel of intimacy' spreading its wings over them, after Wharton's famous outburst in which she decried 'the miserable poverty. . . of any love that lies outside of marriage, of any love that is not a living together, a sharing of all!'[53] Du Bos noted that while Wharton was shy, he was not, yet he hardly understood Wharton for all his sense of communion, because he was deeply disappointed that this moment led to no deeper intimacy between them. Surely Wharton wanted more than *silence* when she cried out to Du Bos – this pained exposure of herself was not met by any such admission of Du Bos. He did nothing to share and validate her pain and ease the two of them into further conversation; perhaps he was embarrassed and surprised by her outburst.

Again and again in Wharton's fiction, feelings of shame which are central to the character's actions are only partially resolved, if at all. We find no mutual unburdening at the end of *The Touchstone*, no real resolution of shame because Wharton 'lacked the vocabulary of happiness.'[54] This novella is a touchstone both for Wharton's life and her career because she herself was always haunted by shame, expressed most evidently in social circumstances where she was often a victim of 'incorrigible shyness'[55] – that is, shame in the presence of strangers. We do not have to look far for an understanding of the roots of Wharton's shame. Kaufman finds that one of the most critical ways in which shame generates in childhood is when children consistently feel rejected, whether openly or unconsciously by a parent. If the child's needs are consistently not met, the 'conditions for basic security are absent and the child will come to feel lacking and deficient.'[56] We all need to feel worthwhile and valued, and 'through having someone significant provide that affirmation of self for us we gradually, and over time, learn how to give it to ourselves.'[57]

Wharton's earliest years seem in some ways to have been positive, though in photographs she looks fearful; she says that she felt 'safe and guarded' thanks to her nurse Doyley, whose 'presence was the warm cocoon in which [her] infancy lived safe and sheltered.'[58] But this warm, compassionate woman and Wharton's apparently kind but distant father were quite eclipsed by Wharton's mother Lucretia, and the family atmosphere as a whole. As she grew up, Wharton was made to feel inferior, deficient and shameful in an environment that praised the uniformity she could not achieve and the beauty she would never have, while suspecting the creativity she could not suppress. The dominant notes in her memoirs are terrible isolation, loneliness, and a sense of being deficient and different from everyone around her: a 'helpless blundering thing': 'My little corner of the cosmos seemed like a dark trackless region. . . [and] I was oppressed by the sense that I was too small & ignorant & alone to find my way about in it. . .' (Wharton's ellipsis)[59]

While critics discussing the opening of *A Backward Glance* tend to focus on Wharton's description of a childhood walk with her father, and their closeness, they have not noted that Wharton describes herself there as 'a soft, anonymous *morsel* of humanity [my emphasis].'[60] The phrase calls up images of insignificance, helplessness, and being devoured. No wonder, then, that Wharton had such a deep and lifelong identification with small animals, particularly dogs. This affinity is very revealing in another way. Darwin was the first to observe that the dog is the most sociophilic of animals, and characteristically the most readily observed to display the head and eyes lowered in shame. Wharton describes herself as feeling in touch with the unexpressed feelings of small animals, and 'possessed by a haunting consciousness of [their] sufferings,' longing to 'protect them against pain & cruelty.'[61] How 'safe and sheltered,' then, was her childhood really, if she was drawn to the helpless and felt so herself?

Wharton's family, typical of her society, was one where 'everything [was] ordered according to convention' and the only form of wrong-doing she remembered hearing condemned was 'Ill-breeding.'[62] At an early age, Wharton tried rebelling against that environment. With the energy we see in child evangelists, Wharton embarked on a career of 'making up' – telling stories that went on with volcanic facility and invention. This act required the prop of a book with densely-packed type which she would hold as she stomped back and forth 'reading' from it. This remarkable performance had to be solitary, though she says she was peered at around doors by her parents and servants. Cynthia Griffin Wolff reads Wharton's 'making up' as an episode in the power struggle with her controlling mother (who would later censor Wharton's reading), Wharton relegating her mother here to the wings while *she* dramatically takes center stage.[63] But it is also an attempt to deal with the shame of being different, inferior, ignored. By 'making up,' by becoming a whirlwind of story-telling which tumbled out too fast to be recorded, Wharton asserted herself as important, special, worthy of attention.

One wonders what specific events precipitated the onrushes of story-telling, and how Wharton treated the people in them who apparently resembled her family and friends. Certainly to catch them all 'in the same daily coil of "things that might have happened"'[64] was to assert the control her family denied her, as Wolff points out. Kaufman notes that powerlessness is a fertile ground for the development of shame, reactivating early 'governing scene[s] of initial primary helplessness' as an infant.[65] Not surprisingly in such a restricted environment, when Wharton left her playmates and went off to her room to 'make up' she felt 'the exquisite relief of those moments of escape from the effort of trying to "be like other children!"'[66] She could thus triumph in her difference, rather than feel it an intolerable source of shame. No wonder that 'making up' was 'ecstacy' for Wharton, though she struggled against the urge to give way because she was 'a very conscientious little girl.'[67] As Cynthia Griffin Wolff puts it, 'the society that had produced Edith Jones Wharton had developed the art of repression to an excessive degree'[68] – and Wharton *embraced* this repression. I would argue that she strove to be the perfect little girl as a defense against her shame, against feeling flawed, bad, and deficient for everything she was and felt that seemed wrong, objectionable. Perfectionism is a frequent response to the burden of shame, magically seeming to banish it from possibility.[69]

Wharton's conscientiousness led to an important early scene of disgust and shame she felt was really her own fault. Wharton recalls telling another child in her dancing class that the mother of their French dancing teacher looked like an old goat. Wharton claims that she had never been told 'that it was "naughty" to lie' and that all by herself she had worked out 'a rigid rule of absolute, unmitigated truth-telling, the least imperceptible deviation from which would inevitably be punished by the dark Power I knew as "God."'[70] She went even further to decide that merely thinking such a thing was 'naughty' and only confession could save her. Surely Wharton had already internalized the rigid 'standards of honor and conduct' of her culture and family, rather than having *invented* them? What circumscription – she shamed herself for even *thinking* ill of someone. Her strategy of confession did not, however, work in this particular case. She subjected herself to an unnecessary public humiliation, and was deeply disappointed that this confession was not hailed as honest reparation, but criticized by her teacher.[71] As we have seen in *The Touchstone* and will observe in other works, characters in her fiction sometimes choose to shame themselves further in the hope of escaping the burdens of a shameful act they find already intolerable.

Perhaps part of what fueled this event was her teacher's ugliness. While in *A Backward Glance* she notes she was 'always vaguely frightened by ugliness',[72] in the far more revealing, unpublished 'Life and I' Wharton says that she was never able to overcome 'feeling for ugly people an abhorrence, a kind of cold cruel hate.'[73] On the first page of that memoir she says one of her greatest and earliest desires was to look pretty. We know from photographs that she never really was, which was not only a deep disappointment for a girl of her era, but for *this* girl, whose mother was considered beautiful, and whom Wharton thought New York's best-dressed woman.[74] Conceiving so powerful a hatred of ugliness is certainly one way to diminish the shame of not being attractive in a society where 'there was an almost pagan worship of physical beauty, and the first question asked about any youthful newcomer on the social scene was invariably: "Is she pretty?" or: "Is he handsome?"'[75] Detesting people and places that were ugly, and later dressing so well and creating beautiful, elegant homes and gardens, she could hold herself superior via contempt for others deemed inferior (which does not, of course, discount her love of beauty and joy in creating it).

Wharton clearly grew up in an environment that praised surfaces and preferred to ignore depths. Wharton asserts that she 'never exchanged a word with a really intelligent human being until [she] was over twenty.'[76] For a writer, what could be more damaging than to experience as a child 'complete mental isolation', an 'intellectual desert' where she was 'starving for mental nourishment'?[77] She was an anomaly in her family, unable to claim literary ancestors so that she could feel herself truly part of her family. There was only one other 'bookworm' in her family, which may 'have held literature in great esteem, [but] stood in nervous dread of those who produced it. . . They were genuinely modest and shy in the presence of any one who wrote or painted.'[78] Writing was considered both mysterious and beneath them by her parents and their friends – 'manual labour.'[79] While Wharton's mother encouraged her 'making up,' or at least did not discourage it, when she started writing, Wharton was not given any paper to write on: 'I was driven to begging for the wrappings of parcels delivered at the house.'[80] Eventually all the wrapping paper was hers to use, but what contempt and disgust her family's attitude suggests about her creativity! And surely the excitement of composition would have been underlaid for Wharton by the association of her work with something transitory, unimportant, even with trash, since she was not at first given *good* paper to use.

The story is much quoted of her mother's response to her first novel, written at the age of eleven. Wharton's heroine greets a guest with 'If only I had known you were going to call I should have tidied up the drawing-room.' Her mother's 'icy' comment was, 'Drawing-rooms are always tidy.'[81] Now, one such shaming remark is not enough to be crippling, but this incident is typical of a pattern in Lucretia's behavior, borne out by Wharton's early sense that her mother was more inscrutable and distant even than God. Did Lucretia ever bond with her daughter? Did Wharton ever feel valued and loved· by her mother? What evidence there is strongly suggests Wharton never was able to please her mother, and never felt a sense of belonging and security. This childhood isolation left her feeling 'humiliated. . . to be so "different."'[82]

Another often discussed example of her mother's coldness and contempt occurs on the eve of Wharton's marriage, when she nervously begs her mother to vanquish the fog of sexual ignorance she has grown up in. What will happen to her? Greeting her question 'with the look of icy disapproval [Wharton] most dreaded,' her mother's response is contemptuous, shaming: 'I never heard such a ridiculous question!' But Wharton is *desperate* for information, and persists. With difficulty (is she disgusted? ashamed?), her mother asks Wharton if she hadn't noticed that male statues were made differently than female ones. Unable to extrapolate, Wharton falls silent, which makes her mother burst out, 'You can't be as stupid as you pretend!' Thus Wharton was ridiculed, shamed for not knowing what she ruefully noted she 'had been expressly forbidden to ask about, or even think of!' Such questions had always been 'not nice', or she was told she was too young to understand. Wondering about sex, and keeping silent about it were equal sources of shame.[83]

Why was Lucretia so dismissive, so unkind? In some measure, she seems to have treated Wharton as she herself was treated as a girl. Wharton related that her mother 'never ceased to resent the indignity inflicted on her' at her own coming out; Lucretia wore a home-made dress and her mother's ill-fitting satin slippers: 'She suffered martyrdom.' Lucretia's younger sisters 'were prettier and probably more indulged. . . given new slippers when their turn came.'[84] While this offers us only a glimpse into Lucretia's family, the incident certainly establishes a sense of its·values and exclusions. When Wharton herself was to come out, her mother in a way recreated the scene of humiliation, by visiting a different and perhaps more damaging set of disabilities on her daughter. Lucretia decided that the usual social procedure for bringing a daughter out, 'a series of coming-out entertainments. . . leading off with a huge tea and an expensive ball,' was absurd.[85] Wharton was more informally launched at this moment when a girl was at her most exposed and vulnerable to shame; well-dressed and coiffed, she was simply brought to a friend's ball. Scenes which take root in the personality and begin to govern it also compel re-enactment, according to Kaufman.[86] Tomkins describes this process as recasting the scene.[87] Lucretia re-enacted the scene of her *own* coming out, a scene infused with shame, by reversing roles and playing her own mother's part in the original scene, here in relation to Wharton. That is one way to understand their analogous coming out experiences. Given what we know of her environment, and given that Lucretia seemed to be expressing quite clearly that her daughter wasn't worth the standard effort (Edith Wharton was, after all 'much less pretty than many of the girls'),[88] can we wonder that Wharton experienced 'a long cold agony of shyness' that night, cowering in 'speechless misery' at her mother's side? Her shyness 'long troubled [her] in general company. . .'[89]

Kaufman notes that parental 'expressions of contempt either directly toward the child or towards others profoundly shape the family culture into a breeding ground for shame. Considerably older siblings. . . often can function significantly as activators of shame.'[90] And indeed, this seems to have been the case for Wharton, her adult brothers playing an important stifling role as well. Wharton, for instance, was shamed by them *and* her mother into speaking well:

> I still wince under my mother's ironic smile when I said that some visitor had stayed 'quite a while', and her dry: 'Where did you pick *that* up?' The wholesome derision of my grown-up brothers saved me from pomposity as my mother's smile guarded me against slovenliness; I still tingle with the sting of their ridicule when, excusing myself for having forgotten something I had been told to do, I said, with an assumption of grown-up dignity (*aetat* ten or eleven): 'I didn't know that it was *imperative.*'[91]

While Wharton praises her parents' use of and reverence for clear and beautiful English in *A Backward Glance*, this passage reveals far more pain than praise: 'I still wince,' 'I still tingle with the sting of their ridicule – and how 'wholesome' is derision?[92] Wharton also says that she was compared to her brothers, made to feel inferior to them because she wasn't expressive enough, had 'less "heart"' – a characteristic that might have been different, she notes, if she 'had been praised a little now and then.'[93] It is painfully ironic that in some ways Wharton became like her mother: concerned with dress and appearances, cool, critical, at least on the surface. And she could certainly be contemptuous; one wonders how deeply she understood this dynamic of her personality. Many who knew Wharton later in life commented on her hauteur, though others pointed out that beneath this facade was the 'incorrigible shyness' Wharton felt to be a lifelong affliction. Contempt indeed functions as a defense against shame, as does perfectionism, which Kaufman notes 'is an attempt to compensate for feeling inherently defective.'[94] In the 'arid emotional climate' of her family and society, Wharton 'chose to become the perfect model of propriety and "niceness."'[95]

Adolescence is a period of particular vulnerability to shame,[96] and it was at this time she notes what amounts to a family conspiracy against her:

> I was laughed at by my brothers for my red hair, & for the supposed abnormal size of my hands & feet; as I was much the least good-looking of the family, the consciousness of my physical shortcomings was heightened by the beauty of the persons about me. My parents – or at least my mother – laughed at me for using 'long words,' & for caring for dress (in which heaven knows she set me the example!); & under this perpetual cross-fire of criticism I became a painfully shy self-conscious child.[97]

Ostensibly, Wharton says, the goal here was a socially approved one: to keep children from becoming vain and spoiled. That pedagogical aim dovetailed quite well with a family's predisposition to criticism and contempt. The role her father played in this criticism is unclear (note the qualifying 'or at least my mother'). Was it perhaps important for Wharton to exclude him from among the list of her tormentors, or was he actually not involved? Wharton seems to have identified with him through literature, because it was his well-stocked library that was a precious treasure to her growing up. Wharton's father appears remote, hard to pinpoint in the memoirs, but she writes of him as her mother's victim in a way, his interest in poetry 'shrivelled' by his wife's 'matter-of-factness.' Wharton saw him as stifled, a lonely man, 'haunted by something always unexpressed and unattained.'[98] The look in her eyes in many photographs throughout her life (consider the dust jacket of Wolff's *A Feast of Words*) can be quite adequately described in just those words.

Wharton was also shamed less directly, in the form of indifference, a word that occurs with some frequency in *The Touchstone* (and throughout her fiction), linked with shame sometimes in the same sentence, and is clearly of great significance to the author, often seen as toxic and destructive. Her every aspiration was 'ignored, or looked at askance' and she had to fight her way 'to expression through a thick fog of indifference.'[99] Wharton writes that her growing literary success was 'avoided as though it were a kind of family disgrace, which might be condoned but could not be forgotten.'[100] In *A Backward Glance* she speculates on the impact of this indifference on her career as a writer, and though she posits that too easy a path makes artists ineffectual, she cannot decide if she was 'really hindered.' Yet the text emphasizes struggle and pain when Wharton considers: 'a case like my own, where a development no doubt naturally slow was certainly retarded by the indifference of every one about me [note her father is not made an exception here].' She seems to include herself with the 'baffled, the derided or the ignored. . . who have fought their way to achievement.'[101]

Wharton also suffered a public humiliation in New York when she was twenty. Her engagement to Harry Stevens, the intelligent and handsome son of a wealthy *nouveau riche* society hostess, Mrs Paran Stevens, was broken off. R.W.B. Lewis cites social slights that Mrs Stevens experienced from the established old-money Joneses as a possible cause, but weighs in for Mrs Stevens' desire to prolong her control of her son's sizable trust fund. Whatever the reason, Wharton must surely have suffered being gossiped about and rejected so completely. Returning to New York a year later, she appeared 'shaken. . . under the watchful and knowing eyes of the other guests' at a ball.[102]

The early years of Wharton's career as a writer were marked by her shame. When her editor at Scribner's asked for some revisions on an early story, she was 'unaccountably' unable to make them, R.W.B. Lewis notes. Wharton's editor even offered to make the revisions himself, but Wharton finally returned the story months later without any changes. Like many novice writers, she seems to have been unable to adequately disguise her own life in this story, which draws on her feelings of isolation in her marriage. She may have been unable to deal with the story because it was nakedly about herself, but just as powerfully, she seems to have been crushed by what she interpreted as a negative response. The ghost of Lucretia-as-critic would not be an easy one to banish; in 1917 she would write to Bernard Berenson: 'I'm so used, these many years, to contracting at a word. . .'[103]

A year after her inability, to revise the story, another request for revisions brought a more dramatic response from Wharton than mere silence. In a letter suggesting her editor have 'no tender-hearted compunctions about criticizing' her stories, she thanks him for the 'justice' of his comments (the word suggests trial and sentencing). The gratitude throughout this letter is undercut by her confession of having 'fallen into a period of groping,' having 'lost confidence' in herself. 'Pray don't regard this as the wail of the rejected authoress,' she instructs - but of course that is what her whole sad letter is.[104] Lewis observes that Wharton seemed to have internalized her 'society's and her mother's distrust of a person of good family who took seriously to writing.'[105] I would go even further and call this internalization *shame* – how could she not be somewhat ashamed and uncertain when her family had never encouraged her to write, and by virtue of her interests and burgeoning talent, 'there was no [woman] quite like her in her New York generation.'[106]

Looking back at the start of her career, Wharton notes in *A Backward Glance* that she read reviews of her first book, *The Greater Inclination*, with 'a sense of mingled guilt and self-satisfaction. . . They were unbelievably kind, but for the most part their praise only humbled me; and often I found it bewildering.'[107] Growing up in an environment that consistently tore her down, is it any wonder that she had trouble assimilating praise, and even more, was humbled by it, felt *lesser*, rather than buoyed and excited? Shame-bound individuals have a great deal of trouble with compliments and praise, which collide so violently with their sense of inadequacy and worthlessness.

Wharton was quite cruelly trapped, a prisoner of shame – criticized for being different, for being creative and literary, for the way she spoke, for her lack of beauty, for the coolness she developed both in response to criticism and perhaps in unconscious emulation of her mother, for her very body (so important and terrifying in adolescence), for wanting to be like her mother – in other words ineluctably for who she was and what she felt. Cynthia Griffin Wolff notes that there 'were no particularities [of Wharton's] that had not been *humiliatingly* compromised [my emphasis].'[108]

Wharton's shame was most obviously expressed in what she called her 'incorrigible shyness'. Kaufman considers shyness a manifestation of shame '*either* in the presence of *or* at the prospect of approaching strangers' – we feel 'socially awkward, dumb, speechless.'[109] We have all seen small children exhibit this shyness, hiding their faces, or hiding themselves behind their parents, and have probably all suffered such social inhibition at various times in our lives. For Wharton, this shyness was an essential part of her personality, and never left her. She was, for instance, 'struck dumb in the presence of greatness'[110] and thus too shy to speak to Henry James the first two times she was in his company. Even when she was already a famous writer, she was unable to tell the poet Rilke how very much his work meant to her, or talk to Yeats. This shyness may explain why she preferred skimming over subjects in conversation rather than delving deeply into them – to linger too long might have left her exposed in some way. Her conversational style unnerved some people, and Charles Du Bos, the young translator into French of *The House of Mirth*, says he was struck shy by it, but it seems more likely that he was responding to her underlying lack of ease. Tomkins notes that affect is contagious. Only gradually did Du Bos realize that her shyness was 'such an inveterate trait' and 'the key to all her social demeanour outside the circle of close friendship.'[111]

Those familiar with Henry James' and others' reminiscences of Wharton as often imposing and sometimes impossible may find it hard to believe that Wharton was at all shy. Such hauteur and even force were in no way inconsistent with her shyness, however, but clearly defenses against it. Among others, her friend Logan Pearsall Smith recognized as much: 'Edith Wharton was an extraordinarily shy person; meeting strangers frightened her, and to protect herself against them she would assume the air and manner of the aristocratic New Yorker she happened to be born. This assumption of a great lady's manner was unfortunate, as it tended to terrify the people of whom she herself stood in terror.'[112] Terrify – or outrage. Smith, Bernard Berenson's brother-in-law, records that when he, his wife and Berenson first met Wharton, they indignantly found themselves treated with a mixture of 'intellectual and social contempt.'[113] Wharton later would not admit to her hauteur on this occasion, but did say that she was terrified of meeting Berenson. While Wharton refers to her shyness a number of times in *A Backward Glance*, she seems not to have fully understood its hold on her, even though shame often appears as a central motivation in her work, and her characters sometimes even reflect on shame and its consequences.[114] In discussing her instant communion with Paul Bourget's gentle wife Minnie, she insists that they were completely unlike one another, yet she notes that 'Everything about [Minnie] was shy.'[115]

Given how shame-bound Wharton was, it is not surprising that the two most important men Wharton was involved with – Walter Berry and Morton Fullerton – 'withheld themselves from her in critical, heartbreaking ways.'[116] One cannot underestimate Berry's invaluable support of her writing over the thirty years of their friendship, his 'painstaking efforts' and 'meticulous criticism', whether by mail or in person, and even when he was ill.[117] Indeed Wharton credits him with teaching her everything she knew 'about the writing of clear, concise English.'[118] However, he seems to have taught her an ambiguous lesson about her writing: 'Never to be satisfied with my own work. . .'[119] One can applaud such high standards, but they hold within them the seeds of disappointment and shame. To never be pleased is to hold off satisfaction indefinitely; surely at some point one must say, 'this is good enough.' His impossible standards make him chillingly similar to Lucretia. His first response to her writing was quite cruel; when Wharton 'shyly' asked him to look at the 'lumpy' manuscript of *The Decoration of Houses*, he responded with a 'shout of laughter'! Wharton explains this away by saying 'he never flattered or pretended' and that he 'good-naturedly' went on to help her – but his initial response must have been devastating (the unpleasant Culwin responds this way to a novelist in 'The Eyes').

Leon Edel sees Berry as having offered Wharton 'sanction' for her career as a writer, and something more – *identification*:

> By becoming an ally of authority she could have authority. By an alliance with power and even coercion, she could wield power and coerce as well. Her friends, who disliked Berry [they found him cold, aloof, supercilious], said that he endowed her with the things they liked least. Perhaps it is truer to say that her less pleasant qualities had always been there, unexpressed, until he freed her to express them.[120]

When they first met, she was twenty-one, and Berry, a distant relative, gave Wharton something entirely new: 'The sense of a genuine communion of intelligence and literary appreciation.'[121] But he was also a potent source of shame. Her first engagement, with Harry Stevens, had recently been broken off by the young man's mother, and as Wharton and Berry grew closer in the summer of 1883, she was further humiliated by his never proposing marriage, and one assumes, by her own 'shy ignorance of the arts of lovemaking.'[122] This early experience of being shamed seems to have continued when they resumed their friendship some years later. Though he inspired her, and helped her hone her craft, Berry was 'a source of anguish to the sensitive and emotional woman. She was sure of her affection for him, but unfortunately, she could not be sure of his for her.'[123]

Despite his role as sexual Prometheus for Wharton, Morton Fullerton was apparently quite critical, and made Wharton often feel ashamed, conscious of her flaws, her inexperience:

'I'm so afraid that the treasures I long to unpack for you, that have come to me in magic ships from enchanted islands, are only, to you, the old familiar red calico & beads of the clever trader, who has had dealings in every latitude, & knows just what to carry in the hold to please the simple native – I'm so afraid of this, that often & often I stuff my shining treasures back into their box, lest I should see you smiling at them!'[124]

'I know how unequal the exchange is between us, how little I have to give that a man like you can care for. . .'[125]

'Don't you suppose I know that the blessedness is all on my side?'[126]

'I'm not worthy to write to or think about. . .'[127]

' . . . what I might be to you. . . is little enough, heaven knows, for the reasons we know: the fact of all I lack. . .'[128]

Early in their correspondence, she is 'ashamed to write so often,'[129] and stingingly remembers Fullerton's chilling sarcasm while writing one of her most 'vibrant and openhearted' letters.[130] ' . . . you once told me that, on this topic [love], I serve up the stalest of platitudes with an air of triumphant discovery!'[131] Are we not witnessing here a re-enactment of the analogous scenes of disapproval and criticism with her mother?

What seems to have been most painful to Wharton in her affair with Fullerton was his *indifference*. 'This incomprehensible silence, the sense of your utter indifference to everything that concerns me, has stunned me.'[132] She wrote, 'the pain within my pain, the last turn of the screw, has been the impossibility of knowing what you wanted of me, and what you felt for me.'[133] Wharton could have felt this about her mother as well. She could not please Fullerton, just as she could not please her mother, and experienced his rejection as just as fundamental a repudiation of herself. Fullerton, too, was inscrutable, someone she struggled unsuccessfully to understand, to please. When she met him, she had already written a version of a relationship with a famous novelist and an uncaring man, and in 1899 she had thought of destroying the manuscript of this novella. Did it reveal too much? Her affair with Fullerton seems to have been in part an attempt to master those early childhood scenes of indifference, just as *The Touchstone* was in part an attempt to master them, and in so doing, master her shame. Her actual affair re-enacted the analogous scene she initially re-created through writing; in a sense, first she wrote the script, and then lived it out.

It is easy to dismiss Teddy Wharton because of his later embezzling of Wharton's money and his erratic behavior, but until around 1902 he was almost unanimously found to be 'warm-hearted, gracious, and utterly accommodating' and a man of 'intuitive good breeding.'[134] One can almost feel a bit sorry for this apparently affable and ordinary fellow. How could someone as unexceptional as he was have possibly understood and helped a woman as complex and wounded as Wharton? Their empty and increasingly disastrous marriage ended after thirty dreary years, and throughout those years, many Wharton characters pronounce about the prison of marriage. The last ten or so years were particularly difficult, punctuated by Teddy's erratic behavior that seems to have included psychosomatic complaints and possibly manic depression. Teddy also embezzled Wharton's money and had at least one mistress. Even though Wharton had already had her affair with Fullerton when Teddy announced his infidelity, surely someone as insecure about her sexuality would have found this news humiliating, no matter what she felt about Teddy at the time?

The divorce proved a significant source of shame for Wharton. She wrote many of her friends afterwards, concerned about what people in Boston, people of her class, and relations would think of her. What would they say? This vulnerability to the opinions of others appears in many of Wharton's characters, and the question of divorce being shameful is powerfully dramatized in her 1913 story 'Autre Temps. . .' Divorce 'was not readily accepted among Wharton's circle of genteel acquaintances. . .'[135] Clearly, the fear of social consequences, and their emotional impact on her, kept her in the marriage so long, and even governed how she wanted the divorce to be thought of *after* her death. During her final slow illness, Wharton prepared papers for her future biographer that contained letters and doctors' reports that in effect made the case for her divorcing Teddy because of his instability. Cynthia Griffin Wolff notes that Wharton's most formidable critic was herself in this instance, since she did know people who 'had survived the trauma of divorce.'[136] Wolff speculates that Wharton was in conflict over what the consequences of her new freedom would be, but I think that Wharton was quite understandably ashamed: by the public failure of her marriage (reporters apparently asked Fullerton what *he* knew about it!), by her affair (which Teddy must have guessed at in some way), and by the unfortunate but devastating impact her success and wealth seemed to have on Teddy, diminishing his self-respect and undermining his mental health. Despite the ease and proliferation of divorce in our own time, many people still suffer the pangs of shame at this public exposure of a failure in marriage.

I think it is a mistake to argue, as Gilbert and Gubar do, that *The Touchstone* offers a portrait of 'a woman artist who is empowered by her talent to transcend what is supposedly for women the insurmountable pain of unrequited love.'[137] This reading completely overlooks the emotional core of the novella, which is not at all a comforting book. Wharton does indeed want us to sympathize with Aubyn's plight before and after her death. What is actually *central*, though, is *Glennard's* suffering, his deepening humiliations, which are created with such psychological accuracy and depth because of Wharton's own visceral knowledge of shame. If she had intended to keep ironic distance from her protagonist, his descent into one ordeal of humiliation after another completely destroyed that distance. Like Wharton herself, part of his misfortune is to love too late.[138] His manifestations of shame – the sense of exposure, failure and deficiency – appear chillingly dramatized in her autobiographies, in the letters to Fullerton, and in the other novels, novellas and short stories to be discussed here. Tomkins writes that 'in order to understand shame one must have experienced' it deeply.[139] There can be no doubt that Wharton certainly did; how else are we to understand that despite her success, fame, wealth, her loving friends and devoted servants, her gorgeous homes and gardens, 'throughout her life, Wharton carried within her the conviction that she was at base a small, hungry, helpless creature'?[140] The phenomenological portrayal of shame is pervasive in her works to be examined here: in the consistent blushing and turning away, the covering of eyes or face that signal poignant responses the characters cannot speak of because shame is tabooed and because to talk of it is to seemingly confirm oneself as shameful. Even the language of shame is ever present: 'humiliation,' 'humiliated,' 'humiliatingly,' 'ashamed,' 'shame,' 'mortified,' 'mortifyingly,' 'mortification,' 'abased,' 'abasement,' 'self-abasement,' 'humility' – and the consistent concern with 'pride,' which is invariably being 'humbled'.

Shame-bound characters appear throughout the fiction: in men and women who feel isolated, lonely, deficient, helpless, unlovable, outcast, unwanted, disappointed, self-conscious, discouraged, blundering, clumsy, shy; who invidiously compare themselves to others and find themselves deeply lacking; whose family and environment send the unequivocal message that they are inferior, unworthy. These are men and women whose relationships are almost invariably doomed to failure, whether with children, lovers or parents (though sometimes Wharton adds a happy ending, as in *The Touchstone*, which contradicts the emotional movement of the work); who like Godwin's Caleb Williams find that their 'fairest prospects have been blasted;'[141] who struggle unsuccessfully to salvage their pride and self-esteem; who are driven to strange and even implausible acts because of shame, but in a terrible paradox experience renewed shame precisely because of the acts that were meant to free them.

Edith Wharton's prisoners of shame are, understandably, the product of a brilliant and talented woman who was 'far more aware of what [her life] cost [her], of loss and dissatisfaction and failure, than of accomplishment, scope achieved, experience garnered.'[142] We must not only recognize the impact of shame on

Wharton's fiction and her life, but do what is more difficult and challenging: *experience* the shame she writes about with such devastating accuracy and deep intuition. Even though at times we may feel that we are 'listening at a keyhole.'

2
Flights from Shame

Edith Wharton apparently thought so little of her 1903 novella *Sanctuary* that she called it 'Sank' at The Mount,[1] and discussed it less than any other of her books before or after publication.[2] Recent assessments have more than confirmed Wharton's dim estimation of the work. R.W.B. Lewis calls it 'relatively undistinguished.'[3] Cynthia Griffin Wolff dismisses it in a footnote as 'a really bad little novel' that deserves to be 'mercifully forgotten,' and does not discuss it further.[4] Elizabeth Ammons finds elements of the book 'preposterous' and 'ludicrous.'[5]

On the face of it, *Sanctuary* is somewhat hard to take seriously. Kate Orme discovers that her fiancé Denis Peyton has dishonestly inherited a fortune by hiding his knowledge of his stepbrother's marriage. He is thus indirectly responsible for the suicide of the woman his brother married and the death of the woman's child. But instead of breaking off the engagement, Kate decides that she must marry Denis to save any child he might have from the moral taint of his behavior. Years later, she does indeed save her son from appropriating a fellow architect's plans to win a competition – by a sort of sympathetic emotional telepathy.

Central to any discussion of this novella is the nature of Kate's unusual decision to devote herself to Denis Peyton's unborn child. An anonymous reviewer in 1904 labeled this aspect of *Sanctuary* 'absurd,' and most modern readers would no doubt agree.[6] What reviewers and critics alike have not understood, however, is the crucial role of shame in shaping Kate Orme's decision, and indeed her whole life. Examining her struggles with shame illuminates the novella's unappreciated strengths and clarifies its weaknesses.

At the opening of the novella, Kate Orme seems to be experiencing the very opposite of the failure and isolation that are inherent to shame. She is irradiated by happiness, which is more precious for having been threatened by a vague story about her fiancé's brother and some 'dreadful' woman who had a 'shadowy' claim on him. Much like the upbringing Wharton describes in *A Backward Glance*, Kate has been sheltered from 'any open dis-

34

cussion of life,'[7] which her father points out 'isn't any Sunday school story' (109). Even her prospective mother-in-law remarks that *her* husband always spared her 'the painful side of life' (104). Kate is not at all spared, however, when Denis announces that the 'dreadful' woman and her child have drowned in a nearby lake. Kate hides her eyes, a clear sign of shame, and soon after feels herself lost in 'indistinguishable blackness' (93). She is seeing life, and the sexuality in it, for the first time. What she seems to see is an abyss with anguished figures, 'striving together in the darkness' (94) like a vision of Hell. And she discovers a strange, shameful affinity in herself with the drowned woman – *she* could have been that woman, and Denis, his stepbrother.

Sharing her distress and confusion triggers Denis' own shame over having acted dishonorably, and his response to that shame is anger, which serves to insulate him from Kate, the immediate source of his shame. Denis speaks to Kate 'with a kind of violence' (95), revealing the truth to Kate 'almost savagely' (96) – much like Glennard confessing to his wife in *The Touchstone*. Denis' shame builds as he tries to explain his actions to Kate:

> The money, of course, had made a difference – he was too honest not to own it – but not till afterward, he declared – would have declared on his honour, but that the word tripped him up, and sent a flush to his forehead (99) [note his blushing, and the cause].

One of Denis' excuses for hushing up his step-brother's marriage is having wanted to save his family from scandal and humiliation, but Kate urges a different response. 'Imprisoned. . . in this dreadful thing' (100), Kate seeks to cast the guilt – the shame over a transgression – from her by having Denis publicly confess what he did, and return the money that is not rightfully his. Apparently she believes he must first pay in public humiliation for a shameful act that has been kept private (as Wharton records herself doing, early in 'Life and I').

Until Denis' confession, Kate has been tolerant, even somewhat amused by his 'clear-eyed directness' (86), his beefy self-satisfaction. Now, however, she is seeing him 'for the first time in an unmitigated glare' (note the sense of exposure and observation) as extremely weak (97). The plunge for her from contentment and joy to disappointment and disgust can only result in shame, which

Tomkins observes can be triggered vicariously by another's *failures* as well as successes.[8] Even worse for Kate, her vision of Denis and the world has proven wildly inaccurate. The bridge between them is broken: 'a chasm had opened at their feet and they found themselves on different sides' (102). Kate is terribly isolated in her feelings, unable to communicate their nature to Denis' less sensitive mother, and especially to her own father, who is readily able to 'resign himself to the misfortunes of others' (109).

Kate's sense of being soiled and defiled deepens when her father dismisses a similar scandal in their own family as merely a 'disagreeable accident' (109). Denis' weakness is thus not an anomaly; Kate begins to feel 'that the fair surface of life was honeycombed by a vast system of moral sewage' (110), with many families covering up similar disgraceful episodes. The disgust she feels is significant, especially when we remember that she felt herself strangely, unexpectedly connected with the 'dreadful woman.' She is utterly alone, suffering 'an isolation more complete, more impenetrable, than that in which the discovery of Denis's act had plunged her' (111). The 'golden haze' in which she has pictured her marriage as 'the exquisite prolongation of wooing' (112) has vanished, and Kate's loathing for herself and her situation is complete: 'For here, at last life lay before her as it was: not brave, garlanded and victorious, but naked, grovelling and diseased, dragging its maimed limbs through the mud. . .' (111)

Her shame and disappointment are so disturbing that the only way she can escape is to hurl herself into an entirely new vision of life. Kate makes an almost frenzied decision to 'expiate and redeem' (112) Denis' fault – which has become hers by association – by going ahead with the marriage and protecting the child she assumes they will have. In a series of imaginative leaps she has found a grander solution than that of having Denis confess to a judge. It is not coincidental that her new vision of 'spiritual motherhood' (113) *is* spiritual. Kate has fled from the shameful vision of sexuality conjured up by this scandal, from her profound disillusionment with Denis, and from the ruins of her vision of wifehood. She feels safe now, free, will no longer have to fear striving in the darkness.

But Kate's fervent decision is not only a strategy for dealing with shame in terms of high emotional drama. Her decision grows out of and confirms deep-seated feelings about herself. Shame did not enter her life for the first time through Denis' revelations and her response to them; she had been bound by it all along. Consider Kate's relationship with her father (which critics do not discuss). For Mr Orme, she is a non-person whose attentions to his dinner mean more than her being his daughter. He is a self-centered man for whom Kate is merely 'an outlying region, a subject province' (109). As noted in Chapter 1, continued rejection of a child by parents – whether consciously or not – will lead children to believe they are deficient and prevent them from learning how to affirm themselves. Mr Orme's coldness and distance clearly explain why Kate had never completely yielded to happiness before her engagement – how could she?

Though likable and charming, Denis is more egotistical and obtuse than Kate's father. When Kate fell in love with him, she felt that 'the first stranger in the street could have interpreted her happiness for her more easily than Denis' (85) – quite an indictment. Like Mr Orme, Denis is not used to trouble, does not expect to brush against the hard edges of life which would disturb his 'incurious cheerfulness' (88). Marriage to such a man is a clear continuation of the pattern of relating between herself and her father. Thus the 'mystic climax of effacement' (113) Kate imagines in becoming a mother is not so much a change as a more complex re-enactment of her earlier scenes of indifference. Kate's aim of saving the child Denis will father from 'secret weakness, a vice of the moral fibre' (112) may to some readers appear positive. After all, the argument could go, if she is so shame-bound, how can she picture herself saving *anyone*? This 'rescue' is not, however, the act of someone with self-esteem, but born out of desperation. And while it seems to be a solution that will free her from shame, it does the opposite. She is like someone lunging for a tree branch to pull herself from quicksand only to have it break and plunge her deeper in.

Kate's effacement is carried to a consummation in her relationship with her son, the 'solution' to the problem of her marriage. Her life as a mother is one of 'ever-renewed and indefatigable effort' (138):

It was because her intimacy with her son was the one need of her life that she had, with infinite tact and discretion, but with equal persistency, clung to every step of his growth, dissembling herself, adapting herself, rejuvenating herself in the passionate effort to be always within reach, but never in the way (115).

The 'passive attitude she had adopted' (139) condemns her to wretched waiting while her son Dick struggles with his own sense of honor and shame about plans his friend Darrow bequeathed him, plans that are so exceptionally good they will surely win Dick his first major commission.[9] Kaufman writes that a common strategy for compensating for 'the sense of defectiveness which underlies internalized shame' is striving for power or success.[10] The irony in *Sanctuary* of course is that Kate 'had come to sacrifice everything to the one passion of ambition for her boy' (131). Deepening her humiliation is a sense that Clemence Verney, the woman Dick loves, has outmaneuvered her by offering herself as a 'prize' if Dick uses the plans. Not surprisingly, Clemence makes Kate blush and look down.

Kate is not without insight, however. The passivity tears her apart and she sees more deeply into the existence she has chosen than ever before. It begins to seem that her 'faith and hope [in Dick] had been marsh-lights luring her to the wilderness, her love a vain edifice created on shifting ground' (155). She feels ashamed of having created a situation in which she has consistently submerged her own self to her son's:

> A mortal *loneliness* enveloped her. She felt as though she had fallen by the way, spent and broken in a struggle of which even its object had been unconscious. She had tried to deflect the natural course of events, she had sacrificed her personal happiness to a fantastic ideal of duty, and it was her punishment to be left *alone* with her *failure, outside* the normal current of human strivings and regrets (151) [my emphases].

The bold solution she found to deal with her shame over Denis' culpability and her growing knowledge of sexual 'darkness' has been a dismal failure, and produced an entirely *new* source of shame. At one point, she asserts to herself that only she 'who held the clue to the labyrinth could thread a way through the confusions and contradiction of Dick's past' (156). The metaphor is not merely one of mastery and control; it calls up the image of what lurked at the center of the Cretan labyrinth: the Minotaur, devourer of young lives. Kate's own youth has been devoured, yielded up to others.

Unfortunately, Wharton falters. The novella's end seems to endorse Kate's wasted life of 'sterile misery' (111)[11] by showing

Dick as grateful and redeemed. He has not used the plans; her sacrifices have kept him honest. There *is* some psychological believability in Kate's having become a sort of internalized conscience for Dick, who tells his mother that

> old things you'd said and done kept coming back to me, crowding between me and what I was trying for, looking at me without speaking, like old friends I'd gone back on, till I simply couldn't stand it any longer (162).

Here we see a *healthy* sense of shame operating, keeping Dick from a dishonorable act. However, the conclusion (with a sentimental tableau like that ending *The Touchstone*) seems at wide variance with what has gone before, given the very real pain one feels for Kate's suffering and desolation. Wharton has movingly and realistically portrayed a young woman shocked and shamed into what is a deeper betrayal of her own independence and potential, but the ending denies the emotions powering the text. Kates 'reward' for a lifetime of sacrifice seems paltry when measured against what she has given up. The hopelessness of *Bunner Sisters* would be a far more fitting conclusion. This assessment is confirmed by R.W.B. Lewis' report of what Wharton was reading while she wrote *Sanctuary*: Flaubert's *Madame Bovary*. Lewis concludes that Wharton identified with Emma Bovary's 'sense of suffocation,' and records that she 'transcribed, underlined, and wrote marginal strokes next to' the following revealing passage: 'Her life was as cold as a garret whose windows face north, and boredom like a spider spun its web in the shadows, to all the corners of her heart.'[12] Though the second part of *Sanctuary* suffers from *longueurs* (it is almost twice the length of the first), the real 'problem' with the novella is its inappropriately happy ending and not Kate's decision, which is perfectly consonant with her personality as Wharton presents it. A second, minor flaw is the sketchiness of Kate's background, which has, in a way, encouraged critics to overlook its influence in shaping her character.

What stopped Wharton from carrying the book through to its organic conclusion? Her courage may have failed her as she created with deepening intensity one of her 'landscapes of desolation' (as Cynthia Griffin Wolff terms them), yet she felt compelled to resist its implications, as she had in ending *The Touchstone*. The story may have drawn too heavily and explicitly on her own sense of entrapment with her husband Teddy – and earlier, with her mother. In *A Backward Glance*, Wharton records having found out from her mother that a family member had been scandalously involved with 'some woman!'[13] Writing in 1933, the incident may have seemed amusing; perhaps what she felt at the time was something closer to Kate Orme's sense of desolation in the face of ugly truths. I would guess that Wharton said so little about *Sanctuary* at The Mount for several reasons. She may well have been ashamed of her very real artistic failure (especially with an exalted model like Flaubert!) and her failure of nerve in this novella, which unlike *The Touchstone* focuses on a *woman's* disappointment, shame and despair. Despite the tacked-on ending, however, *Sanctuary* is a moving study in hopelessness and living with shame. Wharton so deeply and intuitively understands the way shame can distort and limit a woman's life that we should value her very real achievement in *Sanctuary*, and not let the novella sink any further into critical disregard.

The Mother's Recompense is a far more powerful and effective evocation of a woman's life stunted by shame. Though the novel has not benefited from the resurgence in Wharton studies, that may be changing. It has recently become widely available, in American and English paperback editions, and was the partial focus of a panel at the first Edith Wharton Society Conference held in 1987 at The Mount. In a paper at this session it was suggested that Kate Clephane's return to France at the end of the novel was a sign of growth and insight, even redemptive.[14] In the subsequent lively discussion, this view was vigorously supported by those in the audience who ridiculed the idea of Kate marrying fat and red-faced Fred Landers. Others defended Fred as Kate's last chance for happiness. Marriage to him, or a tentatively hopeful return to France thus emerged as Kate's polar possibilities.

That same split also appears in the recent criticism of this not highly regarded novel. Adeline Tintner argues that Kate finds 'she has a new identity' at the novel's conclusion and has at last 'become an individual.'[15] R.W.B. Lewis and Elizabeth Ammons acknowledge loneliness and abnegation in Kate's return, but balance it – as does Blake Nevius – by her commendable decision not to cause her daughter 'sterile pain.'[16] Conversely, Louis Auchincloss is convinced that Kate and Fred would have had 'happier and better lives married to each other.'[17] With more sensitivity, Cynthia Griffin Wolff suggests that Kate must reject Fred's steady, uncapricious and comfortable love because she wishes to avoid plunging 'into time and change and the compromises of reality.'[18] Somewhat similarly, Marilyn French holds that 'kindly' Fred offered Kate 'a place to be her "real self".'[19]

Both interpretations seriously misread the novel. Kate's return to France is anything but positive and hopeful because it caps a lifetime marked by hiding, silence, and flight. Nor could she marry Fred – but not for the reasons critics point to. What sends her back to France and what keeps her from marrying Fred, in fact, what dominates her entire life is shame. *The Mother's Recompense* is a profound and disturbing study of the ways in which internalized, unconscious shame can cripple an individual's emotional development and poison each and every one of her relationships. It is a compelling, haunting novel of great psychological depth and impact that deserves to be ranked among Wharton's best. It is also a book that haunted Wharton in one form or another from 1900 to 1925, and indeed she started a version of it called 'Disintegration' in 1902.[20]

Examining the role of shame in this novel not only helps us reassess its value, but will explain many of the problems critics have had with its ending, its point of view, its moral focus or dilemma, and the intense emotion that at one particularly crucial moment seems incongruent with the events recorded in the text. The much-discussed incest motif of this novel will also be seen as a *metaphor* for shame.

The novel opens in the South of France where Kate Clephane, in her forties, leads an aimless, impersonal life in the wake of a failed affair with Chris Fenno, whom she still longs for. Twenty years earlier, Kate had abandoned her husband and baby daughter Anne in New York because she felt stifled and constricted. Leaving New York with rich Hylton Davies (their affair lasted two years), she soon repented and tried to see her child again, but was always forbidden access, and had her letters returned. After her ex-husband and implacable mother-in-law are dead, Kate receives an invitation from Anne to return to New York. Kate's past is avoided there, and her discomfort (though balanced by the joy of seeing Anne) becomes overwhelming when she learns Anne is in love with Chris Fenno, whom Kate had an affair with during the war. Her desperate (and outwardly inexplicable) attempts to stop the marriage without letting Anne know why are a failure, and Kate flees back to France, refusing an offer of marriage from Fred

Landers, an old friend and Anne's former guardian.

In the earlier 'Disintegration,' which is only seventy pages in manuscript, the center is the heroine's loneliness and deprivation – Wharton's similar concern in *The Mother's Recompense*. Kate Clephane is the very embodiment of the vulnerability and alienation Kaufman describes as the 'result of internalized shame. Marilyn French has noted that after her return to New York, Kate frequently is overwhelmed by feelings of 'unworthiness' and 'illegitimacy.'[21] But these intrusions into consciousness of her internalized feelings of shame actually predate her return and are rooted in her childhood. Shame has permeated and distorted her relationships, because it is inextricably bound with her identity. Kate has always felt 'awfully alone,'[22] that within her 'all was darkness' (149).

While we know almost nothing specific about Kate's background prior to her marriage, she behaves like a woman irreparably and unspeakably wounded by an early environment in which she never felt quite good enough, never felt valued or wanted. She has learned these beliefs about herself by the ways in which she was treated, and has come to act on them. Why else would she marry a man like boorish, stifling, stingy, rigid, stubborn, ill-tempered John Clephane, who intensified this sense of isolation, of being deficient and unworthy? Her marriage was marked by a 'continual vain effort to adapt herself to her husband's point of view, to her mother-in-law's standards' (58). Marriage did not bring her freedom, merely an exchange of prisons; she re-enacted the analogous scene she experienced growing up – like Kate Orme exchanging Denis for her father. Kate's two-year affair with Hylton Davies after leaving her husband may have offered travel and luxury, but he too was stifling: a man with the 'soul of a club steward' (243). In some ways Kate seems like a portrait of what Wharton might have become without her fierce intelligence, her creativity, her friends, her drive and her good luck.

Kate's desperate escape from the Clephanes deepens her shame because not only has she abandoned her husband, she has done what 'a mother couldn't confess, even to her most secret self' (13) – abandoned her young child. It is not surprising that she keeps Anne's existence a secret from her Riviera set, even when after twenty years, Anne calls her back to New York. Kate could not bear the sense of exposure which would cause her to re-experience the overwhelming shame of her double abandonment, along with the deeper internalized shame stemming from childhood. Tomkins notes that 'every individual. . . is vulnerable to shame. . . whenever he violates the social norms which he inherits by virtue of his membership in society.'[23]

Just as flight brings her imprisonment, so her war-time love affair with Chris Fenno confirms and intensifies her shame. The 'central fact of her experience' (42), this love for Fenno (whose name suggests being trapped – fen, marsh) is portrayed very negatively, despite its having awakened her sexually. Kate's love was 'an isolated and devouring emotion' (82). Fenno's 'restless mind and capricious fancy' (44) forced her to keep him amused, 'and herself amusing' (43). 'His ways of being cruel were innumerable' (205) – like subtly acting boyish to make her feel older than she really was. In this affair, when 'had there ever been a question of what *she* wanted?' (91). Her own needs were insignificant and she was reduced to 'scheming, planning, ignoring, enduring, accepting' (5).[24] Ultimately, she and the simple pleasures she wanted to share with Chris were not enough. Not being able to understand this deficiency (and how can any of us 'understand' being rejected so fundamentally?), was the 'torment of her torments, the inmost pang of her misery' (16).

Kate's longing for closeness, understanding and harmony with Chris continues well after the affair ends, in her futile hope that Chris will telegram and ask her to come back. In fact the first chapter of the novel is dominated by this vain expectation:

> There was no reason why, this very day, this day on which the sunshine had waked her with such a promise, there shouldn't be a message at last, the message for which she had waited for two years, three years; yes, exactly three years and one month – just a word from him to say: '*Take me back.*' (7)

She cannot let go of her need for him, though he 'inflicted on her the bitterest pain she had ever suffered' (15). Chris has even become a sort of mental roadblock; whenever she tries recollecting the years since her flight from the Clephanes, she seldom goes 'farther than the episode with Chris' (13) – he is woven into the very texture of her past (62). She behaves much like contemporary women who remain caught in unsatisfying and even abusive relationships, unable to leave them because of their own shame, and driven by shame to re-enact them.[25]

With Chris, Kate re-enacted almost the identical scenario she had escaped from, once more submerging her own separate self in another's. Such loss of self is a continuing source of shame, Kaufman writes.[26] Kate seems driven to repeat this pattern in her relationships because of her own deep abiding sense of worthlessness and inner deficiency – the shame which remains unconscious. Typically, the roots of such a relationship pattern lie in early failed relationships which induced shame that eventually came to be internalized. In the course of those failures, Kate would also have internalized images of the significant others she was identifying with, and in her subsequent relationships projected onto others 'feelings and reactions learned in the original situation without any question of appropriateness or accuracy.'[27] Internalized shame and internalized images operate at an unconscious level, according to Kaufman.[28]

Taking on the 'role' of Anne's mother when she returns to New York is commended by their family and social circle as touching and beautiful, but it is a move that is rooted in shame just as much as Kate Orme's decision to 'save' Denis' child. This role is doomed to be unsuccessful because Kate repeats the pattern of her previous unfulfilling relationships. She is still an outsider, first of all, only a 'guest' or even 'intruder' in what was once her own home. And she can't ask questions about her daughter, whom she pictures as – for all her kindness – a 'citadel.' The gap between Kate and Anne (as with Kate and everyone) is enormous: there is an 'abyss of all she didn't know about her daughter' (34). This gap helps Kate completely submerge herself in Anne; indeed, she fantasizes becoming Anne's 'background.' For Kate, 'serving Anne, pleasing Anne. . . getting closer to Anne' (82) has the same 'morbid intensity' of her own love for Chris. It is a form of submission. As with her husband and Chris, Kate is forced into silence, withholding the truth about herself and her feelings; she must keep silent in order to be the perfect mother or at least companion. Her relationship with Anne is indeed a fantasy, as some critics have noted.[29]

When Kate begs Chris not to marry Anne, her entreaty cuts to the heart of all her relationships, in which she can never get what she wants:

> He stood leaning against the chimney-piece, his arms crossed, his head a little bent and thrust forward, in the attitude of sullen obstinacy that she knew so well. And all at once in her own cry

she heard the echo of other cries, other entreaties. She saw herself in another scene, stretching her arms to him in the same desperate entreaty, with the same sense of her inability to move him, even to reach him (176).

One almost has the picture here of a hurt and desperate child holding out her arms to a parent, begging to be held, begging for security to be restored. Kaufman notes that after the rupture of relationship between pre-verbal child and parent, reaching 'to be held at such a cataclysmic moment' is the young child's only way 'to affirm himself or the relationship, and thereby feel restored. Asking to be held enables him to find out for certain. . . that he is still loved and wanted, to affirm his own value and well-being.'[30] Those 'other cries, other entreaties,' aren't they Kate's lifetime longing to feel loved and worthwhile? When Anne invites Kate back to New York, Kate cables her old response to little Anne's insistent cries of 'I want my Mummy!' Kate lovingly repeats this phrase to herself, remembering the scene of early communion between them, but couldn't that cry be Kate's as well, calling out to her *own* mother?

Kate's return to New York is no escape from shame (Mrs Lidcote's identical problem in Wharton's 1913 'Autre Temps. . .'), not only because she meets Chris there, but because she still bears that shame deep within her. Though Kate is often on the verge of sharing her sense of inner desolation, 'she dare not,' because 'it was easier to think of speaking than to speak' (230). The facts of her past must be kept secret because her shame is still secret even from herself (hence her forgetfulness and haziness about dates and even her age in the opening chapter). Those critics who say society has forgiven Kate miss the point; her past has simply been ignored in an environment of 'glazed and impenetrable surfaces' (106) where it is unpleasant and embarrassing. Everyone conspires to avoid shame in the novel – it is, after all, under strict social taboo; 'no one wants to hear. . . anything that touches the heart.'[31] Even Fred blushingly urges Kate to not try finding out what Anne knows about her past, to look forward and not back. Kate accurately assesses him early on as a terrified 'man who has tried to buy off fate by one optimistic evasion after another' (40). Tomkins suggests that because 'the free expression of innate affects is extremely contagious and because these are very high-powered phenomena, all societies. . . exercise substantial control over the unfettered expression of affect. . . whether used in speech or [directly].'[32] At several points in the novel, Fred, intending kindness, no doubt, serves this societal function by keeping Kate from freely expressing herself through speech or tears.

People 'typically hide their own shame and avoid approaching anyone else's,' Kaufman finds,[33] and that is the case in *The Mother's Recompense*. Kate returns to a New York, or at least a generation of 'people who dreaded scandal more than disease.'[34] A conspiracy of silence among her family and in-laws echoes her own silence: 'Whatever I'm afraid to ask they'll be equally afraid to tell' (74). Her in-laws are experts at screening out the unpleasant:

> The Drovers and the Tresseltons were great at acting in concert, and at pretending that whatever happened was natural, usual, and not of a character to interfere with one's lunch. When a member of the tribe was ill, the best doctors and most expensive nurses were summoned, but the illness was spoken of as a trifling indisposition; when misfortune befell any one of them, it was not spoken of at all (183).

Kate doesn't want to *have* to confess her secret – that would activate the unconscious shame that she has attempted to banish from her life by 'the narcotic tricks of evasion and ignoring' (266). But we do not have to stay trapped in shame. Helen Merrell Lynd notes that revealing one's shame 'can be in itself an experience of release and expansion, a coming forward of belief in oneself.'[35] Kate, however, never reaches such a moment and remains bound by shame to the last. She wants to avoid the 'peril of explanation' (253) and be 'lifted beyond that miserable moment of avowal' (252). She wants not to be seen, *exposed*, hence her attraction to the anonymous confessional even after she has spoken to Reverend Arklow about 'a friend' with a situation like hers.

The moment of revelation that Kate feared is far more than miserable, it is the most painful and isolating experience in the book. She does not, in fact, confess, but humiliatingly blunders into an acknowledgement of her affair with Chris, having assumed that Fred Landers knew and forgave her. In Tomkins' view, what she experiences is a sharp though partial drop in positive affect, specifically interest or enjoyment, the result of which is shame.[36] From feeling at last joyfully released, understood and forgiven, she plunges into being the object of Fred's amazement and even scorn.

Like everyone else, he believes that Kate had led a blameless life in Europe after breaking off with Hylton Davies. All along, Kate has felt surrounded by 'averted eyes' and 'shrinking voices' (214), and Fred responds in *just* this way. He turns from her, twice covers his eyes – clear indications of the shame he is experiencing – himself shamed by what he finally understands of her past, and for a while has great difficulty looking at Kate. Fred blushes deeply in this scene, and there is a good deal of blushing throughout the novel.

Until that point, Kate did fully intend to marry Fred, as another escape, so that 'there would always be some one [sic] between herself and her thoughts' (243). His reaction makes such a plan hopeless. Kate's refusal of Fred's marriage proposal and her return to the Riviera are really the acts of a woman fleeing the scene of what must feel like perpetual humiliation. 'It was impossible to analyze her anguish. She knew only that she must fly from it, fly as far as she could from the setting of these last indelible impressions' (221). Whether Fred would be an appropriate partner or not is immaterial at this point. He has responded in the worst possible way, deepening her shame, not releasing or comforting it. Having been further made to feel like an outcast, Kate will of course reject his attempts to restore the bond between them. Fred does not forgive her at the right time, and the critics who see no real obstacle in his marriage to Kate have lacked an understanding of shame and its potentially paralyzing impact. At least in the south of France, Kate can surround herself with comforts and distractions in a group of outcasts who themselves have shameful pasts, and to whom she feels superior ('she could carry her head fairly high, and even condescended a little to certain newcomers' [12]). It is both a retreat, and all that she deems herself worthy of. Tomkins observes that 'successful renunciation. . . will reduce the feeling of shame,'[37] and this observation offers insight into what has seemed a puzzling and unsatisfying conclusion. Readers and critics alike have no doubt felt that this renunciation is not – as the text seems to assert – *positive*, but in reality, as Marilyn French notes, a turning away from life, 'a rejection of intimacy and experience in favour of rigid isolation.'[38] Kate *is* withdrawing deeper from life, deeper into herself, rejecting any further emotional intimacies because they have brought her so much pain, and she is driven to this unpleasant extreme because of her shame.

From the first days of her return to New York, Kate senses revulsion in 'every one to whom she had tried to communicate her secret without betraying it' (213). As we learn, she is fairly accurate in assessing her environment, but her own deep sense of transgression and failure inevitably distorts her perceptions. Is the secret of her affair with Chris so *very* great? Partly Kate seems to feel ashamed of Chris himself, to find him unworthy, inferior, but it is not his age that is central to her concern. The Beatrice Cenci portrait and the 'incest motif' in this novel have been read too literally by many critics. The painting – with its lurid associations of incest, torture and death – seems to be in part a straightforwardly ironic comment on John Clephane, the stodgy and dim owner, who has kept this relic of his parents' European travels out of 'a mixture of thrift and filial piety' (36). The 'mundane souvenir' hangs in the Clephanes' New York home 'over the bed reserved for married guests.' John Clephane apparently had no 'knowledge of its subject's history'[39] – an example of the 'naive incongruities' (like 'Caravaggio gamblers' hanging in the dining-room) of Kate's past in this home (36). If its presence is metaphorical, lurking in one of the 'obscure corners' (36) of the Clephane house, the associations are less direct and obvious than the admittedly sensational theme of incest. In the Clephanes' world, pain is ignored (this refrain appears in *The Age of Innocence, Twilight Sleep, The Children,* and *Hudson River Bracketed*), just as this picture, with its sad, red-eyed heroine, has been relegated to a corner of the house. Imprisoned by her father in a remote fortress, tortured and executed for planning to kill him, Beatrice Cenci became legendary as 'an archtypal damsel in distress who had been abused by patriarchal power.'[40] Her story resonates just as powerfully with *betrayal* and *suffocation* as incest, and thus connects quite forcefully with Wharton's 'familiar themes' of 'domination, entrapment, the longing and the failure to escape.'[41] The presence of this portrait copy over a bed for married guests, in conjunction with the failure of Kate's marriage to John Clephane, also offers a dim, doomed view of that state. The Cenci portrait additionally represents the breakdown of family ties into chaos, betrayal and revenge, auguring ill for Kate's return to New York.

Despite critics' claims that Kate 'transgressed generational boundaries,'[42] Chris is not quite young enough to be her son; the age difference between Anne's friend Lilla and Horace MacClew in the novel is far greater. Chris has, however, gotten others to talk about him as having been a 'boy' when he knew Kate in Europe. Louis Auchincloss is correct in noting that 'the prospect of a sexual union between Anne and Chris Fenno' is not 'sufficiently revolting to cause Kate such trauma' as she experiences thinking about the marriage.[43] Where then is the horror? Why does Kate recoil from the vision of Chris marrying Anne, and from the image of the two of them standing, with Chris' arm around Anne, their lips almost touching?

The 'incest motif' here can be viewed within the larger context of shame. Throughout the book, Kate feels outside 'the mysterious circle' (106). Seeing Chris and Anne hug triggers her shame over the liaison with Chris and the ways in which it left her feeling more deficient and unlovable. But more significantly, seeing them reactivates Kate's unconscious shame over a life of failed relationships. Note that their backs are turned to her and that we are twice told she is 'invisible and inaudible' (221). Kate is indeed a 'ghost' whose 'real self' was 'blown about on a lonely wind of anguish' (167); Kaufman notes that shame can appear 'as a sense of feeling insubstantial, not whole, or even empty inside.'[44] She has no warm and accepting family, no loving relationship with a man, has never really had children (because she abandoned Anne), and has no valued friends (could her Riviera set speak of her with the admiration and regard Fred and Nolly speak of Anne?). But Anne has and will have everything her mother does not. Tomkins notes that the vicarious shame caused by other's successes 'increases the distance between the self and the goal,'. . . 'stimulating longing [and heightening] the awareness of what is lacking in one's own experience.'[45] Chris and Anne together are the visible symbol of Kate's lifelong defeat, one that she has always run from because she could not face the shame that is even now unconscious.

We should note that incest in the novel is introduced by way of Kate's thoughts as a *metaphor* of transgression:[46]

> Jealous? Was she jealous of her daughter? Was she physically jealous? Was that the real secret of her repugnance, her instinctive revulsion? Was that why she had felt from the first *as if* some incestuous horror hung between them? (221) [my emphasis]

Implicit in this jealousy are all the possible invidious comparisons Kate could make with her daughter: Anne is young, rich, desired, secure. For a woman with such deep-rooted shame, it would be impossible to simply revel in her daughter's successes – they translate, instead, into reminders, into *proofs* of her own real and imagined inferiority. Now her daughter will have the man she could not keep; she has failed where her daughter will succeed.

Tomkins' affect theory perspective enlarges the traditional psychoanalytical view of incest. In psychoanalytic thought, incest is generally viewed in the context of the family romance, the Oedipal construct. While psychoanalytic theory interprets it narrowly, in specifically sexual terms, Tomkins views the family romance as actually representing more general wishes to *be* the mother and father and to *possess* both of them. But the possession of the good scene is invariably spoiled because the Oedipal scene is a triangular one, according to Tomkins; it is the result of a rival's appearance. That rival can be either the same sex parent or a newborn sibling, and the intrusion of a rival makes a previously good scene turn bad by generating shame. 'In the psychoanalytic myth,' Tomkins holds, 'the crime of the son is voyeuristic by witnessing the "primal scene" and Oedipus is punished, in kind, by blindness.'[47] Affectively, the theme of incest is always infused with shame and disgust, both of which Kate experiences here.

In *The Mother's Recompense* incest can be viewed as a metaphor for the appearance of a rival upon the scene. Kate returns to New York anticipating the good scene of reunion, yet ultimately experiences that scene turned bad because she discovers that her daughter is to marry her former lover. No incest has actually occured, *even in imagination*. And the transgression that horrifies Kate is not violation of the incest taboo, it is the intrusion into consciousness of her lifetime of failure and humiliation. She has never had 'success in human affairs,' but only 'at best the doubtful gift of discerning. . . why she failed' (258). More so than ever before, Kate feels herself inherently deficient and flawed, a failure at the core of her being. She comes face to face with the truth: the lover who had rejected her desires the daughter she herself abandoned twenty years before. Chris Fenno is a rival for her daughter's affections every bit as much as her daughter has become a rival for his. Each poisons Kate's relationship with the other.

However Kate proceeds, there is inevitable shame – the shame of having abandoned her daughter, the shame of having been rejected by Chris, and ultimately her internalized unconscious shame that predates both. The scene in which she 'discovers' Anne and Chris together fuses two powerful post-childhood scenes of shame, confirming her loss of both Anne and Chris, for she can possess neither, and further magnifying her already corrosive sense of failure and isolation.

Kate must flee such an environment, but running away has not been Kate's only way of confronting the enormity of her shame. Like Glennard in *The Touchstone*, she has utilized contempt to lift herself above others to neutralize her shame (living among her expatriate community she has ample opportunity for this feeling). The book is full of satirical observations of those around Kate, which are not, as Cynthia Griffin Wolff suggests, Wharton's authorial intrusions,[48] but Kate's *own* response, flowing naturally out of her shame. In these situations, she first finds herself feeling either out of place, insignificant or even frightened in a group, then she observes those around her with irony verging on contempt. When Kate seeks Anne, for instance, after their rupture over Chris, at the Drovers' Long Island mansion, her shame quickly modulates to contempt. At first she feels 'tenuous and spectral' (183), completely insignificant, and then wonders whether the Drovers or the Tresseltons have the smaller noses. Likewise, at an earlier party at which she feels shockingly unremarkable to those around her, she observes that the blandness of American youths made them look like 'miles and miles between two railway stations' (71). In response to feeling excluded and unimportant, to what she perceives as 'indifference' at one point (and we know how loaded the term is for Wharton), Kate has temporarily made herself superior through contemptuous irony. Contempt may insulate against shame, 'but only at the expense of distorted relationships with others.'[49] Like her silence, it further stifles the real woman inside of her, and is not enough to keep shame from overwhelming her.

Kate Clephane has never been deeply understood as a woman crippled by internalized, unconscious shame, and driven into lonely exile and silence. That lack of understanding has hindered an appreciation of Wharton's real achievement in *The Mother's Recompense*. Among recent critics, Margaret McDowell, for instance, calls the book 'inferior,'[50] Elizabeth Ammons terms it 'stale' and finds that Wharton treats the reunion of Kate and Anne 'unrealistically,' which seems a confusion of Wharton's perspective with Kate's.[51] Louis Auchincloss has trouble understanding Kate's renunciation[52] and Cynthia Griffin Wolff holds that the point of view is seriously flawed.[53] The lists of complaints could go on, but they seem less relevant when one carefully considers the centrality of shame in this novel, which is full of the rhetoric of that affect: 'embarrassment,' 'embarrassed,' 'embarrassingly,' 'shyness,' 'humiliated,' 'humiliatingly.' In addition, the characters often talk about their 'pride,' and as noted before, there is a good deal of blushing throughout. Perhaps now we can extoll this novel for its true, compelling, even hypnotic portrait of Kate Clephane, and Wharton's rich evocation of shame's crippling impact on personality and relationships. Its hitherto unappreciated power lends credence to Gaillard Lapsley's claim that Wharton 'was possessed by a sense of compassion deeper and more authentic than I have ever seen in any other human being.'[54]

Like so many of Wharton's doomed and defeated heroines, Kate Orme and Kate Clephane face an insidious enemy that was once external but has become inextricably part of them through internalization; this we have not seen, but can clearly infer from their actions, the way they think about themselves, and the tenor of their relationships. Kate Orme fled into a marriage where she hoped to salvage some positive vision of life, but wound up involved in deeper suffering. Wharton's happy ending does little to counteract the negative arc of the book. Kate Clephane has committed a series of acts that grow out of and confirm the worst she feels about herself: marrying a jailor instead of a husband, abandoning her baby and her home, engaging in two affairs with somewhat shabby men. Returning to her former home exposes her to even deeper humiliations and she has no recourse but to flee to a narrow environment that is the best she thinks she deserves. In these two books (whose characters bear the same first name perhaps because their fates are so similar), the emphasis has been on shame distorting and shrinking an individual's possibilities, forcing that individual into seemingly illogical and self-destructive actions. Wharton was just as astute an observer of the ways in which shame could destroy relationships, and could make readers experience both sides of the dissolution. The books to be discussed in Chapter 3 powerfully convey the loss of hope and connection that two people can suffer when shame thrusts them ineluctably apart.

3

Divided by Shame

Elizabeth Ammons makes the important point that Wharton 'began her novel-writing career by courting popular taste.'[1] *The Valley of Decision* was a historical romance, one of the widely-read genres of the period, but even though Wharton wanted to appeal to a popular audience, she 'did not want to be pigeonholed as a lightweight author of diverting ladies' fiction.'[2] This goal, Ammons says, explains Wharton's 'burdensome show of knowledge' in the two-volume novel, set in eighteenth-century Italy.[3] Janet Goodwyn offers some ways of taking Ammons' observation even further and understanding this unusual choice of a first novel. Goodwyn notes the similarities with George Eliot's first novel, *Romola*, which she points out that Elaine Showalter sees

> as an illustration of general shamefastness or anxiety in women concerning their lack of education or simple ability to write. . . The act of research then is a strategy of self-protection; better to make a display of pedantry than to expose one's efforts to charges of ignorance and ridicule.[4]

That Wharton's choice of launching her career as a novelist with this particular book partly has its roots not just in her admiration for Eliot and her love of the period, but in her *shame* is also clear from *A Backward Glance*. As Goodwyn points out, Wharton 'assumes a potentially hostile critic'[5] when she writes that she did not study hard at all to write the book, but rather absorbed the details, and was 'compelled to write it' after 'years of intimacy with the Italian eighteenth century [which] gradually and imperceptibly fashioned the tale.'[6] It is a ridiculous claim, if we do not understand it as defensive, a proud denial. We would not need Wharton's extensive notes for the novel's historical details to know that a book so steeped in its time was the product of hard work, not osmosis. Cynthia Griffin Wolff notes that though the book at first seems both different from Wharton's subsequent novels, and an 'irreconcilable distance' from Wharton herself, the problems in the book 'exhibit a direct relationship to Wharton's life, and the language here as elsewhere bears her characteristic stamp.'[7] I would add that the language of shame is present in the most significant and interesting relationship of the book – that of Odo and Fulvia. Shame and disappointment divide them throughout the novel.

Despite the wealth of period details in what reads like a guide book straining to be colorful and charming, the story is not very complicated. Odo Valseca, a poor and lonely relation of the ducal family of Pianura, ends up inheriting the title. Attracted to Enlightenment ideas through the education of the very learned Fulvia Vivaldi, who becomes his mistress, Odo eventually turns conservative after she is assassinated. His attempts to reform his Duchy have run up against entrenched interests and popular ignorance and superstition, and Odo ultimately 'has failed at living up to the ideals that Fulvia taught him.' Like Newland Archer in *The Age of Innocence*, he is really bound by convention, Carol Wershoven explains, and has only flirted 'with the new.'[8]

Like many other poor relations of noble houses in a time of Italy's 'abasement' (I,100), Odo lives an impoverished life, 'taunted. . . for being a beggar's brat' (I,3). He feels 'a melancholy kinship' (I,4) with the suffering face of St Francis in a ruined chapel, and suffers 'in a dumb animal way, without understanding why life was so hard on little boys' (I,7). Odo will be plucked by his selfish cold mother from this 'mist of indifference' (I,9) and brought to court, but his emotional environment hardly changes, and he is all but ignored by his mother. Like Wharton herself, as she writes in *A Backward Glance*, he discovers a library and spends 'many blissful hours' reading (I,51). His intelligence and his feeling for nature isolate him in a 'stifling' atmosphere of 'emptiness' (I,110–11).

Meeting Fulvia Vivaldi, the daughter of a scholar, puts Odo's 'ignorance to the blush' (I,139), but she herself blushes under his 'wondering gaze' (I,140). She becomes his touchstone, because he compares her to the frivolous woman he pays court to, and sees his role as rather shameful: he is nothing more than 'a puny doll condemned, as the strings of custom pulled, to feign the gestures of immortal passions' (I,134). Odo makes many visits to her house, attracted by the free-wheeling intellectual discussions there, but his presence alerts the state's security apparatus. One evening she greets him at the door with a strange and fierce kiss. Alone with him, 'her face hidden,' and referring to what just happened, she flushes 'to the brow' (I,160). Furious at his confusion, she asks if he thinks 'by feigning ignorance, to prolong [her] humiliation?' (I,161). It is Odo's turn to feel humiliated when she explains that her father is now under surveillance: 'It was Odo whose gaze fell. Never perhaps had he been conscious of cutting a meaner figure' (I,162), but his shame is mixed with admiration for Fulvia's courage and he confesses: 'I have been blind indeed, and what you say *abases* me to earth' (162) [my emphasis]. Fulvia doesn't believe him, and the scene ends with his feeling rebuked, and Fulvia flushed and distant when he asks how he can repair his mistake.

Odo spends 'a restless night face to face with his first humiliation. Though the girl's rebuff had cut him to the quick, it was the vision of the havoc his folly had wrought that stood between him and sleep' (I,165). Having endangered the life of a man he respects is deeply disturbing, and Odo cannot even tell a friend what happened, after he's been warned to stay away from the Vivaldi home, because 'shame restrained him' (I,177). Odo is thus not only attracted to Fulvia, but it is a desire to overcome his shame that draws him even closer, despite the enormous differences between them. As Carol Wershoven notes,

> Fulvia wants to show Odo. . . the value of free inquiry, the possibilities of change and improvement that enlightenment may bring. She is fully committed to a political, intellectual ideal. Odo will only be committed (and never fully) to Fulvia. The results of such a mismatch will be disastrous for both people.[9]

A road accident brings him together with Vivaldi and his daughter, in whom Odo discovers 'a blush of recognition' (I,188). They are in flight, and Odo flushes 'to the forehead' wondering if they suspect him as 'the cause of [the] misadventure' – but he insists on helping them get across the border, 'if not to atone, at least to give practical evidence of his contrition' (I,191–192). Odo blushes when Fulvia suggests he save himself the inconvenience, and blushes 'furiously' to have to admit that his servant may not be entirely trustworthy (I,193). Fulvia is not at all grateful, and when he helps her into his carriage, 'to his *mortification* she merely laid two reluctant finger-tips in his hand and took her seat without a word of thanks or so much as a glance at her rescuer' (I,194) [my emphasis]. Soon after, hailed in a crowded square for his looks, he finds that 'so modest a success was not without solace to his vanity' (I,196). Though he has promised to help the Vivaldis escape the next day, a night of revelry makes him oversleep and miss the rendezvous: 'He dropped into a chair and hid his face with a groan. He had failed them again, then, and this time how cruelly and basely!' (I,216). He is bitter and full of criticism: 'He who had fed his fancy on high visions, cherishing in himself the latent patriot and hero [had broken] the first law of manliness and honor!. . . in a flash of self-contempt he saw himself as [Fulvia] no doubt beheld him' (I,220).

When he meets her again in Venice, she is a nun. She shrinks from him, and where he was once 'humbled at her feet' (II,72) the positions now seem reversed. Still, when he asks why she won't trust him, 'he burned with blushes in the darkness' (II,73). He longs to help her escape her convent, where she has been dumped by her relatives, who do not want to support her, but he wonders if 'having been the witness of her *humiliation* must insensibly turn her against him' (II,83) [my emphasis]. At an arranged meeting in the convent, she keeps blushing in his presence, but *he* is mortified to realize that she thinks of him as a friend, not a possible lover: 'Once again he found himself the prisoner of his folly' (II,88). Determined to rescue her, he is 'resolved to let no rashness or negligence hinder the attempt, and to prove, by the discretion of his course, that he was no longer the light fool who had once hazarded her safety' (II,90). Successful in his attempt to rescue her, he is embarrassed recalling when he first tried to help her and her father, and failed, as well as feeling ashamed to realize that she is happier being free than being with him.

Gaining the throne, he is determined 'to redeem the credit of his house' (II,139) as he is to have Fulvia at his side. But she has rejected him because 'his duty to his country must take precedence over his love for [her].'[10] Several years later, she returns to Pianura as his mistress, and Fulvia 'became the fashion. The literati celebrated her scholarship, the sonneteers her eloquence and beauty'– so much so, that Odo feels 'deserted' (II,190) and almost jealous of her renown. It is not a joyous reunion.

Odo remembered that he had once thought her nearness would dispel his hesitations. At first it had been so; but gradually the contact with her fixed enthusiasm had set up within him an opposing sense of the claims she ignored. The element of dogmatism in her faith showed the discouraging sameness of the human mind (II,223).

Their union has come 'too late. . . when delay and disillusionment had imperceptibly weakened the springs of passion' (II,220). Even worse, Fulvia realizes that 'she had become to him the embodiment of a single thought – a formula, rather than a woman' (II,222). Odo's attempted reforms in Pianura only leave him feeling 'his impotence' (II,229) and Odo ends up facing indifference and even hostility on a large, public scale. 'Honor and power had come to him, and they had *abased* him in the dust' (II,229) [my emphasis]. Despite her fierce independence of thought, Fulvia ends up stung by gossip, realizing that Odo's heart is not fully in the new constitution she has urged him to implement. When she is shot by enemies of reform, Odo lashes out briefly in reprisals, becomes ill, retreats to a monastery and ends up reassuming the throne being 'as repressive a leader as any of his ancestors ever were.'[11] Forced to abdicate, he ends up utterly disillusioned, riding off to fight the invading French armies.

Carol Wershoven reads the conservative turn of Odo and Fulvia's increasing dogmatism as evidence that *The Valley of Decision* is like *Ethan Frome* 'a novel about destruction. . . about the warping and distortion of personalities through imprisonment in a static nightmare world.'[12] That indeed is the emotional core of the novel. Odo and Fulvia's relationship is dominated by shame and humiliation, anger and contempt in response to it, and when they do become lovers, it is in the context of deep personal and political disillusionment for both of them – a shameful ending. One could say that despite their physical relationship, they had always been divided, first by Odo's sense of inferiority, then his need to atone for having failed her, and finally his sense of distance and superiority.

Among the books Wharton wrote in the tremendously productive years immediately after *The House of Mirth* was the novella *Madame de Treymes*, and critics are sharply divided about its worth, though few discuss it at length. Some class the story of an American encountering the 'convolutions of French family customs and social restrictions for the first time'[13] as inferior Henry James, and the novella certainly owes a great deal to James's *The American*, 'Madame de Mauves,' and even *The Ambassadors*. Other critics find the novel superior to James' *The American*, subtler and more realistic.

The question of Jamesian influence aside, I think that Louis Auchincloss is right in calling the novella a lively, subtle and humorous story.[14] The book is enjoyable simply for its hero's clear admiration of Paris compared to New York (which reads like Wharton's own feelings). But even more intriguing is Wharton's skillful social contrast of Americans who are either innocent and travelling or quirky and transplanted, with, on the other hand, snobbish French nobles of the Faubourg Saint-Germain who prey on them in various ways.

R.W.B. Lewis notes that though Wharton's novella was the discerning 'fruit of her first long dip into Parisian society,' it was another working out of her 'dominant theme,' 'Wharton. . . suggesting that the psychic imprisonment of women could occur anywhere and even under the most gracious of conditions.'[15] I would add that Wharton also works more subtly with the international theme than has been recognized, because she contrasts different notions of honor and shame in this novella. While the French here are socially adept at hiding embarrassment and Americans seem unable to, it is the French whose behavior is deeply shameful, and the Americans (for the most part) who resist dishonorable actions, though shame also plays a role in their motivation.

Visiting with his old friend Fanny Frisbee (now the Marquise de Malrive) in Paris, John Durham is intensely struck by the city's 'vast and consummately ordered spectacle.'[16] It is a city 'boldly and deliberately planned as a background for the enjoyment of life,' unlike his native 'lamentable New York,' a place of 'unenlightened ugliness' (165). Fanny strikes him somewhat similarly: '. . . completely equipped. . . made up of exquisitely cared for and finely related details' (166). She has absorbed French manners and ease, and can even calmly accept his moved silence in her presence, without any sign of embarrassment, whereas 'in her Frisbee days' (167) she might have filled the silence with nervous chatter. His recognition of the change marks his awareness that such moments are embarrassing to Americans, who he sees clearly and even with a little pity. Fanny has indeed become so French that she marvels at Durham's mother and sisters as 'fresh and innocent and simple' (169); nothing proves how French she has become as this 'exotic enjoyment of Americanism' (179).

it was the finish, the modelling, which Madame de Malrive's experience had given her that set her apart from the fresh uncomplicated personalities of which she had once been simply the most charming type. The influences that had lowered her voice, regulated her gestures, toned her down to a harmony with the warm dim background of a long social past – these influences had lent to her natural fineness of perception a command of expression adopted to complex conditions (179).

But Fanny's mysterious changes also hint at 'unprobed depths of initiation' (178), depths Durham begins to sound when he proposes to her. Though Fanny has been separated from her 'reprehensible' husband, she cannot divorce the Marquis, and indeed she flushes deeply when Durham mentions the word. The Marquis' family will not allow it, and she tries to explain to Durham that for the French, family is more important than the individual and divorce completely unacceptable, therefore, on more than just religious grounds. Divorce is inherently, then, a source of profound shame. She herself wants to do nothing that would cause a scandal, because her son has 'been brought up in the French tradition of scrupulously preserved appearances' (176). Indeed, she seems dedicated to fighting a spiritual battle for control of her son, who she has already lost in many ways. The boy will be 'taught to see vileness and corruption in everyone not of his own way of thinking' and his whole life will be planned – 'his political and religious convictions, his judgments of people, his sense of honour, his ideas of women, his whole view of life' (172). She must be there to throw her own moral weight into the balance. (The situation is thus vaguely reminiscent of *Sanctuary* and also bears some resemblance to a story discussed in Chapter 5, 'The Quicksand.') Fanny seems afraid of her husband's family's machinations and power, and Durham swears that he will find out from Fanny's sister-in-law, Madame de Treymes, what the family's intentions are, since Madame de Treymes both likes Fanny and hates the Marquis, her brother.

Durham seeks information about Madame de Treymes and her family from friends, the Boykins, after having briefly met her and found out that she has never seen an American before! It is a fact Fanny reveals about her sister-in-law 'with a faintly embarrassed smile' (181). The Boykins, expatriates who live in a Little America, exist in perpetual contempt of France and the French: 'Chronic opposition toward a society chronically unaware of them' (182). Actively disapproving of the life around them, and clinging to the memory of each slight, each distasteful act of 'the abominable foreigner,' the Boykins remind Durham 'of persons peacefully following the course of a horrible war by pricking red pins in a map' (183). The military metaphor is an appropriate one for the social battle that is to follow. Apparently Fanny 'dropped all her American friends since her marriage' (183), the Boykins relate, and has even avoided them in her 'five or six years' of being separated. Surely, we assume, Fanny was at first pressured by her family and not motivated by snobbery, but has kept her *recent* isolation because of shame, unwilling to expose the unhappiness of her married life, and to cause any kind of scandal that would hurt her son. The dynamics of scandal inevitably involve dishonor and loss of face – the dynamics of shame. The Boykins also reveal that Madame de Treymes has had quite a checkered romantic history and is currently ruining herself to pay the debts of a charming, debt-ridden prince.

Durham manages to get some time with Madame de Treymes by spending a good deal of money at a charity bazaar she is part of (a traditional way in which the French of the Faubourg fleece Americans). When they are alone, this dark exotic creature point-blank asks him if he wants to marry Fanny. After some fencing she makes clear that her brother the Marquis will never agree to a divorce, but she agrees to meet Durham again (marking the privilege of even a little time with her!) at the Boykins. *They* had always asserted it was shameful to curry favor with the French and see 'thrusting' oneself into French society as a 'loss of self-respect' (184), but the Boykins are flustered by the idea of having a dinner for Madame de Treymes and out of shame, they overdo it. The too elaborate meal is the mark of their 'national determination not to be "downed" by the despised foreigner, to show a wealth of material resource obscurely felt to compensate for the possible lack of other distinctions' (194). But Madame de Treymes is cool, especially when her lover the prince is crudely referred to and she does not show 'anything so simple and unprepared as embarrassment' (194).

In a *tête-à-tête* with Durham, Madame de Treymes reveals she is willing to help him. And then she confesses unspeakable unhappiness in her marriage, shocking and embarrassing Durham into asking how he can help her. Confessing her financial straits because of the prince (though she says she borrowed her brother's and husband's money and cannot repay it) she so astonishes Durham that she has to explain 'humiliating [herself] before a stranger . . .' (197–8). She is not as lucky as an American woman, who can 'seek liberation without dishonour' (198), and she intimates clearly that she 'was ready to sell her influence' (199). Disgusted both by her willingness to help him if paid and her lying (because she hasn't actually mentioned the prince), Durham refuses the deal. A contemporary reviewer for *La Revue de Deux Mondes* said that 'one is astonished that a well-born woman gives up the most intimate and most shameful secret of her heart to a stranger, almost a first-comer.'[17] Wharton notes that Americans do not understand how centuries of confession have made this possible – and while her reasoning may be simplistic, Madame de Treymes's outburst is not 'unbelievable.' Her secret is gossiped about, anyway (even the Boykins know), but her revealing it to Durham makes a certain kind of sense – he is someone who can help her, and she is desperate. Even *more* humiliating would be admitting the truth of her need to a family member, where the condemnation risked would be in the context of deep emotional ties, and thus more devastating.

In any event, Durham does not tell Fanny exactly what transpired in his talk with Madame de Treymes. And though he later feels guilty about hiding the truth from Fanny, he unambivalently feels that he cannot be involved in such a dishonorable, shameful transaction, or involve Fanny. His love for her cannot be placed on the same level as an adulterous affair. Yet Fanny hears from Madame de Treymes that the divorce will go through because the family is satisfied that Fanny had not intended to proceed despite their opposition. She was not, in other words, about to disgrace, to shame them, and they can thus relent – or so says Madame de Treymes. When Durham next unexpectedly meets Madame de Treymes at Fanny's she once again is gracious, as 'her surprises never wore the awkward form of embarrassment' (206). Yet Durham can see how distraught she is about the prince: 'accustomed to the pale inward grief of the inexpressive races. . . [he] was positively startled by the way in which she seemed to have been openly stretched on the pyre; he felt almost an indelicacy in the ravages so tragically confessed' (206). Rather than hide her grief, Madame de Treymes seems to be shamefully forcing it on his attention, and he feels disgusted. Ironically, he is ashamed of his own reaction: 'Such sensations required, for his own relief, some immediate penitential escape' (206) and in their following conversation he flushes deeply twice, noting that this is an occasion for him to 'abase' himself for having failed her, and he offers his help. More ironically, Madame de Treymes cryptically warns that accepting help would be 'robbing [him] shamelessly' because she has already taken something in return for her 'service' (209).

Appearances require Durham and Fanny to separate for 'a decent interval' (211) while the divorce goes through, but in a final long interview with Madame de Treymes, Durham learns that Fanny and he have been tricked: French law will require that the Marquis de Malrive will gain sole custody of his son in this case – which had always been the plan. Though Madame de Treymes has said, 'we are of different races, with a different point of honour' (215), for the first time she drops her eyes, blushes, looks down and blushes again to reveal her duplicity. Now, she displays her shame openly and facially. Fanny is lost to him, Durham realizes, because she will never consent to giving up her son.

The same reviewer who doubted that Madame de Treymes would confess anything so shameful to Durham also felt that the novella's real truth was its revelation of what Americans thought of the French. To some extent that is accurate; the novella reveals what Wharton – at that particular point – thought about the French and Americans in terms of honor and shame. Though France and Paris are magnetic and admirable, the French are clearly more dissolute, less honorable underneath a facade of manners and respectability. That respectability crushes the individual even more than the American variety, and has ruined Fanny Frisbee's life, making her fearful of plots and undercurrents, and desolately committed to 'saving' her son when she knows that he is in many ways lost. Embarrassment – which is shame in a social context – is clearly *de trop*, something to be avoided, and Madame de Treymes is exemplary in this regard. Social shame thus becomes a source of further shame. Durham, on the other hand, blushes freely because he cannot hide his feelings as well; *his* feelings are much less regulated and suppressed. Thus 'the whole width of the civilization' (167) between himself and Fanny includes differing notions of honorable behavior at the level of action, and at the level of social interaction. Also at work are different display rules governing the expression of shame in the two cultures. Durham and Madame de Treymes are representatives of their respective cultures and therefore reflect *differences* in the display of shame in social contexts.

What ultimately divides Durham from Fanny is his initial inability to do something dishonorable, to overcome his disgust over

Madame de Treymes' private life, in order to gain what he wants. His inability to act dishonorably is admirable and American here, but Wharton would not develop this contrast much in her fiction, perhaps partly because James had been there before her so successfully. More to the point, however, E.K. Brown writes that this broad international contrast was not as interesting to Wharton as moral issues.[18] If Durham is honest, then the Boykins are a comic example of dishonesty and lack of insight into themselves and their situation. Their nervous delight at suddenly scraping acquaintance with the Faubourg Saint-Germain, which they have professed to abhor, is an amusing cultural comment. They have clearly acted out of shame, out of feeling inferior, and end up hiding that by airily claiming to know Madame de Treymes quite well.

Wharton seems to have been amused and stimulated by the contrasts she saw in French and American society, and especially by the contrasts in the kinds of feelings one could acceptably express or reveal in public. The rules governing the open display of affect, shame being one, are decidedly culture-specific. And the open expression of shame is clearly problematic. Shame is an emotion that is ambivalently experienced and inherently so, because one part of the self still longs for reunion while another part of the self hides and covers the face. Therefore shame is both deeply disturbing and deeply divided, with the self feeling divided within and from others. Wharton tends in this novella to stay on the surface in her observations about shame, perhaps because the setting was so relatively new to her. In *The Reef*, also set in France, Wharton's characters would not be French, and her observations would be far more profound.

Upon its publication in 1912, *The Reef* was given a grandiloquent (though guarded) blessing by Henry James, and for many years after was his 'godchild.'[19] James wrote Wharton that the novel was 'the finest thing' she had done, praising its 'psychologic Racinian unity, intensity and gracility,' and ranking her above George Eliot.[20] That blessing turned into something of a curse. As James' reputation continued to decline, Wharton's ostensibly most Jamesian novel suffered as well.[21] The Anglo–American revival of James in the late 1930s and after World War II did not bring about a subsequent rehabilitation of Wharton. The Wharton revival of the mid-1970s, sparked by R.W.B. Lewis' Pulitzer-winning biography and the rise of feminist criticism, did not help the novel's reputation either. Only recently has the novel begun to be reclaimed from James' heavy benediction.

Yet one of James' comments about the novel's protagonist, Anna Leath, pinpointed a significant side of the book that critics have not examined. Admiring Wharton's creation of this 'exquisite thing' whose 'finest, scarce differentiated notes are sounded with a wonder of delicacy,' James mused: 'I'm not sure her oscillations are not beyond our notation.'[22]

Recent critics have explained Anna's character in terms of a sexist and repressive society, or the double standard for male and female sexual conduct, or seen her as conflicted about her sexuality and aggression, or narcissistic.[23] While the novel is certainly open to these various interpretations, some of which overlap, there are *indeed* 'oscillations' in the novel that have eluded critics who have lacked an accurate terminology to describe what is deepest in Anna's character: a fundamental sense of her own inadequacy and failure. James perceived but could not pinpoint Anna Leath's *shame*. Shame and humiliation can be read as central to the entire novel, the catalysts of its major actions. George Darrow and Anna Leath both unsuccessfully struggle against the shame that shapes their behavior and destroys their chances of happiness by inexorably dividing them from each other and themselves.

Twenty years before the novel begins, George Darrow, now a diplomat, was in love with Anna, but their relationship disintegrated for reasons no longer clear to him. When they meet in England after a twelve-year separation, Anna is now widowed, and they fall in love again. Having proposed to her, Darrow is twice put off from getting an answer. Her second postponement of his visit – this time while he is en route to Givré, her late husband's chateau in France – precipitates the action that will help unravel their relationship once again, but more painfully for everyone involved.

Anna sends Darrow a telegram that reaches him as his train for Dover is about to leave: 'Unexpected obstacle. Please don't come till the thirtieth.'[24] The book opens with this distancing delay. Some critics have characterized Darrow's response to Anna's telegram as resentment, annoyance or peevishness[25] – but it goes far beyond that. All the way to Dover he feels *hammered* by the telegram's words, and in a rain storm at Dover feels 'stung and blinded' by 'a fresh fury of derision' (3). Anna's message leaves a 'mocking echo' (9) and twice more we are told that Darrow is struck by 'the derision of his case' (5). Struggling through the crowded station, he is 'obscurely outraged':

> It was as though all the people about him had taken his measure and known his plight; as though they were contemptuously bumping and shoving him like the inconsiderable thing he had become. 'She doesn't want you, doesn't want you, doesn't want you,' their umbrellas and their elbows seemed to say (11).

Note not only Darrow's sense of exposure to the contempt and mockery of strangers, and an almost paranoid sense of his inner life being spread out for all to see, but his sense of a physical assault that comes as the symbol of his insignificance. Anna's telegram, her second delay, has clearly plunged him into the torment of shame, which is the affective core of Darrow's sense of being fooled and abandoned, and of his doubts that she truly wants him. Darrow worries about Anna's indifference, a word we know has deep resonance in Wharton's fictional world and in her psyche. The intensity of his response, and the shape it takes, make mere annoyance or peevishness completely out of the question, and help explain the disturbing sequel of Anna's temporary rejection.

After their long separation, Darrow found Anna subtly and beautifully changed by marriage and widowhood; she is now 'a finer and surer. . . instrument of expression' (4) who is no longer 'elusive and inaccessible,' but 'communicative and kind' (6). Darrow senses that 'his meeting with her had annihilated the intervening years' (6). Surely he can expect this more reachable woman to not put him off as she apparently had in the past? But she does, and by postponing their *tête-à-tête*, she inadvertently triggers his shame, and then rage – both of which divide him from Anna.

Imagine Darrow's state: after all these years he has found Anna again and pictures a future together, one in which she will help him reach his goal of being a writer and scholar. We do not have to approve of his visions of happiness to recognize their importance to Darrow, and that they are quite shattered, as Kate Orme's were in *Sanctuary*. We see his hopes destroyed again when he pictures finding a letter from Anna at his Paris hotel. He 'had even gone so far as to imagine that its contents might annul the writer's telegraphed injunction, and call him to her side at once. . .' (46) [Wharton's ellipsis]:

Mrs Leath had not written – she had not taken the trouble to explain her telegram. Darrow turned away [from the front desk] with a sharp pang of *humiliation*. Her frugal silence *mocked* his prodigality of hopes and fears (47) [my emphases].

Shame is an ambivalent affect, because in the midst of a rupture with others one longs for réunion, as Darrow longs here for Anna to reverse her decision, to explain, *to reach out to him*. In *The Touchstone* Glennard experienced an analogous conflict, wanting to confess to Alexa, but distancing her, and Kate Clephane in *The Mother's Recompense* longed to yield up her secret, while remaining desperate to keep it. Darrow's sense of mockery and derision is not accidental; as we have seen, exposure is essential to the phenomenological experience of shame. Darrow has plummeted from the heights of being a man in love, a man with an exciting future, to nothing more than an 'inconsiderable being,' an 'anonymous rag' (17) shoved around at a train station. Later, when he is certain that Anna has not written, he feels deeply disappointed in her, another source of shame. Thinking of Anna as 'trivial or insincere' is so painful, such a violation of his image of her, that he feels 'a blind desire to punish someone else for the pain' of this perception (55). Rage is a frequent response to shame, which insulates oneself from the person who triggers the shame; because of socialization, in our culture men are more likely to respond with rage directed outwards than inwards as women do (this rage is frequently misread as depression, which is actually conjoined shame and distress).[26]

The 'someone' Darrow can punish is close at hand, in the next hotel room: Sophy Viner, whom he met at Dover and accompanied to Paris. In London, Sophy had been the secretary of a vulgar hostess, Mrs Murrett, whose barely respectable 'salon' he used to visit in amorous pursuit of Lady Ulrica, who was apparently no lady. At Dover, where Darrow shared his umbrella with Sophy, offering to help locate her lost luggage, he only recognized her face, though Sophy remembered him well. Darrow is intrigued by natural, comradely, enthusiastic Sophy, but his already keen sense of exposure is unexpectedly heightened early in their first conversation. He discovers that Sophy and others had observed him at Mrs Murrett's, talked about him and mocked Lady Ulrica as well: 'It was odd. . . to discover suddenly that the blurred tapestry of Mrs Murrett's background had all the while been alive and *full of eyes*' (17–18) [my emphasis].

Orphaned and poor, 'alone in a busy and indifferent world' (23), Sophy has had a sad, lonely life with little joy in it, and Darrow soon realizes through her conversations about acting and Paris that she has been starved for experience, for someone to talk to and share her enthusiasms with. He finds great pleasure in squiring her around Paris and to the theater, enjoying her enjoyment and his ability to provide it. Even more than delighting in her exuberance and freshness, Darrow feels proud again, important and strong in her presence. Sophy appeals to him as an expert on the theater, for example, 'and the deference with which she received his comments called from him more ideas about the theatre than he had ever supposed himself to possess' (49). When they dine out, he does not feel at all sorry 'to be seen with her in public' (48) [my emphasis] and at the theater, he basks in 'the primitive complacency of the man at whose companion other men stare' (50). With Sophy, in short, Darrow is anything but an inconsiderable being – he is a man who attracts admiring and not mocking attention, or at least *perceives* himself that way.

Clearly Darrow is extremely vulnerable to shame because he measures himself through the imagined opinions of people he doesn't even know. Later in the novel, at Givré, Anna's chateau, Darrow thinks of Anna in terms of ownership and public display. He imagines her as 'a picture so hung that it can be seen only at. . . an angle known to no one but the possessor':

> He reflected with satisfaction that she was the kind of woman with whom one would like *to be seen* in public. It would be distinctly agreeable to follow her into the drawing-rooms, to walk after her down the aisle of a theatre, to get in and out of trains with her, to say 'my wife' of her to all sorts of people (130) [my emphasis].

Darrow feels something quite different about Anna from that real and imagined satisfaction when he is with Sophy in Dover and Paris. Sophy's presence sparks 'the dormant habit of comparison' (27) in Darrow. As we have seen in discussing *The Mother's Recompense*, contempt is a common response to the unbearable nature of shame, lifting oneself above the cause of that shame. Anna, Darrow muses with disdainful insight, is the end result of 'the deadening process of forming a "lady"' (29), hemmed in by 'inscrutable abandonments and reluctances' (27), 'reticences and evasions,' 'hesitations and reserves' (29). He imagines Anna in Sophy's place. Alone in a train compartment with him, not knowing him well, *she* would be restless, embarrassed, uncomfortable, not unruffled like Sophy. These observations are of course a response to his great disappointment in Anna's not responding to his proposal; to diminish and criticize her is to ease his own pain and make himself feel superior. Glennard in *The Touchstone* followed a similar strategy after he understood that his wife knew he had sold the Aubyn letters, but wouldn't speak of it to him. Tomkins notes that when 'shame proves too painful to be tolerated – as, for example. . . [when] the shamed one despairs of ever achieving communion again. . . then [he] may defend himself against his longing by renouncing the love object and expressing contempt for the person he cannot have. . .'[27] A sense of superiority is obviously vital to Darrow, and suggests deep-rooted shame. Though he is intrigued by not being able to categorize Sophy Viner, he definitely feels she is his aesthetic and intellectual inferior: 'He did not believe there were ever any echoes in her soul' (62) – a cold-blooded, distancing observation.

Darrow's disparagement of Anna helps lay the foundation for his brief liaison with Sophy, as does his disappointment: 'In the reaction of his wounded vanity [after not getting a telegram from Anna] he found [Sophy] prettier and more interesting than before' (47). He can do more than give Sophy 'a few hours of amusement between a depressing past and a not particularly cheerful future' (69). He can restore his sense of power and control, can try to overcome his feelings of humiliation by imposing himself on a powerless, virtually friendless young woman who is without a job, without character references and without any resources but her own charm. It is not callousness, libertinism, boredom, or cruelty that makes him seduce Sophy – it is ultimately the shame and humiliation Anna has all unknowingly triggered in him. This analysis is not meant in any way to excuse what Darrow does, but instead to offer a far more nuanced description of his motivations, to make him more than simply the sexist, egotistical cad he figures as in many critics' discussions. Wharton creates in Darrow a multi-dimensional character, *not* a cartoon, who is somewhat more sympathetic than a number of critics charge.[28]

When Darrow forgets to mail Sophy's letter to friends who might have found employment for her, he is not just prolonging his enjoyment of her company, or unconsciously preparing to seduce her. To send her letter and thus speed her departure is to deliver himself up to the painful feelings he has been trying to stave off: 'The fruitless contemplation of his private grievance' (34). In Sophy's company, Darrow has been progressively feeling more powerful, and this change also guarantees that Sophy's letter will remain in his pocket. Shame explains his unwillingness to admit to Sophy that he never sent her letter, and also why he throws Anna's letter, which comes on the last day of his leave, into the fire. Anyone trying to bridge a rupture after having triggered shame will likely be dismissed as summarily as Anna's letter is.

The excitement of his pursuit of Sophy (which may affectively sedate his shame) quickly turns into boredom and disgust, however. Before he remembered her name back in Dover, he sensed that she was connected with 'something uncomfortable and distasteful' (14). That connection to his chase after Lady Ulrica seems to balance and overpower his feeling that this adventure is outside of any category of experience he has known. Surely he also feels ashamed of the mixed motives that lead him to take advantage of Sophy's apparent innocence? His rage at Anna sullies any real attraction he had to Sophy.

When Darrow answers another letter of Anna's four months later and arrives at her chateau, he finds Sophy there as governess to Anna's daughter. This discovery begins what is a long nightmare for Darrow of lying and subterfuge, a period when each evening seems to bring 'its new problem and its new distress' (192). Initially, Darrow must at all costs keep his liaison with Sophy a secret from Anna, who wants to know more about the woman caring for her daughter, as she and Darrow intend to travel to South America after their marriage, without the little girl. These 'interviews' in which Anna seeks information about Sophy are intensely painful for Darrow, who is fighting 'the insidious taint' (156) of his affair with her. Seeing Sophy again, Darrow is ashamed to realize that in their liaison he 'had fallen below his own standard of sentimental loyalty' (152) to any woman, let alone Anna. Even worse, he discovers that Sophy is afraid that he will harm her, though she is not ashamed of their relationship. Once again, this man who has such high expectations of his future, and whose sense of self is precariously at the mercy of others' opinions, is 'left face to face with the mere graceless fact of his *inferiority*' (150) [my emphasis].

This sense of inferiority – which is at root shame, of course – will be the keynote of his experience at Givré. At first it is 'the essential cheapness of the affair – as far as his share in it was concerned,' that strikes Darrow 'with humiliating distinctness' (167). He feels his pride 'humbled' by his having invested so little when Sophy gave so much, as he sees it (167). Darrow also feels ashamed at having to counsel Anna on Sophy's suitability as a governess when he not only has to lie, but actually knows almost nothing about her fitness for such a post.

Darrow's confusion deepens to 'utter helplessness' (188) when he discovers that Sophy is engaged to Anna's stepson, Owen. Critics have accused Darrow (and through him, Wharton) of class prejudice against Sophy,[29] or of chauvinistic (and perhaps unconscious) adherence to the double standard,[30] or a horror of incest.[31] I read 'the blind motion of his blood,' his 'instinctive recoil' (188) from the situation of Sophy becoming a sort of daughter-in-law as none of these. Imagine his future: Sophy would be present at family gatherings, holidays, or at the very least, always close through correspondence, because Owen and Anna are so devoted to each other. There would be grandchildren. The affair he is now so ashamed of would never be over because Darrow would have no opportunity to forget having fallen beneath his own standards, of having betrayed Anna and subsequently lied to her.

More painfully than that, his mixed motives for getting involved with Sophy, and his humiliation and rage over Anna's earlier apparent rejections would be perpetually renewed in the context of social embarrassment and fear of exposure whenever he and Sophy were together. She would become a very avatar of shame, and Darrow understandably feels trapped in 'a startled vision of the inevitable occasions of contact, confidence, familiarity, which his future relationship to the girl would entail, and the countless chances of betrayal that every one of them involved' (194).

The continuing shocks and suprises at Givré undo Darrow's confidence in his judgment and perception as 'a man of the world' who can 'deal adequately with the most delicate situations' (257). Darrow is 'more and more aware of his *inability* to test the moral atmosphere about him: he was like a man in fever testing another's temperature by the touch' (208) [my emphasis]. Even the announcement of his engagement to Anna is no source of satisfaction, but embarrassing:

The state of being 'engaged,' in itself an absurd enough predicament, even to a man only intermittently *exposed*, became intolerable under the *continuous scrutiny* of a small circle quivering with participation (224) [my emphases].

It is Darrow's relentless sense of exposure and inferiority – manifestations of his shame – that make him far more than the egotistical and even uninteresting man critics describe.[32] Every event seems to exacerbate his feelings of shame, and confound his ability to cope with those feelings. When he tries, for instance, to convince Sophy that Owen is not the right husband for her, Darrow first feels ashamed at apparently not having mattered much to her, having been an inconsiderable thing again. Then, when Sophy justifiably suspects his motives, he is ashamed, but he is also ashamed when she shifts a moment later to trusting him. This scene, like a great many others in the novel, is filled with blushing, revealing the characters' shame even when they try to dissemble it. Tomkins notes that blushing, a response to shame, paradoxically compounds it.[33]

Later, after Darrow knows that Sophy loves him and is breaking off her engagement with Owen and planning to leave the chateau, Darrow admits to Anna 'there's my shame!' (314) – he had never guessed at Sophy's deep feelings for him. Once Anna has divined the nature of Darrow's previous relationship with Sophy, Darrow has to deal with her almost morbid curiosity about the liaison and her struggles to understand it and the man she thought she knew. But despite defending Sophy as a woman steeped in 'miseries and *humiliations*' (290) [my emphasis], Darrow refuses to tell Anna 'everything' about their affair: '"I've done a thing I loathe," he says, "and to atone for it you ask me to do another. What sort of satisfaction would that give you? It would put something irremediable between us"' (358). What could be more humiliating than for Darrow to have to tell Anna every detail of the affair? Shame cannot be healed in this way – there must be a *mutual* unburdening, which Anna is incapable of.

Something irremediable has *always* been between them, and that is Anna Leath's deep and abiding sense of shame. We have seen how Darrow has been shamed by recent events and actions, but Anna offers a poignant study of a woman whose entire life has been distorted by shame. Shame can be internalized, we have noted, when a child is consistently, and over many years, disparaged, criticized, thwarted in significant ways. Growing up in New York, Anna was profoundly rejected by her family and milieu, made to feel deficient and inferior. A girl with an innate appreciation of poetry and adventure, Anna had the misfortune to be raised in a 'well-regulated well-fed. . . world [where] the unusual was regarded as either immoral or ill-bred, and people with emotions were not visited' (86). It was a 'starved youth' for Anna, who eventually came to see life as ordinary and unexciting, 'swept and fenced and tended' (87).

More critically, she also learned to see herself in this way, particularly *in comparison with* other girls who seemed more alive and knowing, 'possessed of some vital secret that escaped her':

> There seemed to be a kind of freemasonry between them; they were wider awake than she, more alert, and surer of their wants if not their opinions. . . the resulting sense of *exclusion*, of being somehow laughingly but firmly *debarred* from a share of their privileges, threw her back on herself and deepened the reserve which made envious mothers cite her as a model of lady-like repression (87) [my emphases].

To live with shame as Anna does 'is to feel alienated and defeated, never quite good enough to belong.'[34] Her reserve leaves a lifetime stamp on her social behavior in the form of shyness, which we know was an affliction of Wharton's, who described it as a 'dread disease.'[35] Anna is not just sexually repressed – the heavy hand of repression has crushed her essential self. She is so bound by shame, that talking to Darrow as a girl, 'the things she really wanted to say choked in her throat and burned the palms of her hands' (89). Her inability to share what she felt with Darrow was a continuous source of self-mockery, adding to the mockery of other girls ('laughingly but firmly debarred').

Making invidious comparisons with others is a potent source of shame,[36] and for Anna, her sense of herself as deficient in comparison with other girls helped destroy her early relationship with Darrow. At a dinner party, Anna observed him talking to a 'luminous, perilous obscurely menacing' (89) young girl, Kitty Mayne, with a look in his eyes Anna both detested and longed for. Darrow's response to Kitty thus inadvertently triggered shame in Anna, calling forth her sense of being less attractive and exciting than other girls – a reaction Darrow was apparently unable to recognize. Shame frequently paralyzes speech; the 'alienating, isolating effect of shame. . . prevents us from conversing directly about the experience. However much we long to approach, to voice the inner pain and need, we feel immobilized, trapped and alone.'[37] In this case, Anna was afterwards unable to tell Darrow that she felt

> as if he were leagues and leagues away from her. All her hopes dissolved, and she was conscious of sitting rigidly, with *high head* and straight lips, while the irresistible word fled with a last wing-beat into the golden mist of her illusions (90) [my emphasis].

Holding one's head high is a way of countering the shame one is feeling, an anti-affect response,[38] because sustained 'eye contact with others becomes intolerable' and 'the head is hung'[39] when one is feeling shame. We live in a society that taboos open admission of shame: to say one feels shame is equivalent to admitting that one actually is shameful. Anna suffers deeply from this cultural prohibition all her life. She is also ashamed of feeling, and of not feeling – just as Wharton described herself in 'Life and I.'

The poetry and passion in Anna have been silenced, 'conquered' by her stifling environment (87). It is no wonder, then, that she married Fraser Leath, a dilettante living 'in an atmosphere of art and beauty' (91). He offered her escape. Leath did more than flatter her taste; he restored her self-confidence and countered her shame, or seemed to, by respecting her opinions and implying that he thought her superior to her surroundings. Leath 'made her feel for the first time that she was understood' (91). For a girl feeling inept in her intercourse with men, less womanly and attractive than her friends, such sentiments were an anodyne. Discovering that a handsome, dignified, impressive man whom she admired for his values and taste deemed *her* his equal partially restored her self-confidence. But basing her self-esteem on the opinions of others made no real and lasting change in how she had come to feel about herself (consider how precarious Darrow's self-esteem is).

Perhaps predictably, the marriage was a great disappointment for Anna. Though late in the novel she decides that she was cold to Leath, soon after their marriage she discovered him to be rigid and conventional: 'Life, to Mr Leath, was like a walk through a carefully classified museum, where, in moments of doubt, one had only to look at the number and refer to one's catalogue' (95). Like Kate Clephane in *The Mother's Recompense*, Anna exchanges one prison for another. To have hoped for freedom but to have found only a different kind of restriction is to suffer shame once again:

We experience *expectations* phenomenologically as imagined scenes of positive affect: desired outcomes in relation to people, events, or accomplishments. Individuals depend on those vital interpersonal scenes. . . expecting and needing them. Shame becomes activated whenever fundamental expectations of significant others [in the form of] imagined scenes of interpersonal need – or those equally fundamental expectations of oneself [in the form of] scenes of accomplishment or purpose are either suddenly exposed as wrong or thwarted.[40]

Her visions laden with excitement and joy have been shattered, and her chateau in France is 'the very symbol of narrowness and monotony' – a dull, 'inconvenient' place of 'duties,' 'habits,' 'defects,' 'discomforts,' and 'shabbiness' (84–85). If Anna were not shame-based, this disappointment would not have so lasting an impact. Such a marriage, however, ultimately confirms her sense of not being valuable and worthwhile.

That desperate need to feel wanted for who she is fuels her renewed love for Darrow when they meet again in London. At Givré, she feels him transfixed just by her presence. The unassailable happiness he seems to offer is loving her without desiring any change:

She knew that every inflexion of her voice, every gesture, every characteristic of her person – its very defects, the fact that her forehead was too high, that her eyes were not large enough, that her hands, though slender, were not small, and that the fingers did not taper – she knew that these deficiencies were so many channels through which her influence streamed to him; that she pleased him in spite of them, perhaps because of them; that he wanted her *as she was*, and not as she would have liked to be; and for the first time she felt in her veins the security and lightness of happy love (122) [my emphasis].

Later, at the end of a long and tiring day, Anna gazes into her mirror:

'I want him to see me as I am,' Anna thought.
   Deeper than the deepest fibre of her vanity was the triumphant sense that *as she was*, with her flattened hair, her tired pallor, her thin sleeves a little tumbled by the weight of her

jacket, he would like her even better, feel her nearer, dearer, more desirable, than in all the splendours she might put on for him (124) [my emphasis].

For a woman who has suffered a marriage in which she felt like a prisoner tapping out messages on her cell wall, what could be more deliriously liberating? Darrow's love of the flawed and human woman she is can perhaps give her permission to love herself and give up longing to be 'as she would have liked to be' – like those girls of her youth.

Yet even in such a state of excitement, in which her feelings are 'richer, deeper, more complete' (124) than they have ever been, Anna's shame still colors her experience. Anna feels exposed when Darrow wants to know that she will not regret leaving Givré. To readily admit that would be to disclose her long empty years; Anna wonders why he presses her 'to *uncover* to him her poor starved past?' (119) [my emphasis]. And going to sleep the first night that he is at the chateau, she feels 'like a slave, and a goddess, and a girl in her teens. . .' (125) [Wharton's ellipsis]. Each image is quite revealing. Darrow has too much power over her if she is a slave, power that would be all hers, however, as a goddess. Goddesses are not just above humans, but above their feelings as well, feelings whose shadow returns with the final image. After all, we know how miserable Anna really was as a teenage girl.

Elizabeth Ammons has brilliantly demonstrated the fairy-tale pattern underlying *The Reef* in which Anna awaits a man to wake her from her sleep.[42] What she awakens to, however, after a brief time of joy, is a nightmare far worse than Darrow's. The first blow comes with discovering that Sophy loves Darrow. From feeling completely secure in his arms, Anna plunges into a vision of Darrow looking at her from 'a place of graves' (274). And when she realizes that Sophy and Darrow have been lovers, it seems to Anna that 'her life had ended just as she had dreamed it was beginning' (299). All her previous years of pain seem dim, historical, as she is 'stretched on this fiery rack of the irreparable. . . suffering as a hurt animal must, blindly, furiously' (284–85).

Critics have discussed Anna's attempt to reconstruct her moral universe in the wake of these discoveries, and many see her struggling successfully for moral integrity.[41] But what they have uniformly missed is the scene that she is reliving: betrayal by Darrow. He *did* eventually have an affair with Kitty Mayne all those years ago; once again, while engaged to *her*, he has chosen a more seductive and attractive woman. The devastation is complete, but in shame's ambivalence, Anna is split, just as Darrow longed for reunion with her at the beginning of the novel. Anna's ambivalence does much to explain her subsequent wavering which may trouble some readers. Consider the interchange where Anna mentions to Darrow having seen Sophy in Paris. At one point, 'she had lowered her head, but through her dropped lids seemed to be watching the crowded scene of his face' (331). She is both cutting off contact with him, hiding, and peeking like a shy little girl afraid of strangers. Anna is often lowering her eyes or head in the book, or attempting to hold it up; looking back on herself before she knew of Darrow's betrayal, she remembers with longing a time when she feels 'she had walked with her head high and her eyes unguarded' (300).

Darrow has not only proven to be untrustworthy, she herself has once more, humiliatingly, been reminded of her deficiencies as a woman. Even before the discovery, Sophy had called forth in Anna her

romantic and almost *humble* admiration for those members of her sex, who, from a force of will, or the constraint of circumstances, had plunged into the conflict from which fate had so *persistently excluded* her. There were even moments when she fancied herself vaguely to blame for the immunity, and felt that she ought somehow to have affronted the perils and hardships which refused to come to her (234) [my emphases].

Shame makes us feel 'revealed as lesser, painfully diminished in our own eyes and the eyes of others. . . [and] secretly we feel to blame,' as Anna does here, because the 'deficiency [seems to] lie within ourselves alone.'[43]

Still, Anna desperately needs to believe that what has happened to her was 'a hideous accident,' that 'Life was not like that' (302). Above all, she needs to believe that 'she was worthy' (302) of the love she had dreamed about – because everything seems to confirm her *unworthiness*. The whole seemingly inexplicable business torments Anna with 'the desire to know more, to understand better, to feel herself less *ignorant* and *inexpert* in matters which made so much of the stuff of human experience' (290) [my emphases]. Sophy knows all of that, Anna believes, daunted by Sophy's knowledge and her 'intenser passion' (307). Anna fears that she will never be to Darrow what Sophy was. Even worse, Anna's shame keeps her from fully expressing her curiosity to Darrow: 'The colour rose to her forehead. How could she tell him what she scarcely dared own to herself?' (331)

But perhaps more humbling is Anna's sexual desire. She wants to be Darrow's lover, which makes it impossible for her to feel herself different from Sophy, superior. She even spends a night with Darrow out of humiliation at thinking that he doesn't want her, and fury at her own inability to express her longing: 'Don't I feel things as other women do?' she wonders (342). Rather than releasing her, this night leaves her with a new reason to feel ashamed. In a train compartment the next day, Anna hides her eyes from Darrow, flushes with 'the desire to shield herself' (345), and is surprised and ashamed 'to detect a new element in her love for him: a sort of suspicious tyrannical tenderness that seemed to deprive it of all serenity' (345–46). Sophy seems stronger to Anna, 'surer of her power to carry out her purpose' (345) of giving Owen up, while Anna vacillates between rejecting Darrow and claiming him forever. Sophy, Anna thinks, would also have guessed about an affair sooner than she; Anna has always been painfully aware 'of her lack of penetration' (246).

It is not quite Sophy's strengths and superiorities as a woman that make Anna rush to Paris at the novel's end to find her. Anna is not seeking advice, though that seems to be her aim: 'It was Sophy Viner only who could save her – Sophy Viner only who could give her back her lost serenity' (360). Anna has been incredibly humiliated thus far: by not knowing about the brief affair and hiring Sophy, who could have become her daughter-in-law; by discovering Darrow to be utterly different from her expectations, and untruthful; by being made to feel once again unwomanly, unwanted. Can we imagine that 'offering' Darrow to Sophy, as Anna intends to do, would be anything but a further humiliation? She is seeking freedom from her humiliation through what Tomkins calls 'a bath of shame,' like a losing gambler tossing his last chips down on the table. The aim of such a masochistic plan is 'to increase negative affect to such a point that it produces an explosive overt eruption of affect which ultimately thereby reduces itself.' One would emerge purified, released, as Wharton herself hoped to do by confessing to her dance teacher (as discussed in Chapter 1). Tomkins labels this process 'reduction by magnification' and it goes a long way to explaining Anna's apparently inexplicable action here.[44] Her shame is so intolerable that she can only seek refuge in this seemingly wild and improbable act, but the explosion never comes. Sophy is already gone, and Anna is faced with a ménage in which Sophy's sister seems to be a prostitute. It is an ending that has been deplored for its 'cruelty' to Sophy. But Sophy has escaped, after having had one rich experience she intends to keep in her heart, and Sophy is a survivor. She bore five years at Mrs Murrett's, after all, with her spirit undimmed.

Others read the cruelty as directed towards Anna (and by extension, Wharton herself).[45] Anna is indeed still trapped, and the ending does resonate with 'the futility of every attempt to reconstruct her ruined world' (312). However, the *real* cruelty in this novel is the devastating impact of shame. Though Darrow is on his way to see Anna that afternoon, if they were to marry, what sort of marriage could we imagine between two lovers whose relationship has been torn apart on the hidden reef of shame? Though he may have some conception of the shabbiness of his behavior, Darrow seems to have no idea what the *impact* of his former and recent actions have had on Anna, and he seems only dimly aware of what led to his affair with Sophy. Despite his pain, he lacks understanding that might release them both. Anna likewise does not guess at her impact on Darrow, just as why they originally broke up in her teens is beyond her comprehension. And she cannot completely reveal the pain he has caused her now, for the wounds of shame are too deep and destructive. How can she 'openly express what must seem [her] inescapable flaw as a human being?'[46] Tomkins observes that 'shame is often intimately related to and easily confused with contempt, particularly self-contempt; indeed, it is sometimes not possible to separate them.'[47] The entire experience has filled Anna with even more contempt for her limitations:

> She looked back with a melancholy derision on her old conceptions of life, as a kind of well-lit and well-policed suburb to dark places one need never know about. Here they were, those dark places, in one's own bosom. . . (353)

R.W.B. Lewis records that six years after *The Reef* was published, Wharton thanked a friend for praising the novel she felt she had put most of herself into. Upon its publication, however, when she sent a copy to Bernard Berenson, she begged him, 'Please don't read it! Put it in the visitors' rooms, or lend it to somebody to read in the train and let it get lost.'[48] Lewis speculates that Wharton was displeased with the novel on aesthetic grounds, but more to the point, he says, was its being her most autobiographical novel to date. There are indeed echoes of Wharton's family, her husband and her affair with Morton Fullerton, but her self-revelation goes beyond facts here. It also goes well beyond 'the immensely convoluted, many-sided problem of sexuality'[49] that Cynthia Griffin Wolff reads not only as central to the book, but to Wharton's entire life.

The novel is terribly exposing because it is more than anything else about the role of shame in distorting personality and destroying love, trust and hope between men and women. The continued repetition (sometimes in the same paragraph) of the words 'shame,' 'ashamed,' 'humiliation,' 'humiliated,' the references to pride being humbled and humiliated, and the persistent blushing are not accidental, but undoubtedly central to Wharton's conception of Anna and Darrow's relationship.[50] Both of them at various times feel exposed, helpless, longing, inferior – and angry and contemptuous in response to those feelings. They seem unable to recapture hope in the other, or their own self-respect. The book's title calls up images of crashing, rending, drowning and destruction; those violent associations are perfectly suited to Darrow and Anna's emotional devastation. Wharton already had deep insight into the destructive power of shame when she wrote *The Touchstone*. In *The Reef*, however, she has given even more compelling voice to the most isolating and divisive of human experiences. It is the doubling of perspective that makes the novel so very disturbing and is one of its chief strengths.[51] Wharton offers no palliative, no sentimental tableau at the end to heal the overwhelming pain of the protagonists. The plunge into shame for Darrow and Anna is completely unrelieved in what is perhaps her most brilliant novel, and certainly one of her saddest. It is anything but 'dated,' or a 'failure.'[52]

Sadness and longing predominate in Wharton's eleventh novel, *The Children*, which, as Carol Wershoven has pointed out, has received considerable negative criticism.[53] Major critics like Q.D. Leavis, Louis Auchincloss, Irving Howe, Blake Nevius, and James Tuttleton have found the book variously 'not worthy of [Wharton],' 'superficial,' 'heavy-handed,' 'shoddy,' 'fragmentary,' and 'seriously defective' – clear 'proof' of a decline in her talent after 1920.[54] The underlying argument has been that Wharton lost touch with America, her material and the postwar world. More recently, R.W.B. Lewis finds it to be 'a novel of surfaces,' and Elizabeth Ammons judges the book neither intellectually nor artistically up to the standards of her earlier works.[55]

The novel was a Book of the Month Club best seller in 1928, but has been – not surprisingly, given the earlier critical blast – out of print for decades, and is unavailable in an American paperback. Marilyn French ascribes this virtual disappearance of *The Children* in part to the novel's 'forbidden subject – the desire of an older man for a girl of fifteen.'[56] Perhaps predictably, even approaches like French's that are not specifically Freudian are influenced by the psychoanalytic emphasis on sexuality and aggression. French finds the novel 'poignant and penetrating'[57] and Cynthia Griffin Wolff ranks it among 'the best novels of [Wharton's] later years.'[58] I agree with these assessments, but think that it is through an understanding of the dynamics of shame that this unjustly neglected novel comes into clearer focus as one of Wharton's strongest. Shame shapes Martin Boyne's and Rose Sellars' identity, limiting their actions, destroying their relationship and leading each into deeper loneliness, resignation and despair.

On the way from Egypt to propose to recently widowed Rose Sellars, whom he has loved for many years, Martin Boyne, an engineer, runs into the 'riotous and cosmopolitan'[59] Wheater brood, the natural and 'adopted' children of rich, old friends of his – Cliffe and Joyce Wheater. The Wheaters' tempestuous marital life of 'careless coupling and careless divorce,'[60] has convinced their eldest daughter Judith that she must keep the band of children together, and resist any further divorces, remarriages and the subsequent ugly custody squabbles. Fascinated by the children's plight and by their spontaneity, Boyne drifts into becoming their temporary ward after they flee their parents in Venice for Cortina, his and Rose's Swiss retreat. Boyne's increasing involvement in their future, and growing unconscious attraction to Judith, alienate his fiancée Rose, who breaks their engagement, and end in his leaving for South America desolate and alone, to throw himself into his work.

Though a competent and successful engineer with a 'life of practical activities and swift decisions,'[61] Boyne is definitely haunted by a sense of his own inadequacy. At the opening of the novel, on a boat in the Algiers harbor, he dwells on his bad luck in never meeting interesting travelling companions. Indeed, it will be his fate on board to dine with dismally boring 'waifs and strays like himself' (18). But this complaint is not isolated or insignificant – it has roots in his family history, and is a key to understanding his personality. Boyne's Great Uncle Edward is the stick he beats himself with. Uncle Edward's family reputation rests on over sixty years of unparalleled social success while travelling. Though he was 'the model of complacent dulness [sic] at home' (1), Edward had fabulous encounters with English nobility and the likes of Ruskin and Rachel, all of whom he apparently impressed. Despite *his* own extensive and exotic travels, however, Boyne is painfully aware that 'adventure worthy of the name perpetually eluded him' (2). This is by no means a new insight for Boyne. Later in the novel we learn that Boyne 'had often mocked at himself as a man who, in spite of all his wanderings, had never had a real adventure' (235) – unlike most other men. His self mockery is somewhat reminiscent of Anna Leath's in *The Reef*: he is different from most men, inferior, less masculine (by implication), as she was less feminine than her friends. Boyne is not 'peevish' in this assessment of himself, as Cynthia Griffin Wolff has it,[62] but *ashamed*:

> Some men's luck in travelling was inconceivable. They had only to get into a train or on board a boat to run across an old friend; or, what was more exciting, make a new one. They were always finding themselves with some wandering celebrity, with the owner of a famous house, of a noted collection, or of an odd and amusing personality. . . (1)
> . . . he could hardly believe he really looked to the rest of the world as he had seen himself that morning [in the mirror]: a critical cautious man of forty-six, whom nobody could possibly associate with the romantic or the unexpected (3).

We have seen before that shame is frequently generated by invidious comparison, a particular problem because of our 'culture-wide phenomenon of unwitting, lifetime immersion in competition, which compels us to attribute significance to all performance on a comparative basis.'[63] This comparison making, which confuses one characteristic of the self with the entire person, actively devalues and undermines the self. Such invidious comparisons can sometimes force us into behavior that is not necessarily appropriate for ourselves, but which we long to feel is natural. Perhaps allowing his involvement with the children to develop at *all* is more what one would expect of his Uncle Edward than of a cautious man of forty-six, who 'despite a lively imagination. . . had so often managed to resist' his impulses (81).

Uncharacteristic actions are only one of many possible responses to shame – we have seen how contempt variously served Stephen Glennard, Kate Clephane, and George Darrow. If Boyne feels inferior to Uncle Edward's social success, he can attempt to neutralize that feeling by making himself superior to his uncle. Sixty years of social success do not seem to have affected his uncle, but Boyne is convinced that *he* would not go through such adventures with 'benignant blindness': 'No tremor of thought or emotion would. . . have escaped [him]: he would have burst all the grapes against his palate' (2).

Margaret McDowell notes that the gap between Boyne's inflated sense of his own potential, and his actual meager achievements in the novel is a source of comedy. It is easy to read Boyne's comparison with his uncle as comic self-mockery, but for Boyne to devalue his actual 'good nature and genuine sympathy'[64] in favor of qualities he does not have is to treat himself in ways that are guaranteed to perpetuate shame. The note of dissatisfaction and failure struck in the opening scene of the novel is a clear indication that his relationship with Rose Sellars is doomed from the start.

What sort of woman is she, high in her Swiss fastnesses, this 'lady in the Dolomites' (37)? The woman he intends proposing to is not at all adventurous, but a sort of chic and self-possessed incarnation of Patience. Rose waited for him through the long lonely years of her marriage, but now that she is a widow, Boyne has 'begun to wonder how much of her attraction had been due to the fact that she was unattainable' (40). Boyne's ambivalence has its roots in his shame, and in how Rose has dealt with her own.

Rose Sellars is perfect, exquisite, widely admired back in New York for her cleverness and originality:

> if Rose Sellars excelled in one special art it was undoubtedly that of preparation. She led up to things – the simplest things – with the skill of a clever rider putting a horse at a five-barred gate. All her life had been a series of adaptations, arrangements, shifting of lights, lowering of veils, pulling about of screens and curtains. No one could arrange a room half so well; and she had arranged herself and her life just as skillfully (38).

Note that the predominant imagery here is of hiding, concealment, and that even 'the simplest things' seem to call up energy greatly in excess of the occasion. She strikes one as a woman whose defense against shame is striving for perfection. It is as if she has felt that her 'sole means of escaping from the prison that is shame is to erase all signs that might point to its presence.'[65] Rose's marital circumstances certainly have given her much to be ashamed of: 'mediocre means, a mediocre husband, an ugly New York house, and a dull New York set' – all of which was 'in every way unworthy of her' (38–9). Her life has been 'too vacant for hurry, too hopeless for impatience' (91), and she has sought refuge in culturally approved 'occupations' for women – creating atmosphere, a background, for men, of course. Here as elsewhere Wharton is indicting our society for its 'devaluation of woman's mind. . . the objects to which women are to devote themselves are inherently incommensurate with the energy brought to them.'[66] Helen Block Lewis, a psychoanalytic writer on shame, has noted that our Western 'sexist intellectual inheritance contains an explicit devaluation of women, and an implicit, insoluble demand that they accept their inferior place without shame.'[67]

Predictably, for Boyne, the order Rose has created has been extremely satisfying: her 'world had always been the pole-star of his whirling skies' (82). And what she offers now is a rarified sort of adventure on an aesthetic, nostalgic level: in an age of 'standardised' beauty, 'Mrs Sellars's deepest attraction lay in her belonging to a day when women still wore their charm with a difference' (105). She is almost a human souvenir, larger than life, but as Oscar Wilde puts it, 'not nearly so natural.'[68] Indeed, Boyne pictures Rose as a mountain, 'aloof and aloft' (83).

Their present age, in which she sets a formidable standard, is one where, as Rose puts it, there are no manners left, 'but customs' (38). Marilyn French feels that Boyne always found Rose's manners admirable until he meets the free-spirited Wheater children,[69] but Rose's manners are his own, and he is clearly unhappy with himself, his mannerliness, *before* he meets the young Wheaters. The attitudes he expresses about himself at the novel's opening are deep-rooted. Is it any wonder, then, that he is somewhat uneasy about seeing Rose after their long separation: 'He had schooled himself to think that what he most wanted was to see Rose Sellars again. Deep within him he knew it was not so; at least not certainly so' (81).

Boyne is not afraid of Rose's 'mature sexuality', as Ammons believes.[70] Rose is the very avatar of the values he finds burdensome in himself - respectability, order and tact. She comes to represent all the inner obstacles (the internalized standards of behavior) that keep him from being 'spontaneous, honest, himself' (270): 'She seemed hemmed in by little restrictions and inhibitions' (171). The language here strongly reminds us of Darrow surveying Anna Leath. For a man who is likewise restricted and painfully conscious of that limitation, Rose is bound to trigger Boyne's shame when she is being most herself:

> It was not necessary for Rose Sellars to formulate objections: they were latent everywhere in her delicate person, in the movement of her slim apprehensive fingers, the guarded stir of her lashes. But the sense of their lurking there, vigilant guardians of the threshhold, gave a peculiar quality to every token of her approval (169).

Once again we are struck by the sense of something being hidden, protected by those 'guardians of the threshold.'

What precipitates the decline in their relationship is the arrival of the children, under Judith's and a nanny's stewardship. The undercurrent of criticism in Boyne's earliest perceptions of Rose in the text (all that *arranging* – life as interior decorating!) grows more intense as he attempts to balance taking charge of the children with his and Rose's relationship. Rose quite correctly points out that the Wheater brood is not his concern, but before they begin to disagree about the children, their bond is undermined by a quarrel over something more immediate.

For many years Rose was a mirage for Boyne (270), the oasis seen across a blistering desert. When Boyne heard of her being widowed, he'd cried out to himself 'At last. . .' (221) [Wharton's ellipsis] – and their reunion is not disappointing. He finds her 'so much younger and more vivid than his remembrance' (85) and he enjoys 'the glow of long-imagined caresses. . . the whole enchanting harmony of her presence' (237). But Rose deeply, though unintentionally, shames him. After a few days of blissful lingering over the past and in the present, during which Rose still wants to be his 'perfect friend' (84), Boyne presses to get married as soon as possible. She does not respond positively, she *recoils*, and asks for a five-month delay until her husband has been dead for a full year, so as to consider the feelings of a rich aunt who has made Rose her legatee. We have already seen how when Darrow is disappointed by Anna's telegram, shame is triggered by his expectations being thwarted, proven wrong; the intensity of such a disappointment cannot be overestimated.

Boyne angrily objects to Rose's suggestion of a delay, feeling that agreement would by 'unmanly' on his part. He does at last give in, but only after shouting, and taking 'the coward's way out,' as he sees it (96), by saying that *he* wants what *she* does. Labeling his stand unmanly, Boyne further shames himself through self-contempt. This disagreement has far more than a 'minimal effect' on their romance.[71] While Rose does not gloat, Boyne knows that 'the sweetness of her smile was distilled out of satisfaction at his defeat.' He has not merely acquiesced; he feels that Rose has made a meal of him: 'Damn it,' he thinks, 'what cannibals marriage makes of people' (96). A wedge has been driven between himself and Rose, just as happened when Anna Leath was unable to tell Darrow that his attraction to Kitty Mayne shamed her. Neither Boyne nor Rose can verbalize their shame, which traps and immobilizes them further. Shame will drive them further apart as each experiences it as a result of the other's actions, but neither can discuss what is happening to them. Rose can only wonder, with some dim awareness of the predicament: 'I wonder why we're trying to hurt each other?' (220).

The almost completely imperturbable tact that suffuses Rose's life like the scent of the carefully arranged flowers on her dinner table becomes more oppressive to Boyne: 'Damn tact!' (108) Boyne thinks when she leaves him alone with Judith on Judith's first night in Switzerland, and 'there's nothing I hate as much as tact,' Boyne erupts later in the novel (268), damning it again. Boyne feels restricted by Rose's coolness and control, and because Boyne feels inferior to her, as with his uncle, he must pull her down with criticism. After all, though they are of the same class and can mock the *nouveaux riches* at Cortina together, Boyne never quite matches the social poise Rose gathers about her as gracefully as her beautiful shawl.

Shame-bound as he is, Boyne not surprisingly feels 'doomed to blunder' (191) in his dealings with women. When he buys souvenirs from Venice, he gets Rose a conventional engagement ring, but accidentally shows Rose the lovely antique brooch he got for Judith. Because it is original, Rose is struck by the brooch, but

Boyne stuffs it back into his messy pocket 'with the exasperated sense of blushing like a boy over his blunder' (172). Tomkins writes that 'when the face blushes, shame is compounded. And so it happens that one is ashamed of being ashamed as of anything else.'[72] Here as elsewhere through the novel and in Wharton's fiction as a whole, shame is revealed through facial manifestations – characters flush, colour, crimson, redden. Boyne compounds his error by putting Rose's ring on the wrong finger, and though Rose 'tepidly' and then 'diligently' (173) admires it, Boyne knows she would rather have had the unusual brooch, though her 'tact' prevents her from saying so. Still, she has not quite hidden what she felt, and has thus further magnified Boyne's shame: he is left feeling clumsy and foolish.

But he is even more ashamed when Rose accuses him of having fallen in love with Judith. At a picnic arranged by Rose's punctilious lawyer, Dobree, Boyne is uncomfortably aware of how attractive Judith is. The sensation is heightened by feeling that the elderly but fit Dobree is also staring at her with the same thought. Boyne is disgusted to see Dobree's 'clear cautious eyes grown blurred and furtive' (205). We should remember that Boyne characterized himself as looking 'cautious' in the opening pages of the novel. Imagine seeing one's private thoughts exposed in someone else's face, someone whom you detest, as Boyne does Dobree, whose tact seems a monstrous parody of Rose's. Boyne wonders if his own eyes have been 'like that' and if 'the muscles of his face [had] been stretched in the effort to [look away]. The thing was not pleasant to visualize; and he disliked Mr Dobree the more for serving as his mirror. . .' (206) [Wharton's ellipsis].

Donald Nathanson notes that shame involves two kinds of discovery: when '*we* are revealed, and when we are caught looking at someone else.'[73] Tomkins writes that 'the taboo on looking directly into the eyes of the other' is matched by 'the equal taboo on looking away too visibly.'[74] Dobree blushes at the picnic, after Boyne stares at him: 'Mr Dobree's habitual pinkness turned to a red which suffused even his temples and eyelids, so that his carefully brushed white hair looked like a sunlit cloud against an angry sky' (206). And Boyne himself blushes when he gazes into Judith's 'sleepy eyes' (208), hoping that he does not look like Dobree. Boyne misreads Dobree's blush as proof that Dobree is interested in Judith, but we discover that Dobree has actually been watching *him* watch Judith. The dynamics of this complicated and important scene are not sexual, but related to shame.

> There are universal taboos on looking too directly into the eyes of the other because of the likelihood of affect contagion, as well as escalation, because of the unwillingness to express affect promiscuously, and because of concern lest others achieve control through knowledge of one's otherwise private feelings. Humans are primarily voyeuristic, not only because vision is their most informative sense, but because the shared eye-to-eye interaction is the most intimate relationship possible between human beings. There is, in this way, complete mutuality between two selves, each of whom simultaneously is aware of the self and the other.[75]

What is violated here is the taboo on *looking* too directly and intently into the face and eyes of the other.[76]

Dobree takes the opportunity of a walk that afternoon to propose to Rose. When she reveals this to Boyne, who is insultingly sure that Dobree wants to marry Judith, he shames Rose by laughing at the idea of Dobree's proposal. His mocking laughter at his own self-deception produces 'a faint note of vexation' (217) in Rose's voice – to begin with. Boyne is relieved to know that Dobree had wanted nothing more, and this unflattering assessment naturally makes Rose blush. She sees Dobree's proposal as the highest honor she can receive from a man, but Boyne seems to think it trivial. When Boyne asks if she wants her freedom, she plunges ahead, revealing that Dobree is convinced that Boyne is in love with Judith. Exposed at last, Boyne explodes, shouting, wondering how anyone could suggest such an unnatural thing! Just before, *he* had been smugly assuring Rose that Dobree intended to marry Judith; he has obviously revealed too much. 'He dropped down into the nearest chair, hot, angry, ashamed, with a throat as dry as if he had been haranguing an open-air meeting on a dusty day. . . He felt self-conscious and clumsy' (219–20).

Pathetically eager to please now, Rose blames the whole contretemps on herself, 'with a distressing humility. . . [her] self-abasement humiliated [Boyne]' (221). 'No matter what our age, shame resonates with the worst of our fears of abandonment'[77] and Rose is clearly trying to bridge the terrible gap between them. The next day, Rose is no longer cool and in control; she has become unravelled. She is 'timorously anxious' that Boyne notice she is *not* making a scene: 'The only sign she gave of a latent embarrassment was in her too great ease, her too blithe determination to deny it' (226–27). This is a major change in Rose, for until now she was better able to conceal what she is feeling; she is clearly losing control, and Boyne is not at all helpful. He does not, for example, wax appropriately nostalgic when Rose mentions they will be leaving Cortina now that her Aunt Julia has come to Paris.

Some critics consider what happens next a 'tactic' – Rose's attempt to manipulate Boyne. She offers herself up to him, 'to be cherished or shattered' (230), ready to get married. But what happens here is far more complex and unconscious, revolving around shame. Telling Boyne that she is ready to get married now, or at least soon, she is like Tomkins' defeated gambler throwing his last chips on the table 'to take a bath.' Like Glennard trying to humiliate Flamel, or Anna hurrying to Paris to give Darrow to Sophy, Rose is *bathing* in shame, a strategy we are forced into whenever we have not learned to tolerate and otherwise neutralize our own negative affects, as Rose and so many of Wharton's characters clearly have not.

Rose's sudden conversion is not convincing. Can we believe that she has actually been 'set free' by Boyne, who has rejected her for another woman, free to proclaim 'I've been imprisoned in my past, I see it now; I had become the slave of all those years of conformity. . . How monstrous to have waited so long for happiness, and then be afraid to seize it when it comes!' (230–31). Given Boyne's deep commitment to the children, and his now obvious attachment to Judith, Rose must know that he will reject her. He does, and she accuses him of being in love with Judith, but the release from shame expected by the 'reduction by magnification,' the bathing in shame, does not seem to come for Rose, and she is still trapped. Boyne exhibits a classic response to shame (hers and his own): 'He lifted his hands to his face, and covered his eyes' (234). Blushing occurs as well in this painful scene.

Nathanson notes that when we look down or away in shame, it is as if 'we hope to prevent others from knowing what we are thinking.'[78] Rose and Boyne 'stand in silence, with eyes averted' (234), until Boyne realizes something awful: *he* has been 'Rose Sellar's Great Adventure, the risk and the enchantment of her life':

While she had continued, during the weary years of her marriage, to be blameless, exemplary, patient and heroically gay, the thought of Boyne was storing up treasures for her which she would one day put out her hand and take – no matter how long she might have to wait. . . . She had trained herself to go on waiting for happiness, day after day, month after month, year after year, with the same air of bright unruffled vigilance, like a tireless animal waiting for its prey (235).

The tremendous shift in imagery here that casts Rose in such a harsh light is Boyne's unpleasant, even shocking, but nonetheless natural response to the desolation he now sees himself having caused in her life. How else can he deal with having created such grief, been such a disappointment, face his own shame, in other words, except by picturing himself as her victim? In a sense, he *has* been victimized by Rose (and she by him) in that her behavior, her very identity have been sources of shame, but not to so great a degree as the predator image suggests. Kaufman notes that the external transfer of blame, which is fundamentally an attempt to transfer shame away from the self, can itself 'come to function as a defense against experiencing shame through empathy or identification,'[79] which is exactly what happens in this case: 'It was. . . painful [for Boyne] to be entering so acutely into her feelings' (235).

Rose has reached her nadir. Like Kate Clephane, she flees the scene of her humiliation so that she does not have to see Boyne, and *be seen.* But Rose demeans herself even further in a letter: 'I feel that I have made. . . an understanding [about our future] impossible by my unreasonableness, my impatience, my apparent inability to see your point of view' (250).[80] She offers to adopt with Boyne the two children Boyne rightly recognizes she will be least threatened by. Such a plan could not possibly please him, and Boyne's curt rejection brings his engagement ring back. Rose musters her tact for the perfect farewell message: 'I shall always remember; I shall never resent' (261). Such beautifully balanced words are, Boyne realizes, 'the devices of decent people who hated to give pain, and were even capable of self-sacrifice to avoid it' (270).

When Boyne sees her again in Paris, she is calm, controlled, even though Boyne commits another immediate blunder by announcing that he has failed to keep the children together, rather than first asking Rose to forgive him. His embarrassment does not blind him, though, to Rose's 'victorious smile' (318). When Boyne erupts at hearing that Judith's flighty mother is being advised and reformed by Dobree, and is apparently leading a more respectable life, her fragile command of the situation is shaken. She is nervous, sharp, helpless, and this last meeting drifts into a terrible silence in which Rose is struggling with 'a pain as benumbing as his own' (323). All that is eventually left to Rose is the 'small preoccupations' of her life in New York. The overwhelming shame she experienced in her failed relationship with Boyne has reduced her to little more than a ghost.

Near the end of the novel, when Martin Boyne is returning to Europe after a three-year absence, he feels that Rose's fate is more grim than his own, and some critics agree.[81] But everything in the text points to his restricted, sterile life, to the emptiness inside of him despite his achievements. The last words of the book leave him standing by himself, 'a lonely man' (387). What young Judith Wheater seemed to offer Boyne was of course not real, because he sought in her a chimerical freedom from 'a wilderness of evasions and courtesies, where nothing is said directly and nothing is done and happiness is endlessly deferred.'[82] He seeks freedom from shame, without the shamelessness of Judith's parents, whose life is a 'perverse summer camp.'[83]

If Rose represents his emotional withholding, his caution, a confusion of timidity with stability,[84] Judith is her very opposite, and not just because of youth. As Cynthia Griffin Wolff points out, 'Judith has no evasions' because she has developed 'a completely different set of emotional habits.'[85] She is not mincing and given to 'premeditated spontaneity' (127), but open, enthusiastic, natural, clumsy (in her, clumsiness is somehow redeeming), and Boyne is struck throughout by her changeableness. Unlike the cool and deliberate Rose, Judith's face is open, vivid, dramatic, arresting, a face in which 'things happened so suddenly and overwhelmingly' (193). Throughout the book, Boyne is struck by the openness and readability of her face with all the hunger of someone paralyzed watching a brilliant dancer on stage. Her body is elusive, not fixed – 'the mere vehicle of her moods, the projection of successive fears, hopes, ardours. . .' (36). I think it is important to note that she is emotional and expressive (which Boyne and Rose are not), and not yet ashamed of being so. Rose after all comes from an environment, like Anna Leath's, in which 'people with emotions were not visited.' Boyne at one point pictures Judith as Mercury, the perfect representation of youth, speed and freedom.

But Judith also consistently embarrasses Martin by acting more grown-up than she is, by being more knowledgeable about the adult world than he expects her to be, and by asking tactless questions about his feelings that make him explode: 'Can't you ever keep from treading on people's toes?' (268) She is like the children she is trying to protect from further dislocation. They are 'not nice children; they are childish and unpleasantly precocious by turns; they are selfish, quarrelsome, lying and thieving.'[86] In other words, they are not idealized, they are not controlled and discreet arrangers of veils. Late in the novel, when Boyne's relationship with Rose has almost completely collapsed, Boyne wonders whether he would like her more if jealousy, 'the most passionate and irrational of sentiments lurked under [her] calm and reasonable exterior. If it were so, it certainly made her more interesting' (253) – more human and complete, though one doubts Boyne would respond positively if Rose erupted into a Medea-like frenzy, given how Judith's lapses unnerve him.

The seven Wheater children Boyne takes up offer him a completely different vision of life than Rose does, and this vision goes well beyond manners. I noted in Chapter 2 that Tomkins comments on the intensity of 'the unfettered expression of affect' and how society controls it. The Wheater children are not old or disciplined enough to have learned to do anything *but* express themselves without fetters. They are angry, loud, jealous, affectionate: a perpetual roar of feelings, and Boyne is increasingly conscious of the precious difference between their spontaneity and Rose's calculation as the novel progresses. This cold and cautious man admires the children's 'animal warmth': 'Uninterrupted communion with the little Wheaters always gave Boyne the same feeling of liberation. It was like getting back from a constrained bodily position to a natural one' (245).

Boyne also admires Judith's ability to keep the children together amid 'a welter of change,' to inspire hired help with 'her own passionate fidelity' (288). But while he is both pleased and annoyed by Judith's freedom from the restrictions that bind his life, one can hardly say that he *sees* her, as Elizabeth Ammons points out.[87] At their first trip together, a stopover with the children in Sicily, he is, the narrator tells us drily, 'already busy at the masculine task of endowing the woman of the moment with every quality which made life interesting to himself' (35). He completely misjudges her after Rose has sent back his ring and the children are sure to be split up by the Wheaters' coming divorce. His lack of insight here is due to his shame. It isn't lust that drives him to make an oblique marriage proposal to Judith, or a 'masculine desire to escape adult life,'[88] but an almost hysterical flight from an empty past and a deeper emptiness inside, from a life of restriction, caution, a life that is the antithesis of his Uncle Edward's, a life of no adventures. He feels at last 'free to chuck his life away on any madness; and madness this was, he knew. Well, he'd had enough of reason for the rest of his days' (307).

What happens next is perhaps the most devastating scene of shame in Wharton's fiction. When he offers to take care of her, Judith thinks he wants to *adopt* her and the children. 'Boyne felt like a man who has blundered along in the dark to the edge of a precipice. He trembled inwardly with the effort of recovery' (310). When he goes further and laughingly (because of his shame), less obliquely presents himself as a hypothetical husband, Judith laughs too. Of course, now his greatest fear is that Judith will understand that he really *meant* to propose, and then his humiliation would be complete, he would be utterly exposed as ridiculous. As it is, Boyne alone bears the burden of the shame here. Further humiliations await him, however. Mr Dobree has apparently helped Judith's mother reform her wayward life, and in Paris, Judith's loyalty seems transferred to Dobree as someone who can effectively keep her family together. Dobree has apparently succeeded where Boyne has miserably failed; once again he has been bested by another man. Like Rose, Boyne ultimately now has 'nothing to sound in the long empty corridors of his future but his loneliness.'[89] He flees the scene of his disasters.

When one considers the role of shame in undermining Rose's and Boyne's self-esteem here, and in destroying their relationship, Margaret McDowell's complaint that 'Wharton could have penetrated more deeply and more subtly into the central situation'[90] seems less tenable. The book is far more subtle and compelling than most critics have acknowledged, and in its own way, a masterpiece of 'renunciation and bleak resignation.'[91] Soon after meeting the Wheater children, Boyne is struck by their being 'so exposed, so bared to the blast' (44), which strongly reminds us of Wharton's own identification and empathy for objects of persecution. It is also a metaphor that just as adequately captures his and

Rose's own sense of helplessness, their inner precariousness. He and Rose are indeed fossils, as Cynthia Griffin Wolff labels them,[92] trapped by shame which prevents honesty and intimacy, which perpetually divides where it might connect. George Darrow and Anna Leath were likewise driven apart by their own shame, and the shame that they inadvertently kept triggering in each other with such devastating results. They waited for years to be together, just as Rose and Boyne did, only to be deeply, cruelly disappointed. Both couples are prisoners of shame quite unable to understand the nature of their entrapment.

The original plan for *The Children* called for Boyne's marrying Judith at the end[93] – but that would clearly have made this novel end as falsely and disappointingly as *Sanctuary*. Instead, it is emotionally true, in that the shame that lies under the surface of human relationships – toxic, threatening, inescapable – is allowed to lead the characters to their fates, without wavering. It is shame that explains why in Wharton's fiction, 'human beings seem always to prove inadequate, always to fail each other, always to be the victims of an innate disharmony between love and response, need and capacity.'[94] We have seen Wharton examine this terrible disharmony in individuals and in relationships; now we will turn to exploring the ways in which she observes shame poison family and marital ties.

4

Shameful Relations

Given what we have seen about how Wharton was treated in her family, at least by her brothers and mother, there is nothing surprising in finding that from her first fictions onward, Wharton saw the family as an environment in which shame could crush or at least maim individuals. Shame works not only through parent-child relationships (with the echoes therein of larger cultural shaming patterns) but also between siblings and other close relations, as in Wharton's first long piece of fiction, *Bunner Sisters*, written in 1896 but unpublished until 1916.

On a shabby side street in 1870s New York, Ann Eliza and Evelina Bunner have a little sundries shop that is the 'shrunken image of their earlier ambitions'[1] – though it pays their rent and keeps them modestly comfortable. Into their uneventful life 'of habitually repressed emotion' (228) comes Herman Ramy, an immigrant German clockmaker. Ann Eliza, the elder sister, buys a clock from him for Evelina's birthday. Lonely, the clockmaker begins spending time with the sisters, proposes to the eldest, who rejects him so that he can marry Evelina, the younger and prettier one. Ramy, a drug addict, eventually cheats the sisters out of their life savings, and after marriage to Evelina the pair go to St Louis where he runs off with another woman; Evelina's baby dies; she temporarily has 'brain fever' and has to beg her way back to New York where she dies of tuberculosis. The shop, having declined after Evelina left it, has to be given up, and Ann Eliza is reduced to looking for a sales position which her age and faded appearance make unlikely.

This novella is not just a story of poverty and isolation, but a sad playing out of envy and shame between sisters, who were able to coexist only when feelings were unexpressed, and everything in their meager life was shared. Mr Ramy, however, bent on marriage, will end up being only one sister's portion, and shame comes to spoil the little family, which is devastated by the results of an unfortunate match.

Elizabeth Ammons' assessment that Ramy is 'a monster' seems a

94

somewhat schematic reading of a work that is more subtle and effective than Ammons and other critics hold.[2] Ramy is the catalyst that undermines what has been a fairly uncontentious and harmonious relationship. Hoping to meet Mr Ramy after she has bought the clock, for instance, Ann Eliza experiences shame as she imagines doing the marketing in place of her sister: 'She shrank back shyly. . . A plan so steeped in duplicity had never before taken shape in her crystalline soul. How was it possible to consider such a step?' (234). Lurking at the butcher's in the hope of running into Ramy, she is both 'ashamed of staying longer' and critical of herself. We have often seen Wharton's characters in this same pattern of reacting to their own shame with criticism, contempt or disgust. How, Ann Eliza now wonders, could she 'have been foolish enough' to think that Ramy would be there? (236).

This unexpected emergence of a double life, a variance between how Ann Eliza acts and what she is really thinking, is echoed by a surge of dissatisfaction: 'For the first time in her long years of drudgery she rebelled at the dullness of her life' (236). Though she has always felt sympathy for her younger and more attractive sister's lack of romantic success, Ann Eliza now starts thinking about 'lost opportunities of her own' (237). So of course her 'face burned' when Evelina says Ann Eliza has to take the clock back because it doesn't work, and she is utterly silenced when mischance prevents her and Evelina goes in her place. As her sister rattles on about having seen Ramy and relates their conversation, Ann Eliza is both cool and sneering in her responses. When a neighbor later implies that Ramy is interested in her sister, Ann Eliza will be even more contemptuous in response to her shame, and she discovers flaws in her sister's beauty for the first time: 'her involuntary criticism startled her like a secret disloyalty' (248). She is also ashamed to talk about Ramy and her sister: 'Ann Eliza could bear to connive at Evelina's bliss, but not to acknowledge it to others' (254).

Evelina, too, is dissatisfied, beginning to see their life as it might be seen by an outsider, when Ramy is to come over after dinner. Her shame about living in one room behind their store makes her complain about the dinner dishes and the bed being in plain sight. Her shame is infectious: 'Ann Eliza coloured. There was something vaguely embarrassing in Evelina's suggestion' (241). Ramy's unexciting visit, which the sisters do not discuss, is nevertheless so different from anything in their past that life afterwards seems

'monotonous', 'colourless', and 'aimless' (245). And Ramy's presence
in their crimped little world leads to an unprecedented explosion
of feeling in which Evelina reveals how interested she is in Ramy,
and fliply questions her sister's honesty. This unheard of emotion-
ality leaves 'Ann Eliza. . . burning with the *shame* of Evelina's
self-exposure. She was shocked that, even to her, Evelina should *lay
bare the nakedness* of her emotion; and she tried to turn her thoughts
from it as though its recollection made her a sharer in her sister's
abasement' (257–58) [my emphases]. Simply to feel, and to express
feeling is as forbidden here as it is in the higher reaches of New
York society that Wharton would chronicle in later novels.

Yet when Ramy proposes to Ann Eliza, and she pushes him in
the direction of her sister, she is ashamed of that habitual damp-
ening of emotion between herself and Evelina, mortified and
feeling 'a touch of humiliation' that her sister can't see something
momentous has happened to her (268). What makes Ramy's proposal especially important for Ann Eliza is the temporary triumph
over shame: she may be older, more faded, but Ramy was attracted
to *her*, and she critically assesses her sister as 'dull, and even
slightly absurd' for not realizing 'at last that they were equals'
(268). This triumph is short-lived, however, and Ann Eliza finds
herself criticizing her sister's taste for the first time, 'and she was
frightened at the insidious change in her attitude' (269). Superiority and contempt are one way she can adjust to her sister's perceived superiority; 'self-effacement' is another, and she finds
refuge in 'idolatrous acceptance of the cruelties of fate.' Having
rarely thought herself worthy of anything good that life has to
offer, 'this exclusion seemed both natural and just' (271).

Nothing in her past can prepare her, though, for the terrible
loneliness and despair she will feel when Evelina goes off to St
Louis with her husband; the intensity of her emotions leaves her
with 'a trembling sense of her *insufficiency*' (278) [my emphasis].
When her sister's impersonal and evasive letters (in which Evelina
asserts her superiority as a married woman) drop off, Ann Eliza's
attempts to track her sister down force the shy shrinking woman
into encounters she is fairly crushed by. Thus, when a battered
and desperately ill Evelina returns, Ann Eliza moans in 'triumph'
(296), though she attempts to hide what has happened from prying
neighbors. Just as Evelina says she was ashamed to let Ann Eliza
know how much she was suffering, Ann Eliza is ashamed to let
anyone know how dreadful 'a tale of misery and humiliation' (298)

her sister's marriage turned out to be. Yet because she has pawned so many of her belongings, she needs to borrow money for Evelina's medical care – a 'shameful' extremity (304) as humiliating as letting 'Evelina's miserable secret' slip out of her grasp (305). The story movingly presents not just the results of disaster in a precariously balanced life, but the impact courtship and marriage can have on siblings, especially in a relationship based on factitious harmony. The entrance of a man cracked it, and left one of the sisters ashamed in many ways and isolated, 'an exile from her closest affections' (307).

The novellas in *Old New York* revolve around shame, inasmuch as they discuss a society in which 'appearances were more important than reality,' as Marilyn French notes. Social standing is determined by 'what other people knew and thought' in this 'society of wealth and leisure' whose 'morality was based in negations, narrowness, omissions and avoidances.'³ What French is describing is a society heavily bound by shame, and the main characters of each novella endure social condemnation or ostracism because they have shamefully defied their families or New York itself. Cynthia Griffin Wolff notes the failure of connection between parents and children in this volume, and that failure is a powerful source of shame, as Kaufman observes. The first two novellas, which emphasize family-induced shame, will be discussed here, and the others, more centrally about marriage, below.

Lewis Raycie in *False Dawn* has the misfortune of being the 'shrinking and inadequate' son of a big, booming egotistical man who values Lewis only because Lewis is *his*.⁴ Raycie senior longs to found a dynasty, but his material is a 'lean little runt' who was 'a shrimp of a baby, a shaver of a boy, and now a youth as scant as an ordinary man's midday shadow' (6). Tight-fisted Raycie senior, who subjects his wife to humiliating 'little economies' (28), consistently humiliates his son, calls him 'a sparrow' in front of guests, and keeps him on a short financial rein. Even when Lewis is of age and headed for a Grand Tour, he has to sneak off to see Beatrice, the young girl he loves, but whom his father would not approve of as a match. Raycie senior may say that Lewis is his 'own master' now, 'but it's only his own terms,' Lewis despairingly explains to Beatrice, 'only while I do what he wants!. . . If you knew how it humiliates me –' (18).

Though Lewis still feels 'a lurking and abeyant fear of Mr Raycie senior' (33) when he is in Europe, the trip gives him both confidence and a new perspective (at least temporarily): his father's 'thunders were now no more than the far-off murmur of summer lightning on a perfect evening' (36). What digs the grave of his father's 'self-importance' (43) for Lewis is learning from people he meets in Europe, like John Ruskin, that his father's taste is abysmal. That knowledge, which Lewis blushingly acquires in Ruskin's company, is profoundly corrosive of his fear, so that when he returns home with a collection of Italian Primitives, 'the image of Mr Raycie had meanwhile dwindled':

> Everything about him, as his son looked back, seemed narrow, juvenile, almost childish. . . his fussy tyranny of his woman-kind; his unconscious but total ignorance of most of the things, books, people, ideas, that now filled his son's mind; above all, the arrogance and incompetence of his artistic judgments (42).

But Lewis, in the flush of discovery, has misjudged his father, who is mortified at not knowing any of the painters his son claims are important. Raycie senior imagines a shameful public exposure of what he takes to be his son's incompetence. Visitors to the gallery he had planned will be as perplexed as he is, stare blankly and ask for the painter's name again: 'In going the round of the gallery (the Raycie Gallery!) the same stare and the same request were likely to be repeated before each painter' (49).

Raycie senior falls ill, makes a new will disinheriting Lewis but leaving him the 'worthless' paintings, and 'New York agreed it was the affair of the pictures that had killed him' (54). For Lewis, the undisplayed pictures he bought with his father's money are closely tied with his shame. Not only has he been exposed and expelled from his family (at least symbolically) and socially exiled by New York – but the scenes he imagined have not come true. Before leaving Beatrice, he had rhapsodically promised that he would return from Europe his own master, 'independent, free,' able to claim her 'in face of everything and everybody!' (19). In Europe, however, his imagined scene of triumph becomes more explicit and even evangelical. 'His eyes had been opened to a new world of art. And this world it was his mission to reveal to others – he, the insignificant and ignorant Lewis Raycie' (41). Thus the pictures were meant to prove his competence, his worth, his *superiority*.

When he inherits a home in New York, he opens his gallery

there, acting as tour guide even though his wife (Beatrice) is painfully aware of the embarrassing public attention that will accrue. For Lewis, though, this opportunity must be taken; he has to show the world that he was right, that the pictures he brought back are indeed masterpieces – even if it hurts his wife:

> He could hear all the town echoing with this new *scandal* of his showing the pictures himself – and she, so much more sensitive to *ridicule*, so much less carried away by apostolic ardour, how much louder must that *mocking echo* ring in her ears! But his pang was only momentary. The one thought that possessed him for any length of time was that *he must vindicate himself* by making the pictures known (60) [my emphases].

The gallery is not a success, though it does get some initial attention. One of Lewis's married sister's pleads with him to spare the family and his wife 'the humiliation. . . the public slight on [their] name' (63), offering to double his income if he closes the gallery, while his other sister offers him enough money to keep the gallery open for a year. The obvious irony will be, of course, that the pictures, unvalued in Lewis' lifetime, will be worth millions years later.

At one level, the story is almost a fable of old New York's blindness expressed through a son victimized by his father's grandiosity. But more broadly, shame withers a number of lives here – Lewis's, his wife's, even his father's. In his dogged determination to prove that he is right, Lewis becomes in his own way as limited a person as his father, as concerned with his name, his reputation. If Raycie senior has been monomaniacally determined to carry on his name through the glory of an art gallery, his son is equally as obsessed, and with his name too – inasmuch as he has become identified with the paintings. His efforts to overcome the ways in which he has been consistently shamed by his father lead him into more shaming situations. John Amherst in *The Fruit of the Tree* (discussed below) is another character similarly over-identified with his career or work.

In *The Old Maid* Wharton returns to the subject of her first novella, *Bunner Sisters* – the jealousy and shame that distort a relationship between two women – but her treatment here is far more complex, and the novella has a great deal more to say about stifled lives. Delia and Charlotte Ralston are cousins whose widely-married family is one of those ruling New York in the 1850s, 'in simplicity and affluence.'[5] These fourth generation Ralstons have no convictions left but 'an acute sense of honour in private and business matters' (79) and their society is one marked by extreme complacency. When Charlotte confesses to having borne an illegitimate child, Tina, something deeply dishonorable will come into their lives. For nearly two decades the cousins' relationship, in which 'there was nothing open' (125) will be marked by secrecy, jealousy, anger and shame. Charlotte loses her rightful place as Tina's mother to Delia, whom the girl comes to think of as her mother. Delia will eventually adopt Tina in her teens, giving her the shelter of the Ralston name and also some of her own money so that she can marry well. Charlotte, 'at considerable personal sacrifice, agrees to the end that the truth must never be exposed to the girl.'[6]

Contemplating her cousin Charlotte's marriage to a cousin of her husband, Jim, Delia Ralston is an expression of New York complacency, well aware that though Charlotte will have a married life similar to hers, 'Charlotte's bedroom would certainly not be as pretty' (83). (We will see in *The House of Mirth* the power of such comparisons.) Delia's complacency about the beauty of her own home is somewhat undercut, however, by her sense that Charlotte's affection for the paupers in a day-nursery that she runs is a 'fierce passion' while what *she* feels for her children is only 'a mild and measured sentiment' (86). Years later, in a crucial confrontation with Charlotte, Delia will feel much the same: 'It seemed to her that for the first time she had sounded [in Charlotte] the deepest depths of maternal passion, and she stood awed of the echoes it gave back' (168). Charlotte will seem to speak 'with the voice of all the dark destinies coiled under the safe surface of life' (137). Though smugly superior to Charlotte, her poor cousin, Delia thus also feels deeply and consistently inferior – and that bifurcation will mark their relationship, and even unexpectedly intensify as the novella progresses. For though Delia is a Ralston (by marriage), and steeped in Ralston-ism, she sometimes has moments of 'secret questioning' of everything in her life, moments that leave her 'breathless and a little pale' (81). These vertiginous moments are the seeds of deeper, more isolating doubts and regrets for an unlived life.

On the eve of her own wedding, Charlotte declares that she absolutely cannot marry, and her subsequent confession about the hidden child changes the two women's lives irrevocably, binding them in a secret. With *lowered head*, Charlotte at first says she wants to get away from 'the Ralston ideas' (89) which of course makes Delia – who lives them – angry. What really haunts Charlotte, though, is having to give up Tina, her favorite child at the day-nursery, because her Ralston husband-to-be is afraid of their future children catching some illness from the paupers. But the child is *her* child. This revelation makes Delia look away, and leaves her

> dumb with the horror and amazement of learning that her own blood ran in the veins of the anonymous foundling. . . It was her first contact with the nether side of the smooth social surface, and she sickened at the thought that such things were, and that she, Delia Ralston, should be hearing of them in her own house, and from the lips of the victim! (92).

This awful moment of discovery and disillusionment reverberates back to *Sanctuary* (see Chapter 2). Trying to explain how it happened, Charlotte dismisses her cousin with 'You wouldn't understand.'

> A slow blush rose to Delia's cheek: she felt oddly *humiliated* by the rebuke conveyed in that contemptuous retort. She seemed to herself *shy, ineffectual*, as *incapable* as an *ignorant* girl of dealing with the abominations that Charlotte was thrusting on her (94) [my emphases].

Pressing to find out who the father is, Delia is plunged into deeper 'revelations of dishonour' (95), because the little girl is the daughter of Clement Spender, a handsome but 'irresolute, impecunious' (135) suitor Delia had loved but rejected for the security of the Ralstons. Charlotte's confession will vault Delia 'farther than ever before beyond the Ralston horizon' (104), and fill her with 'secret envy' as she thinks of 'Charlotte's eyes – so much the more expressive for all that they had looked upon' (107). She even identifies with Charlotte so much that she feels as if 'this other woman were telling her of her own secret past, putting into crude words all the trembling silences of her own heart' (96).

Delia's solution to the problem of Charlotte's child is to use Charlotte's recurrence of tuberculosis to halt the marriage, and she goes further by taking the child into her own home, to protect

Charlotte's shameful secret, and by extension, her secret as well. Charlotte moves in as well, and becomes the quintessential old maid: 'Precise, methodical, absorbed in trifles, and attaching an exaggerated importance to the smallest social and domestic observances' (120). Her carapace hardens over the years because it is Charlotte's 'ruling purpose that her child should never guess the tie between them' – even though Charlotte opens herself up to suffering and abuse, as when Tina complains that her aunt is 'so dreadfully old-maidish!' (122). Charlotte, of course, turns harshly red when she overhears this offhand remark.

Yet for all the terrible distance between Charlotte and the truth, between herself and her child, Charlotte is not entirely powerless, at least in Delia's view. Delia feels she always seems to yield 'whenever any question arose about the girl' (127), subdued by her cousin's 'mute obstinate way' (127). And even trying to understand what makes her cousin tick leaves Delia '*humiliated* and *abashed* by the base motives she found herself attributing to Charlotte' (129) [my emphases]:

> How was it that she, Delia Ralston, whose happiness had been open and avowed to the world, so often found herself envying poor Charlotte the secret of her scanted motherhood? She hated herself for this movement of envy whenever she detected it, and tried to atone for it by a softened manner and a more anxious regard for Charlotte's feeling; but the attempt was not always successful (129).

The greatest irony of this intriguing novella is that despite having had her own children and a husband who loved her, Delia Ralston comes to feel that she is 'living the life meant for another woman' (141). She experiences a 'deep central indifference' and looking around her she sees 'the walls of her own grave'; she is 'doomed to dwell among shadows. Life had passed her by, and left her with the Ralstons' (142).

To ensure that Tina marries someone in their set, and does not end up being seduced like her mother, Delia adopts the girl, winning a confrontation with Charlotte, who declares that she has never been ashamed of what happened. Charlotte's actions demonstrate the untruth of her assertion, however:

> Charlotte *hid her face* in the cushions, clenching them with

violent hands. The same fierce maternal passion that had once flung her upon those same cushions was now bowing her still lower, in the throes of bitter renunciation (155) [my emphasis].

The cousins have tangled before, and will again, climactically, over who should talk to Tina about married life the evening before her wedding. Who is her real mother? Charlotte at last speaks the word she feels describes what has always been between them: hate. In her loneliness and frustration she accuses Delia of having been jealous that Clement Spender found consolation with *her*, and of having found revenge and triumph in taking his child away from Charlotte. Much of what Charlotte spews out is true, and Delia is overcome by an 'embittering sense of failure' (169).

Tina's socially correct marriage may fill Delia with excitement, unlike her own 'placid bridal' which had 'nothing to quicken the pulse' (161). And she may identify with Tina so much, 'living the girl's life,' that Tina's 'bridal joy' is 'mysteriously her own. . . the compensation for all she had missed and yet never renounced' (169). But it is only when she is old that 'for the first time, without shame, without self-reproach, without a pang or a scruple, Delia could yield to that vision of requited love from which her imagination had always turned away' (169). Because it is her point of view through which we experience the story, it is not inappropriately her losses that seem greater. We never learn the full extent of Charlotte's pain, only infer it, but the lives of both women force us to contemplate what it is to 'grow old and to be lonely – with all life's options already taken and all life's expectations harshly foreclosed.'[7]

Loneliness permeates 'Her Son', a powerful and haunting long story that documents the lengths a woman will go to in order to overcome the shame of having abandoned her child. It has been inexplicably ignored by most Wharton critics. Norcutt, the narrator, a minor American diplomat, meets the recently widowed Catherine Glenn on board a ship headed for Cherbourg. She is a woman he has always seen as 'aloof and abstracted, shut off from the world behind the high walls of a happy domesticity.'[8] In fact, looking at her, he imagines that 'in that smooth marble surface there was no crack in which detraction could take root,' (622), even though she had been orphaned, penniless, and 'passed about from one reluctant relation to another' (621). After marriage to Stephen Glenn, a handsome, well-respected and unexceptional lawyer who was something of a social arbiter in New York, the pair gradually evolved into a couple widely perceived as 'wooden, pompous and slightly absurd' (623). Only the death of their son in World War I revived interest in the couple.

Mrs Glenn will soon reveal to Norcutt at the consulate in Paris that she bore her husband a child while he was still married to an insane woman, a child that had to be given up for adoption. Her life has ever since been one of silence, lies and deep regret, especially because she was unable to adopt the child after she married Glenn when his wife died. Any breath of scandal would have damaged his career, and even almost thirty years later, she hangs her head and blushes to give these reasons to Norcutt. But now, alone, she is determined to comb Italy with the few clues she has to find her lost son, Stephen, and the couple that adopted him – the Browns.

Norcutt next sees Mrs Glenn in the South of France after she has cabled him that she found her son. Seeing how joyful she looks, he understands that

> during all those years, the unsatisfied longing for her eldest child, the *shame* at her own *cowardice* in disowning and deserting him, and perhaps her *secret contempt* for her husband for having abetted (or more probably exacted) that desertion, must have been eating into her soul, deeper, far deeper, than satisfied affections could reach (628) [my emphases].

The young man is pleasant enough, though tubercular, but Mr and Mrs Brown are a somewhat unlikely and unlikable couple – he, rather dandified and possibly alcoholic, she, the 'perfect specimen of the middle-aged flapper' (632), and rude as well. She criticizes Catherine Glenn's comparative inattention to her appearance, making her flush in front of Norcutt. Two weeks with these people make the situation even more perplexing to Norcutt – how could such a couple have raised the 'whimsical dreamy charming' (632) man who is a 'brilliant' painter? Norcutt finds the Browns, Boyden (nicknamed 'Boy') and Chrissy, a bit hard to stomach and can see that with their airs and familiarities Catherine does as well, but her attempts to get some time alone with Stephen fail. Norcutt is ashamed to see that Catherine is growing increasingly intimate with the Browns, and she seems equally ashamed, blushing and looking down when Norcutt refers to their apparent selfishness.

Catherine, of course, is trapped by her shame; and so she cannot suggest separating Stephen from his adopted mother: 'She brought him up. She was there – all the years when I'd failed him' (637).

When Norcutt next sees Catherine, the situation has become deeply mysterious. Stephen has apparently argued with the Browns, moved to his own studio, and Mrs Brown discourages Norcutt from seeing Catherine, who herself hasn't seen Stephen. Why would Mrs Brown try to keep them apart, and why has she discouraged Stephen from marrying the nice young woman he recently met? And why did Stephen ask Norcutt – to their great mutual embarrassment – if Catherine had written the Browns into her will? When Norcutt does talk with Catherine, she seems frightened and cowed, unable to do anything that might offend the Browns; a talk with Mrs Brown is even stranger. She tells him that Stephen is cruelly refusing Catherine's money, 'in his crazy pride. . . depriving himself of the most necessary things' (650). She urges Norcutt to get Catherine to write her monthly check for Stephen to *her*, because then Stephen will take the money, and then Catherine presses him to give money to Stephen, which he ends up passing on to Mrs Brown in what almost seems a sort of bribe for seeing Stephen.

Quite ill, unable to paint anymore, Stephen not only expresses his disgust for the Browns and tenderness for Catherine, he reveals that it's all been a 'conspiracy,' relating the 'sordid tale of a trio of society adventurers come to the end of their resources, and suddenly clutching at this unheard-of chance of rescue, affluence, peace' (655). Too ill now to paint the portrait of Catherine he hoped would in some way atone for his imposture, Stephen wants to confess to her, struggling as he is with the 'naked shame' of what he's done. But Norcutt swears that the truth will kill Catherine and that keeping up the pose can be 'a sort of expiation' (656).

Stephen is reunited with Catherine, and after his death, Mrs Brown, who suffers the loss 'more bleakly and bitterly' (658), becomes 'Mrs Glenn's chief consolation in her sorrow' (657). 'The two women, so incessantly at odds while Stephen lived, were now joined in a common desolation' (657). Catherine tells Norcutt that she has had more of Stephen than his adopted mother, because she carried him, and finding him was such a miracle. She even seems ashamed of Stephen having loved her more than Mrs Brown, which makes her sorry that she hasn't been kinder to

Chrissy Brown. 'Every turn to the strange story had been improbable and incalculable, and this new freak of fate was the most unexpected' – still, Catherine has 'a new pretext for her self-devotion,' so Norcutt makes no comment (658). Catherine also criticizes herself for having been too hard on Mrs Brown after they have argued about Stephen's paintings. Exhibited, they stimulate attractive offers, but Catherine refuses to sell a single one, and ends up giving the angry Mrs Brown a sum equivalent to what the buyers offered, by way of consolation.

Norcutt doesn't see 'the incongruous trio' (660) for two years, though he hears occasionally from Catherine, and knows she has been ill. Searching for her in Nice, he discovers that lack of funds has forced them to settle in Monaco, where their rooms are 'wretched' and 'tawdry' (662); he overhears Mrs Brown berating Catherine, and in his presence, she taunts Catherine: 'The fact that for years I looked after the child she deserted weighs nothing with her. She doesn't seem to think she owes us anything' (663). To Catherine's simple statement that there's simply no money left, Mrs Brown explodes:

> No money! No money! That's always the tune nowadays. There was always plenty of money for her precious – money for all his whims and fancies, for journeys, for motors, for doctors, for – well, what's the use of going on? But now that there's nobody left but Boy and me, who slaved for her darling for years, who spent our last penny on him when his mother'd forgotten his existence – now there's nothing left! Now she can't afford anything; now she won't even pay her own bills; now she'd sooner starve herself to death than let us have what she owes us. . . (663–64) [Wharton's ellipsis].

Drunk and incoherent, badgering Catherine, the sloppy Mrs Brown responds to Norcutt's unspoken threat to reveal the truth about Stephen by contemptuously doing just that, and implicating Norcutt in the fraud. In response to Catherine's questions, Norcutt can only urge her to leave that terrible place with him, and when Mrs Brown triumphantly flings out the fact that she and Stephen were really lovers, Catherine has suffered a stroke, and is too far gone to understand.

The Browns and Stephen have heartlessly taken advantage of Catherine Glenn's shame over her abandonment of her child, reminding her at every opportunity that she abandoned her baby, and bilking her for every penny they could get. While the scam eventually left Stephen ashamed of his role, Mrs Brown has only suffered a few pangs of embarrassment. Her relationship with Catherine is one in which she, common and vulgar, can triumph over a true lady to whom she feels consistently superior because of her attention to appearances, but more importantly, because she is defrauding Catherine. Her contempt and Catherine's shame make for a deep and dark relationship – which Norcutt recognized from the beginning: 'The women were so different, so diametrically opposed to each other in appearance, dress, manner, and all the inherited standards, that if they had met as strangers it would have been hard for them to find a common ground of understanding' (631). From the beginning, though she felt distaste for the Browns, Catherine buried her qualms, and was in fact oversolicitous of *their* feelings.

But Norcutt's relationship to Catherine is also complicated, since he is responsible to some extent for her final decline in the hands of the Browns. He had until then been convinced that 'after all, her life had been richer and deeper than if she had spent it, childless and purposeless, in the solemn upholstery of her New York house' (661–62). Has he done the right thing? He can't admit to Catherine that Stephen was not in fact her lost son, and that he knew this was so, which seems to indicate his own shame for having let the situation deteriorate. Catherine's longing for family connectedness (and for an easing of her shame) leads her into a twisted and masochistic relationship which she can only escape through the partial loss of her faculties.

Another dark and perplexing relationship arises out of family life in 'Confession,' which focuses on a shameful secret that we never learn, but whose existence shapes several lives. Convalescing in a fashionable Swiss hotel, the narrator, Severance, is drawn to an interesting shy woman, Mrs Ingram, but put off by Cassie Wilpert, her vulgar and over-dressed *dame de compagnie*. Attempting to inquire about the companion makes Mrs Ingram blush and explain her away. The narrator is uncomfortably piqued, though 'not given to prying into other people's secrets,'[9] he wants to understand what on earth can link these two so different women.

A journalist friend appears on the scene and swears that 'Mrs Ingram' is really the notorious Kate Spain who was tried for killing her tyrannical, miserly rich father, and the vulgar woman was her servant, by whose testimony Kate was acquitted of murder. Ezra Spain, universally disliked, was a man 'reported to have let his wife die of neglect because he would not send for a doctor till it was too late, and who had been too mean to supply her with food and medicines'. After her death, his daughter was likewise 'browbeaten and starved' (813). Severance insists that the identification of Mrs Ingram as Kate Spain can't be accurate, and that she had *not* recognized his journalist friend and hurried off – but alone at night, he begins to wonder. And to feel like a fool, 'ridiculously, fatuously drawn on' by her gifts as a listener; he has told her everything about himself, yet he knows nothing about her (815). But even though he is falling in love with her, there is still the mystery of her rude, unpleasant companion. 'What conceivable interest or obligation could make a woman like Mrs Ingram endure such an intimacy?' (816)

In the morning he is stunned to find she has left the hotel, and he is plunged into doubt about her past. Even if she were Kate Spain, and innocent, she could never 'live it down, her name would always remain associated with that sordid tragedy' (817). Understanding why she might have fled 'a scandal-mongering journalist,' he tracks her down at a small Italian inn where she confesses herself to be Kate Spain, but he proposes marriage anyway. She presents him with a vision of public humiliation: 'How would you like, wherever you went, to have some one suddenly whisper behind you: "Look. That's Kate Spain?"' And her question momentarily halts Severance as he imagines being pursued by 'the ugly whisper. . . from place to place, from house to house' (820). Kate reveals her own torment of always being discovered, criticized and suspected no matter how she comported herself, and of having been unable to seek refuge with family because she could never escape her past.

Severance offers a bold alternative to her shame:

'Your real name is Kate Spain, Well – what of it? Why try to disguise it? You've never done anything to disgrace it. You've suffered through it, but never been abased. If you want to get rid of it there's a much simpler way; and that is to take mine instead. But meanwhile, if people ask you if you're Kate Spain, try saying yes, you are, instead of running from them' (821).

Kate listens *'with bent head.'* Though they spend a beautiful day together, her companion is still the mystery – what is her hold on Kate and why can't Kate get rid of her? We do not even find out when the companion barges into Severance's room the next day, flushed, glaring, possibly drunk, accusing him of prying into Kate's life, and declaring Kate cannot, must not marry him. When she threatens to reveal something about Kate that he will take as his 'death sentence' (827), she has a stroke. After Miss Wilpert's death, Kate still insists that she can't marry Severance, and gives him the sealed envelope Cassie had meant to force on him.

Severance takes the envelope but refuses to read what's in it. Kate's willingness to hand it over when the secret it revealed 'would doubtless have destroyed her in the eyes of the world' (831), has revealed her character to him. Severance judges her not by her past, but by who she is to him *now*, and even says he doesn't care if she has concealed knowledge of who really killed her father. The story ends with Kate having died after five years of marriage, and Severance about to burn the unopened letter. We never learn whether she did murder her father, and if so, why. But Cassie Wilpert's threat that what she knows will destroy Severance suggests that rape or incest could really have been the secret of the Spain family.

What is remarkable about this story is Severance's almost un-flinching devotion to Kate. Though he has his initial doubts about their relationship because she has revealed comparatively little about herself (and *he* feels exposed), once he knows who she is, he is unwavering in his love. The potential of shame does not really faze him, and thus he is utterly unlike men like George Darrow in *The Reef* imagining the glory of being married to a woman people will admire. Severance offers Kate complete freedom from shame – or at any rate, he will not shame her by bringing up her past or digging into it any further. The moment in which Kate gives up her shameful secret in the envelope to him is a rare one in Wharton's fiction. Confessions, like Kate Clephane's in *The Mother's Recompense*, tend to be sources of *further* shame. Severance is quite aptly named, having attempted to sever the ties between Kate and her former servant, and having successfully, it seems, severed her from her shameful past. His advice that she look people in the eye and not hide is extremely unusual counsel in Wharton's fiction – silence is more often the advised response – and their marriage acting to heal shame is equally unusual. For the most part, mar-riages in her fiction are a deep and painful source of shame, largely because one partner becomes profoundly disappointed by the other, yet feels trapped. As R.W.B. Lewis points out, Wharton's dim view of marriage was clear as early as her stories 'The Valley of Childish Things and Other Emblems' and 'The Lamp of Psyche.'[10]

The Fruit of the Tree is a long novel which 'analyzes the psychological complexities of marriage'[11] as well as demonstrating the interconnectedness of the personal and the social. The means are two marriages, that of social reformer John Amherst to Bessy Westmore, a wealthy New England mill-owner, and subsequently to Justine Brent, a nurse and friend of Bessy who performs euthanasia on Bessy after she is crippled by a riding accident and condemned to useless suffering.

Both marriages John Amherst makes in *The Fruit of the Tree* ultimately founder, and shame is certainly a key culprit in each case. To begin with, like Lily Bart in *The House of Mirth*, John Amherst has suffered a shameful social decline:

> In adopting a manual trade, instead of one of the gentlemanly professions which the men of [his mother's] family had always followed, he had not only disappointed her hopes, and to a great extent thrown away the benefits of the education she had pinched herself to give him, but had disturbed all the habits of her life by removing her from her normal surroundings to the depressing exile of a factory-settlement. . . her self-effacement made him the more alive to his own obligations.[12]

Mrs Amherst's shame also clearly communicates itself to him: she flushes 'like a girl' telling him his job is not the kind she 'ever wanted to see [him] in!' (28). And after meeting Bessy Westmore, Amherst will realize that though he had never thought of money in choosing his work, 'without its aid, he was powerless to accomplish the object to which his personal desires had been sacrificed' (97) – that is, reform at the mills.

Amherst is keenly sensitive to the drop in his family's status. Meeting Bessy Westmore for the first time to discuss the mills, he is aware that his mother would have been pleased by her 'murmur of surprise' (42) at seeing a mere assistant manager cut such a fine figure. But he is annoyed at the impression created by his being well-dressed. In his 'everyday clothes' the difference between what Bessy expected and how he appeared would not be so great, and so embarrassing; her murmur may be a compliment but it is also a clear reminder of the current social distance between them. When Bessy's father obviously can't place him, Amherst is offended to be so much less important than he imagines himself to be: 'The discovery stung Amherst to a somewhat unreasoning resentment' (43).

A close family friend of the Westmore's, Mrs Ansell, turns out to have previously known Amherst's mother, and her visit with Bessy to the Amhersts' little house is deeply embarrassing:

[Amherst] was too proud of his mother to feel any doubt of the impression she would produce; but what would Mrs Westmore think of their way of living, of the cheap jauntiness of the cottage, and the smell of cooking penetrating all of its thin partitions?. . . [H]e detected the uneasy desire that Mrs Westmore should not regard him as less of her own class than his connections and his bringing-up entitled him to be thought. In a flash he saw what he had forfeited by his choice of a calling – equal contact with the little circle of people who gave life its crowning grace and facility. . . (68).

As we have seen before, like other characters of Wharton's, Amherst is ashamed of his shame; he blushes 'at this reversal of his standards,' and then wonders 'almost contemptuously' about Bessy as the trigger of this shame (68–9). Despite all that, he cannot help imagining 'his house as it must appear to Mrs Westmore,' and he notes the fence's shabby paint job, a neighbor's poor garden, 'the week's wash *flaunting itself indecently* through the *denuded* shrubs about the kitchen porch' (69). The language of exposure here is appropriate to his shamed state, and even after his marriage to Bessy he will be painfully aware of their social differences. Temporarily parted by their continued and growing misunderstandings, he will at one point feel quite embarrassed to return to their Long Island estate with houseguests on the scene, because he is 'inexpert in the art of easy transitions, and his inability to bridge over awkward gaps had often put him at a disadvantage with his wife and friends' (246).[13]

Amherst's shame about his social position is clear in his second visit to the Westmore home, this time in 'rough clothes' that strike him as 'incongruous' in an 'atmosphere of after-dinner ease' (73).

He is so identified with the way he looks (which is a trait that is very common in Wharton's women), that it is as if 'the mud on his walking-boots' and 'the clinging cotton-dust' from the mills 'seemed to have entered into the very pores of his skin' (73). Attempting to argue for improvements at the mills, and put off from seeing Bessy, Amherst is consistently embarrassed at this meeting by her lawyer, Mr Tredegar, to whom 'he was no more than an underling' (75). The lawyer uses silence to deliberately embarrass Amherst, calmly questions Amherst's recital of facts, suggests he may be underhanded in complaining about the mill's manager, and implies that Amherst is criticizing Bessy. Tredegar is so socially adept that a mere 'Ah–' can make Amherst feel as if he has been whipped. He has of course blushed throughout this interview – as he was meant to.

This meeting with the Westmore family lawyer, and Bessy Westmore's beauty, which has stimulated him as never before, leave Amherst 'humbled' (91) and full of 'self-derision' (92). Captivated by Bessy, he had attempted to win her over to his vision of reform at the mills, and endangered his position by complaining to her about the current manager. Thinking it all over, he is left 'blushing at his own insincerity' (93):

> he saw now that he had risked his future not because of his zeal for the welfare of the millhands, but because Mrs Westmore's look was like sunshine on his frozen senses, and because he was resolved, at any cost, to arrest her attention, to associate himself with her by the only means in his power. . . In the cold light of disenchantment it seemed as though he had tried to build an impregnable fortress out of nursery blocks (93).

For a while, however, Bessy *does* take up his plans of reform, even though he is not the mill's appropriate representative, and Amherst, not surprisingly, enjoys the 'sense of being the glove flung by her hand in the face of convention' (109). After all, what 'he really wanted was to speak out, and yet escape the consequences' (54). Bessy's departure, however, removes his protection, and he is fired. When she returns at Christmas, Amherst is mortified at the idea of her *insisting* that he be re-employed; that would be owing her far too much, and impossible, he vehemently tells her. Their talk ends with Bessy's tears at the thought of losing him, and they subsequently marry. Carol Wershoven notes that Amherst marries her 'not out of genuine love, but to further his ambitions.'[14]

As we have seen, Amherst feels himself Bessy's equal socially, but he is absolutely certain that he is *superior* to her in terms of intelligence, insight and social consciousness, and part of his attraction to her is a patronizing desire to make her over. He thus is in some ways in love with the woman he sees himself helping to create, in love with the image of his own power affecting a change in her. Taking her to the mills and bringing her 'face to face with her people,' he hopes 'to see the angel of pity stir the depths of those unfathomable eyes, when they rested, perhaps for the first time, on suffering that it was in their power to smile away as easily as they had smiled away his own distrust' (47). The scene he imagines is highly sentimental and unrealistic – the Lady Bountiful changing the world through the intercession of her beautiful charity – all, of course, set in motion by Amherst himself. But his expectations of her from the very beginning have been unrealistic. Based merely on their very first talk, and her visit to his home, Amherst has 'the sense of having penetrated so far into her intimacy that a new [town of] Westmore must inevitably result from their next meeting' (70). And though he finds her like his mother far more drawn to the personal than the social, he soon comes to romanticize what he formerly considered a problem: didn't concentrating on 'the personal issue' as women did 'offer a warm tint of human inconsistency to eyes chilled by contemplating life in the mass' (119)? Indeed, Amherst believes that Bessy's physical beauty must surely be a reflection of her beautiful soul. These flights of fancy are undercut by the narrator pointing out that for 'a young man ruled by high enthusiasms there can be no more dazzling adventure than to work this miracle [of transformation] in the tender creature who yields her mind to his' (120). To conquer Bessy's ignorance, and through her, reform the mills and change the lives of all those who work for the Westmores is to become powerful, a success. This vision will wipe the slate clean – no more talk of letting his family down, of being a disappointment. Amherst will instead be a hero.

Amherst's egotism and obsession with reform help destroy his peace in their subsequent marriage, in which he will of course be profoundly disappointed, ashamed of his self-deception and critical both of himself and Bessy. Two years after their marriage, it is with intense 'self-derision' that he remembers deluding himself about Bessy as a woman, and Amherst is 'more ashamed of [his current] insight than of the blindness' (183) to what Bessy was like. He may have wanted to believe that he showed frivolous Bessy a higher meaning in life, but he understands that she married him for much more prosaic reasons: 'because he was young, handsome, persecuted, an ardent lover. . . because her family had opposed the marriage' (180). Bessy's interest in Amherst's plans is partly based on this opposition: she was 'too much the wife – and the wife in love – to consent that her husband's views on the management of the mills should be totally disregarded' (183). But with her 'dense misintelligence of both sides of the question' she ends up uncomfortably in between her husband and his opponents in her family and at the mills. It is an 'ugly *impasse*' (187) for Amherst, who had hoped to do great things with the opportunity his marriage afforded him. Throughout the book he will continue to try persuading Bessy to follow his lead even though 'all about her spoke a language so different from his own' and there was little 'hope to make himself heard' (249). Even after many bruising arguments about the cost of making changes at the mills, and the necessary reduction in their own living expenses, Amherst will still hope 'to reawaken in Bessy some feeling for the urgency of his task,' but he will only be met by 'her cold anticipation of his demands as part of a disagreeable business to be despatched and put out of mind' (286). This is not what he expected; Amherst was certain that his wife 'would abound in the adaptabilities and pliancies which the lords of the earth have seen fit to cultivate in their companions' (179).

Amherst seems absolutely stuck in his *own* 'dense misintelligence' of Bessy. Having had an image of her that was romantically untrue, he persists in badgering her, trying to convert and reform her – as if to relent, to accept the reality of what she is and live peaceably with that reality would be too shameful an admission of failure. It is humiliating enough to realize that he is unable to convince his wife by 'argument and exposition' when he knows that he can 'trick her into a confused surrender to the personal influence he still possessed over her' (185). He knows he's failed, but will not give up trying – and his persistence is not admirable, but extremely ill-advised. 'Between them, forever, were the insurmountable barriers of character, of education, of habit – and yet it was not in him to believe that any barrier was insurmountable' (290). He will continue to misread his wife and their situation, imagining after they make up once again that they 'were at length reaching some semblance of that moral harmony which should grow out of the physical accord, and that, poor and incomplete as the understanding was, it must lift and strengthen their relation' (321).

What will precipitate the final rift between them is in part social shame. Amherst learns that his wife is letting a married friend, Mrs Carbury, meet her lover at their Long Island estate, while she is in residence, and though he had 'tried to deaden himself to the situation,. . . all his traditions. . . were roused to revolt by the receipt of a newspaper clipping' about the scandalous situation (310). Bessy's father will not help Amherst deal with the insult to the family honor, merely suggesting that if Amherst take Bessy away, the adulterous couple will have to rendezvous elsewhere. To Amherst this advice is 'but a part of the ingenious system of evasion whereby a society bent on the undisturbed pursuit of amusement had contrived to protect itself from the intrusion of the disagreeable' (313). But his father-in-law's lack of concern is also a reminder of the social gap between them. Mrs Carbury's husband apparently has no complaint, and that is what determines the prevailing opinion, Langhope explains, as always, politely 'elucidating the social code to his son-in-law' (312). Amherst still finds the business disgraceful, and feels publicly shamed, telling Bessy that 'As long as you're my wife we've only one honour between us, and that honour is mine to take care of' (322). This paternalism makes Bessy blush (of course!) and their subsequent argument leads to another separation.

Accidentally meeting Justine Brent in New York, on his way to take a job in the South, he will be convinced to return. Justine's questions about his plans embarrass him, especially when she points out that leaving Bessy as he plans to will 'subject her to. . . unkind criticism,' and if he takes a job to support himself, people's gossip will 'make Bessy suffer,' and it will be Amherst's 'fault if she is humiliated in that way' (336–37). Amherst does go back, but only to face more humiliation when his staff knows that his wife has gone to stay with the disreputable Mrs Carbury, and he obviously does not. A 'well-bred man' would have disguised his surprise, but he is humiliatingly unable to avoid 'laying bare his discomfiture to his dependents,' embarrassing his butler by the 'manifest impropriety of the situation' (342).

Who is the 'tender creature' that Amherst has treated as if he were a missionary in some pagan land? Mrs Ansell, the family confidante, sees Bessy Westmore as 'one of those most harrowing victims of the plan of bringing up our girls in the double bondage of expediency and unreality, corrupting their bodies and their brains with sentiment, and leaving them to reconcile the two as best they can' (281). Indeed, Bessy has led a life 'so free from tiresome obligations that she had but a small stock of patience to meet them with' (40). That patience will be tried and exhausted in her marriage with Amherst, to whom she has felt inferior from the beginning, confessing her ignorance of business affairs. This ignorance, we should note, is shared by her father, but he does not belittle himself the way he belittles his daughter. Commenting on her control of the mills after her husband's death, Mr Langhope sneers: 'Apply yourself, Bessy. Bring your masterly intellect to bear on the industrial problem' (36). Mrs Ansell asks him not to tease Bessy, and it is she who has 'the faculty of restoring to [Bessy] the belief in her reasoning powers that her father could dissolve in a monosyllable' (109). Without Mrs Ansell, Bessy finds reflection difficult – as she has been brought up to do. This lack of insight helps draw her to John Amherst without real awareness of what she is experiencing:

> Bessy Westmore had in full measure that gift of unconscious hypocrisy which enables a woman to make the man in whom she is interested believe that she enters into all his thoughts. She had – more than this – the gift of self-deception, supreme happiness of the unreflecting nature. . . (120)

Bessy can thus start to spend time with Amherst without feeling constrained, and Amherst has interpreted her 'unconscious hypocrisy' as 'the good faith of a child' committing to him 'her ignorance, her credulity, her little rudimentary convictions and her little tentative aspirations' (100).

Amherst theoretically admires 'the woman who kept a calm exterior in emergencies, [but] he had all a man's desire to know that the springs of feelings lay close to the unruffled surface' (27), and it is significant that Bessy 'blushed easily' (113). Her blushing has a powerful impact on him when they meet a second time, and he decides to be completely honest about conditions at the mills: 'All thoughts of personal prudence were flung to the winds – her blush and tone had routed the waiting policy' (52). Susan Brownmiller notes in *Femininity* that the maidenly blush in nineteenth-century fiction 'was an excellent indicator of innocent virginal shyness in contrast to the worldliness and sophistication of men.'[15] It serves just such a purpose here. But Bessy resists being trapped by Amherst's infantilizing and degrading conception of her. Trying to soothe her after another argument about the mills when they are married, Amherst is aware of having reached a stage in their marriage where 'he went through all these accustomed acts of pacification as mechanically as a nurse soothing a fretful child' (198). He dismissingly tells her to 'be reasonable and try to sleep.' Understandably, Bessy erupts: 'Don't talk like that! I can't endure to be humoured like a baby' (199), and she also reveals how controlled she is by shame, blushingly telling him that she is worried what people will say about his spending *her* money 'imprudently' (203). This conversation ends with Amherst once again talking to her in 'his soothing way of speech,' and saying he is leaving for Chicago instead of staying to attend a business meeting the next day. Bessy is of course shamed again, 'turning her face away,' and she begs him not to hate her: 'I'll do anything. . . only say you don't hate me!' (206) He stays the night with her, claiming a small, momentary victory, having disgustedly played on her intense need for him to get what he wants at the mills.

When her old school friend Justine Brent eventually becomes a sort of governess and companion, Bessy asks her for advice on what to do about the rift in her marriage, but Justine's advice 'that she should *humble herself* still farther to Amherst. . . left in Bessy's mind a rankling sense of being *misunderstood* and *undervalued* by those to whom she turned in her extremity' (259) [my emphases]. Being misunderstood and undervalued has of course been her fate all along – and she marries a man who overvalues himself. Thus their marriage becomes what Carol Wershoven calls 'a war of wills and egos,' with Amherst's self-esteem on the line as he pushes for reforms, and Bessy's self-esteem dependent on her resisting and clinging 'to her money, knowing it to be the only thing she has that "interests" her husband.'[16]

Bessy's disappointment in being treated as a child is not the only source of discontent in her marriage. While her 'mind could revolve in the same grievance as interminably as a squirrel in a cage,' Amherst is seemingly able to slough off his problems after initially wrestling with them, which to Bessy 'seemed to betoken poverty of feeling' (265). When he returns after an absence, he is cool, 'tongue-tied and helpless' (266), and his wondering if it's inconvenient for her to have him back while there are guests makes her blush. Worse still is his attempt to 'humble himself still farther by saying he should pay more attention to "appearances."'

> Appearances! He spoke as if she had been reproaching him for a breach of etiquette. . . it never occurred to him that the cry came from her humiliated heart! The tide of warmth that always enveloped her in his presence was receding, and in its place a chill fluid seemed to creep up slowly to her throat and lips (267) [Wharton's ellipsis].

This particular meeting after an absence is like so many others, filled by their mutual embarrassment and unhappiness, and ends with Bessy turning her head away.

In addition to seeming unfeeling (a friend of Justine's finds him 'so cold and sarcastic' after his marriage [149]), Amherst has proven to be a distinct social embarrassment to Bessy. Her friends treat her now with elements of 'criticism and compassion' (262). If he had hoped to convert her, *she* had hoped that his good looks and other qualities 'would immediately make him free of the charmed circle in which she moved; but she was discouraged by his disregard of his opportunities, and above all by the fundamental differences in his view of life. . . he would never acquire the small social facilities' (262). And Bessy's circle takes those facilities quite seriously, while Amherst is bored by stocks, cards, billiards, smoking-room anecdotes, and talking about sports. Amherst's 'social insufficiency' makes him a liability for Bessy, and worse, opens her to the possibility of shame in her circle, leaving her 'miserably persuaded that she and her husband were the butt of some of their most effective stories' (263). Like Darrow in *The Reef*, she is overly concerned with other people's opinions of herself.

Bessy will also be likewise ruled by what her friends think (by a desire to avoid shame, in other words), when she launches a project to have an extravagant addition to her mansion that would include a swimming pool and other luxurious recreational accoutrements. Bessy says yes to everything, because she is 'filled. . . with the dread of appearing, under Blanche Carbury's eyes, subject to any restraining influences of economy.' Why should she be subject to her husband's 'mute criticism' when he keeps away from her? 'The accomplished Blanche did not have to say this – she conveyed it by the raising of painted brows, by a smile of mocking interrogation, a judiciously placed silence or a resigned glance at the architect' (364–65). The discovery that improvements already underway at the mills will make Bessy's pleasure dome impossible soon after leaves her crying out to Justine, 'the humiliation – before my friends!' (368). This addition was meant to prove her independence, her power, her indifference to her husband, but it has done just the opposite. Her expectations of marriage to Amherst have all been frustrated; he seems to prefer the mills to being with her; can't fill his social place as her husband; badgers her for money; and makes her feel lesser, despite all his talk of being the guardian of 'her dreams and her hopes, her belief in justice and goodness and decency' (323–24). As she sensibly points out in their last argument about the mills and money, 'I don't see why you should expect me to give up all the ideas I was brought up in. Our standards *are* different – but why should yours always be right?' (324). In a similar vein, Bessy asks Justine why she and Mrs Ansell push her to try getting Amherst back: 'I don't know why my friends should treat me like a puppet without any preferences of my own, and press me upon a man who has done his best to show that he doesn't want me' (375).

Justine Brent, Bessy Westmore's old school friend and John Amherst's second wife, has also suffered a shameful social fall like Amherst's, and feels that she belongs to no society at all (141). She had led a 'childhood nestled in beauty and gentle ways, before her handsome prodigal father had died, and her mother's face had grown pinched in the long struggle with poverty' (146). For Justine, a career in nursing had helped support herself and her mother, and after her mother's death, had carried her through her grief. It has been a 'crowded yet lonely life' (5), in which she, with a 'lonely heart' (222), has felt herself a superior person 'imprisoned in a circle of well-to-do mediocrity' (151). 'Her world. . . had been chiefly peopled by the dull or the crude,' and Justine's refuge is an 'inner kingdom' ruled by 'fastidiousness' which she has never shared because there has been no one worthy of entrance (152). Like Lily Bart imagining what she would do if she had the wealth of her friends whose taste and judgment are so inferior to hers, Justine

rebelled at the conditions that tied a spirit like hers to its monotonous task, while others, without a quiver of wings on their dull shoulders, or a note of music in their hearts, had the whole wide world to range through, and saw in it no more than a frightful emptiness to be shut out with tight walls of habit. . . (147) [Wharton's ellipsis].

As nurse for Bessy's child from her first marriage, Justine finds even more injustice in her surroundings at the Westmore estate of Lynbrook, where 'finer graces of luxurious living' are a welcome relief from the 'ugliness, pain and hard work' of nursing (221). While she is 'not in the least ashamed of her position in the household,' (220) she keeps herself somewhat aloof from Bessy's houseguests who she thinks 'missed the poetry of their situation, transacting their pleasures with the dreary method and shortness of view of a race tethered to the ledger' (221).

But despite her feelings of superiority to those around her, she can experience shame arising from her anomalous position as a cross between companion and employee. Westy Gaines, one of Bessy's cousins, is attracted to Justine, but when she encounters him with a number of Bessy's guests at Lynbrook, he is obviously embarrassed to be seen paying any attention to her: 'she recognized with a sting of mortification the resemblance between her view of the Lynbrook set and its estimate of herself. If Bessy's friends were negligible to her she was almost non-existent to them' (236–37). Brushing Westy Gaines off leaves Justine's 'pride quivering with a hurt the more painful because she would not acknowledge it' (237). Like Amherst wondering about seeing his home through Bessy's eyes, and becoming angry at this shift in his standards, Justine is annoyed at wasting even 'a moment's resentment' on someone as insignificant as Gaines (237). More evidence of the Lynbrook influence greets her when she is soon after met by Bessy's doctor, Wyant, who has proposed to her, and to whom she has promised an answer. Justine is rather rude to him, and is humiliated to be struck by 'the possibility that [her] resistance might be due to some sense of his social defects, his lack of measure and facility' (245). Living in Bessy's house, she has been unavoidably influenced by Bessy's standards.

The 'falseness of her position' (237) there extends to her feeling caught between Bessy, who has confided her anguish about the deteriorating marriage to her, and Amherst, whom Justine admires, and feels somewhat drawn to. She is appealed to by Mrs Ansell to write Amherst and ask him to come back, because she is 'the only one of Bessy's friends who is in the least in her husband's confidence.' The assertion increases Justine's embarrassment in this conversation, but she is aware that 'to betray embarrassment under Mrs Ansell's eyes was to risk giving it a dangerous significance' (358). Justine does, however, decide to write Amherst, and his letter leads to a significant shame scene between Justine and Bessy, who as we have seen above, resents Justine's advice that she relent somewhat to get her husband back. Bessy opens the letter by mistake, and then hands it to the blushing Justine, who finds it altogether too personal. When she hands it to Bessy, she sees 'the blood mount under her clear skin, invade the temples, the nape, even the little flower-like ears' (373). Bessy of course feels exposed, talked about, not considered, and she furiously mocks Justine and her obvious influence on Amherst, who wrote only because Justine asked him to. Justine can make no reply, and fears having missed her 'last opportunity' to make peace between Bessy and Amherst. She is silenced by shame: 'The blow to her pride had been too deep, had been dealt too unexpectedly – for one miserable moment she had thought first of herself!' (378).

In a rage, Bessy goes out riding on a dangerous horse, and is brought back with a broken spine. Crippled for life, in agony, she is tended to by Justine and Dr Wyant. Amherst is unreachable at first, but Justine, terribly moved by Bessy's wrenching and – to her – useless pain, decides to end the cruelty of keeping her alive and administers an overdose of morphine. This act of euthanasia – which she keeps secret from Amherst – destroys the foundations of her marriage with him a year and half later. Unlike his first marriage, Justine and Amherst are deeply united from the first: 'Every fresh discovery they made about each other, every new agreement of ideas and feelings, offered itself to these intrepid explorers as a friendly coast where they might beach their keel and take bearings' (472). A storm brews, however, when Dr Wyant, who knows what Justine did, begins writing to her for money, implying he will tell Amherst what happened if he doesn't get it. Justine assumes that the last large sum she sends him will leave him 'on his feet again, and ashamed – unutterably ashamed – of the threat that despair had wrung from him. She felt almost sure that his shame would keep him from ever attempting to see her, or even from writing again' (492).

But she is wrong, because Wyant has told her he is 'past shame' now (481). He shows up, asking Justine to get him the job of house-physician at a hospital Bessy's father and Mrs Ansell are involved with, but she refuses, and their confrontation drags on while she realizes Amherst is due any minute: 'There was no knowing how long the humiliating scene might be prolonged: and she must be rid of the creature at any cost' (507). Wyant ends up blurting out the truth to Amherst when he arrives, and Wyant's exit relieves Justine: 'She had suffered less from the fear of what her husband might think than from the shame of making her avowal in her defamer's presence' (516). Justine explains everything, even how she felt inspired and encouraged by things Amherst had said and written down, but she realizes that while *she* was able to 'rise above conventional restrictions,. . . he would never be able to free himself from the traditional view of her act' (525). Amherst has 'dishonoured her by the most wounding suspicions. The tie between them was forever stained and debased' (526–27). After a painful and ineffective separation, which leaves Bessy's daughter unhappily longing for Justine, they reunite, with nothing 'left of that secret inner union which had so enriched and beautified their outward lives' (623). Amherst has fallen in love again with Bessy, in 'retrospective sympathy' (589) with the image of her he first had, and Justine sees Bessy's plans for the addition become accepted as plans for a building devoted to the workers of Westmore! The dedication ceremony, and Amherst's speech are 'grotesque and pitiable' – but Justine, 'with bent head' (629), has no choice but to endure the often petty and vindictive Bessy paraded as the model of 'self-devotion and idealism' (628). It is the final humiliation of a woman who had longed for 'a life in which high chances of doing should be mated with the finer forms of enjoying' (223).

Elizabeth Ammons reads this novel as an attack on the socially crippling force of patriarchal power.[17] Indeed, the culture at work here as Amherst has internalized its values, destroys the possibility of true happiness and understanding in both of his marriages. He is attracted to the ignorant girlishness that has been cultivated in Bessy, rather fantastically imagining that he can transform the very qualities in her that he finds so alluring. It is an act of romantic colonization. Yet when Bessy struggles in the only ways she knows how to maintain some sense of herself as an individual, resisting being bludgeoned into believing what *he* believes, Amherst is furious and depressed. How dare she not follow his lead? Likewise with Justine, a far more developed and independent woman, with rich impulses of charity and kindness. As Carol Wershoven notes, when Justine kills Bessy, 'freeing Amherst from his detested wife, [she] has also placed Amherst under a certain obligation to her; he owes, in effect, his position to her, and she has thus doubly upset the balance of power in their marriage.'[18] Amherst retreats at the end to a fantasy woman – thus rejecting the real, suffering, humiliated woman who still loves him, and accepting Bessy in memory as he never could in life.

Wharton's rivetting story 'The Pretext' appeared in 1908 in a volume which, as R. W. B. Lewis notes, sounded her familiar themes of 'entrapment, the longing and the failure to escape.'[19] As we have seen elsewhere, the crushing of a hoped-for scene brings shame in its wake, and here Margaret Ransom's expectations rise so high because of the dreary marital reality she is trapped in. 'The Pretext' is the painful story of a married middle-aged woman who mistakenly comes to think that the attractive Englishman visiting her college town has fallen in love with her. This belief lights up her dull life and dull marriage, until she finds out that she jumped to conclusions and in fact has only been a pretext for him. The Englishman used her name back home to explain breaking an engagement there. In its arc from elation to disappointment, the story powerfully carries us along through fantasies of release from dullness, to the depths of mortification. It is not only one of Wharton's most compelling treatments of shame, but one of her most compelling and heartbreaking stories.

Just as the inhabitants of old New York are governed by their strict social codes, Mrs Ransom lives in a world as imprisoned by restrictions and taboos: the New England college town of Wentworth, a place of 'inflexible aversions and condemnations.'[20] The tone of this estimable seat of learning 'sits in judgment not only on its own townsmen but on the rest of the world – enlightening, criticizing, ostracizing a heedless universe – and nonconformity to Wentworth standards involves obliteration from Wentworth's consciousness' (636). The satire here cannot diminish the implicit cruelty of such an environment. This world offers its inhabitants security through superiority and feelings of contempt for all others who do not share its 'rich sense of privilege and distinction' (637). But Wentworth is a 'world destitute of personal experience' for Mrs Ransom, who has vainly 'waited for the joys of youth' (632) while married to a thoughtless, self-obsessed man whose casual and 'relentless domesticity' has created 'a massacre of all the privacies' (634).

Into her dull and predictable life, then, comes more experience than she could ever have imagined, in the form of a handsome visiting Englishman, Guy Dawnish. *His* life is 'so rich, so romantic, so packed' (638) in comparison to hers, that she is almost dizzied contrasting his wealth of tradition with Wentworth's 'little teacupful' (639). But these dazzling insights into a world that makes her own seem 'as featureless as the top shelf of a dark closet' (638) are merely the first wave of excitement for Margaret Ransom. They will be followed by her 'flushed tumult of sensation' when she thinks that Dawnish has chosen her; that is, he seems to find *her* company the most delightful in Wentworth, so much so that he will miss her when he returns to England. We have already seen how Wharton's shame-bound women can be intoxicated by the love and attention of men they deem superior. His knowing 'that other life' and seeming 'to set her in the balance against it' leaves Margaret Ransom overwhelmed, 'feeling herself a mere leaf in a blast' (639).

Blushing is foregrounded in this story with dramatic insistence. At the beginning of 'The Pretext' Mrs Ransom hurries up to her room after her epochal talk with Dawnish, impatient 'to bolt herself in. . . with her throbs and her blushes. Her blushes? Was she really blushing?' (632). No longer beautiful, she finds that the unfamiliar color, 'a pretty lingering pink' softens her pale and wrinkled middle-aged face, making her look younger. Appreciating the effect, she blushes more deeply, understanding now 'why bad women rouged' (633). While she may be scornfully sure that none of her Puritan ancestresses had anything to blush about 'in all their frozen lives' (633), prolonged scrutiny in the mirror leaves her critical not only of her appearance and her dress, but of the very tenor of her life. She wonders 'why she had always, so tamely, allowed her aspect to conform to her situation?' Might not 'a gayer exterior have provoked a brighter fate'? (633) Dawnish's attention has embarrassed her so much – to be so important, so unexpectedly! – that she succumbs to criticism. Like so many other women in Wharton's fiction, looking in the mirror is facing a potentially hostile audience, and they 'accept that their selves and their lives are decided in large measure by what they look like in the mirror.'[21]

Waiting with 'burning cheeks' (640) to hear a lecture given by her husband, and feeling stared at, Margaret grows faint and has to be escorted away. She had been ambivalent about going to the lecture, but having left, she is sure it was right to do so: 'the wrong would have been in sitting up there in the glare, pretending to listen to her husband, a dutiful wife among her kind. . . [Wharton's ellipsis] (641). Her shame left her feeling exposed, a transgressor. She and Dawnish then stroll down to the river and when he tries to share something important with her because she's been so understanding, Mrs Ransom – shyly touching his hand – urges him not to spoil their friendship by saying *anything*. In so doing, she reveals her own feelings for him, and is so overwhelmed that she does not pay attention to the fact that he looks away and is both fearful and surprised. She is silenced by 'strangling hands' that 'seemed to reach up from her heart to her throat':

A flush of guilt swept over her – vague reminiscences of French novels and of opera plots. This was what such women felt, then. . . this was 'shame.'. . . Phrases of the newspaper and the pulpit danced before her. She dared not speak (644).

Note her sense of exposure to the denunciations of a priest or minister and the smirking publicity of journalism.

This mood passes after Dawnish leaves, however, and her 'thoughts were no longer vulgarized and defaced by any notion of "guilt." She was ashamed now of her shame' (645). Dawnish, who writes somewhat infrequently, has given her 'a secret life of incommunicable joys, as if all the wasted springs of her youth had been stored in some hidden pool, and she could return there now to bathe in them' (645–46). Though she experiences 'extremes of self-reproach and derision' (646), her joy deepens when she hears from a friend in England that Dawnish has broken a long-standing engagement for a mysterious woman in America. Dawnish has loved her, she reasons, has given her up to keep their love perfect, and given up another woman because of that love – surely a 'transcendent communion' exists between them (649). Mrs Ransom feels 'like some banished princess who learns that she had inherited a domain in her own country, who knows that she will never see it, yet feels, wherever she walks, its soil beneath her feet' (649). She has gone from feeling helpless (a leaf in the storm), to feeling powerful, content and in control.

Margaret Ransom is headed for a terrible disillusionment. Dawnish's aunt comes over from England to find out why he ended a long-planned match, 'upsetting an arrangement that affected a number of people besides himself' (651). Attempting to meet with his 'unfortunate attachment' she has a long, painfully embarrassing interview with Mrs Ransom, who has to explain – with a blush 'fixed. . . on her throbbing forehead' (653) that she has no daughter, no daughter-in-law. *She* is the Mrs Ransom that Dawnish has said he's in love with. Dawnish's aunt is frustrated and disappointed, and presses for more information – surely Margaret knows who Dawnish is *really* in love with? But Margaret says she has no idea who the woman can be.

What a humiliation. She has not merely discovered herself to have been a 'pretext,' but had the discovery thrust upon her. Upstairs, she faces her mirror now with the knowledge that Dawnish must have been as unimpressed by her as his aunt was and why not? There 'was no trace of youth left in her face – and she saw it now as others had doubtless always seen it' (654). Like Newland Archer despairing early in *The Age of Innocence*, she feels trapped in the ordinary: 'the days would go on as usual, bringing the usual obligations. . . She had an aching vision of the length of the years that stretched before her. Strange that one who was not young should still, in all likelihood, have so long to live!' (654). It is fitting that she turns back to a book on the English Gothic – like the Gothic cathedral arching heavenward, her hopes have soared high. And her reading is part of her involvement with Wentworth's Higher Thought Club: no doubt a group of women like those Wharton satirizes in 'Xingu,' who pursue Culture in bands because meeting it alone is dangerous.

The Glimpses of the Moon is perhaps Wharton's least admired book, variously dismissed by James Tuttleton as 'seriously defective,' R.W.B. Lewis as 'not very readable,' Margaret McDowell as 'inconsequential, dull and inferior,' Geoffrey Walton as 'careless and ill-written,' Blake Nevius as 'the weakest of her novels.'[22] One of the most damning charges against the book is that Wharton was unconsciously plagiarizing her earlier work, *The House of Mirth*.[23] To understand the strengths of this vastly underappreciated novel, countering that charge is a good place to start. I do not think that Wharton was cannibalizing previous work, or even unintentionally parodying it; echoes of *The House of Mirth* are deliberate.[24] I think she was intrigued as a writer by the tempting artistic question that is raised by the relationship of Lily Bart and Selden in *The House of Mirth*: what would happen when two people heavily dependent on others for their pleasures get married? What are the costs, the challenges, the pressures of such a marriage? Can it survive? Given that Wharton so often examined marital strains, a novel like *The Glimpses of the Moon* seems inevitable in her oeuvre, and not (as some critics suggest) mere pandering for *The Pictorial Review*, which serialized the work.[25] In the relationship Wharton analyzes here, shame acts both to bring the couple together and separate them, and Wharton's analysis of the ups and downs of their marriage is anything but superficial.

Mixing the 'modern sense of expediency' with an 'old-fashioned standard of good faith,'[26] poor Nick Lansing and Susy Branch – who share 'a kind of free-masonry of precocious tolerance and irony' (17) – have married with the understanding that if either has the chance to find a rich mate who will support them, divorce is not only acceptable but mandatory. Both have always wanted 'the power to get away from dulness [*sic*] and monotony, from constraints and uglinesses' (160) – but 'to get what they liked they so often had to do what they disliked' (15). They have heretofore led 'wretched lives' built out of 'compromises' (25). Who is to blame? Susy pins it on

> the world they had grown up in. . . their own *moral contempt* for it and physical dependence on it. . . his half talents and her half-principles. . . the something in them both that was not stout enough to resist nor yet pliant enough to yield (166) [my emphasis].

That contempt is a key element of their lives, the response of the powerless who are shamed by their situation, to the powerful who seem to control their lives. Each one has a shameful background. Susy Branch has always been in 'tight places' and her past looks like 'a very network of concessions and strivings' (38). Living among rich friends who are terribly unimaginative, Susy hates them:

> People with a balance had always been [her] bugbear. . . She detested them, detested them doubly, as the natural enemies of mankind and as the people one had always to put oneself out for. The greater part of her life having been passed among them,

she knew nearly all that there was to know about them, and judged them with the contemptuous lucidity of nearly twenty years of dependence (5).

Nick sees Susy, 'thrown on the world at seventeen, with only a weak wastrel of a father' as moral guide, as having 'been preserved chiefly by an innate scorn of most of the objects of human folly' (26). Indeed, what else could help her keep her self-respect in continued dependence on others if not an attitude of superiority? Her situation as a poor single woman is all too precarious, and she is afraid of what the future holds for her

as the years passed, and she lost her freshness and novelty, she would more and more be used as a convenience, a stop-gap, writer of notes, runner of errands, nursery governess or companion. She called to mind several elderly women of her acquaintance, pensioners of her own group, who still wore its livery, struck its attitudes and chattered its jargon, but had long since been ruthlessly relegated to these slave-ant offices (176).

Susy is aware that getting married would be socially advantageous: 'I know it would furbish me up tremendously to reappear as a married woman' (22). Indeed, as an impecunious young couple quixotically snatching a year of happiness on other people's money, Nick and Susy become quite fashionable and interesting to their rich friends.

Nick, a would-be writer, has also had a precarious life. Having spent too much of the 'pittance' he had as a young man, 'the best he could look forward to was a middle-age of poorly-paid hackwork, mitigated by brief and frugal holidays' (16). Like Susy, he perceives himself both as threatened and deserving more than he has. 'He had always felt himself to be the superior of his habitual associates' – so much so, that on their honeymoon, partly spent in a Venetian palazzo, Nick is certain that he and Susy alone 'were the only ones who appreciated it, or knew how it was meant to be lived in; and that made it theirs in the only valid sense' (90). This superiority is set in the context of his vulnerability to shame: 'Lansing was irritated with himself for perpetually suspecting his best friends of vague complicities at his expense' (96). Nick has published an art essay and a book of sonnets, neither of which succeeded, and there is 'no prospect of his ever earning money'

(16); fiction seems to be his only hope. It is very revealing that the subject of a philosophical novel Nick is working on is one of the world's most famous conquerors: Alexander the Great. Though Nick wants the book to express his ideas about 'Oriental influences in Western art' (63), surely the immersion in this particular subject as opposed to any other says a great deal more about his inner life than it does about his theories of art.

Both Nick and Susy have shameful pasts and dismal futures, but seizing the possibility of marriage ironically will *increase* their shame because it increases their dependence on the very people they have looked down on. Their wedding presents are a heap of checks and the use of various luxurious residences for their year-long honeymoon – they have thus plunged themselves *further* into obligation. The other side of lending their bright, amusing presence to social scenes has always been the expectation that they will do whatever is required by the host of the moment. Before their marriage, for instance, the wealthy Ursula Gillow sobbingly asked Susy not to pay so much attention to Nick, whom she was fond of. How could Susy say no, when she was wearing a dress Ursula gave her, Ursula's car had just been at her disposal and she expected spending next August at Newport with the Gillows? 'She sounded the lowest depths of subservience' (8). Not surprisingly, then, Susy pictures marriage in terms of her life of gifts and duties: 'I should like, just for a little while, to feel I had something in life of my very own – something that nobody had lent me, like a fancy-dress or a motor or an opera cloak' (22).

The hold of obligations, and the inevitable shame arising from them, will thrust Nick and Susy apart all too soon, cutting short their blissful first months of marriage in which they feel – as one would expect – 'the superior quality of the sympathy that held them together' (80). At their friend Strefford's villa on Lake Como, which they have chosen despite 'the ridicule' (2) of deciding on such a stereotypically romantic place, Nick's vulnerability to shame begins to come between them. Leaving after a month, Susy has gotten the next tenants' chauffeur to drive them to Milan, saving money on the train, and Nick feels himself aware that he is shrinking from renewed evidence of 'her always knowing how to "manage"' (29). This managing of Susy's – proof of her skill, evidence of her exigencies and short-cuts – will come to haunt Nick; even the word will embarrass and annoy both of them. Late in the novel, when they are already reconciled, a mere mention of the word will silence Susy, 'and an agony of crimson suffused her from brow to throat' (352). For Nick it seems deplorable that Susy's 'exquisite insight' and 'swift intelligence' should have 'been spent upon reading the thoughts of vulgar people, and extracting a profit from them – should have been wasted, since her childhood, on all the hideous intricacies of "managing!"' (184). But more disturbing to him now are the five boxes of Strefford's excellent cigars she has packed, acting as if there was nothing wrong with taking them.[27] He orders her to leave them behind: it is their first disagreement and leaves 'ravages. . . deep down and invisible' (32). For Nick, thinking back months later, the whole thing is 'ridiculous and mortifying;' and it briefly made their marriage seem 'unendurable' (93). But Susy only took the cigars for Nick

> because the desire to please him, to make the smallest details of his life easy and agreeable and luxurious, had become her absorbing preoccupation. She had committed, for him, precisely the kind of little baseness she would most have scorned to commit for herself; and, since he hadn't instantly felt the difference, she would never be able to explain it to him (33).

She feels ashamed at having caused their first fight, and afterwards feels *small* in her friend Ellie Vanderlyn's Venetian palace.

The cigar incident is just a prelude. Intent on hiding an affair from her husband, Nelson, Ellie Vanderlyn has left Susy numbered letters to send to her husband a week apart, to disguise where she really is. Susy and Nick know about Ellie's affairs, but Susy 'had never imagined that Ellie would dare to use her in this way. It was unbelievable. . . she had never pictured anything so vile. . .' (34) [Wharton's ellipses]. Blushing and feeling 'weak with shame' (35), Susy becomes enraged and then her rage is deepened by learning that Ellie has left her young daughter in the Lansings' care, and begged Susy on her 'sacred honour' to keep everything private, even from Nick! Susy of course feels trapped: 'Never before had she had such a sense of being tripped up, gagged and pinioned. The little misery of the cigars still galled her, and now this *big humiliation* superposed itself on the raw wound' (38) [my emphasis]. It is one thing for Susy to know about Ellie's affairs, and not feel they are her concern, that is 'the old view that cloaked connivance in an air of decency' (84). It is quite another to participate in the affair. Susy has after all imagined that she and Nick 'would always go on living, fondly and *irreproachably*, in the frame of other people's wealth' (192–93) [my emphasis].

That will be Nick's view, of course, when the 'dirty business' (107) emerges after Ellie has given him and Susy expensive gifts by way of thanks. Nick is angrily inquisitive, and Susy would tell him everything 'if only she could be sure of reaching a responsive cord in him. But the scene of the cigars came back to her, and benumbed her' (105). Badgering the whole story out of her, Nick is flushed and accusatory: 'I've never in my life done people's dirty work for them – least of all for favours in return' (108). Susy blushes too at the difference between their standards, and at the impossibility of getting him to see 'that under his influence her standard had become stricter too, and that it was as much to *hide her humiliation* from herself as to escape his anger that she had held her tongue' (109) [my emphasis]. Nick is brutally frank about their situation, calling himself and Susy 'born parasites,' and doomed to more 'baseness' and 'getting blunted to it' (111). Yet he finds it shameful to let *her* do things he might deem acceptable or at least expedient. This paternalism is clear early in the novel in his anger about her past, in his desire to protect her – as if he were a chic John Amherst telling Bessy that her honor was his. Many months later, Susy will still be haunted by Nick's 'cruel and humiliating words' in this scene (326).

Though he and Susy had promised to break up only if there was a chance of one of them landing a better match, they separate after this fight, Nick intensely ambivalent, alternately convinced that if he were to go back 'he would inevitably be drawn under, slipping downward from concession to concession,' and determined to return 'without conditions' (130–31). But what future do they have beyond 'unconcealed and unconditional dependence on rich friends, the rôle of the acknowledged hangers-on?' (131–32). From this point onward, Nick and Susy drift further apart, occasionally hearing or reading about each other, convinced that the other is going to fulfill the terms of their original agreement, Susy with their friend Strefford, who has unexpectedly inherited great wealth and a title, Nick with Coral Hicks, the daughter of drifting wealthy parvenus. Shame will keep them apart and bring them almost to the brink of divorce. When they do exchange a letter or note, because each is so angry and ashamed, every word will register as a sign of indifference and deepen their shame.

Susy leaves Venice for the Versailles home of an aimless rich friend, Violet Melrose, hoping to 'be alone – alone!' after the 'first exposed days' (142) when Nick was gone and she had to pretend his absence was planned. With Violet unexpectedly showing up, however, with a 'discovered' artist in tow (the Lansings' friend Nat Fulmer), Susy feels 'mysteriously reabsorbed into what had so long been her native element. . . now that she was abandoned, left again to her own devices, she felt herself suddenly at the mercy of the influences from which she thought she had escaped' (145). Asked about Nick, she resonantly declares, 'her *head erect*, her *cheeks aflame*,' [my emphasis] that he's fine – but she has no need to lie for long because in her world nobody

> questioned, nobody wondered any more – because nobody had time to remember. The old risk of prying curiosity, of malicious gossip, was virtually over: one was left with one's drama, one's disaster, on one's hands, because there was nobody to stop and notice the little shrouded object one was carrying (148).

Despite feeling like a ghost, unheard, unnoticed, Susy is still ashamed, and even with Strefford, one of her closest friends, she feels 'the impossibility of confessing to anyone the depths to which Nick's wife had stooped.' When he asks what happened, and how Nick comes to be on a yacht in the Mediterranean with Coral Hicks and her parents, 'Susy flushed, hesitated, looked away'. It is ironic that she feels so ashamed here, because she had hoped that talking to Strefford would help her 'recover something of her shattered self-esteem' (158). Strefford, who now has 'one of the oldest names and one of the greatest fortunes in England,' proposes to Susy, whom he had always loved and flirted with. Though she flushes with shame because Nick had suggested just such a course, she is filled with visions of power:

> She thought of Ursula Gillow, Ellie Vanderlyn, Violet Melrose, of their condescending kindnesses, their last year's dresses, their Christmas cheques, [sic] and all the careless bounties that were so easy to bestow and so hard to accept. 'I should rather enjoy paying them back,' something in her maliciously murmured (162).

Marrying him 'would give her that sense of self-respect which, in such a world as theirs, only wealth and position could ensure'

(165). Though Nick has promised a letter, it doesn't come, and finally Susy has to take 'a step from which her pride had hitherto recoiled' and she goes to the bank and asks for Nick's address, 'embarrassed and hesitating' – but there is none (174).

In Paris to buy clothes, Susy blushes when her friend Ellie assumes that some rich lover is footing the bill, and Susy, three months after the separation, finally blurts out the truth about Nick – that their marriage has failed. There is no reason to keep it a secret, especially since she owes nothing 'to the man who had so humbled her' (211), so she confesses about Strefford, too. Though Ellie's joy that Susy has at last secured 'her incredible prize' is honest, Susy is disturbed to hear not 'a word of sympathy for the ruin of her brief bliss, not even a gleam of curiosity as to its cause!' (213) And she feels 'oppressed and humiliated' (216) to be part of this world again, when wealthy Ellie announces she is divorcing her fond husband Nelson to keep her wealthier lover, Algie, out of the hands of other women! Yet freedom from Ellie's world only seems possible through wealth, 'to attain moral freedom [Susy] must be above material cares' (216), and marriage to Strefford offers something more than freedom: anesthesia. Her new life may not be fulfilling, despite the 'surface-excitement' of buying gowns and jewels, but 'the very absence of sensation would make for peace' (248). Susy's ambivalence about this world has kept her from accepting a ring from Strefford, or being seen in public with him 'among their own group of people' (225). Because she thus 'had humbled his pride,' Strefford insists on being seen at an exhibition with her at which one of his Reynolds's has the place of honor. And when she learns with 'mortification' that Nick is still with the Hickses, the thought of pressing for a divorce, and the physical presence of Strefford seem less appalling.

Speaking to a lawyer about a divorce is not easy, however; Susy is 'humiliated' to admit that Nick is as anxious for a divorce as she is, and 'ashamed to show her agitation' to the lawyer, himself embarrassed by her inexperience (252), and doubtless wondering 'at her childish lack of understanding' (253). Susy is forced to write to Nick to ask for clarification of their situation, but before she hears from him, she learns something from Strefford that stuns her. The couple that had replaced her and Nick at Strefford's villa after the newlyweds' wonderful month was Ellie Vanderlyn and Algie Bockheimer. Susy recoils from the fact that Strefford, living in luxury in Nelson Vanderlyn's house, should at the same time have secretly abetted Ellie Vanderlyn's love-affairs, and allowed her – for a handsome price – to shelter under his own roof. The reproach trembled on her lip – but she remembered her own part in the wretched business, and the impossibility of avowing it to Strefford, and of revealing to him that Nick had left her for that very reason (263).

Strefford would doubtless sneer at her scruples, and her own shame at feeling she has fallen below Nick's genuine standards. Susy feels even more implicated 'in the whole hateful business' by having used Algie's car to get to Milan: 'This seemed to her the most humiliating incident' (262).

Susy realizes that marrying Strefford will not give her the moral freedom she yearns for; she will have to condone her set's 'shifts and compromises' and grow 'blunted' (264). Even the 'triumph of her wounded pride' would mean nothing compared to this new insight into herself and her milieu. Unfortunately, because she cannot explain all this to Strefford, he will end up 'wounded, humiliated, uncomprehending' (269). Susy is at least not cavalier about the breakup: 'She felt ashamed of the hesitations which must cause him so much pain and humiliation. Yes: humiliation chiefly. She knew that what she had to say would hurt his pride, in whatever way she framed her renunciation' (279–80). Susy ends up agreeing to take care of her friends the Fulmers' children in a rundown part of Paris, virtually abandoned by her rich friends, and longing for Nick.

Nick has meanwhile spent months on the Hicks' yacht, feeding on books and the views 'with the careless greed of the sufferer who seeks only to still pain and deaden memory' (179). He has been unable to write because his manuscript reminds him of Ellie Vanderlyn interrupting and giving him the gift for helping with her adultery. It is embarrassing, however, not only to admit to Coral Hicks that he has no plans, and is not working on the book, but to admit that he has no 'assured income' (187). He is of course annoyed with himself for the confession, concerned that it will be taken as some sort of request for help. Like Halo Tarrant will do in *The Gods Arrive*, Nick reads about Susy and Strefford spending time at the Gillow's castle in Scotland only a month after he left her.

He becomes a sort of cultural guide for the Hickses, and at first sees 'nothing humiliating in being in the employ of people he liked and respected' (237) – but his position changes when his social and personal attributes make him helpful as the Hickses expand their restless and unfocused social life to include petty royalty: 'If the young man's value had risen in the eyes of his employers it had deteriorated in his own. He was condemned to play a part he had not bargained for, and it seemed to him more degrading when paid in bank-notes than if his retribution had consisted merely in good dinners and luxurious lodgings' (237–8). It is not a position which builds his self-respect, but what alternatives does he have? Nick is unprepared to deal with his situation, which demands more character and will-power than he has ever had; he has until now lived in the present and taken 'whatever chances it offered' (242). 'He had thought it rather fine to be able to give himself so intensely to the fullness of each moment instead of hurrying past it in pursuit of something more, or something else, in the manner of the over-scrupulous or the under-imaginative, whom he had always grouped together and equally pitied' (243).

Convinced that Susy is going to marry Strefford, Nick drifts into the strong possibility of marrying the intelligent but unexciting Coral Hicks, a match that would bring him at least 'temperate happiness based on a community of tastes and an enlargement of opportunities' – much as Susy pictured her marriage to Strefford (311). Yet in Paris to see his lawyer, Nick feels sunk in apathy, and stalked by shame: 'He had the *exposed* sense of a fugitive in a nightmare, who feels himself the only creature visible in a ghostly and besetting multitude. The *eye* of the metropolis seemed fixed on him in an immense *unblinking stare*' (313) [my emphases]. Surprised to find that Susy is living in an unfashionable neighborhood, he sees her one day with one of the Fulmers' children in her arms and the vision of 'the eternal image of the woman and the child' (319) sends shock waves through him, filling him with 'a tumult of new hopes and old memories' (321). She is not living a life of luxury at all, not sunk in their old world. Yet Strefford arrives just then (to unsuccessfully press his suit on Susy), and Nick disgustedly takes the visit as a sign of continued relations between the two.

Their first meeting after six months is very difficult because of their shame. Nick is cool and aloof, and Susy feels pitied about her broken engagement with Strefford, while she thinks he is still set to marry Coral Hicks: 'The thought stung her pride, and she *lifted her head* and met his eyes with a smile' (333) [my emphasis]. He flushes at her attempt at neutrality, and they embarrassingly blunder through mutual congratulations; Susy reddens when the divorce comes up, and 'the blood rushed to her forehead' when she understands that Nick has to manufacture evidence of infidelity, which she thinks 'too stupid and degrading' (335). Susy does not mention her refusal of Strefford, because 'it helped her wounded pride a little' (336–37); they are both embarrassed at mentioning another possible divorce and remarriage in their set. Susy is struck 'painfully, humiliatingly almost' by Nick's casual reference to fabricating evidence for a divorce; she is silenced by shame:

> It was on the tip of her tongue to cry out: 'But wait – wait! I'm not going to marry Strefford after all!' – but to do so would seem like an appeal to his compassion, to his indulgence; and that was not what she wanted. She could never forget that he had left her because he had not been able to forgive her of 'managing' (337).

The meeting dribbles away into more embarrassed hesitations, and leaves Susy furious at herself for not having been able to bridge the terrible gap between them, 'she, so fertile in strategy, so practised in feminine arts, had stood there before him, helpless, inarticulate, like a school-girl a-choke with her first love-longing' (339). The novel ends on a much different note, however, when Nick finds Susy bundling up all the children in her care to take them to Fontainebleau, and stop him from setting up evidence for the divorce. They all end up going together, the idea of divorce abandoned, and Susy confesses that though Nick returned his present from Ellie Vanderlyn for 'helping' with her affair, Susy never did, and 'her confession had broken up the frozen pride about his heart, and humbled him to the earth' (363). While apparently for the sake of the novel's symmetry, the couple end up looking out at the moon, the more powerful image is of Susy, on her knees, her arms around his, head buried: a position that recalls the ending of *Sanctuary* and *The Touchstone*.

The novel has been criticized as ending melodramatically and unconvincingly on the basis of Nick's vision of Susy with the Fulmer children, but it is important to remember that this is Nick's perception, and it leaves him not just feeling warm to Susy, but a *claimant*: '"But she's mine!" Nick cried, in a fierce triumph of recovery' (320). Wharton surely is not endorsing such a statement

– it is in no way commendable. Nor is Nick's thinking at the end about the differences between how men and women love; though he had been 'a coward in regard to Coral. . . his mind dwelt on Coral with tenderness, with compunction, with remorse,' whereas he is sure that Susy has quite forgotten Strefford, though she was 'sincere and courageous' in dealing with him (363). We know that this perception of his own superiority is false; because Susy was so keenly aware of Strefford's humiliation, it seems unlikely she would forget him. We also know that for Susy, being with the Fulmer children (who seem like an early version of those in *The Children*) did not give her a 'sense of a missed vocation: "mothering" on a large scale would never, she perceived, be her job. Rather it gave her, in odd ways, the sense of being herself mothered' (298). *The Glimpses of the Moon* thus ends with a rather somber sense of their future; Nick and Susy are bound together forever: the 'deep-seated instinctive need that each had of the other, would never again wholly let them go' (363). The moon casts 'her troubled glory' (364) on a couple who despite Nick's sudden sale of some travel articles, is haunted by a shameful past that will not let them go, and who have deeply shamed each other, without being able to fully explore what went wrong between them, as Anna Leath and George Darrow could not do in *The Reef*. Wharton's touch is far less clumsy in this novel than has been believed, despite the fact that her exploration of Nick and Susy is not as deep as it could have been.

The marriage in *The Spark* (part of *Old New York*) is one in which shame plays a central role because the wife is ruled by it, while the husband generally is not. The first words Haley Delane's flirtatious wife address to him in the novella are 'You idiot!' at a poker game.[28] The narrator turns his head away (mentioning this action twice), wanting in his embarrassment 'to blot the whole scene from my memory' (175). He works in the banking firm in which Delane is a partner, and deeply admires this 'shut-up fellow' (181) who seems almost a monument on New York's social scene. There is also some mysterious equanimity, some untouched depth in Delane that the narrator is intrigued by.

The narrator witnesses an even more humiliating incident after a polo match at which Delane's wife's lover, Bolton Byrne, beats his horse. Delane is outraged at the cruelty and strikes Byrne in front of witnesses. Delane's wife says something terrible to her husband that no one hears, but whose effect everyone observes: on Delane's 'dark face [her words] raised a sudden redness' (187). Delane is forced to apologize to Bolton Byrne because otherwise, people will think he beat Byrne out of jealousy, and 'mud was bound to stick to his wife' (190). Since Mrs Delane's infidelities are common knowledge, this apology is merely a tribute offered to hypocrisy. While society gossips about the incident, the narrator, who knows the truth, is 'as pleased as if [he] owed Mrs Delane a grudge, and were exulting in her abasement' (194).

Even more than abhorring cruelty, it is clear that Delane does 'not care a fig for public opinion' (217), however much he can be embarrassed in conversation. In a society marked by 'extreme caution' and suspicion of unsuitable people being involved in committees or movements, Delane only cares about getting things *done*. And Delane's lack of intimidation by the dead hand of social disapproval is evidenced by his having married a woman even though her disgracefully dishonest father was the most typical of those 'figures that rose here and there like warning ruins from the dead-level of old New York's respectability' (183). Years later, Delane even shelters his reprobate father-in-law, who can no longer take care of himself, though New York 'sided unhesitatingly' with his wife. 'Society's attitude towards drink and dishonesty was still inflexible: a man who had to resign from his clubs went down into a pit presumably bottomless' (214). Delane's wife leaves him because of the disgrace, but eventually returns and is a model daughter; New York in the interim had gotten used to the strange situation, especially since Delane didn't bother explaining. His equanimity and lack of concern about the 'right way' to behave is owed, we finally learn, to his having met Walt Whitman in the Civil War, and having learned 'Christian charity' from him (212). Whitman (whose poetry Delane will discover he doesn't like or understand), serves as a sort of conscience for Delane, telling him 'the right and wrong' of things (213), in contrast with the dictates of a society governed by appearances. It is worth noting that Wharton deeply admired Whitman's poetry, a taste she lovingly shared with Henry James.

Lizzie Hazeldean is the protagonist of *New Year's Day* (the last novella of *Old New York*), and observed in its frame narrative. She has gone from being 'the friendless defenseless daughter of a discredited man,'[29] her clergyman father 'under a cloud' (266), to the wife of rich Charlie Hazeldean, after terrible humiliations. Her rescue is affected in the context of a society that 'regarded poverty as so disgraceful that it simply took no account of it' (304). Charlie's aunt took the unprovided-for girl into her home, but eventually accused her of stealing the household keys (which had merely been misplaced). Lizzie is devastated by the implication that she is used to being an object of suspicion, as 'no one had ever before attempted to visit upon her the dimly-guessed shortcomings of her poor old father' (268). 'She had been wounded to the soul' (269), and even her cousins, 'as much humiliated by [her father's] disgrace as they had been puffed-up by his triumphs,' abandon Lizzie once this rupture has occurred (269). Charlie Hazeldean providentially happened to appear when his aunt was unfairly berating Lizzie, and she knows that he took her 'out of misery into blessedness. . . saved [her] from untold humiliation and wretchedness' (284). But she will always be aware that his family is jealous of 'her good looks, her popularity, [and] above all for being, in spite of her origin, treated by poor Charlie as if she were one of them!' (265). And she has to betray her husband to make his last years as an invalid comfortable.

We first see Lizzie Hazeldean publicly discovered leaving a hotel with her lover during a fire, while across the street a New Year's Day gathering of old New Yorkers observing the fire through their parlor windows, turn red at the scandalous sight, and for a while keep 'an embarrassed silence' (236). When we switch to Lizzie's point of view, we are plunged into the consciousness of someone desperate to hide her infidelity, but aware that she, who has heretofore been so careful, has been observed, and by Sillerton Jackson, New York's social arbiter 'who saw everything.' 'Composure and presence of mind were so necessary to a woman in her situation' (239), but she obsessively returns to the moment in which she is almost certain she was observed. She is even tormented by the possibility that her invalid husband, out on a rare stroll, was apparently at the scene of the fire, and might have observed her too.

At a musical evening later that day, she feels utterly exposed, especially to Sillerton Jackson's gaze:

The sense of that tireless attention made Mrs Hazeldean's temples ache as if she sat under a glare of light ever brighter than that of the Struthers' chandeliers – a glare in which each quiver of a half-formed thought might be as visible behind her forehead as the faint lines wrinkling its surface into an uncontrollable frown of anxiety (258–59).

The imagery of exposure here recalls that of *The Touchstone*. The evening (where she chats with her lover, Herbert Prest, *head high*) will bear terrible fruit for Lizzie. She will be cut, and deliberately, for the first time in her life, by Sabina Wesson, one of those witnessing her exit from the hotel. This slight is of great importance, because 'the cut was a deadly injury in old New York':

> For Sabina Wesson to have used it, consciously, deliberately – for there was no doubt that she had purposely advanced toward her victim – she must have done so with intent to kill. And to risk that, she must have been sure of her facts, sure of corroborating witnesses, sure of being backed up by all her clan (265).

The cut will make Lizzie feel 'as if she had received a blow on the forehead' (261), and her response will be twofold. She immediately 'lifted her head very high' (261) and then set out to charm Mrs Wesson's eldest, Hubert, so that he will not gossip about her. Hubert, a boy 'bathed in blushes' (293), 'crimsoned to the forehead' when he saw her, and his low bow (which no doubt served to hide his face) convinced Lizzie he too saw her at the hotel (261). She takes the offensive by mentioning the hotel fire twice to him, in a barrage of flirtation, with this result: 'The blush again swept over young Wesson's face, rose to his forehead, and turned the lobes of his large ears to balls of fire' (262). Like Mrs Manson Mingott mocking May Welland in *The Age of Innocence* (see Chapter 7), she cruelly calls attention to his embarrassment: 'Why, you're actually blushing! I assure you, you're as red as your mother's fan – and visible from as great a distance!' (262–63)

It is only 'passing childish amusement' to torment and exhilarate the young man, but she has done it many times before, and 'better than the other women – more quietly, more insidiously, without ogling, bridling or grimacing.' Clearly, Lizzie's ability to turn 'indifference' into 'beating heart and dazzled eyes' (263) is her one weapon against the shamefulness of having been poor, unwanted, disregarded. She has contempt for her society, for the men she can play with, and among 'all these stupid pretty women she had such a sense of power, of knowing almost everything better than they did' (253). Her power extends to convincing Herbert Prest that she loves him, when she enters into an affair with him solely because her ill husband's income has diminished and she needs money. After her husband's death, when Prest urges that they continue their affair, and then blunders into a marriage proposal, Lizzie reveals that she only loved her husband, and claims to feel no remorse. But the close of the novella contradicts that claim. Lizzie Hazeldean has 'a perpetual need to explain and justify herself – the satisfaction of these two cravings, once she had permitted herself to indulge them, became the luxury of her empty life' (301). Ironically, though she has led a blameless life since her husband's death, she is cut off from society, and has fallen into her own place in New York: she 'was not a lady on whom other ladies called, though she was not, on the other hand, a lady whom it was forbidden to mention to other ladies' (295). The narrator (who had been a child among those watching her leave the hotel fire) comes to know her, and admire her ability, like Lily Bart, 'to put the awkward at ease' (296). But in her presence, the young man discovers 'a humiliating disheartening sense of not understanding: of being too young, too inexperienced' (299) to comprehend how she can talk about the death of Henry Prest so sympathetically, when he is 'the man who had "dishonoured" her!' (299). The narrator learns the truth about her relationship with Prest, which leads him to dwell on the plight of women in her day who had no way of dealing practically with financial trouble. Lizzie Hazeldean 'had known no way of smoothing her husband's last years but by being false to him; but once he was dead she expiated her betrayal by a rigidity of conduct for which she asked no reward' (304). She has thus committed – from New York's perspective – the most shameful act, but for private, honorable reasons. Her motivation does not, however, free her from the consequences of the action which is not performed in a social vacuum, as we can see by her need to explain and justify what she did. The consequences of doing the only thing possible to save her husband are social ostracism.

Twilight Sleep is a powerfully satiric evocation of Twenties' New York's fads and fixations, and as Carol Wershoven aptly describes it, 'a novel of evasion':

Each character in the book, with one exception, has one goal: to get through life without suffering; and each numbs his sensibility in a different way: through the pursuit of pleasure, through bad faith, through false credos, or through self-delusion.[30]

As in *A Son at the Front* (see Chapter 5), one of Wharton's focuses is the fascinating strains and perplexities of relationships in the wake of a divorce when there are children involved, and it is here that we see a prominent manifestation of evasion on a grand scale. We find another 'oddly-assorted trio' that is 'drawn into a kind of inarticulate understanding by their mutual tenderness for their progeny.'[31] The potential for shame created by such a situation is not only disguised but actively battled, primarily by wealthy Pauline Manford, whose 'breathless pursuit of repose' and 'incessant effort to be calm' (47) are furious attempts not to feel. Pauline is a believer in the American virtues of Positive Thinking and Newness, that 'one had only to be brisk, benevolent and fond to prevail against the powers of darkness' (48). In that sense, the book is not at all dated in its satire, but powerfully and even sadly contemporary, the time-bound details less significant than the timeless American cultural characteristics Wharton skewers.

Pauline Manford, a daughter of an auto manufacturer, has to assert 'there is no shame in being in trade' (11), but one sign of her feeling that shame is her first marriage to an old New Yorker, Arthur Wyant. She had been attracted to his 'brilliant figure,' which symbolized 'the tempting contrast between a city absorbed in making money and a society bent on enjoying it' (23), but Arthur Wyant had simply faded. This marriage was a great disappointment to Pauline, and Wyant was both contemptuous of her background and of her plans for him to enter politics and perhaps the diplomatic service. Bent on success, she found him an 'obstacle and a disappointment' (24) – 'from the first he had been one of her failures': 'She had a little cemetery of them – a very small one – planted over with quick-growing things, so that you might have walked all through her life and not noticed there were any graves in it' (23).

Pauline keeps up a restless hum of activity to avoid dealing with the emotional realities of this divorce, her 'breezy optimism relegating to silence and non-existence whatever it was painful or even awkward to discuss' (165). In fact, her determination not to be embarrassed about her ex-husband, with whom she had a son, Jim, has influenced both families to act 'on the assumption that they were all the best friends in the world, and the vocabulary of that convention had become their natural idiom' (165). Pauline has apparently managed things so that Wyant and her second husband get along, Wyant feeling 'a sort of humiliated gratitude for Manford's generosity to his son.' Pauline's second husband seems to take an honest interest in Jim, and thanks to that, 'the two men came together now and then in a spirit of tolerant understanding' (75). Pauline, who feels that people's lives should have 'no corners in them' (60), relishes the relationship between her two husbands, 'always pleased when the two men spoke of each other in [a friendly] tone' (104). Pauline had seen Arthur's 'first bitterness against the man who had supplanted him' as 'barbarous and mediaeval' (48–9). This spurious contact with two families is in contrast with Pauline's real relations with those around her; her daughter is used to being 'squeezed in between faith-healers, art-dealers, social service workers and manicures' when she wants to see her mother (4). And for all the benevolence which is 'the note of the Manford household' (3), Pauline has actually in many ways cut herself off from her family, though appearances argue otherwise. She has even continued, for example, to use Wyant's first cousin, an Italian Marchesa, as a social drawing card and resource at her dinner parties, and pay the debts of the Marchesa's wastrel son.

Deeply disappointed with Wyant's 'inadequacy,' his 'dreaming and dawdling,' the energetic Pauline found a lawyer to settle the divorce 'rapidly, discreetly, *without scandal*,' but her husband was not so easily cut adrift [my emphasis]. At a time in New York when divorce was still beyond the pale, this divorce proved to be a humiliating 'blow to Wyant's pride,' and in his shame he 'sank into a sort of premature old age,' living 'in complete retirement at his mother's' (24–5). Alcoholic, and chronically unwell, he 'was always miserable out of reach of his doctor' (290), and 'when taken out of his rut, became a mass of manias, prejudices and inhibitions' (312).

Feeling guilty for the unforseen changes she has wrought in her ex-husband, after her second marriage to Dexter Manford, her divorce lawyer, Pauline 'came to regard poor Arthur not as a grievance but as a responsibility [and she] prided herself on never neglecting her responsibilities' (25). Though Wyant is a product of 'old New York blood,' (11), Pauline feels superior to him, especially in the way they interact. 'He had never quite acquired the note on which discarded husbands should welcome condescending wives' and typically greeted her 'with his usual rather overdone cordiality.' Pauline, however, 'had found the exact blend of gravity with sisterly friendliness' (102), and has more impact on him at one point than on her husband, ably appealing to his egotism with her assertion 'that the opinion of people like [him] still counts in New York' (108).

Wyant, true to 'his tradition of reticence and decency,' adheres to the family silence about his divorce with Pauline, but the one time he does bring it up, Nona Manford, Pauline's daughter by her second husband, is deeply embarrassed: 'Nona's colour rose through her pale cheeks to her very forehead. The motions of her blood were not impetuous, and she now felt herself blushing for having blushed' (165). Wyant's offhand but bitter remark about Pauline having left him while they were having 'a holiday from each other' (164) is a foretaste of his pivotal role in the novel as a defender of his family's honor.[32] Powerless, and apparently heavily influenced by Dexter Manford's infrequent visits, Wyant has typically retaliated with mockery, using contempt to cover his shame as so many of Wharton's characters do. Discussing his son Jim and his restless, jaded flapper wife Lita, Wyant observes to Manford that

'all the musty old traditions have been superseded. You and your set have seen to that – introduced the breezy code of the prairies. . . But my son's my son; he wasn't brought up in the new way, and, damn it all, Manford, you understand; well, no – I suppose there are some things you never will understand, no matter how devilish clever you are, and how many millions you've made' (257-58).

Wyant grows increasingly angry and ashamed of his son's passivity in his marriage, urging Jim to do something to defend his honor (as Wyant perhaps did not, when *he* was married?). Nona – who is very fond of Wyant – does not take Wyant's complaints at all seriously. She can't help comparing his rhetoric to her own father's silent, purposeful action, while Wyant, 'perpetually inconsequent and hesitating, was never tired of formulating the most truculent plans of action for others' (316).

Lulled by all his years of irony, his passive enjoyment of gossip, Nona cannot possibly predict Wyant's sudden burst into action, late in the novel. She knows Wyant wants to speak to her mother, but Pauline is at their country estate, Cedarledge, and neither can imagine him coming there, though Pauline blushes at the mere thought:

> Wyant had always refused to cross her threshold in New York, though she lived in a house bought after her second marriage; surely he would be still more reluctant to enter Cedarledge, where he and she had spent their early life together, and their son had been born. There were certain things, as he was always saying, that a man didn't do: that was all (328).

Yet Wyant, outraged by the collapsing marriage of his son, *does* show up at Cedarledge, and Pauline's tact is first directed at the butler, 'for once embarrassed and at a loss' (338), who announces Wyant: Pauline makes herself show no surprise at her ex-husband's arrival. They both blush, however, talking about a Sargent portrait of Jim as a child that no longer hangs where it used to. Though he talks to her in a 'queer excited state,' Pauline's graciousness 'put a stop to his ravings, shamed him a little, and so brought him back to his sense of what was due to the occasion, and to his own dignity' (347). Quiet, reasonable, she calms him down enough for him to share his sense of public humiliation about 'Jim's supineness, and Lita's philanderings.' Does she realize that Lita 'was making a laughing-stock of their son' and that 'at the clubs' people are talking about him? (348). Pauline tries to push the whole thing out of her mind, her typical reaction to anything disturbing.

Even though Wyant later returns with a gun to defend his family's honor, he ends up not shooting the faithless Lita or Dexter Manford, who is presumably having an affair with Lita, but accidentally shoots Nona, who it seems has come to Lita's room to break up the argument between Dexter and Wyant. In the subsequent cover-up which leads to everyone scattering from New York, Wyant is rumored to be drying out in Maine, but no one really seems to care: 'He had long since lost his place in the scheme of things' (361). Arthur Wyant's one heroic act, his attempt to wreak vengeance, has been ably whitewashed and after a few days of notoriety, the shooting – blamed on a burglar – disappears from the papers. And 'instead of the discovery of the lovers leading to at least two divorces, multiple recriminations, and emotional scenes, life goes on – serenely.'[33] But the shameful evidence of something terrible having occurred – wounded Nona in her hospital bed – is left behind, 'someone to be avoided.'[34] Nona has all along been not just 'a center of sanity,'[35] but the only one in the novel who registers suffering consciously, who truly experiences not just her own pain – in her love for her cousin Stan, in her loneliness and isolation – but the pain of others, like her suffering half-brother Jim.

Scandal has been averted, but its specter has haunted the novel from the opening pages. As Carol Wershoven notes, the novel's plot line follows 'the Wyant–Manford clan's battle to keep Lita from her satisfactions and to keep her a virtuous wife.'[36] *Twilight Sleep* is indeed pervaded by what Geoffrey Walton calls 'a sort of logical conclusion of old New York's genteel avoidance of unpleasantness.'[37] Pauline Manford, though not an old New Yorker, in her own way carries on the traditional covering up of reality; as she puts it, 'I always take particular pains to avoid hearing anything painful or offensive' (63). Compare that dictum to Mrs Welland in *The Age of Innocence* cheerily noting, 'Having an invalid to care for, I have to keep my mind bright and happy.'[38] The muffling of the unpleasant continues, but in the context of a city whose pace is now frantic; in *Twilight Sleep*, Pauline and others are intent on avoiding 'nasty notoriety' (204) through exposure and public humiliation in the press. In *The Age of Innocence*, Mrs Welland mentions the appalling possibility that a picture of her daughter may *appear* in newspapers, 'and from this unthinkable indecency the clan recoiled with a collective shudder.'[39] In this novel, it takes an *indecent* picture appearing in the paper to cause shudders, as we shall see below.

Storm clouds of scandal threaten to burst in the form of revelations about near-nude dancing of young society women at a chic Mahatma's retreat. This sage, a current spiritual resource of Pauline's, has apparently played host to a good friend's daughter, and a lawsuit is in the offing. Cousins of Pauline's, the Lindons, are outraged that their daughter Bee was among the dancers, and they are determined that the Mahatma 'has got to be shown up' (64). Attempting to save her emotional and financial investment, and stifle public scandal, Pauline first tries intervening with her husband, taking the tack that 'it's out of the question that you should be mixed up in it' (61). Despite her 'famous' tact Pauline loses her self-control talking to Manford, urging him to defend the family honor – Mrs Lindon is a cousin of Pauline's ex-husband. And despite all her appeals, Manford insists that the Lindons have evidence, and Pauline blushes. She tries bringing the potential scandal closer to home. After all, she argues, Bee Lindon is a friend of their daughter Nona, and of Lita, Jim Wyant's wife – won't they all be tarred by the same brush? Manford is still undaunted, and Pauline is equally unsuccessful appealing to the Lindons themselves; her visit to them is an 'utter failure' because she 'had apparently over-estimated her influence on [them], and that discovery in itself was rather mortifying' (101). It is all the more so, given that she knew it would be 'awkward. Any form of untidiness, moral or material, was unpleasant to her' (95).

Pauline will be further shocked that she can't get her ex-husband to see the situation as she does; visited by Mrs Lindon, who he says is intent on having the Mahatma 'in jail if they spend their last penny on it,' he does nothing to stop her. Pauline finds their behavior 'indecent' and 'shameless' (106). She feels trapped until Dexter Manford discovers Lita, his stepson Jim's wife, in the picture of the festive and scantily-clad dancers published in a gossip magazine. The investigation and the outrage die down, and Pauline is sure that her intervention helped. It is crucial to her to feel accomplished and even superior: her household arrangements are the best in New York, she believes, and her management at Cedarledge is likewise perfect – frantic activity and huge expense creating the illusion of seamlessness. In her own way, she is like Lily Bart, creating beautiful pictures – only not with herself as their subject.

Lita's presence in the Mahatma's dancing (which *she* sees as unobjectionable) is partly a sign of her utter boredom. She has wealth, a devoted husband in Jim, a baby, a family anxiously attuned to her vagaries – but she wants more, and her restlessness sends tremors through her family, and ultimately leads to an affair with her husband's stepfather, Dexter Manford. Lita apparently has no sense of shame. Lita can even calmly imply that Jim is really Dexter's son and not Wyant's, stunning Pauline, who feels 'as humiliated as if she had been caught concealing a guilty secret' (232). Lita, however, would find Jim's illegitimacy appealing and romantic.

While the Mahatma scandal dies down, and Pauline turns elsewhere for spiritual guidance and relief, another scandal is not averted, however. Nona Manford is in love with a Wyant cousin,

Stan Heuston, who is unfortunately married to a puritanical woman who refuses, on religious grounds, to give him a divorce. Like Arthur Wyant, Stan might have made something of his life, but has merely become, at thirty-five, 'a disillusioned idler who killed time with cards and drink and motor-speeding' (211). Nona refuses to run off with him, and so Stan settles for flashy Cleo Merrick (also married, and to a Catholic), who as Nona puts it, is willing to give him what he wants – 'his happiness' (242). Houston's distraught and embarrassed wife Aggie embarrassingly tries to convince Nona that *she* should rescue Stan from Cleo Merrick (who 'hadn't a rag of reputation to lose' [211]) to save everyone the public scandal. Hoping to force his wife to give him a divorce, Stan intends to openly live with Cleo 'as if they were husband and wife. . . and everybody will know that they're not' (242). Nona may have felt herself a coward before, but taking Stan away from the vulgar Cleo Merrick, and accepting Aggie's offer of a divorce would be too shameful. It is a strange and affecting scene between them, Aggie blushing when she seems to think Nona is accusing her of frigidity, Nona feeling 'one of her slow secret blushes creeping up to the roots of her hair' after having asked if Aggie ever loved Stan (240). Nona and Aggie in their different ways have lost, and seem to lead stunted lives.

This scene tends to bear out Mary Suzanne Schreiber's analysis of the novel: 'the simple truth of *Twilight Sleep* is that the objects to which women are to devote themselves are inherently incommensurate with the energy brought to them.'[40] And Pauline Manford's case is the apotheosis of this terrible and shameful cultural wasting of potential. 'Pauline's sphere of activity is inadequate for her ability and energy, so limiting her that she must scratch like a bird for some small sense of power, authority, duty, or purpose.'[41] One of the most moving aspects of the novel is Pauline's unrequited search for connection with her husband. But just as she erred significantly in choosing Arthur Wyant, she mistook Dexter Manford. Manford did not imagine a total nullity of a wife, but his vision of what she would offer was severely limited: 'He had dreamed of quiet evenings at home, when Pauline would read instructive books aloud while he sat by the fire and turned over his briefs in some quiet inner chamber of his mind.' Pauline, however, saw this interest in being read to as childish and deplorable, and decided 'to amuse him' (59). The great but undiscussed sorrow in this marriage is that Pauline is losing her hold on Manford and is incapable of discovering how to regain it. Her attempts to fill his life with 'almost incessant social activity' have ceased to be amusing or flattering – he is just bored. And she has become boring, predictable.

> Under his admiration for her brains, and his esteem for her character, he had felt, of late, a stealing boredom. She was too clever, too efficient, too uniformly sagacious and serene. Perhaps his own growing sense of power – professional and social – had secretly undermined his awe of hers, made him feel himself first her equal, then ever so little her superior. He began to detect something obtuse in that unfaltering competence. And as his professional authority grew he had become more jealous of interference with it (66–67).

In *The Gods Arrive* we will see a similar pattern of devaluation; Vance Weston, once so dependent on Halo Tarrant, needs to criticize her and feel superior to her as he develops his own sense of strength and accomplishment (see Chapter 6). Here, Manford pictures marriage as a competition, and while Pauline correctly chose someone who would become successful, that growing success has helped create a barrier between them, which was already in place given Pauline's inherited wealth.

Far more touching than Nona Manford's confusion and isolation in the book is her mother's utter inability to reach her husband, and her continued hope that somehow she can cross the desert that separates them, even though she cannot understand how she herself keeps intimacy at bay. When Dexter suggests that the whole family – including Lita – spend Easter at Cedarledge, Pauline's face lights up 'with blissful incredulity' (142) because it has been so long since he expressed such family feeling. Pauline feels justified in having always pushed him to take time for himself:

> And here at last was her reward – of his own accord he was proposing that they should all be together for a quiet fortnight. A softness came about her heart: the stiff armour of her self-constraint seemed loosened, and she saw the fire through a luminous blur. 'It will be lovely', she murmured.

Even more heartening to Pauline is feeling Dexter's 'obvious solicitude for her [which] was more soothing than any medicine' (143).

Manford is interested in spending more time with Lita, but Pauline mistakenly feels a renewed interest in herself, and this misunderstanding highlights that 'the one thing she had lacked, in all these years, was to feel that some one was worrying about her as she worried about the universe' (143–4). Pauline is ecstatic and tearful to find in this same conversation that her husband has talked the Lindons into dropping their suit against the Mahatma:

> He had actually thought over what she had said to him – when, at the time, he had seemed so obdurate and sneering! Her heart trembled with a happy wonder in which love and satisfied vanity were subtly mingled. Perhaps, after all, what her life really needed was something much simpler than all the complicated things she had put into it.
> 'I'm so glad,' she murmured, not knowing what else to say. She wanted to hold out her arms, to win from him some answering gesture (144–45).

Manford is blind to her reactions, and leaves, but Pauline is still lost in the delirious fantasy of being valued, appreciated, loved. What else can this 'strange presence' (145) in her room be but happiness? The intensity of her response to her husband throws the poverty of their emotional life into high relief. And soon afterwards, she feels herself once again cut off by 'one of those invisible barriers against which she had so often bruised her perceptions. And just as she had thought that he and she were really in touch again!' (156).

Pauline's expert and exhausting attention to all the details of improving Cedarledge is not just an expression of her competence as a manager, but is sadly 'suffused with a romantic glow at the thought that they might lure her husband back to domestic intimacy' (180). She is almost like a child craving for attention, craving to be held, showing off, reaching out, every act a desperate appeal for attention: '*Look* at me. *Love* me.' And she is so needy that any sign of Manford's possibly renewed attention is like manna from heaven. When he cancels a dinner engagement that is the peak of her slow social climb after the divorce from Wyant, surely it means he wants to be alone with her, and 'how many years had passed since he had expressed such a wish?' (197). Pauline is puzzled – what can account for the change in her husband? Her slimmer hips? Her 'renewed optimism'? With no real insight into herself, she doesn't understand her husband either, and is left wishing that 'a woman could guess what inclined a man's heart to her, what withdrew it!' (198).

This evening alone with Dexter is a disappointment, however, because her husband 'apparently had no desire to listen to her' and like Anna Leath in *The Reef*, choked by what she longed to say to Darrow as a young woman, Pauline, after all these years of marriage, does not know 'how to reveal the secret tremors that were rippling through her!' (199). She is silenced by the shame, and by invidiously comparing herself (like Anna Leath in *The Reef*) to other women 'who would have known at once what to say, or how to spell the mute syllables of soul-telegraphy' (199). Pauline, however, is only capable of discoursing on facts, even household facts, and she is 'paralyzed' because Dexter is only interested in his own facts, his own career. While his feelings about Lita churn under the surface of their conversation, Pauline feels distanced, confused, and suddenly realizes he dropped the Mahatma case for Jim and Lita, not her. Despite her beautiful tea-gown, her jewels, her rouge, she feels utterly rejected – as if she does not exist. What could be more humiliating? Pauline is so starved for a sign of affection from her husband that one compliment about her management at Cedarledge 'paid his wife for all she had done, and roused her inventive faculty to fresh endeavor. Wasn't there something else she could devise to provoke his praise?' (262).

Janet Goodwyn has noted that 'critics who see in Wharton's portrait of Pauline only scorn and derision underestimate both her sensitivity as a writer and her capacity for self-analysis and mockery.' Goodwyn writes that Wharton gave Pauline her own 'drive for domestic order and discipline,'[42] her love of gardening and her willingness to exhibit her work. Wharton also gave Pauline a philandering husband who mismanaged an estate and whose family couldn't see the seriousness of his behavior. Pauline Manford is thus 'a self-that-might-have-been': Wharton without her art. But beyond that, Pauline, despite her running after cures and committees, despite the frantic whirlwind of empty activities that fills her life, is strikingly like other Wharton characters in her desperate longing to be loved and appreciated, and in her inability to express what she feels, in her sense of herself as inferior to other women, and neglected. Wharton shows compassion for Pauline, 'pity for the woman with no wider creative outlet for her energies' – but the shame of her wasted activity, of her being unloved, is not resolved, merely covered up, once again.

5
The War Fiction

While friends and acquaintances noted that Edith Wharton 'spoke less of her [war work] than anyone similarly occupied on the Paris scene,'[1] her name became legendary in this connection. With 'organizational genius'[2] she plunged into a 'stupendous contribution to the [French] effort' and was made a Chevalier of the Legion of Honor 'an unprecedented distinction for a woman. . . sparingly awarded to foreigners.' Wharton 'raised funds, organized relief for refugees, founded hospitals and hostels, created jobs for war widows and homeless women, wrote propaganda, took in orphans.'[3] One of her most unusual projects was editing *The Book of the Homeless*, an anthology of poetry, prose, art, and musical scores. Among its seventy contributors were Yeats, Rupert Brooke, Jean Cocteau, Henry James, Monet, Sargent, Renoir and Stravinsky; sales of the volume and an auction of some of the originals brought $15 000 to Wharton's war charities.[4]

Wharton was also the only reporter allowed at the front in the early months of 1915 during which year she published articles in *Scribner's* that would be collected as *Fighting France*, a book of 'close observation' and 'passionate commitment,' as Peter Buitenhuis notes. Given her 'unlimited freedom of movement [due to her wealth], her intelligence and reputation,'[5] perhaps no one could better know the devastating impact of the war, and she saw more of it 'than almost any other woman writer.'[6] Her moving reports about ruined villages, towns and churches, and the strange intensity of front-line trenches in *Fighting France*, and her letters to Henry James about some of her experiences at the front are more than adequate proof of her rich opportunities for observation, and her ability to make use of them.

There has been much speculation on the impact of the war on Wharton's fiction and psyche. Cynthia Griffin Wolff, for instance, makes a strong case that the war did a great deal more than give Wharton an 'outlet for her energies.' Previously, she had 'been inclined to identify tradition with one or another form of repression. . . an external restraining force. But observing at first hand the devastation that war wrought on individuals' lives, she 'began to develop a more ample notion of tradition as the preserver of life.'[7] Elizabeth Ammons observes that after the war Wharton turned to writing novels about the present, 'declaring motherhood woman's best and most fulfilling job in life.'[8] Other, less subtle critics claim that the collapse of Wharton's old world led to conservatism, a reassessment of the values she had suffered under – leading thus to the nostalgic *Age of Innocence*, for instance, and then to what a good many critics see as 'stridency' in the novels until her death.

I am not entirely convinced that the war produced so very great a change in Wharton's sense of social priorities. After all, she had fled rigid and stifling New York for an environment infinitely more restricted and traditional – the Faubourg Saint-Germain. She did *not* flee into bohemianism. In Paris Wharton made herself a true home in 'an intellectual, artistic and cultural milieu in which she moved with ease.'[9] France came to represent the values of old New York which she was cherishing more *consciously*, rather than seeing as solely repressive: reverence, taste, 'the love of continuity or tradition.'[10] Louis Auchincloss writes that Wharton found in France 'a world where everything blended: beautiful surroundings, intellectual companionship, a society that combined respect for the past with a vital concern for the present.'[11] I doubt that the strengths she found admirable in France and praised in *Fighting France* (1915) and *French Ways and Their Meanings* (1919) had only struck her during the war. France had so much that she had longed for: intellectual honesty; the expression of emotion without fear of ridicule or indifference; a lack of shame about the relations between men and women; respect for intelligent women; esteem for 'ideas and their noble expression'; lack of suspicion of culture; a decidedly un-puritanical encouragement of knowing how to enjoy living in small ways. It was country where – as she tartly put it – 'poetry, and imagination and reverence [were] higher and more precious elements of civilization than telephones or plumbing.'[12] So she escaped, and in some ways, her success in Paris seems almost to have been directed at her mother, an attempt to establish herself in an even more exclusive and demanding environment – one in which she was at a great disadvantage as a foreigner. What a challenge – what a coup!

In any event, her successful and indefatigable war work itself seems in no way to have diminished her sensitivity to the impact of shame. The competence, energy, inventiveness, and courage she displayed did not lead to the disappearance of shame in these works. In fact, her two war novels and three short stories about the war do not focus on even the many small victories any war worker would have achieved, and which she undoubtedly had to her credit. Instead, their central characters are in one way or another infused with, bound by or deeply motivated by shame. It can certainly be argued that Wharton – who Mary Berenson finally came to like because she spoke so little of her magnificent efforts[13] – was understandably unwilling to seem to be trumpeting her own efforts in the war fiction. One can even conclude that only someone who had accomplished as much as she had could so mercilessly skewer slackers and hypocrites, the self-interested and self-important hangers-on of the home front. Yet despite the massive upheaval of the war, what fiction she wrote directly relating to that chaos is still concerned with shame in ways that are similar to the fiction before the war. What has shifted somewhat is the social context of shame, and the nature of the individuals' attempts to heal it.

The two war novels have suffered a long eclipse since their publication – Louis Auchincloss observed that reading them 'gives one the feeling of taking an old enlistment poster out of an attic trunk.'[14] They are currently among her least regarded books, derided as sentimental, boring, propagandistic and beneath her, and the three stories are seldom discussed. In seventy years, for instance, *The Marne* has become a mere footnote to Wharton's long career. This simple and affecting story of Troy Belknap, a young American Francophile who volunteers for ambulance service and is then wounded in the second battle of the Marne, was enthusiastically received in 1918. Reviewers praised its truth and called it 'almost flawless,' 'a beautiful and enlarging tale.' *The New York Times* raved: 'The reader's first sensation on closing the volume is one of sheer wonder at its richness.'[15]

Almost twenty years later, E.K. Brown found the novella disappointing because he felt Wharton was trying to cover more time – four years – than was appropriate for a novella. He even damningly quoted Wharton's own *The Writing of Fiction* to support his point.[16] In 1961 Blake Nevius agreed with Brown, adding that in this banal and slapdash tale Wharton was 'guilty of presenting the war too narrowly' as a French struggle, 'belaboring her compatriots,' and 'not adding a single individualizing trait' to her main character.[17] A few years later Peter Buitenhuis dismissed the novella as Wharton's 'most naive and sentimental fiction. . . an almost total embarrassment to read.'[18] While a few voices were raised in somewhat mixed defense of *The Marne* in the 1960s, the last two decades of Wharton criticism have utterly swept this little book aside as 'dated,' 'very inferior,' and mere 'propaganda.'[19]

My purpose here is not to claim that *The Marne* is a neglected masterpiece. But examining the dynamics and impact of shame illuminates the novella's artistic problems in an entirely new way, and pinpoints its previously unacknowledged strength.

As we have already seen, Wharton's novels are full of protagonists who feel isolated, worthless, weak. Troy Belknap in *The Marne* is not merely the vehicle for Wharton's intensely pro-French and anti-German feelings, but a typical Whartonian hero, if only in miniature, so to speak. It is not simply a love of *la belle France* that ultimately leads Troy Belknap into battle. Troy desperately needs to *prove* that he is brave, important, strong – to overcome his shame.

Well-travelled and well-schooled in the glories of France, Troy feels quite helpless at the outbreak of the war when he is in Switzerland. Suffering under 'all the shafts of the world's woe,'[20] Troy thinks that he alone is concerned, while his parents and their friends worry 'that they could get no money, no seat in the trains, no assurance that the Swiss frontier would not be closed' (10). Wharton is merciless in lampooning the 'indignant chorus of [Americans] stranded in Paris, and obscurely convinced that France ought to have seen them safely home before turning her attention to the invader.'

> 'Of course I don't pretend to be a strategist,' whimpering or wrathful ladies used to declare, their jewel-boxes clutched in one hand, their passports in the other, 'but one can't help feeling that if only the French government had told our Ambassador in *time* trains might have been provided. . .'
> 'Or why couldn't *Germany* have let our government know? After all, Germany has no grievance against *America*. . .'
> 'And we've really spent enough money in Europe for some consideration to be shown us. . .' (17–18).

Expressing typical adolescent contempt for adults (all too familiar to parents with teenage children!), Troy wonders how these people can be so disloyal to France, 'the world of his fancy and imagination' (10).

That world has come to be personified for Troy in the figure of his tutor, Paul Gantier, 'whose companionship [had] opened fresh fields and pastimes to Troy's dawning imagination' (5). When Troy hears that war has been declared, he immediately thinks of the tragedy in terms of losing Paul:

> War against his beautiful France! And this young man, his dearest friend and companion, was to be torn from him suddenly, senselessly, torn from their endless talks, their long walks in the mountains, their elaborately planned courses of study. . . and vistas and vistas beyond – to be torn from all this, and to disappear from Troy Belknap's life into the black gulf of this unfathomable thing called War (8–9).

Agonizing over not being able to help the 'attacked, invaded, outraged' France because he is 'a poor helpless American boy' Troy feels there is nothing he can do for France, '. . . not even cry, as a girl might! It was bitter' (10).

Few strivings are as important in adolescence as the 'compelling. . . need to identify with someone, to feel a part of something, to belong somewhere.'[21] Paul is Troy's link to France, embodying as he does France's 'ideas in his own impatient, questioning and yet ardent spirit' (39). It is Paul's advice Troy most treasures: 'Whatever happens,' Paul tells him, 'keep your mind keen and clear; open as many windows on the universe as you can' (39). But parallel with the adolescent need to belong is the powerful need to pull away from one's parents. Through Paul, Troy can abandon his parents and claim a different heritage as one of *France*'s children, with 'that long rich past' in his blood. Later in the novella, the image of France as mother takes on biblical resonance: she is the 'Naomi-country that had but to beckon, and her children rose and came. . .' (107) [Wharton's ellipsis]. It is not unlikely that Wharton felt equally as wanted and protected by her adopted home, valued as she had not been in New York. Indeed, French reviews of her work until her death were far more respectful and admiring than American reviews tended to be. Robert Morss Lovett noted in 1925 that Wharton's articles on France, collected in the 1908 *A Motor Flight Through France*, clearly showed that France was the country 'of her heart.'[22]

Wharton attacks American *complacency* about the war 'at every opportunity' in the novella.[23] All around Troy at the war's onset,

Americans 'whose affluence and social prestige had previously
protected them from the unpleasant and the violent'[24] are scheming to get out of the country. 'If [the Germans] *do* come,' one
woman whispers at Mrs Belknap's tea-table, 'what do you mean to
do about your pearls?' (21). Troy, 'long-limbed, strong-limbed, old
enough for evening clothes, champagne. . . and views on international politics,' faces an altogether different trap (15). He is
'sullen, *humiliated* [my emphasis], resentful at being associated
with all the rich Americans flying from France' (16). Adolescence is
'a time of especially heightened self-consciousness and thus a
'critical period of. . . vulnerability to shame.'[25] The Americans'
self-interest and lack of concern for France shame Troy. Watching
refugees pouring into Paris from the Marne, Troy is miserable
about his 'inability to do more than gape and pity' (20). Shame is an
isolating experience, in which one longs to hide, to avoid further
exposure – which is what Troy does here. He avoids the streets
where he might find those refugees coming into the city. Their
very presence is a terrible reminder of his helplessness, of his
feeling 'small and useless' (21).

Back in the United States, Troy is irritated by the way Americans
respond to the waves of returning Americans reporting on their
own experiences in France. 'No one was listened to for long, and
the most eagerly sought-for were like the figures in a moving-
picture show, forever breathlessly whisking past to make way for
others' (36). Outraged that the 'Americans had neglected a moral
responsibility,'[26] Troy at dinner one night calls for America's entry
into the war. He blushes furiously at the sound of his own voice,
and again when he is condescended to by a distinguished senator
(we have already seen the connection between blushing and shame
in *The Touchstone* and elsewhere). The adults see this war as an
alien concern, and his fervor as just an adolescent phase, which of
course in a sense it is. Troy's shame is triggered by their disdain;
his fervent commitment to France, which distinguishes him from
his family, friends and country, is brushed aside as unimportant,
even silly by pompous adults.

The reaction at school is more painful for Troy because public
humiliation 'creates a far deeper wound than the same action done
in private.'[27] In addition, the peer group rivals the family's importance in adolescence and is thus a potent source of shame. Troy is
'laughed at, scolded, snubbed, ridiculed, nicknamed, commemor-
ated in a school-magazine skit in which "Marne" and "yarn" and

"oh, darn," formed the refrain of a lyric [apparently to the tune of 'The Star Spangled Banner'] beginning "Oh, *say*, have you *heard* Belknap *flap* in the breeze?"' (51). Even the young woman he is most attracted to embarrasses him by her flippant assertion that the war is 'boring,' as late as 1917 when such a claim is no longer clever. When America's involvement seems increasingly likely, Troy is stung by sensing that friends see him 'as a little boy' because he is not old enough to join the army.

After America finally enters the war, and Troy insists on going to France to be an ambulance driver, he angrily interprets his mother's natural fearfulness as her treating him like a child not 'out of the nursery.' Given what his veritable *worship* of France means to him, how it is the focus of his emerging identity as an adult, this reaction is not surprising. 'Shame carries a multiplicity of meanings for the self,' depending on such things as the 'actual importance of the part of the self that has been exposed or shamed.'[28] France is so important to Troy – and to Wharton – that there is an uncomfortable adolescent rawness to his feelings, which critics have, I think, often read merely as crude jingoism. En route to France, Troy will also be deeply ashamed of Americans who are fatuously convinced that they are in the war to teach France 'human values' – as well as defeat the Germans.

Driving an ambulance, however, is no solution to Troy's problem. It *is* important for him to be 'relieving a little fraction of the immense anguish' (76) through his 'humble job' (103). But Troy still feels 'almost as helpless' as when the war broke out, a mere spectator (85), 'an infinitesimal cog' in this 'turning point of history' (86). Near the front, in a YMCA shelter full of American soldiers, none of whom he feels could be 'more passionately eager' than he, Troy feels more 'keenly than ever, the *humiliation* [my emphasis]' of being 'so hopelessly divided from [them] by [the] stupid difference' in their ages (90–91). Invidious comparisons like this one are a potent source of shame; we have already seen their corrosive impact on Anna Leath in *The Reef*.

When his ambulance breaks down close to the front, Troy grabs a fallen rifle and is swept into battle by an American unit. Once again, along with his fierce desire to fight, he feels ashamed. He fears anyone discovering that he is not really a soldier; 'his heart sank at the dread of doing something stupid, inopportune, idiotic' (113). Troy is driven by shame into the war where he is only confronted by shame at every turn. Now he is afraid of being *exposed* as the *helpless* thing he is, and worse, as a deserter. Guilt is shame over a moral transgression, according to Tomkins and Kaufman, and Troy feels guilty about having deserted two refugees and a wounded soldier in his ambulance because of his war fervor. Wondering if he will be court-martialled, he volunteers for a scouting party, which seems 'the one chance to wash his guilt away' (119).

His training as an ambulance driver betrays him, because Troy tries to rescue a wounded soldier and is himself wounded. Waking in a hospital, he at first has absolutely no sense of accomplishment or satisfaction; rather, he is 'filled with the bitter sense of his failure. He had abandoned his job to plunge into battle, and before he had seen a German or fired a shot he found himself *ignominiously* [my emphasis] laid by his heels' (123). The novella ends more positively with Troy's relief that the Germans were turned back, France and the wounded in his ambulance saved. He is especially joyful to have been part of the action, and there is an unexpected conclusion. Troy tells no one that he is convinced he was brought to safety by the ghost of his beloved tutor, Paul, who died four years before in the first battle of the Marne, and is buried nearby.

David Clough is fairly accurate in assessing *The Marne* as showing 'no evidence. . . of [Wharton's] considerable direct experience of the war' or her talent in the years she wrote *Summer* and 'Xingu.'[29] It *is* laden with stock scenes, and burdened by the myth of American troops as virtuous, noble Galahads winning the war in a sort of adolescent daydream. The book's weakness is perplexing to Clough, and he concludes that the tremendous personal significance of France as avatar of Western civilization for Wharton led to her gross simplification of the war in this novella. This latter conclusion, shared by Patricia Plante, is only partly accurate. What consistently appears in the novel is Troy's shame – in response to American lack of concern for France, to those around him who do not take his adoration of France seriously, and to events that dwarf his potential for action.

At each turning point in the novella, Troy's sense of himself as worthless, helpless, exposed, dominates the action and even the demagogic rhetoric. If the novella is thin, it is because Wharton's *own* shame, more successfully integrated and given richer context and substance in novels like *The Reef* and *The Mother's Recompense*, overwhelms the frail narrative. The novella is too insistent in reiterating 'over and over again how worthy of adoration France is.'[30] Wharton's shame about America's failure to enter the war before 1917 is what sometimes turns *The Marne* strident and makes it a sketchy performance. And like Paul, she must have initially felt helpless and despondent when America failed to appreciate and defend France as she had done and was heroically doing. In *A Son at the Front*, completed well after the war, the stridency, the simplification is not quite so glaring.

Yet for all its problems, *The Marne* is a precise and moving little study of the impact of shame on an adolescent, and here is Wharton's unacknowledged success. She intuitively understood how shame could leave one feeling worthless and outcast, and dramatized that understanding here with admirable acuity. What has escaped decades of critics is the centrality of shame in this novella; we see it in the iteration of words like 'humiliation,' 'humiliated,' 'ashamed,' and various synonyms, in the blushing, and in the situations where Troy consistently feels exposed, worthless, inferior, helpless, guilty – all manifestations of the affect of shame.

Patricia Plante is rather charitable in her reading of the novella's surprising supernatural ending. She explains Paul's ghost saving Troy from certain death on the battlefield as 'a symbol for [Wharton's] belief in the immortality of the French ideals and the French civilization.'[31] But I think that beyond this possible 'moral' purpose behind the book – in Plante's terms – the ending says more about Wharton herself than her artistic engagement with this material. It is no accident that Wharton chose as her protagonist someone young, 'shy and awkward' (48), helpless, someone racked by shame, who is not saved by his *own* effort, but by ghostly intervention. She could imagine no other resolution for Troy's shame.

As Wharton's spokesman, Troy found America's long delayed entry into the war intensely dishonorable, shameful; a question of honor and shame as seen primarily from the French standpoint is central to her long story early in the war, 'Coming Home.' Reviewers found it the best story in her collection *Xingu and Other Stories*, no doubt because of its 'topicality,' as R.W.B. Lewis suggests.[32] The story opens with an unnamed narrator telling us that the story that he has written down was told to him by H. Macy Greer, a young member of the American Relief Corps. Now that the immediate horrors of the war have passed and people are becoming 'disciplined' to them, such coherent narratives as the one to follow are possible. At the beginning of the war, however, things were 'too wild and grim. . . such fragments of experience as one got were torn from their setting like bits of flesh scattered by shrapnel.'[33] Not everyone, though, is capable of offering compelling stories based on what they've seen; Greer is an astute observer (despite his drawling bland delivery).

The story hinges on the fear, discovery, and actions of Count Jean de Réchamp, a wounded cavalry lieutenant Greer meets at the front. Réchamp is in agony for news from his hometown which has been 'retaken' by the Germans. His whole helpless family and his fiancee are there, and Réchamp has had no letters from them. His anxiety is heightened by having overheard, while he was in hospital, wounded German soldiers formerly stationed in his region talking about their commanding officer, von Scharlach, with terror. They have apparently committed 'abominations' at his order, and in an atmosphere of stories of terrible German atrocities, Réchamp is frantic to know if Yvonne and his family are safe. As Réchamp and Greer get to know each other better, we learn that Réchamp's family opposed his engagement to the free-thinking Yvonne, orphaned at ten, and the ward of a neighboring old Marquis who left Yvonne all his money. This inheritance gave rise to gossip in their town, and intense opposition from the Réchamps to a marriage. Réchamp won out, however.

Greer and Réchamp travel East as the Germans are slowly pushed back. They drive an ambulance into an eerie land with no clear boundaries: 'The sense of loneliness and remoteness that the absence of the civil population produces everywhere in eastern France is increased by the fact that all the names and distances on the milestones have been scratched out and the signposts at the crossroads thrown down. . . one is forever losing one's way' (240). Réchamp's fear builds when he knows for sure that Scharlach was stationed near his family's chateau. At home, despite his joyous reception, he is uneasy about not having time alone with Yvonne. It is uniformly agreed on that Yvonne's 'coolness and courage had saved the chateau and the village. The officer in command had arrived full of threats and insolence: [Yvonne] had placated and disarmed him, turned his suspicions to ridicule, entertained him and his comrades at dinner' (252), saved her father and brother, and even earned protection from other Germans by instructions left by the German commander, whom everyone calls 'Charlot.'

Yvonne unexpectedly urges Greer to take her fiance away, and in an inconclusive confrontation, Réchamp demands to know the whole story of the German occupation there, finding out that Charlot was, of course, Scharlach. Réchamp cannot be content that everyone was saved, but suffers an attack of shame at what he suspects Yvonne did: 'He *covered his face* with his hands. "Scharlach – Scharlach" I heard him repeat' (251) [my emphasis]. On the return trip they end up taking on a wounded German officer in desperate condition. He later turns out to be Scharlach, who Réchamp has previously had described to him. When the ambulance runs out of gas, Greer is gone for twelve hours getting more, and the officer is dead when he returns; we assume, of course that Réchamp has killed Scharlach and avenged himself for Yvonne's 'dishonor' which of course is his own because he has been sexually humiliated, and by a *Boche*.

The story is marred by predictability and coincidence: Réchamp happens to be hospitalized with two of Scharlach's men; Scharlach happens to be the wounded German officer he and Greer take charge of. And the central act, which presumably shows a man of a traditional background forced into murder, seems less dramatic than Wharton intended, perhaps because we have all along sensed such a confrontation is coming. We are familiar with Wharton's re-creation of notions of honor and shame in French families from a novella like *Madame de Treymes*, in which the violence is social, emotional – and more convincing. Réchamp's act is thus not a surprise, though it must have been deeply satisfying to contemporary readers of the story. Also, if Scharlach is a monster, then Yvonne having gotten around him is not infamous so much as intelligent. Another problem is that the passions involved in the story are presented at too much of a distance, vitiating their power. If Réchamp's act is to have meaning, then his sense of dishonor needs to be more directly created; his shame is too distant, as is Yvonne's fear he will discover how she saved everyone. The story's real strength is in its description of wartime conditions, travelling to the front and back – passages that recall Wharton's letters and *Fighting France*.

'Writing a War Story,' published in 1919, is much lighter, but far more successful in offering readers access to the main character's feelings, which are of growing helplessness and embarrassment. Ivy Spang, a volunteer at an Anglo–American hospital in Paris, is asked to contribute 'a rattling war story' to *The Man-at-Arms*, a new journal for wounded and disabled British soldiers.[34] Her qualifications? Before the war, she published a widely unnoticed and unremarkable volume of poetry called 'Vibrations.' Yet she is appealed to as someone who will know just what the soldiers will like: 'A good rousing story. . . a dash of sentiment. . . but nothing to depress or discourage. . . a tragedy with a happy ending' (360). This remark recalls William Deans Howells' assessment of what 'the American public wanted' when he explained to Wharton the failure of the dramatization of *The House of Mirth*.[35]

The volume will include pieces by The Queen of Norromania and other notables, and Miss Spang's picture will accompany her story – an overwhelming honor all around. She is quite 'dizzy with triumph' (360), only how is she to start, and *where*, she who knows so much about the war, but so little about fiction? Ivy discovers to her dismay that she in fact knows absolutely nothing about writing a story, and awkwardly courts her muse by reading other stories in a contemporary journal. She begins to 'hate her Inspiration,' feeling trapped, 'abased and dejected' (363).

Ivy tries to back out by offering her editor poetry, but escape is impossible, and with only a few weeks to go before her deadline, she finds unexpected help in her old governess who has 'picked up many good stories – pathetic, thrilling, moving stories of our poor *poilus*' (363). Even better – the governess has written them down! Ashamed not to have a subject, which Mademoiselle thinks is surely the easiest part of a story, Ivy responds with contempt as well as relief when she sees her governess' notebook: 'the narrative, written in a close, tremulous hand, covered each side of the page, and poured on and on without a paragraph. . . Decidedly poor Mademoiselle did not even know the rudiments of literature!' (364).

The collaboration is not easy, but Ivy's courage is renewed when she sees the photograph which makes her look quite arresting:

exceedingly long, narrow and sinuous, robed in white and monastically veiled, holding out a refreshing beverage to an invisible sufferer with a gesture halfway between Mélisande lowering her braid over the balcony and Florence Nightingale advancing with the lamp (364).

'The photograph was really too charming to be wasted' – how can Ivy resist her 'inexorable fate'? (364) Finished at last, she and Mademoiselle are both moved by the story, a military anecdote 'with sentiment.' When it appears in print, however, the story inspires shame in Ivy who feels *exposed*: 'It seemed to her a pitifully small thing, hopelessly insignificant and yet pitilessly conspicuous' (365). Comparing her prose and her looks to the Queen of Norromania temporarily boosts her self-esteem, but Ivy is subsequently bewildered 'to find that no one about her seemed to have heard of her story' even though the journal is conspicuously displayed in some bookshop windows (366).

Distributing copies of the journal in her ward leaves Ivy feeling 'hot and shy' and her shame is heightened by a review not mentioning her at all. The men in her ward seem unusually cheerful some days later and she stammeringly takes their pleasure and gratitude for a response to her story, when it is really her *picture* everyone admires. Ivy is mortified, painfully aware that 'not one of them had read her story' (368). Worse is to follow; a famous novelist is in her ward and she comes upon him laughing at her story: 'She blushed all colors, and dropped into a seat at his side' (368). But surprisingly, she is able to share her disappointment with the novelist. Pouring tea for him, she asks his honest opinion of the story, and she is of course ashamed when he says she mauled the subject: 'She sat before him with her head dropping. . .' (369). Her disappointment deepens when the novelist too asks for a copy of her photograph.

Wharton's ironic narration here is not cruel but comic: the story 'issued forth in the language that a young lady writing a composition on the Battle of Hastings would have used in Mademoiselle's school days' (364). One is able to feel for Ivy Spang's difficulties and shame though one is all along well aware she is dangerously over her head, and ought to know better. There is something almost Chaplinesque in the picture of this kind but completely untalented young woman striving to plant her little flag on the peak of Literature. Wharton must have observed many such attempts during the war. One wonders too how much of Wharton's own disappointment when her work was poorly received figures here. Even those of us who hope we are better writers than poor Ivy can appreciate her sense of helplessness in the face of an overwhelming project, her exposure, and then her disappointment and defeat. Ultimately, even a fine writer may be faced with 'a plethora of impressions' as Ivy is about the war, and unable to start. We shall see in Chapter 6 how Wharton's Vance Weston faces the similar burden at one point, and he is certainly a figure we are meant to take seriously.

The novelist who undermines Ivy's already low self-esteem is the author of a novel called *Broken Wings*, the title of a 1903 story by Henry James. Wharton's use of James' title gives her story a deeply personal reference as well as an undercurrent of sadness quite appropriate to the material here. James' tale is a powerful and sad account of a writer and an artist who have been estranged for ten years because each has thought the other too famous and popular to be interested. It is a story of keeping up pretenses and being too 'proud,' of those pretenses finally giving way to the truth when each artist reveals a history of failure, defeat and desperate and humiliating attempts to stay afloat. Both were once popular but are now 'at the bottom of the social ladder' and though they are beaten and defeated, they find solace and encouragement in each other. 'Broken Wings' is a story of shame overcome by mutual confession and love, and ends with the cry of 'And now to work!'[36] It is interesting to note that for James, at least in this tale, shame could be healed, whereas for Wharton it could not.

But the reference to James in 'Writing a War Story' is even more meaningful. The novelist's comments to Ivy bring to mind comments Wharton records James having made to her. In *A Backward Glance*, she notes being 'dressed down' by James on the terrace at The Mount in front of her guests. After Teddy Wharton asked James if he had read Wharton's latest *Scribner's* story, James starts with a compliment but ineluctably progresses toward finding the subject 'totally unsuitable' because it permitted only a 'conventional treatment.' Wharton records other instances of his 'withering' criticism that undermine her rather jaunty conclusion that James 'knew I enjoyed our literary rough-and-tumbles, and no doubt for that reason scrupled the less to hit straight from the shoulder.'[37] These painful moments would have been more shaming because they occurred in Wharton's homes, and in front of other guests, and thus were more exposing, in situations where she would have expected to feel most at ease. The impact of James' magisterial inability to steer away from the truth is somewhat reminiscent of Lucretia Jone's smothering comments. No wonder, then, that the novelist in 'Writing a War Story' seems rather fatuous at the end when he criticizes Ivy for rejecting a compliment about her looks.

Wharton's 'The Refugees' focuses even more intensely on shame than 'Writing a War Story.' Its two main figures are more helpless and hapless than Ivy Spang, and the story hinges on hilarious twin cases of mistaken identity. Charlie Durand, an American professor of Romance languages, and holder of an honorary degree from the University of Louvain in Belgium, is swept up at Boulogne in the tide of war refugees bound for England, where he is headed after having spent some sabbatical weeks in Flanders and then Normandy. At Charing Cross station, where refugees are practically being fallen upon by do-gooders, Durand finds himself 'helplessly' gazing at the chaos 'through [misty] spectacles.'[38] Lame, stepped on, stammering and shy, he is immobilized by the surging crowds, through which

> there squeezed, darted, skimmed, and criss-crossed the light battalions of the benevolent. People with badges were everywhere; philanthropists of both sexes and all ages, sorting, directing, exhorting, contradicting, saying 'Wee, wee,' and 'Oh, no,' and 'This way, please – oh dear, what *is* "this way" in French?', and 'I beg your pardon, but that bed warmer belongs to *my* old woman'; and industriously adding, by all the means known to philanthropy, to the distress and bewilderment of their victims (572).

Durand unexpectedly finds himself grabbed and appealed to in French by a shabby little old woman, and despite his lack of money, and being 'of a retiring nature,' he feels proud to have been 'singled out as a rescuer' (572–73). He becomes instantly intent on helping this desperate woman no matter what the sacrifice. They escape the station and he is 'ashamed of his visible incompetence' (574) to have *her* give a hansom driver directions, and somewhat bewildered by her familiarity with London. Taking tea at a modest tearoom, Durand is silenced 'through sheer embarrassment' (576) by her gratitude and even more when he blushingly begins to wonder if perhaps she harbors some amatory fantasy about him, and blushes again when he realizes it must be impossible. But it is only after no little conversation that he realizes they have *each* mistaken the *other* for a refugee. And Miss Rushworth, he decides, is just as shy as he is, despite her loquacity.

Offering his card as a safe and unembarrassing way of clearing up the misunderstanding, Durand accidentally gives her one printed in French, which only further enmeshes him in his false identity as a refugee. Invited to her cottage at Lingerfield, her brother Lord Beausedge's country estate, Durand is sorely tempted:

'He had always pined to see what an English country seat was like. . .' (579). Deciding not to go doesn't work: he is unable to escape because his luggage has already been sent on. This shy, lame, 'naturally modest' man who 'stammered whenever it was all important to speak fluently' is actually a secret romantic 'without the power of expression' (579). Can he not, then, 'permit himself forty-eight hours of romance. . .' (580) since events seem to conspire against his clearing up the error? In any event, his next attempt to explain the truth is futile because Miss Rushworth misunderstands him as explaining that he actually doesn't *need* the help, because he is – or was – rich. This is a further humiliation, since Durand had been cursing his poverty.

Durand faces further assaults on his confidence at Lingerfield. Lord and Lady Beausedge – perfect English types to Durand's eye – and their children treat him with respectful coolness, but he is humiliated to find that a visiting duchess who has come expressly to see him is less than fascinated: 'Each time she was about to remember who he was something else distracted her.' It 'was painful even to his disciplined humility' (585–86). Still, the general inattentiveness he finds among his hosts comes to seem comforting – at least he will not be unmasked. Squabbling over who will take charge of Durand heightens his embarrassment, and he is even asked to lecture on Atrocities! On the point of confessing to the entire family and their guests, Durand is hustled off by Lord Beausedge's daughter Clio, who knew as soon as she saw him that he wasn't a refugee. He confesses everything, to her great amusement, but she pleads with him to continue the masquerade, his *own* 'adventure of England,' because he is offering her aunt 'the first thing that's ever happened to her' (589). Not surprisingly, 'Professor Durand blushed to the roots of his hair' – embarrassed to figure so grandly in anyone's life.

Durand next returns to France in 1918, self-conscious in a tight YMCA uniform, wishing he were young enough to have joined the army. Unfortunately, he knows 'he was never to get beyond the second-best in such matters' (590). Standing on the pier at Boulogne, waiting for help, he meets Clio Rushworth again and reminisces – apparently only her father, Lord Beausedge found out that Durand was a fraud, and was delighted. Her aunt (Durand's 'refugee') turns out to be in charge of a canteen, and though Durand is anxious about meeting her, she brusquely sends Clio and him away, thinking that Durand is just another refugee –

when there's 'not a hole left to put them in' (592). Durand, who was her first adventure, is 'aware of a distinct humiliation' at not having been recognized (593). He is, after all, as unimportant a man as he always thought he was.

Durand's personal shame and social embarrassment, expressed in his stammering, his blushing, are made humorous by being set in the context of battling for refugees. Wharton here takes the selfishness of Americans stuck in Europe – pilloried in *The Marne* – one large step forward. Clio's aunt is clearly aware that having captured her very own refugee is a definite humiliation to her sister-in-law, who is her superior in rank, wealth, beauty and force of personality. In an atmosphere of 'unscrupulous women. . . as wild as. . . sales days at Harrod's' snatching up refugees as soon as they disembark, Miss Rushworth crows at her triumph: 'How humiliating for her to go back to the Hall without a single refugee!' (577) For Miss Rushworth, her victory means almost too much, and she is ashamed of being unable to communicate it: 'Her blushes deepened, and she lost herself again in the abasing sense of her inability to explain' (578). When she and Durand travel to Lingerfield and are joined on the train by Lady Beausedge and her daughters, Lady Beausedge delivers herself of lines worthy of Oscar Wilde's Lady Bracknell. She laments the paltry refugee she was able to snatch:

'it's almost an insult to have dragged us all up to town. . . They'd promised us a large family, with a prima donna from the Brussels Opera (so useful for Agatha's music) and two orphans besides. . . I suppose Ivy Tranthem got them all, as usual. . . [Wharton's ellipses] I've no doubt the Bolchester set has taken all but the utterly impossible [refugees]' (582).

In the end however, Audrey Rushworth has become forceful and competent, rather like her sister-in-law Lady Beausedge, and slated for an important marriage, while Durand is still Durand. The story has the sharpness and comedy of 'Xingu' (another extended play on embarrassment) and deserves to be better known.

A sense of inadequacy and failure, of helplessness in the face of overwhelming events – treated seriously or comically – unites Troy Belknap in *The Marne* aching to be a hero, Charlie Durand longing for just a bit of adventure, Ivy Spang struggling to write fiction, betrayed Jean de Réchamp and even the narrator of 'Coming Home' who relates a tale of betrayal and vengeance he was unable to avert. These are not war stories *per se*, but rather stories that deal with the impact of war or its consequences, which would be the powerful context of Wharton's richest war fiction, *A Son at the Front*.

Far less strident than *The Marne*, the novel at the most obvious level considers the larger issues of national honor and shame and how they affect individuals. Germany is clearly seen as dishonorable, an outlaw nation, but not all the characters instantly rush to enter the French war effort. In fact, the relationship to one's adopted country at war is made rather more complex than in *The Marne*. The perspective here is not that of an ardent young Francophile, but of a mature, troubled man in conflict over his and his son's role in a war that he at first wants nothing to do with. John Campton struggles with the nature of his duty, and more importantly, his French-born son's duty, and the novel charts his slow painful change of consciousness from critic to zealot. But in many ways, the novel is more deeply concerned with personal issues, and considers the role of the artist in a global conflict, the protagonist's personal and social shame, his poignant sense of aging and failure (despite outward success), his difficult relationship with his ex-wife and her husband, and his attempt to build a life of openness and choice for the son he has only recently grown close to. As Cynthia Griffin Wolff and R.W.B. Lewis have suggested, this is the first novel in which Wharton began to face the issue of relationships between the generations. In that sense, it is an entrance to the world of her later books, though it is clearly connected to those that came before it.

The novel starts just before the outbreak of World War I and ends with the entrance of America and the arrival of American troops in 1917. The book follows Campton's initial efforts to keep George, who like him was accidentally born in France, away from the front lines. Campton is aided by his ex-wife Julia's banker husband Anderson Brant, an adept wire-puller. They all believe George feels the uselessness of the war as they do, and agree that it is not *his* to fight, since George – educated in America – is only French by birth (an admittedly specious argument, given that George has already done his military service). Unknown to them, however, George has himself transferred from the staff position they have wangled for him to the front – which they discover only when he is seriously wounded. Despite being in love with an empty, arty married woman in Paris whom Campton and the Brants detest, George ultimately returns to the front and is fatally wounded. Eddying around this quartet of parents, step-parent and son are various American and French citizens with varying degrees of honest self-interest or enthusiasm about the war. The intricate family drama – and Campton's troubled and fascinating relationship with Brant – is played out against the 'conflict between courage and fear, whether justifiable or not, experienced by those on the home front. . . [Wharton scrutinizing] on the one hand, their selfish and narrow lives; on the other, their grief and bereavements, which they face with endurance, if not always dignity.'[39]

In a world at war, John Campton has long been at war with himself and his circumstances. Though he is greatly in demand as a portrait painter in 1914, that success has come to Campton late, and after a sad and lonely life which he considers very much a failure. Looking back, he muses that though he has been ever hopeful, or tried to be, 'life had perpetually knocked him down just as he had his hand on her gifts.'[40] Campton is so popular now that he can afford to be peremptory and turn sitters away, but these recent few years of achievement and recognition only throw the rest of his life into higher relief. Even amid his acclaim, he is perpetually aware of 'how frail a screen of activity divided him from depths of loneliness he dared not sound' (68). The observation recalls Wharton's own lament to Sara Norton in 1908, 'the change & movement carry me along, help to form an *outer surface*. But the mortal desolation is there, will always be there.'[41] Campton has never been able to 'get on easily with people nor live without them; could never wholly isolate himself in his art, nor yet resign himself to any permanent human communion that left it out, or worse still, dragged it in irrelevantly' (40).

A lonely, thwarted man, Campton feels that every one of his important plans in life has been a failure – starting with his 'stupid ill-fated marriage' (40) which ended in divorce. Julia Ambrose had attracted French-born but America-dwelling Campton because she had been educated in 'a fashionable Parisian convent' and lived in Venice (41). '[A]ll the ideas that most terrified and scandalized Campton's family were part of the only air she had breathed. . . The jargon of art was merely one of her many languages; but she talked it so fluently that he had taken it for her mother-tongue' (41). Like Anna Leath in *The Reef* discovering what her husband

Fraser was really like, Campton was profoundly disappointed when he realized that Julia was boring and always would be. And the result of such a plunge from expectation into disillusionment is inevitably shame (as in *Sanctuary*, for instance). After so many years of divorce, Campton is still ashamed to think about his realization that Julia would always bore him, proving as it does how mistaken he was in marrying her.

When they married, Julia unenthusiastically agreed to share his quest for artistic recognition, in humble circumstances, rather than prosper in the family business in Utica. But Campton's early career was sabotaged when Beausite, an artist for whom he had 'exaggerated reverence', unkindly dropped a sneering epigram upon seeing a painting of Campton's. This powerfully damning remark 'went the round of Paris' despite what it revealed to *Campton* 'of the great man's ineptitude' (4). Campton was thus exposed, humiliated in the very artistic circles he had hoped to conquer. Subsequent years of struggling to make a career in Paris and then Spain ended when Campton had a vision spying a young Spanish woman from a train window, and returned to paint her and became her lover. This desertion gave Julia grounds for divorce. Campton unsuccessfully fought to keep his son, without even his own family's support.

Despite his uneasiness with people, Campton's relationship with his son is foremost in his mind when the novel opens on the eve of the war which many say cannot possibly happen. He and George are just about to travel to Southern Italy and North Africa or Spain after years in which Campton 'had seen his son only in snatches, hurriedly, incompletely, uncomprehendingly' (7). He has just begun to build their relationship in the last few years and dreams of strengthening it. In the coming winter, George will be leaving for New York, to join a branch of his stepfather's bank, so this trip is for Campton

> their last chance, as it was almost their first, of being together quietly, confidentially, uninterruptedly. . . he, poor devil, was trembling for the chance to lay the foundation of a complete and lasting friendship with his only son, at the moment when such understandings do most to shape a youth's future. . . [Wharton's ellipsis] (11–12).

Though one of Campton's most famous works is an early portrait of his son, George is in many ways as mysterious and inaccessible to him as Anne is to Kate Clephane in *The Mother's Recompense*. Like Kate, he is fired by a vision of being a parent, shaping and guiding his son's life – though he doesn't submerge himself as completely as Kate does (*she* has no career). Like Kate, however, Campton abandoned his child many years before, and Margaret McDowell is astute in noting that his 'strong attachment to his son. . . suggests feelings of guilt about his long neglect.'[42] Indeed, like Kate, Campton's learning how to be a father seems designed to erase the shame of having abandoned George as a young child, by turning himself into his son's *rescuer*.

Because Julia's remarriage may have freed Campton (or, humiliatingly, his family) of alimony payments, it brought into his life a maddening and profound source of shame. Julia's new rich husband – Anderson Brant – was able to support Campton's son as *he* could not, and the triangle of Campton–George–Brant, in which shame plays a significant role for the two older men, is the most intriguing element of this book, and almost unique in Wharton's novels.

Campton has been working harder than ever, and sometimes taking sitters he doesn't like, so that he can afford to – as he sees it – free his son from Brant's influence and money. The assumed future for George is a position with Brant's bank, but Campton has an entirely different vision, in which he is 'guide' and 'companion' to George (128). With the money he has been saving, he will extricate George 'from the stifling atmosphere of his stepfather's millions' (122). His weapon will be the gift of George's own bank account which will, he hopes, make George think about his life more seriously. Campton at first even imagines that the war – a 'brief and harmless plunge into a military career' – will 'mature' and 'discipline' George, who will 'come back with a finer sense of values, and a soul steeled against the vulgar opportunities of wealth' (123).

That vulgar wealth has from the beginning, Campton believes, estranged George from him. The first time Campton ever felt some sort of communion with George, who was twelve then, is overlaid by bitterness about Anderson Brant's money. With limited access to his son, Campton had 'resigned himself to the probability of seeing [George] grow up into the ordinary pleasant young fellow,' without a taste for books (29). But on this day he discovered George engrossed in *Lavengro* – a gorgeous first edition, with the price tag still on it! Though from that moment on Campton believed that for himself and George 'their ardour for beauty had the same root,' Brant's money and influence rankled deeply (30). The very phrase 'Anderson's influence,' infuriates Campton, because it had always 'been invoked – and none knew better than Campton himself how justly – when the boy's future was under discussion' (21). That influence shapes Campton's *own* plans for his son, plans that spring in part from 'jealous worship' of his son. Months into the war, it occurs to Campton that

> when the war was over, and George came back, it would be pleasant to hunt out a little apartment in an old house in the Faubourg St Germain, put some good furniture in it, and oppose the discreeter charm of such an interior to the heavy splendours of the [Brants' home]. How could he expect to hold a luxury-loving youth if he had only [a] dingy studio to receive him in? (178)

The Brants' apartments even make him feel physically ashamed, because he is painfully aware of 'the contrast between his clumsy person and [their] expensive and irreproachable [rooms]' (16). Late in the book, after George has been seriously wounded for the second time and is recuperating in Paris, Campton still fantasizes taking 'a jolly apartment somewhere' for the two of them, though an old family friend, Adele Anthony, crisply says that 'it's natural – it's human' for George to want to stay with his mother, as he always has, and simply visit his father (317). It is Adele who has pointedly reminded him of Brant's necessary role in George's life:

> 'poor Anderson really *was* a dry-nurse to the boy. Who else was there to look after him? You were painting Spanish beauties at the time. . . I see perfectly that if you'd let everything else go to keep George you'd never have become the great John Campton: the *real* John Campton you were meant to be. And it wouldn't have been half as satisfactory for you – or for George either. Only, in the meanwhile, somebody had to blow the child's nose, and pay his dentist and doctor; and you ought to be grateful to Anderson for doing it' (117).

Campton has never been grateful, but perpetually jealous: 'Was it always to be Brant who thought first of the things to make George happy – always Brant who would alone have the power to carry them out?' (378) Indeed there is a 'Brant nerve in him' (196) that tingles and stings whenever he thinks about the man, and the turn of fate that made Anderson Brant so important in George's life. Campton cannot 'prevent a stiffening of his whole self at any summons or suggestion from the Brants' (74).

Campton's deep shame about his long inability to take care of George, and the invidious comparisons between himself and Brant, have apparently even affected his ex-wife, who blushes in embarrassment when she accidentally slips in speaking of herself and Brant as 'we.' This conversational 'blunder' turns Campton 'hard-lipped and grim.'

> Through the years of his poverty it had been impossible not to put up, on occasions, with that odious first person plural: as long as his *wretched inability* to make money had made it necessary that his wife's second husband should pay for his son's keep, such allusions had been part of Campton's *long expiation*. But even then he had tacitly made his former wife understand that, when they had to talk of the boy, he could bear her saying 'I think,' or 'Anderson thinks,' this or that, but not *we* think it (19–20) [my emphases].

Though Julia always meets him 'with her usual embarrassment' (236), such conversational lapses are infrequent now, because Anderson's name had just before the war hardly been coming up at all between Campton and his ex-wife, given that Campton has achieved a surprising financial independence. That Campton finds 'we' odious is a powerful indication of how ashamed he is of having abandoned George – the very mention of his ex-wife's marital relation is taboo even *grammatically*. Between George and himself, Julia and Brant are referred to as 'they,' yet another masking of their identity. For Campton, to have been bested is intolerable – and Wharton's insight into how shame has made Campton hyper-sensitive is an unrecognized marvel of acuteness here.

Campton is able to see that Julia's life has not been enviable, 'throning year after year in an awful emptiness of wealth and luxury and respectability, seeing only dull people, doing only dull things' (89). But he is throughout most of the novel unable to consider Anderson Brant with any such equanimity, and in fact deliberately attempts to humiliate Brant. Before the novel opens, the last time they had met was two years earlier, 'when Mr Brant, furtively one day at dusk, had come to his studio to offer to buy George's portrait. . .' (22–3). Campton refused, saying it wasn't for sale, and then donated this famous early portrait of George to the Luxembourg Museum because he dreaded Brant ever getting a hold of it after his death. It is enormously satisfying to Campton to think 'how it must have humiliated Brant to have the picture given to France.' Campton vindictively muses '"he could have understood my keeping it to myself – or holding it for a bigger price – but *giving it* – !"' The satisfaction was worth the sacrifice of the best record he would ever have of that phase of his son's youth' (59). When Campton wants to sell a sketch of George during the war so as to donate money to a dead artist's family, his one fear is that if 'the picture were sold at auction, Anderson Brant would be sure to buy it!' (158) He 'reddens' at the thought – and as we might expect, throughout the novel characters blush, colour, redden, and lower their eyes, indicating the operation of shame in their faces as well as in their speech or interactions with each other.

Margaret McDowell notes that one problem of *A Son at the Front* is that Wharton did not 'adequately exploit. . . the complicated relationship between John Campton and Anderson Brant or their rivalry for the possession of George's affections.' She goes on to find Campton's behavior 'irrational' because he blames Brant for his own situation and 'domineers over the self-deprecatory Anderson Brant as if to prove that the artist surpasses the businessman and that the father outranks the stepfather.'[43] An understanding of the dynamics of shame and its significance in motivation illuminates the relationship between these two men, as I have begun to suggest, and reveals a subtlety of characterization and exploration of the two men's behavior that critics have previously passed over. In almost every one of Campton's and Brant's meetings, shame is present, central and even dominant, and the conflict between the two men will intensify through the novel as they are increasingly thrown together because of the war, and their attempts to keep George from combat.

We have seen in part how Julia Brant is embarrassed in the presence of her ex-husband; Anderson Brant is even more uncomfortable, and Campton recognizes this. 'It had been Campton's lot, on the rare occasions of his meeting Mr Brant, always to see this perfectly balanced man in moments of disequilibrium, when the attempt to simulate poise probably made him more rigid than nature had created him' (23). Their very first meeting to discuss the threat of war, and how to keep George – recently recovered from tuberculosis – out of danger begins with a blush. As 'their eyes met, the memory [of Brant's attempt to buy George's portrait] reddened both their faces' (23). The simplest interaction between them is cause for shame; Brant offers Campton an expensive cigar, for instance, and is 'overwhelmed' by Campton's refusal in this meeting.

Campton delights in Brant's embarrassment, watching him standing 'helplessly, and trying to hide the twitching of his lip.'

> 'Poor devil – he'd give all his millions if the boy were safe,' [Campton] thought, 'and he doesn't even dare to say so.'
>
> It satisfied Campton's sense of his rights that these two powerful people were hanging on his decision like frightened children (24).

Campton urges caution, that is, keeping their plans to save George secret from George himself, though Julia does not exactly agree, and Campton finds himself unexpectedly feeling a bit closer to Brant, sensing 'a common ground of understanding [he] had never found in his wife' (25). Indeed he will feel this shared understanding at other times, brought together with Brant by Julia's incomprehension of events. Campton felt similarly warm, or at least understanding (but suppressed it)

> on the day when Mr Brant, apologetic but determined, had come to the studio to buy George's portrait. Campton had seen then how the man suffered from his failure, but had chosen to attribute his distress to the humiliation of finding there were things his money could not purchase. Now [in their first meeting since], that judgment seemed as unimaginative as he had once thought Mr Brant's overture (25–6).

In response to Campton's 'almost brotherly' glance now, Brant flushes and practically scuttles off, 'as if frightened at the consequences of such complicity' (26). This ebb and flow of anger, contempt, and understanding will characterize Campton's stance throughout the novel, while Brant will remain fairly consistent: mute, shy, embarrassed. It is as if for Brant, any expression of emotion between men is profoundly disturbing and even distasteful. A contemporary review of the novel was keenly aware of this stifling of feelings – which also occurs between Campton and his son, and which Campton condemns as 'hopelessly Anglo-Saxon, so curt and casual' (101). At one point, for instance, he realizes that he cannot possibly tell George how he feels about his return to the front. One reviewer praised 'the sense of emotion held in check, never allowed to cross for a moment the boundary set by the instinctive artist, but always present.'[44]

Brant is perpetually awkward, blushing when he is around Campton, hardly the powerful and competent banker one would expect him to be. And if Julia is sensitive to using 'we' to refer to herself and Brant, Brant likewise hesitates at calling her 'my wife' when he talks to Campton. Brant also seems uncomfortable mentioning George's name to his father, always preceding it with a cough. When he is discovered at the Luxembourg Museum looking at Campton's portrait of George, he turns 'red as a beet' (116). Both Brant and Julia treat Campton with kid gloves, as if he is dangerous, or the humiliation he lives with is in permanent danger of erupting into violence. Campton does not really reciprocate, and George (like Adele Anthony) recognizes this, urging him in one letter 'Don't be too savage to Uncle Andy' (207). It is a request that stumps Campton, for he has difficulty thinking of anything polite to say.

Their relationship is not improved when Anderson Brant uses his influence to attempt to see George at his army post, because Campton has been opposed to George asking for leave. In this scene, it is Brant who is stuck when he refers to himself and Julia not having seen George in a long time: 'The "we," pulling him up short, spread a brick-red blush over his baldness' (249). Campton angrily sneers that *he* has not seen George either. 'Though he had grown kindly disposed toward Mr Brant when they were apart, the old resentments still broke out in his presence' (250). Campton, whose own meager influence was also helpful, he thinks, in keeping George from the front, has not wanted George to call attention to himself, or for anyone to do that either. He accuses blushing Brant of having threatened George's safety in a non-combatant's post.

At last he had Mr Brant at a disadvantage. Their respective situations were reversed, and he saw that the banker was aware of it, and oppressed by the fear that he might have done harm to

George. He evidently wanted to say all this and did not know how (251).

Campton is not entirely governed by his shame, by his resentment and bitterness, however. He is moved by Brant's distress, and actually confesses the torment of helplessly watching Brant over the years give George everything *he* wished he could. He even admits to wanting George back as his and only his son, no longer doomed 'to waste his youth in [Brant's] bank, learning how to multiply [Brant's] millions' (252).

Campton is of course 'embarrassed by the sound of his own words,' but seems almost to be plunging into further humiliation so as to purge himself: he sees 'no escape save to bury [his words] under more and more. . . from the depth of some unutterable plea for understanding.' Afterwards, Campton recoils at his own behavior, 'thoroughly ashamed of what he had said' (252) and face to face with 'a deep disgust at his own weakness' (253). He has revealed too much about himself, and to his rival, his enemy.

Indeed, not only does this outbreak leave Campton ashamed, but it caps many years of what he sees as a sort of cowardice in 'accepting Mr Brant's heavy benefactions for George' (253). We shall see below that contempt for himself grows because of the war, and as with Martin Boyne in *The Children*, this contempt further undermines his self-esteem. Campton is also irked by the fact that George accepts what Brant has done for him easily, with no apparent sense of obligation or burden. Ease, poise, lucidity are the keynotes of George's behavior throughout the book, and he seems perfectly able to balance his obligations to all the adults in his life without conflict. A remarkable achievement, to be sure.

Matters between Campton and Brant do not substantially improve when they discover George has actually been at the front for months, and is now seriously wounded; they are able to go to his hospital only because of Brant's influence. In Brant's luxurious limousine, Campton at first refuses to speak to Brant or even use one of the soft, furry lap robes even though he's cold. It is not only grief that silences him, but shame and rage. When they are stopped by a sentry at one spot, Campton keeps Brant from attempting to bribe the man so they can proceed. It would have been, as Brant admits after a mortified silence, 'an inexcusable blunder' (272). The attempt enrages Campton, and leads to despairing reflections on his own inadequacy:

He said to himself that [Brant] was no doubt suffering horribly; but he was not conscious of any impulse of compassion. He and Brant were like two strangers pinned down together in a railway-smash: the shared agony did not bring them nearer. . . as the hours passed, [he] felt himself more and more exasperated by the mute anguish at his side. What right had this man to be suffering as he himself was suffering, what right to be 'here with him at all? It was simply in the exercise of what the banker called his 'habit' – the habit of paying, of buying everything, people and privileges and possessions – that he had acquired this ghastly claim to share in an agony which was not his.

'I shan't even have my boy to myself on his deathbed,' the father thought in desperation; and the mute presence at his side became once more the symbol of his own failure (273).

Brant, he fears, has finally succeeded in robbing him of his rights. Yet Brant is sensitive enough to blushingly allow Campton to be the first to see wounded George, and alone. After they have both seen George, they are unable to share their feelings, 'the same passion of anxiety consuming them, and no means left of communicating it' (282). Again, the terrible inability to give innermost feelings speech bars any possibility of relief.

With George possibly near death, inoperable until his fever diminishes, the two men end up in a quarrel. Brant had asked a noted surgeon to return to the hospital, but he doesn't come when he promised, and Campton yells at Brant, deriding his influence as 'sawdust.' For once, though, Campton apologizes for 'his senseless violence' (293) before the offended Brant can head back to Paris. Such lulls in the hostilities between them are brief, or at any rate, do not create a permanent change of heart in Campton. Brant is punctilious in attempting to make sure Campton 'has' George, like not coming to the station when George is later recovered and returning to the front, but Campton is unregenerate. When George is wounded a second time and the Brants want him to be brought to Paris, Campton's opposition is 'violent enough to check his growing friendliness with the Brants' (401). Campton has responded like this before, after his divorce, in a 'spirit of aimless random defiance – revolt for revolt's sake,' as *he* sees it (235).

After George dies, the Brants want a monument, and want Campton to sculpt it, further enraging him. The request, relayed indirectly by a friend, Boylston, brings up all the old bitterness in comparing his formerly pinched life to 'their hospitals, their motors, their bribes, their orchids, and now their monument, *their* monument!' (417) Even when he agrees to do it, having come to accept George's loss in an awareness that George will always be a part of him, and even when he realizes that Brant, too, is suffering and unable to express it, he still responds from shame, contemptuously sneering at Brant. The monument, he tells Boylston, will be costly – but of course Brant will *like* that, won't he? Boylston blushes and then so does Campton, who has repentant visions of all the times Brant remembered 'to do or say the one thing the father's lacerated soul could bear' (425) while Brant really had 'nothing!' He urges Boylston to keep Brant away, and in the last lines of the novel turns to his work.

I believe that Wharton consciously saw Campton as experiencing some sort of transcendence as he turns to his clay. But that he is still responding as he did in the novel's first scene between himself and Brant, counteracts the intended positive arc of the book, and reveals him as just as trapped by shame as he was in the beginning. As with *The Marne*, Wharton wanted a happy ending of some kind, but the issues she raises do not get resolved. Campton has after all had charitable thoughts about Brant before, and their relationship has not changed, because shame is still such a significant part of how Campton functions internally.

Shame is also a major theme in how he and others respond to the war itself. For instance Julia Brant refers to her 'son at the front' when a French woman who has lost a son asks Julia if she is not having bridge parties. The mourning mother disagrees, holding her head high (an anti-shame response), and flushing, she says 'one owes it' to the sons to go on as before, even to those who have died. Julia flushes in return, and her color deepens when Campton asks why she had to lie about George (220). Other Americans are ashamed of their country's neutrality, and Campton is not alone in feeling this neutrality to be a 'national humiliation' (255).

Though Campton is initially convinced that the war is more European stupidity that has no connection with Americans, after a while he is not whole-hearted in his denunciations of the foolishness of taking someone like George into the military. His protestations begin to seem excessive, and as he defends himself in having attempted to save George, he also attacks the Brants.

> The Brants had acted [in using their influence] through sheer selfish cowardice, the desire to safeguard something which

belonged to them, something they valued as they valued their pictures and tapestries, though of course in a greater degree; whereas he, Campton, was sustained by a principle which he could openly avow, and was ready to discuss with any one who had the leisure to listen (116).

Thus there is absolutely nothing shameful about trying to keep his son from combat, but he thinks of the Brants with contempt for their similar aim. At first Campton believes he acted as George would have wanted, in the sense that George believed the war was meaningless slaughter, but gradually Campton comes to feel unsure about his own position, and ashamed of having done what he could to help George. As the war continues and the whole world seems to sink into chaos, he begins to wonder how he could have ever justified 'an attitude of moral aloofness' (173). He even begins to criticize *George*, who is writing breezy letters that disguise his actually being at the front. The tone of those letters starts to offend Campton. George is obviously glad he's safe, Campton assumes, and this 'penetrated Campton. . . with a fresh reaction of shame. Ashamed – yes, he had begun to be ashamed of George as well as himself' (213). Campton longs to share these feelings with Adele Anthony (a war relief worker), but is unwilling to expose them, and not really sure how to express 'a feeling so contradictory that it seemed to be made up of anxiety for his son's safety, shame at that anxiety, shame at George's complacent acceptance of his lot, and terror of a possible change. . .' (214). Adele (who knows George is at the front) demands to know how Campton would respond if that were the case. 'A sense of humiliation, a longing to lay his weakness bare, suddenly rose in him, and he bowed his head. "I couldn't. . . I couldn't bear it," he stammered' (212). It is not surprising that after such exposure in this scene, Campton sneers at Adele as childless and unable to understand what he's experiencing. He lifts himself above her through contempt.

Campton begins to feel himself 'part of a greater whole' (183) and understands the terrible damage war does to civilization, but that does not essentially change him or how he responds to people. First of all, Campton is both overweight and lame, and his sense of physical inadequacy is heightened at a time when one needs to push through crowds, hurry up and down stairs – his body is simply incapable of meeting the challenge of this crisis. His limp is significant enough for Wharton to mention it easily a half a dozen times, and for Campton to refer to himself as a 'carcass.' It is as if the limp is an outward sign of his pain, his struggle, his shame.

He imagines that the 'capacity for passion' in himself is dead (176), and despite what one might expect, he does not feel the war bringing it to life. 'He wanted to help. . . but the longing was not an inspiration to him.. . .' With the news of each new tragedy (and they come with deadly regularity), each death of someone he knows, he grows 'more acutely aware of his own inadequacy' (208), struck by his 'curious incapacity to deal with the raw fact of sorrow' (199–200). He even contemptuously mocks his own sentiments about the war: 'Anything a man like me can do is too easy to be worth doing. As for anything one can *say*: how dare one say anything. . . As soon as I open my lips to blame or praise I see myself in white petticoats, with a long beard held on by an elastic, goading on the combatants in a cracked voice from a safe corner of the ramparts' (190). He is likewise helpless and hapless in defending Adele Anthony when there are trumped-up charges about malfeasance in her war charity, and 'speculators' take over, since there is a lot of money being generated: 'His eyes filled with tears of rage and self-pity at his own incompetence' (370). The book is full of such moments, and though Campton is certainly not the most sympathetic or deeply-developed of Wharton's characters, he is a convincing example of someone already deeply divided within himself who is crushed by circumstance. How will he be able to support George after the war if no more requests for portraits come in? How can he even paint again, when 'his artist's vision had been strangely unsettled' (95), and what on earth can he do to stem the tide of human misery, especially when there is enough 'at the rear for every civilian volunteer to find his task.'

> Among them all, Campton could not see his place. His lameness put him at a disadvantage, since taxi-cabs were few, and it was difficult for him to travel in the crowded metro. He had no head for figures, and would have thrown the best-kept accounts into confusion; he could not climb steep stairs to seek out refugees, nor should he have known what to say to them when he reached their attics. And so it would have been at the railway canteens; he choked with rage and commiseration at all the suffering about him, but found no word to cheer the sufferers (129).

This 'abject, irresolute' man is as helpless as Martin Boyne fumbling when he presents Rose with her present from Venice.

I cannot agree with David Clough's assessment that as a character John Campton 'lacks any depth of thought or personality.'[45] It
is an inability to see how his actions are so often determined by
shame that reduces him to a one-dimensional figure. For Campton, one response to the sense of inferiority and inadequacy is
contempt, which lifts him above others in a wide range of situations. We have seen how he treats his friend Adele Anthony (a sort
of aunt for George) in this way. In passing, it is interesting to note
that Adele followed a worthless 'artistic' brother to Europe and
stayed on when he failed, *'ashamed.* . . to go back and face the
righteous triumph of a family connection who had unanimously
disbelieved in the possibility of her brother's success as a sculptor'
(42) [my emphasis]. When Adele wonders if George is aware of the
plan everyone is hatching to keep him from battle, Campton
blushes, accuses her of telling George, *she* blushes, and then
Campton soon jeers at her for using slang when she dresses so
old-fashionedly (83–84). It is a childish remark, but not as insulting
as when he accuses her of being too detached about George's fate,
sneering 'you've never had a child' (214).

Adele is a friend, but there is a whole range of characters in the
book Campton views with great contempt, and here is where
Wharton's clear satire of their self-centered responses to the war
mixes not always comfortably with Campton's natural irascibility.
For instance, Campton consistently responds with disgust and
contempt to the very mention of the financier Jorgenstein's name,
but because we never meet the character, it is hard to know what is
so contemptible about him. Is his being a 'cosmopolitan' a code
word for being Jewish, perhaps, as Communists and Fascists
might use the term? Is this then an example of what Louis Harap
calls genteel anti-semitism in Wharton's fiction?[46] Or is it simply
that Jorgenstein is even richer than Brant, more powerful, and thus
more despicable? The case seems somewhat clearer with Ladislas
Isador, a 'fat middle-aged philanderer with his Jewish eyes, his
Slav eloquence, his Levantine gift for getting on, and for getting
out from under' (180). Isador is the lover of 'idiotic' Madame de
Dolmetsch, who tries to save 'the clever contriving devil' (180), this
'supple middle-aged adventurer' from combat (154). Campton is
disgusted when Madame de Dolmetsch begs him to help her keep
Isador at the War Office, since he has obviously helped his son –
Campton is *outraged* by 'this monstrous coupling of their names'
(154) – as if Isador is a creature utterly beyond the pale, and

mentioning his name profanes all good people. To some extent, Campton is here clearly ashamed, exposed, because evidently Madame de Dolmetsch has found out that Campton pulled strings for George. But because the rhetoric is simply all out of proportion to the character, whom we never meet, we cannot simply read these animadversions as reflections of Campton's own extremely troubled state of mind. Unsympathetic portraits of Jewish characters appear in, most obviously, *The House of Mirth*, but also in *Hudson River Bracketed*, *The Gods Arrive*, 'The Potboiler,' as well, and this use of offensive stereotypes is a weakness not enough discussed in Wharton criticism.

At any rate, other observations of 'war-workers' are pitched exactly right. There is the famous painter's wife, Madame Beausite, who flits about in 'the background, tragic and ineffectual. . . effacing herself behind a desk, where she bent her beautiful white head over a card-catalogue without any perceptible results' (198–99). And one of her confederates is a florid cousin of Campton's, Harvey Mayhew, who abandons his identity as a delegate to a peace conference after imprisonment by the Germans. 'Atrocities' become his career – he lectures about them in ringing declarations of defiance, accompanied by mournful keening by Madame de Dolmetsch for 'atmosphere,' and becomes something of a bigwig in the war charities field. The woman George loves, Mrs Talkett, is in a circle of *soi-disant* bohemians whose desire for pleasure becomes a mission after years of war: surely they must make life beautiful, after so much death and pain? Their empty ambitions are like lurid bright advertisements for a carnival. Wharton demolishes their self-deception here even more effectively than in *The Marne*, but with more insight:

> The war still raged; wild hopes had given way to dogged resignation; each day added to the sum of public anguish and private woe. But the strain had been too long, the tragedy too awful. The idle and the useless had reached their emotional limit, and once more they dressed and painted, smiled, gossiped, flirted as though the long agony were over (325).

I have focused here primarily on Campton's relationships and interactions, and his internal struggles, because most discussions of this novel (and there are not many), highlight the 'jingoistic' attitudes toward the war, and discuss how propaganda and unreflectiveness create a shallow, even dreadful, book. To go over these questions once again is pointless because Wharton's sentiments about the war, relayed through Campton and others, are indeed often heavy-handed, written with no subtlety at all. Cynthia Griffin Wolff acutely notes that Wharton fails in this novel 'when she reaches for blazing, dramatic generalization.'[47] True. Surprisingly, Wharton's writing in *Fighting France* seems a good deal more balanced and even detailed. Yet one can easily be blinded by this failure of language and miss the book's strengths, one of which Margaret McDowell has brilliantly analyzed. She has read *A Son at the Front* as 'not a battlefield novel' but one that 'consummately re-created the tragic impact of a worldwide cataclysm as it affected a group of people whose affluence and social prestige had previously protected them from the unpleasant and the violent.' In this world 'convulsed by war. . . driven apart by the opportunism of the few and the grief of the many. . . people suffer so much that they can see nothing beyond war and nothing unrelated to war.'[48] The sense of a world ground down by anxiety, mourning and pain is superbly realized throughout the novel, as are the pictures of the Paris Wharton and Campton loved.

What has been missing even in a critic as insightful as McDowell, however, is an appreciation of John Campton's wrestling with his internalized shame, the shame of his divorce and of his subsequent years of jealousy and failure. Wharton certainly felt some of what Campton is feeling about the death of his marriage and its painful aftermath. She powerfully expressed these feelings a few years after her divorce in 'Autre Temps. . . ', the widely read and frequently reprinted story which is all about shame and social ostracism, and in which blushing has the power of a thunderclap to shake and alert. Wharton's insights into the potentially crippling legacy of divorce, and the tangled family relationships it can produce, seem startlingly fresh and painful in *A Son at the Front*, making this perhaps not the novel she intended, but a good deal more.

Wharton also raises interesting questions in the novel about artistic inspiration, and failure and success. We have already seen how Campton's career was blighted at the start by the master, Beausite, making fun of his work. The power of this major figure of Paris' artistic establishment apparently kept others from seeing Campton's work at the beginning with their own eyes, and caused Campton great suffering. Julia was after some time able to wangle an invitation to a Beausite soiree for herself and Campton, but obviously ashamed and angry, Campton refused to go, and missed the chance to get Beausite's help. Giving up on portraits in which he did not prettify his subjects, lack of resources forced him and Julia to travel to Spain, where he had the dazzling vision of the Spanish girl whom he *had* to paint, a vision that seemed to liberate him from Julia, but led to many long years of loneliness and failure.

His recent success, however, has brought different burdens; he may be much more comfortable than he has ever been, yet the majority of his sitters are the type 'he least cared to paint. . . but they were usually those who paid the highest prices.' They bored him, and 'the more of their fatuous faces he recorded the more he hated the task' (5). His painting thus seems less organic, less a product of his creativity at the height of his fame, and more a job, an obligation, and even a tool. When war seems inevitable, Campton realizes that he can use the offer of doing a portrait to aid his son. Fortin-Lecluze, a famous physician, has pestered Campton to do a portrait of the doctor's mistress, and Campton agrees when he realizes he might need the doctor's influence to certify George as physically unfit to fight (due to his bout of tuberculosis). It is a decision he blushes about when George asks why he has changed his mind about doing the portrait. Still, when the war has broken out, Campton resists cheapening his painting further by doing portraits for charity – which would no doubt force him to paint people he had previously refused as sitters.

The war crushes his gift, as it seemed to crush Wharton's in the beginning. In *A Backward Glance* she writes that

> The noting of my impressions at the front had the effect of rousing in me an intense longing to write, at a moment when my mind was burdened with practical responsibilities, and my soul wrung with the anguish of the war. Even had I leisure to take up my story-telling I should have had no heart for it; yet I was tormented by a fever of creation.[49]

Well into the war, Campton is beseeched to return to the painting he has abandoned because it is the duty of 'every artist and every creator' to 'save Beauty for the world' (224). The argument is made by Madge Talkett before Campton and the Brants know George is in love with her. Mrs Talkett acknowledges that *her* means of creation are limited to personal adornment and interior decoration (Rose Sellars' gift in *The Children*) – but *he* can do so much more, and must. Mrs Talkett's rather smarmy importunities end up stirring Campton more than he would have expected, and indeed he has been feeling he must begin painting again. But it is Mrs Talkett's person that is far more convincing than her argument; when she blushingly prepares to leave his studio, assuming she has said too much, he is struck by her pose being eminently 'paintable' and instantly drags out an easel and canvas. He is, at last, 'transported into the lost world which was the only real one' and he gains a month of 'transcendent bliss' (227).

He paints Madge Talkett in her salon full of assorted arty types who have unashamedly, he thinks, 'decided, for a certain number of hours each day, to forget the war' (233). He wants to 'drug himself with work and frivolity' (234) and he finds the release into this atmosphere stimulating and enjoyable at first. It is not long, however, before he comes to see that these so-called 'subversives' (who attack ideas no one defends!) have never really thought about the war 'except as it interfered with their plans or cut down their amusements or increased their fortunes' (234). Campton gives up, but he is once again stirred by springtime 'in spite of himself' a year later, and does a charcoal of his concierge, and attempts to do her portrait in oil. All he feels able to do, after he has seen finagling in the war charity Adele Anthony worked for, is to 'shut himself up, for long solitary hours, in the empty and echoing temple of his art' (373).

Campton feverishly tries to do a sketch of George right after he leaves for the front after recovering from his second wound, but 'the violent emotions. . . clarified and transmuted into vision' do not last (385–86). He is ultimately unable to bridge the terrible gap between his vision of George and George's life at the front. The entrance of American troops into Paris, after George's death, stirs Campton once again; he feels 'the inspiration and the power returning' (412) and studies American soldiers and officers, completely, obsessively absorbed.

> To think of them all as George's brothers, to study out the secret likeness to him in their young dedicated faces: that was now his one passion, his sustaining task; it was at such times that his son came back and sat among them. . . [Wharton's ellipsis] (418).

Their presence helps him fight the loneliness 'like his [that] took all a man's strength from him. . . ' [Wharton's ellipsis] (419).

What is perhaps most striking about the way Wharton pictures Campton's relationship to his work is the intense ambivalence he exhibits about his art. Campton revels in the creativity, the excitement, and the clarity of his vision, yet at times seems burdened by his own gift, trapped by the life it has forced him to create. The man who in effect abandoned a marriage to paint and bed a passing Spanish beauty, this man of impulse, has become a society portraitist! His success cannot erase for him the years of failure, and in itself seems to bring him little joy. The sense of one's artistic gift both as a source of pleasure and restriction strikes me as realistic and acute, and such acuteness is an unrecognized element of Wharton's generally unappreciated portraits of artists and writers, to which we will now turn.

6

Writers and Artists

It is almost a critical truism that Edith Wharton could not write convincingly about artists. Blake Nevius roundly asserted in 1961 that none 'of her artists bears the stamp of authenticity' and that 'her view of the artistic life remained an enchanted one, essentially the romanticized version of an outsider' – even in her two novels about a writer, *Hudson River Bracketed* and *The Gods Arrive*. She was, he assures us, no James, no Flaubert, no Joyce. Nevius even damned her as 'a divine amateur,' and extraordinarily thoughtless, condemning her for making terrible demands on Henry James's time. A *real* artist would have been more considerate! If anything, Nevius adds, she was best suited to write about impotent artists who could not overcome the obstacles she in fact did: 'Social position, too much money, lack of sympathy, and an everyday environment that is indifferent, if not hostile to art.' Why? Because she was surrounded by dilettantes.[1]

R.W.B. Lewis and others have generally echoed the major charge of Nevius's assessment – that Wharton's artists were unconvincing – without challenge, but I find the claim that Wharton was an 'outsider' without substance. How can anyone dismiss her as an amateur when she negotiated with publishers so doggedly; was fiercely interested in the production, illustration and advertising of her books; produced not only twenty-three novels and novellas, eighty-seven stories, but also a dozen miscellaneous volumes: travel writing, poetry, autobiography, war reportage, interior design? Despite Nevius' sneering (and rather sexist) comment that Wharton's 'art had to take its place always among the gardening, entertaining, and traveling that crowded her schedule,'[2] she was indisputably a working writer. Nevius' emphasis is curious. Wharton had learned from working on *The House of Mirth* 'the importance of systematic daily effort in sustaining the intensity of her imagination'[3] – but rather than note that she wrote *every day*, Nevius belittles her devoting just her *mornings* to writing.[4] The crowded schedule he deplores seems less an example of her lack of seriousness about writing and more what she praised in *French*

Ways and Their Meanings: the French ability to take time to *enjoy* life and make it beautiful, an ability Anglo-Saxons were suspicious of.

How could so productive a writer, with so many friends and acquaintances who were writers, possibly have had a blinkered view of her profession? Indeed, I suspect that it is Nevius who had a 'romantic' view of the artist, when he suggests that Wharton could not understand 'the artist who is so absorbed in his task that he is all knees and elbows in the drawing room.'[5] Absorption in one's craft does not necessarily preclude social ease, *or* a social life, and it is often the social aspect of artists' lives that Wharton focuses on: 'The real world where money, love, manners, houses, clothes, food, or lack of them, impinge on [the] inner world as well as being the material from which [they] create.'[6] Is that side of life unworthy of consideration? After all, for Wharton, one of the essential qualities of fiction was 'the social relations of the characters presented in all concreteness.'[7] Why is that focus less believable when the subject is a writer or painter as opposed to a society woman?

In discussing one aspect of *Hudson River Bracketed*, Louis Auchincloss notes that the book may be clearer 'to those who write novels than to those who read them.'[8] Perhaps that astute observation can be applied more generally. As a widely-published writer of fiction and non-fiction, with many friends and acquaintances who are writers and editors, I have found Wharton's fiction about artists and writers striking and authentic. She deftly examines cases of artistic failure; the burden of telling the truth in one's art; the conflict between creating for oneself and for a public; the weaknesses of the reading and viewing public; the impact of publicity on a writer and the unexpected problems of success; and individuals caught in painful and demanding relationships with writers. These are *all* issues that have great currency, and in most of her fiction about writers and artists, shame plays a pivotal role, appearing phenomenologically, linguistically or both. It will in fact be impossible to note here all the times characters in these stories blush, look down or away, or list every reference to shame. While a few of the stories discussed here are quite well known, they are included along with the more neglected stories because they have never been considered in terms of the dynamics of shame, and never as a group.[9]

I

John Campton in *A Son at the Front* is not the only one of Edith Wharton's artists haunted by the specter of failure. 'The Bolted Door' is a fascinating study in artistic failure, with clear debts to Poe's 'The Tell-tale Heart' and his other studies in madness. Through 'ten years of dogged work,' Hubert Granice has been living out his 'deepest-seated instinct'[10] – playwriting – but working to fulfill this compulsion has only brought him 'unrelieved failure' (7). He has tried *everything*:

> comedy, tragedy, prose and verse, the light curtain-raiser, the short sharp drama, the bourgeois-realistic and the lyrical-romantic – finally deciding that he would no longer 'prostitute his talent' to win popularity, but would impose on the public his own theory of art in the form of five acts of blank verse. Yes, he had offered them everything – and always with the same result (5).

No one wants to produce his plays, and the only one ever staged was paid for by Granice himself. The complete failure of this piece was humiliating; Granice fled 'to Europe to escape the condolence of his friends!' (5) Granice is so trapped by his failure and shame that he cannot help re-reading his most recent rejection letter, full of searing lines like 'If this was your first play I'd say: *Try Again*' (5). For anyone who has striven to please editors and failed over a long period of time, that letter produces poignant shivers of recognition.

The struggle is over. Granice is a 'soul in misery' (4), 'baffled, beaten, worn out' (3). He even has contempt for his inability to end the pain by suicide: 'his attempts at self-destruction were as futile as his snatches at fame! He couldn't make himself a real life, and he couldn't get rid of the life he had' (6). Despite his friends and acquaintances, Granice feels utterly isolated: 'It was easier to go on automatically with the social gestures than to uncover to any human eye the abyss within him' (6). Not surprisingly, his shame has kept him silent – how can one easily expose ten years of dreary failure? The latest disappointment, however, which seems a death sentence to his career, makes him long for an end to the pain, for death, and pushes him over the edge.

Here is where the story takes on elements of Poe. Granice decides that he must be put to death, and he attempts to reveal, first to his lawyer, then to an editor, and next, to the District Attorney, that he killed his cousin ten years before, to inherit the money that would make his writing career possible. (His cousin was a rich, miserly man bizarrely obsessed with growing melons, as grotesque and 'deserving' of death in his own way as the victim in 'The Tell-tale Heart.') Granice's lawyer urges him to see a doctor – thus Granice, a failed playwright, cannot be taken seriously as a murderer either. Granice's second confession is preceded by his learning 'a new measure of his *insignificance*' [my emphasis]. His friend Denver, a successful editor, 'did not even know that [Granice] had been a failure'! (17) The bulk of the story follows Granice's more and more desperate re-tellings of the story of his crime, but he unfortunately provided himself with so good an alibi that his story is not believed. Increasingly obsessed by the need to convince *someone* of the truth, and the need to have his life ended for him, he is widely suspected of mental illness, and is finally put away in a rest home, where he endlessly re-tells his story, producing more and more precise confessions.

Ironically, Granice never learns that he *has* convinced an eager reporter, whose own research confirmed the murder, but that man doesn't have the heart to see Granice convicted and executed. Thus Granice has turned his life into something worse than the 'stagnant backwater' (30) he felt it had become because of his literary failure. The very ordinariness of his early years of deadening work in a brokerage house to support his sister make his ultimate plunge into lunacy more affecting and convincing.

Pellerin in the somewhat long-winded 'The Legend' is driven by *his* shameful failure into exile. Twenty-five years before the story begins, this philosopher-writer simply disappeared from New York, he says,

'in a rage of disappointment, of wounded pride–no, vanity! I don't know which cut deepest – the sneers or the silence – but between the two of them there wasn't an inch of me that wasn't raw. I had just the one thing in me: the message, the cry, the revelation. But nobody saw and nobody listened. Nobody wanted what I had to give.'[11]

We have already seen in Wharton's autobiographies (discussed in

Chapter 1) the shaming impact that contempt and indifference ('sneers' and 'silence') can have. Pellerin luckily found spiritual peace in the Far East (*pèlerin* is French for pilgrim) and returned to New York only out of curiosity when he accidentally discovered his books were widely read. Indeed they have not only become 'textbooks of modern thought' (104), but downright fashionable, the focus of Pellerin clubs and gushing, breathlessly stupid social- ites. Arthur Bernald, a writer and student of Pellerin's work, is the only man in New York to recognize the older, bearded Pellerin who is using a pseudonym – through the genius and warmth of his conversation. Bernald is not surprised that Pellerin's new writing is ironically dismissed as garbage by Howland Wade, Pellerin's 'greatest' interpreter. Bernald himself has written a deep and thoughtful book on Pellerin which he knows could never survive the howling publicity granted to Wade's shallow and meretricious study. Bernald is also cheated of laughing over Wade's blindness when Pellerin not surprisingly leaves New York again, with his work already beginning to fall out of style. The story thus exam- ines two failures 'in the world' – that of a genius, and of the man who can intelligently, sensitively explore the nature of that genius, all in the context of a public that fails to accurately discriminate between flash and substance.

'April Showers' takes a much lighter look at shameful failure, and at the beginning of a career – or potential career – as opposed to the end. This delightful and tenderly mocking story opens as teenaged Theodora writes the plaintive last line of her first novel: 'But Guy's heart slept under the violets on Muriel's grave.'[12] She has been encouraged to write her five-hundred-page novel by hearing of her uncle's neighbor, Kathleen Kyd, the 'famous society novelist' (190), author of *Fashion and Passion* and *An American Duchess*. Kyd's career started with a story sent to *Home Circle*, and grew from there. As an inveterate novel reader, Theodora feels convinced that her novel *April Showers* 'was a remarkable book' (190), and even more emotionally intense than Kathleen Kyd's work:

> Theodora did not care to amuse her readers; she left that to frivolous talents. Her aim was to stir the depths of human nature, and she felt she had succeeded. It was a great thing for a girl to be able to feel that about her first novel. Theodora was only seventeen; and she remembered, with a touch of retrospec-

tive compassion, that George Eliot had not become famous till she was nearly forty (190).

Theodora even imagines herself following in the steps of great writers who had not compromised their standards and had no 'thought of conciliating an unappreciative public. . . Better obscure failure than a vulgar triumph' (191). What young artist hasn't had such grandiose thoughts and been brought down to earth by household duties, as Theodora is: 'Unfortunately the writing of a great novel leaves little time or memory for the lesser obligations of life' (191). Guilty about neglecting her chores, Theodora is sure that her neglect will be atoned for when she becomes rich and famous (Kathleen Kyd gets $10,000 for each serialized novel) and can indulge her family.

Theodora goes through an agony terribly familiar to all writers: waiting for the mail, which unfortunately comes three times a day! But she survives the strain of waiting, and when *April Showers* is accepted by *Home Circle*, Theodora modestly becomes the cynosure of her town. Then she buys her copy of the magazine and finds the first installment of *April Showers* is not from *her* book, and the author is none other than Kathleen Kyd. Theodora flees her home without permission or explanation, ashamed, enraged, disappointed, to the Boston offices of *Home Circle* where she finds out that *her* manuscript and Kathleen Kyd's came in at the same time. The identical titles account for Theodora's letter of acceptance. Theodora expects her return home will be greeted by anger, but her father tenderly shares his own story of disappointment. Right after graduating college, he had wanted to be a writer rather than a doctor, but 'the public wouldn't have [his novel]; not at any price' (196). While he tells her his story, 'Theodora clung to him in a mute passion of commiseration. It was as if a drowning creature caught a live hand through the murderous fury of the waves' (196). For her, at least, the shame of having failed so publicly is healed by hearing about her father's past disappointment, and experiencing his present kindness. It is a rare moment in Wharton's fiction as a whole, but not quite so uncommon in her writing about artists and writers, where there is at least some chance for shame to be healed. Failure does not automatically or ineluctably lead to isolation, and we shall see in *Hudson River Bracketed* how shame can sometimes also be the source and spur of creative work.

In 'The Recovery,' shame brings an artist to a new and deeper stage in his career, when he finally realizes the emptiness of all his previous work. Keniston's painting has become famous in Hillbridge, Massachusetts mostly because of snobbish pride that he is *in* Hillbridge, the Oxford of the state (especially as seen by those from smaller towns). In a delicious example of intellectual boosterism, Hillbridge's citizens, scholars and collectors are convinced that 'to "know" Keniston one must come to Hillbridge. Never was work more dependent for its effect on "atmosphere," on *milieu*.'[13]

The story follows young, small-town Claudia Day from her first awed visit to this 'antique seat of learning' (260), where she hopes to learn the truth of the Hillbridgian dictum that 'The man and the art interpret each other' (261) and Keniston can only be truly valued and understood in his studio. Like today's New York clubs whose cachet depends on their inaccessibility to the hoi polloi, Keniston is hard to know and Claudia is afraid she will never have this privilege. The irony is that she will gradually come to know him far better than he knows himself. When she does meet him for the first time, her 'fancy instantly hailed in him that favorite figure of imaginative youth, the artist who would rather starve than paint a potboiler' (261). Claudia had felt ashamed of how little she knew about him until she read a journal article about his work en route to Hillbridge, and Keniston's taciturnity leaves her full of shame and contempt for her social failure:

> Claudia was able to indulge to the full the *harrowing sense of her inadequacy*. No wonder she had not been one of the few that he cared to talk to; every word she uttered must so obviously have diminished the inducement! She had been *cheap, trivial, conventional*; at once gushing and inexpressive, eager and constrained. She could feel him counting the minutes till the visit was over, and as the door finally closed on the scene of her *discomfiture* she almost shared the hope with which she confidently credited him – that they might never meet again (262) [my emphases].

After ten years of being married to Keniston, Claudia is no longer a wild admirer of his, but rather prefers 'moderation of speech' in *his* admirers (262). She may still believe in her husband, but not in his acolytes, and she has even begun to wonder 'that her husband remained so uncritical of the quality of admiration accorded him' (262). Keniston is too complacent, too assured of his own success for Claudia to feel the need to encourage him; she has even discovered that Keniston works slowly not because he is a genius, as all Hillbridge asserts and Keniston clearly believes, 'but because he had really so little to express' (263). The exhibition of his works in Paris prompts Keniston to consider visiting Europe, which he has never travelled to before. Though Claudia still feels that he is a great artist, and is satisfied by his paintings, she is pleased to suspect in her husband's desire to go to Europe possible signs of 'a quickened sensibility' (265).

In London's National Gallery, Claudia is overwhelmed by the 'unimagined world' of artistic richness and genius, but her husband is silent, and seems 'to have a sort of provincial dread of showing himself too much impressed' (266). To keep from comparing Keniston's work to what she has seen, Claudia takes 'refuge in a passionate exaggeration of her own ignorance and insufficiency' (267). She at this point would rather feel ashamed of herself than of her husband. In Paris Keniston more volubly visits the Louvre, studiously avoiding his own exhibition, and Claudia begins to see the truth 'amid that ordered beauty which gives a social quality to the very stones and mortar of Paris':

> All about her were evidences of an artistic sensibility pervading every form of life. . . a sensibility so delicate, alert and universal that it seemed to leave no room for obtuseness or error. . . To Claudia the significance of the whole vast revelation was centered in the light it shed on one tiny spot of consciousness – the value of her husband's work (269).

At her husband's exhibition, she realizes that the pictures are simply bad, and is blushingly discovered there by Keniston. After another solo visit to the Louvre, Keniston can confess that he has discovered, at forty, that his work has no value, but he is ready to start over again, ready to *learn*. Seeing the greatest European artists (whom he casually called 'those old chaps' while still in America) has shown him how trivial and untutored his work is, but the invidious comparison is liberating. While still in Hillbridge, he said one should measure oneself against 'big fellows' at least once in a lifetime – but the tone was almost swaggering, as if he would surely hold his own. Now Keniston is humbler. He will stay in Europe and grow not only as an artist, but as a man, we assume. Claudia's fear that he would not be able to face the truth has proven to be groundless, and their potentially destructive insights point the way to a new life. Shame has not crushed or 'silenced' Keniston. He 'demonstrates that he is a true artist by recognizing an absolute standard and that his work does not measure up to that standard, and by his eagerness to learn and see his way forward toward a new vision.'[14]

But shame *has* stopped the successful painter Jack Gisburn in the brittle, amusing 'The Verdict.' Rickham, the narrator, wants to find out why, and why Gisburn's new wife 'had not led him back to the easel.'[15] This flashy painter's popularity was owed almost entirely to women whose portraits he painted 'strongly' but 'sweetly,' and no one in the art world really mourns his 'death.' The narrator gets his chance to unravel the mystery when he stays near the Gisburns on the Riviera, and discovers that Gisburn is – surprisingly – no longer blind to the absurdity of the praises flung at him (as Keniston had also been in 'The Recovery'). Even more perplexing, there are none of Gisburn's paintings in the luxurious house, owing, Mrs Gisburn says, to the painter's 'ridiculous modesty' (657). Rickham knows that this modesty is brand new, and Gisburn blushes when the narrator asks why he's stopped painting. Rickham turns away, 'instinctively embarrassed' when Gisburn says he never thinks of painting now, but his tone and blush betray the truth (659).

Well aware that Rickham loathes his shallow work, Gisburn relates that his crisis came when he was asked to paint a portrait of the just deceased Stroud, a failed, brilliant painter. Confronted with the corpse of this unacknowledged master, Gisburn gradually felt his showy technique collapse under the imagined scrutiny of a *real* artist. The invidious comparison shamed him into giving up his career, and the only one of his paintings Gisburn allows in the house is a portrait of his wife tucked away in 'the dimmest corner of [his wife's] boudoir' (657). Despite hiding this last 'evidence' of his failure, Gisburn is humorously aware that *his* kind of painting will always be around, even if he himself has stopped. He can laugh about his previous career 'without bitterness' (660), Rickham says, but the very fact that he gave up so completely belies this assessment.

For Halston Merrick in 'The Long Run,' failure in his creative work stems from a shameful failure of nerve. Merrick's early writing had 'freshness and audacity,'[16] but it has become conventional and dull, and so has he. These diminutions of an exciting start in politics and writing are due to his failure to make a commitment to Mrs Reardon. Years before, rather than settle for a quiet affair on the margins of society, she had offered herself to him for life, but Merrick stuttered, hesitated, argued, hoping to spare 'her the humiliation of scandal and the misery of self-reproach' (323). In reality, he could not match her passion and vision, was ultimately 'pusillanimous,' and even too ashamed of his failure of spirit to propose two years after her offer when her husband died. He tells a friend 'there wasn't an appeal I could make [to her] that didn't mock the appeal I had rejected' (323). Mrs Reardon wanted him to sell the ironworks his father had left him and 'travel and write,' living the life of the mind, and of his dreams, but he has become merely rich – and terribly alone.

The only hope for Jeff Lithgow's painting in 'Joy in the House' is posthumous success. Because he killed himself when his married mistress returned to her understanding husband, his widow reasons that his paintings might finally sell. His talent, however, has been questionable: even Catherine Ansley, who loved him enough to leave behind her little boy and comfortable home for France and a six-month 'trial marriage,' wonders how talented he is. There 'was something unstable, unreliable in his talent, just as there was in his character.'[17] Catherine was mortified when her husband publicly mocked the first Lithgow painting he saw, but further mortifications related to her lover's talent await Catherine in France. A London dealer returns a painting Lithgow had sent on approval, and Lithgow's offer to pay his hotel bill with a portrait of the hotelier's daughter is greeted with the scornful query, 'Is Monsieur mocking me?' This, after the woman had looked at his work!

Though Catherine's husband permitted her romantic experiment, offering to take her back before six months with nothing but 'Joy in the House' to greet her, she is racked by 'the sense of her iniquity, of her inhumanity' (708) because she abandoned her little boy. She will also abandon her lover, who carries out his threat to kill himself if she leaves. Catherine learns of his death from his wife, whose revelation plunges her into 'humiliation and. . . horror' (720):

> Hadn't she felt, during those last agonizing hours in the hotel at Havre, that what [Lithgow] told her was the truth, hadn't she known that his life was actually falling in ruins, hadn't her only care been to escape before the ruins fell on her and destroyed her

too?. . . [I]f human responsibility counted for anything, wasn't
her place rather in that sordid hotel room where a man sat with
buried face because he could not bear to see the door close on
her forever? (721)

Catherine will feel even more exposed to learn that even though
she felt protected from reporters by her husband (it was a sensational 'elopement'), he and everyone else in the household knew
about Lithgow's death when she returned, and was in fact as
delighted with that news as with her being back. Though Catherine suddenly longs to escape the 'stifling atmosphere of tolerance
and benevolence, of smoothing over and ignoring and dissembling' for 'the live world, where men and women struggled and
loved and hated, and quarreled and came together with redoubled
passion' (721), she comes off as badly as her husband in this story,
and as Lithgow. Her lover was not only embarrassingly cheap
while travelling – and Catherine 'had always held her head so
high, and marked her passage by such liberalities!' (711) – but also
unable to appreciate how torn she was about abandoning her little
boy.

Jack Deering's failures in 'The Letters' have less resonance for
this painter than for his second wife Lizzie West who suffered
them before and after their marriage. Lizzie first met him in France
when she was engaged to tutor his academically uninclined
daughter Juliet. Lizzie is shy, poor and terribly uncertain – 'in
crimson misery'[18] when she has to ask for back wages, blushing to
tell Deering that his feckless daughter needs his 'intervention.'
Lizzie's shame stems from not wanting to confess her own failure
as a tutor, and from not wanting to tell him that Juliet pays too
much attention to the servants' gossip. Deering in turn is 'pained
and shamed' (179) to hear about Juliet, and when Lizzie cries and
he kisses her, Lizzie's immediate feelings are fright, 'shame and
penitence' (179).

What links them is failure. Lizzie had once tried to be a painter,
and thus profoundly sympathizes with this 'baffled, poor, and
disappointed' (179) man who 'had tasted an earlier moment of
success. . . then the tide of publicity had somehow set the other
way, and left him stranded in a noble isolation' (180). Lizzie imagines that it can only be their shared misfortunes in art that could
have made him notice 'so inconspicuous an object as herself [,]'
since she is in awe of him as a painter (180). Their talks about

literature and their visits to galleries and museums leave her 'a little ashamed' to bring back so 'few definite impressions,' but she ascribes this to being dazzled by his person (181). When Deering's invalid wife dies, Lizzie feels the woman's existence can no longer 'shame [Lizzie's] rapture' (183). But Deering has to return to America to see about his wife's estate. The painter makes Lizzie *promise* to write often – even though she wants to be spared 'the embarrassment of [offering him] ill-timed intrusions' (185).

He writes three times, and then no more, and despite her own barrage of letters to him, Lizzie is left comparing herself invidiously to the many other articulate and experienced women whose 'passionate missives' she can imagine speeding to Deering from around the world (186). Her own response to such shaming reflections is the proud assertion, 'head high,' that no one could love him as *she* did. Three years pass, during which she has inherited a good deal of money from a distant relative, and Deering returns like Morris Townsend in *Washington Square*. He claims that he didn't answer her letters because of his desperate poverty, his shame, in other words, at being unable to offer her the life she deserves. Though he managed to sell some paintings in New York, once again his 'moment of success' was followed by failure, debt, and scrounging for jobs. He 'had been humiliated' and blushing Lizzie comes to feel *his* pain more than her own (193).

Lizzie throws over her dim fiancé for Deering. To do him credit, Deering does not take advantage of her wealth – but because he's too lazy, she realizes after three years of marriage. Though Lizzie has built him a studio in their house at Neuilly, he 'failed to settle down to the great work which was to result' from their 'wedded bliss' (198, 197). He seems in fact hardly to have done any painting at all. When trunks 'liberated' from one of Deering's New York landladies are unpacked, Lizzie discovers her letters were never opened, never read. He lied to her, and among her responses to this humiliation (she is with a friend when the letters are found) is disgust at the thought of his dazzling presence and touch, and contempt at his inveterate newspaper reading. Both responses of course distance him and elevate herself. Lizzie wants to thrust the letters at him, but she 'was humiliated by the thought of humiliating him' (203). She ends up accepting him as he is, as she has come to see him: human, flawed, 'not the hero of her dreams' but 'the man she loved, and who loved her' (206). *Their* love can last, and one assumes the issue of his painting will never come up.

Though Lizzie at first thought his work 'remarkable,' there is no sense of how talented Deering really is, and his professional failure seems almost the aesthetic parallel of his slackness of character, his 'smiling irresponsibility' (198). The decision to live with disappointment, found throughout Wharton's early fiction, and based no doubt on her own marriage, here is united with the disappointment and shame of Wharton's affair with Morton Fullerton, who was even more charming and evasive than Deering. The story also draws on Fullerton's engagement with his cousin. Cynthia Griffin Wolff notes the correspondences with real life events and writes that Wharton drew too directly from her own experience with Fullerton here,[19] but I would suggest that the emotional realities make this a compelling and convincing story.

Another twist on the theme of misplaced devotion to an artist or writer is spun in 'The Angel at the Grave.' Paulina Anson, granddaughter of Orestes Anson, a very minor Transcendentalist, is the custodian of his memory, his papers and his house – a 'bleak temple of thought.'[20] She has given up the possibility of marriage to keep tending her flame, and turns to writing a biography of her famous grandfather. Ten years of work blind her to the great decline in his reputation, and her book turns out to be 'worthless,' as a publisher explains. Orestes Anson is still 'a name,' and '[p]eople don't exactly want to be caught not knowing who he is; but they don't want to spend two dollars finding out, when they can look him up for nothing in any biographical dictionary' (251). Returning with the manuscript 'like a wounded thing' (251), Paulina is unwilling to take the manuscript elsewhere – and who could blame her? How can she risk another humiliating disappointment? She is not entirely crushed by the news, however, and rebounds enough to labor to discover what exactly has happened to her grandfather's reputation and why. In the end, a scientific pamphlet of Anson's turns out to be more valuable than his entire works, and she is left 'walled alive into a tomb hung with the effigies of dead ideas' (253). She has submerged and lost her self, like Kate Clephane in *The Mother's Recompense*, and Kate Orme in *Sanctuary*. Ned Silverton's sisters in *The House of Mirth* will likewise lose their identity and their money, trying to keep up with the gambling debts of a brother who 'had meant to live on proof-reading and write an epic,'[21] but became a social butterfly instead.

Devotion to a successful journalist husband and then her even more successful journalist son ruins the life of Mrs Quentin in 'The

Quicksand,' who confesses the shamefulness of her past, and her ties to the scandalous family-owned journal, *Radiator*, in order to save a young woman from making the same mistake by marrying her son Alan. It is a disturbing story of the dark side of success. 'Mrs Quentin had always hungered for perfection' and she has achieved it in a perfect loyal son, a perfect house, and the 'almost morbid finish of every material detail of her life.'[22] It is a somewhat barren existence, but we only learn how barren in her final confession to Alan's beloved, Hope Fenno.

Hope has refused to marry Alan because of his owning *Radiator*, and explaining Hope's stance to his mother, Alan rather contemptuously makes fun of Hope's 'prejudices' – 'she takes in all the moral fashion papers,' he says, 'and wears the newest thing in ethics' (399). Hope wants him to give up the paper or turn it into something less objectionable, hoping that his 'point of view' will change as a result. All through this conversation Mrs Quentin is very careful in her questions and replies, but we do not understand her caution until the story's end. In a subsequent brief attempt to change Hope's mind, Mrs Quentin discovers that Hope sees her own point of view about the newspaper as very different from Mrs Quentin's, and throughout this exchange Hope blushes, ashamed to have to even imply that she has higher standards than Mrs Quentin.

We do not learn what is so objectionable about *Radiator* until Mrs Quentin, oppressed by Alan's pain, runs into Hope six months later at the Metropolitan Museum of Art in New York. When Hope says she has changed her mind, has come to believe that her life with Alan *can* be beautiful and good despite his owning the newspaper, Mrs Quentin cuts her off, unable to see a girl so 'tingling with belief, ambitions, energies. . . walled up alive' (407). It is a powerful metaphor for living with shame, and one Wharton used in 'Angel at the Grave' as well. She has to save Hope, and she tells the story of her shame. When she married Alan's father, a born journalist, *Radiator* was 'less notorious' (408). She had never seen it, and enjoyed the money it earned until she learned what kind of scandal sheet it was. Devastated, she felt she 'would have gone out into the streets barefooted rather than live another hour on the money it brought in' (408). That day, she explains to Hope,

'The paper had stripped bare some family scandal – some miserable bleeding secret that a dozen unhappy people had been struggling to keep out of print – that *would* have been kept out if my husband had not –' (408).

More sensitive than we might expect, her husband was quite upset at Mrs Quentin's reaction and promised to sell the paper. Only, he needed to boost circulation first, and then they needed more money because Alan was a sickly baby, and so it went until talk of selling *Radiator* died away.

Mrs Quentin desperately turned to charity, sure that her husband despised her for never mentioning selling the paper again. And we can understand her perfectionism as an attempt to wipe out the shame at the very core of her life. She made a great mistake, however, in bringing up Alan with a taste for luxury without talking to him honestly about 'the monster that had nourished [them]' (409). What kept her back? Shame, she says. Alan, however, was a more brilliant journalist than his father, and unscrupulous. When *he* inherited the paper, though he didn't need the money, he wouldn't dream of giving it up. He 'loved power, and wanted to have all he could get' (410). Mrs Quentin warns Hope that if she marries Alan she will always suffer the shameful loss of her self-respect, that her gradual moral death will leave one painful 'aching nerve of truth' (410). She disappears from Hope's side as the shocked young woman sits with her head down, obviously shamed by what she has learned. This story is like so many of Wharton's (going as far back as 'The Lamp of Psyche' in 1895), hinging on a woman discovering the shallowness of the man she loves, and being trapped in disappointment, as Wharton was with Teddy, and more tragically, with Fullerton. Wharton skillfully holds back the reader's understanding of the moral shame in Mrs Quentin's life, and how she really feels about her son, until the great outpouring of misery at the end which leaves Hope Fenno crushed.

Many of the writers and artists already discussed were productive, whether talented and successful or not, but what about those who merely *think* they have talent to write or paint, like poor Ivy Spang in 'Writing a War Story'? The results are not always quite so humiliating. Ned Halidon of 'In Trust' has inherited great wealth, an ugly house and no talent. After some time studying art in Paris he was lucky to have discovered that he couldn't paint 'early enough to save himself much labor and his friends many painful efforts at dissimulation.'[23] So far, so good, but Halidon's drive becomes diverted into plans for the 'ultimate aesthetic redemption of the whole human race,' as his friends joke (616). Failing that, he will settle for restoring 'the sense of beauty' to countless Americans suffering 'unperceived and unmitigated ugliness' (616). His great goal is to found an academy, but the scheme consistently founders on his blushing hesitancies, and after his death the money is embarrassingly diverted and re-diverted away from his grandiose aim, which would, no doubt, have erased in his lifetime the shame of not having any talent of his own.

Willis French in 'The Temperate Zone' is luckier and more intelligent. He has learned that 'interesting failures may be worth more in the end than dull successes.'[24] If, for example, he had gotten more out of working in Horace Fingall's studio, he would have missed getting to know that famous painter better. Likewise, when he showed his poetry to the esteemed poet Emily Morland, he might have experienced 'less of her sweet compassion, and her bracing wisdom' (450) had he been more talented. Both artists unequivocally told French to abandon his efforts, but he took their assessment 'without flinching,' which 'no doubt increased their liking, and thus let him further into their intimacy' (450–51). French is thus able to fail without shame, and enjoy the 'leisure to note and enjoy all the incidental compensations of the attempt' (450). He is a rarity in Wharton's fictional world, someone whose disappointments have been the source of insight (as for Keniston in 'The Recovery'), whose shame has not crippled him. But then, the story's focus lies elsewhere; French's enthusiasm is only part of its background, and he does end up as an art critic and biographer. In *The Age of Innocence* M. Rivière, a French tutor, knows Mérimée, the Goncourt brothers and de Maupassant, who all advised him 'not to attempt to write' and he gives up journalism to maintain his intellectual freedom. The choice has left him deeply contented.[25]

Morland and Fingall's advice to Willis French raises a serious question – how honest can one be with a would-be artist or writer? This is a powerful potential scene of shame for all artists. Wharton herself was written to in 1918 by an American soldier who asked her opinion of his poetry. She was quite frank, but not unfeelingly so, telling him that she did not find the echoes in his poetry of Wordsworth, Tennyson or Shelley he thought might be there, but rather those 'of the poet's corner of a daily newspaper.' Poetry, Wharton advised him, was more than feeling – it was 'an art as exact & arduous as playing the violin. . . [presupposing] long training & wide reading, & a saturation in the best that the past has to give.'[26] (She would have a journalist-critic say almost the same things to Vance Weston in *Hudson River Bracketed*). Wharton urged more extensive reading and study on the young man. We know too that in her letters to Fullerton she was unsparingly frank in pointing out the flaws in his unwieldy prose, and seemed to relish the idea of instructing him. Allen Gribben suggests that in her relationship with Fullerton, Wharton had 'a Pygmalion fantasy about discovering and tutoring a writer who did not yet appreciate his own capacities.'[27] Obviously, here she was experienced, gifted, powerful, successful – to re-create Fullerton as a writer of undisputable talent would have been one way to triumph over shame.

Culwin, the contemptuous, sterile dilettante in 'The Eyes' is much less honest than Wharton was to Fullerton, and Culwin's inability to tell a young friend the truth about his lack of literary talent literally haunts him. Years before the story begins, Culwin was under the 'illusion that sustained intellectual effort could engage a man's whole activity' and he 'decided to write a great book' though he can't remember what about.[28] Alice Nowell, an uninteresting cousin, served as his secretary, and Culwin's idle and rather contemptuous flirting with this bland young woman led him into an unexpected engagement. Telling Alice he was about to leave (because he sensed she was too attracted to him), he received a kiss 'worse than any reproach' which, he says, 'made me ashamed to deserve' one (119). So he proposes. That night he is visited by the appearance of spectral aged eyes: grim, derisive, disgusting. Staring eyes are a potent source of shame, as we have seen, in part, in the discussion of *The Children*. Culwin flees and ultimately spends two years in Europe without having explained a thing to his cousin. In Rome, he begins another book that is never finished.

His cousin Alice sends him Gilbert Noyes, a relative destined for an accounting job, but who longs to write. Culwin's task is to judge his talent, and though he knows from the very first that Noyes's writing is 'deplorable,' he doesn't let on, but keeps the charming, beautiful and obliging young man as his companion. He is in part ashamed of how he treated Alice, and doesn't want to disappoint her again. Culwin's view of Noyes's lack of talent was confirmed by editors and critics, but he continued to lie and even got Noyes' time in Europe extended by his family. A confrontation about a terrible novel leaves Culwin 'ashamed' of his 'impulse of egotism' in wanting Noyes forever – but he tells Noyes the novel is fine anyway (125). The eyes return, and Culwin plans to wean Noyes from writing, and marry him off to a rich widow. The eyes only disappear when Noyes, out of money and time, forces Culwin to admit the truth about his lack of talent – which the older man can only deliver as a contemptuous laugh.

The eyes Culwin has seen twice – each time *he* felt he had acted unselfishly – are of course the eyes he now has: those of 'a man who had done a lot of harm in his life, but had always kept just inside the danger lines' (120). Hearing the end of Culwin's story, his current young companion, Phil Frenham, hides his face, ashamed of seeing the truth about the man he has so fiercely admired. Selfishness and shame have stunted Culwin's life (causing Alice and Gilbert great pain), and come back to rob him of his latest intellectual conquest. Cynthia Griffin Wolff suggests that the 'horror of [Culwin's] self-discovery is the ultimate subject of this story.'[29] But it is not so much discovery that occurs – because Culwin does not seem capable of insight and reform, rather, he is *humiliated*. He has told the story *himself*, has thus utterly exposed his own lack of feeling, his own cruelty and egotism.

Shameful exposure is central in a different way to two of Wharton's stories that raise questions of truth versus privacy. What happens when a writer's or artist's revelation or insight is about someone else? Must one publish or paint what one sees? What are the risks, and is hurting another less important than being true to one's craft? Or are there other considerations more important? This question of 'honesty' in one's work bedevils many creative artists (whether they admit it or not), and is intriguingly developed in one of Wharton's earliest stories, 'That Good May Come' and later in 'The Portrait.' Both stories also work with the familiar theme of failure.

In the first story, Maurice Birkton has been unable to publish any of his poetry, and the novel he hoped to write by quitting a clerk's job has not progressed. His greatly reduced income straitens his mother's and sister's life, and financial pressure mounts when his sister needs a new white dress for her confirmation. 'She suffers at the thought of not appearing worthily'[30] – that is, being *exposed* as different and too poor to be dressed like the other girls. Birkton had been offered $150 by the editor of *Social Kite* for a scurrilous poem (which he'd read to friends) about an adulterous society woman, Mrs Tolquitt. He'd refused before, because selling it would have been shameful, yet he goes ahead to help his sister, despite the 'anguish and humiliation' it will cause Mrs Tolquitt, and he feels like a 'blackguard' (40). Though Birkton's best friend argues somewhat sententiously that 'good may come' (40) from this disgraceful act because Birkton may have learned to never do anything similar, he also urges Birkton to keep it secret from his family. The wages of shame thus appear to be a good deal less than the wages of sin, but the ending is inconclusive because we are apparently left with more proof of Mrs Tolquitt's extra-marital relationship – with no authorial comment and no reaction from Birkton.

'The Portrait' opens on a note of exposure, with a debate at a social affair about the merits and demerits of being painted by George Lillo, currently in New York from Paris after a twelve-year absence. He makes people 'look so horrid,' one woman moans, unlike the fashionable and preening portraitist Cumberton, who claims that Lillo only sees his sitters' defects.[31] The hostess, Mrs Mellish, delivers a 'flushed harangue,. . . blushing. . . at her own eloquence.' Lillo is a master, she says, because while 'other painters do the surface – he does the depths; they paint the ripples on the pond, he drags the bottom.' She too argues against being painted by him, but for different reasons: 'If you don't want to be found out – or to find yourself out' (174).

The long-awaited exhibition of Lillo's never-seen portrait of 'Boss' Vard, a corrupt politician who has since committed suicide, is a big disappointment, however. People expected 'the zest of an incriminating document, the scandalous attraction of secret memoirs,' but it was only 'as insipid as an obituary' (175). The painter who reveals so much in his subjects has shown nothing about Vard. As in 'The Verdict,' there is an artistic mystery here, made more intriguing when Lillo says the weakness was deliberate. The painting is a 'lucid failure' (176), and was done to save Vard's worshipful daughter from seeing her father as Lillo did; 'vulgar to the core; vulgar in spite of his force and magnitude. . . a lath-and-plaster bogey' despite his showiness and his demonic reputation (180). Vard's daughter attended all the sittings, and embarrassed, Lillo kept putting off painting Vard's face. Though he ultimately discovers that Miss Vard understands after her father has been arrested, he still botches the face to make her feel 'that her miserable secret *was* a secret' just a bit longer to save her from the shame of further disappointment and exposure (185).

Wharton ironically examines the question of shame and artistic compromise from a different angle in 'The Potboiler.' Its protagonist is Stanwell, a poor but talented painter in love with Kate Arran, the lovely sister of a neighbor who is a dreadful and justly failed sculptor. Caspar Arran produces dreary monumental works no one wants (reminiscent of those committed by Henry James' friend, Hendryk Anderson). Kate Arran is being courted through her brother by Mungold, 'the fashionable painter of the hour,'[32] who can obviously offer Kate more than Stanwell ever could. Mungold is Stanwell's and Caspar Arran's *bête noire*: he paints 'ladies in syrup. . . with marshmallow children against their knees. He was as quick as a dressmaker at catching new ideas, and the style of his pictures changed as rapidly as that of the fashion plates' (671). (Claude Poppel in *The Custom of the Country* will be successful meeting society's expectations of a portrait, 'that the costume should be sufficiently "life-like," and the face not too much so.' Poppel has 'long experience in idealizing flesh and realizing dress-fabrics.'[33]) Stanwell, who once did a painting in Mungold's style, partly as a joke, refuses an art dealer's offer to do a rich woman's portrait in just the same way. But he changes his mind to help the apparently tubercular Arran (and of course Kate).

Why does he compromise his principles? Arran's doctor makes Stanwell realize that Arran's lofty contempt for success and public opinion is only a mask; actually, the little sculptor's 'vanity was starving to death' (675). Arran's standards are hollow in a way, a reaction to the prolonged shame of rejection and failure. Stanwell decides to do the society portrait and anonymously commissions work from Arran with the money. Though he had had ethical reasons for refusing, his own job will not be difficult artistically:

He had *never been very proud* of his adaptability. It had seemed to him to indicate the lack of an individual standpoint, and he had tried to counteract it by the cultivation of an aggressively personal style. But the cursed knack was in his fingers – he was always at the mercy of some other man's sensations, and there were moments when he *blushed* to remember that his grandfather had spent a laborious lifetime in Rome, copying the Old Masters for a generation which lacked the resource of the camera. Now, however, it struck him that the ancestral versatility might be a useful inheritance (673) [my emphasis].

The anonymous commission for Arran does not improve the sculptor's health in the end, and Stanwell has to put up with his and Kate's disdain because he abandoned their mutual high standards to do several society portraits (though he finally quit, disgusted at himself, and disgusting his dealer).

The story ends with Stanwell trying to offer Kate more money for her brother's care. He is 'silenced by her rising blush,' but he goes on to propose marriage, and then cannot look into her eyes (682). Kate flushes 'distressfully' because Stanwell has 'sold [his] talent. . . deliberately.' She accuses him: 'And you're not ashamed – you talk of going on!' Stanwell agrees that he is indeed 'not ashamed,' and justifies painting badly by saying he needed the money, but Kate sees him as lesser than Mungold, who hasn't made any such sacrifices – 'Mr Mungold paints as well as he can' (683). 'Her blush deepened miserably, but she held her head high'; Kate announces she is marrying Mungold 'because, though his pictures are bad, he does not prostitute his art' (684). The implication is clear enough, however, in her blushing and her attempt not to drop her head in shame that Kate knows full well that *she* is prostituting herself to help her brother. An interesting question left open at the end is the nature of Stanwell's talent – if he truly has a gift of imitation, then perhaps he hasn't abandoned his standards so shamefully? Once again in this story, we see the opposition between the struggling artist and the successful one, whose talent is shallow, and the shame of having one's work go unrecognized and unappreciated.

That Wharton wrote so often about artists who have failed and been disappointed, despite her own success, is not surprising, given what we have examined in Chapter 1 concerning her family and relationships. But her early and distinguished successes gave her increasing insights into the unexpected but nonetheless real pitfalls of success, as well as the nature of one's public reception and what we now call 'Public Relations.' Among the stories partly about success is one of her best, the relatively unknown 'Full Circle.' This ironic tour de force examines the relationship between a successful novelist and the failed novelist he unenthusiastically hired as his secretary to deal with the correspondence he expects to flood in after the publication of his second book.

Following the appearance of his first novel, *Diadems and Faggots*, Geoffrey Betton was thrilled by his very first fan letter, and thoroughly enjoyed seeing advertisements for the book, receiving clippings, and being recognized in public. But then 'his success began to submerge him'[34] and the letters became a flood. What irked him most was that the hundreds of letter writers told Betton what his book meant to *them*, but said very little about the book itself, and that, always in the 'same gush of adjectives.' Admiration turned to solicitation:

> His admirers were really unappeasable. . . . they wanted him to do such ridiculous things – to give lectures, to head movements, to be tendered receptions, to speak at banquets, to lead the struggle for sterilized milk. They wanted his photograph for literary supplements, his autograph for charity bazaars, his name on committees, literary, educational, and social; above all, they wanted his opinion on everything: on Christianity, Buddhism, tight lacing, the drug habit, democratic government, female suffrage and love. Perhaps the chief benefit of this demand was his incidentally learning from it how few opinions he really had: the only one that remained with him was a rooted horror of all forms of correspondence (74).

But when he advertised for a secretary to deal with the mail he dreads now that his second novel *Abundance* is due, he did not expect the ad to be answered by his old Harvard friend, Duncan Vyse. In the days when Betton was still only dreaming of a literary career, Vyse had practically given up on getting a novel published, and brought it to Betton, who had a friend in publishing. Betton kept forgetting to contact his friend (who would later publish *Diadems and Faggots*), and thus he understandably feels 'a vague embarrassment' and 'growing awkwardness' that Vyse would accept a job as his secretary (77). Betton disparages the position, asking 'Have you any idea of the deluge of stuff that people write to a successful novelist?' Vyse reddens and Betton blushes more deeply to have reminded him of the difference in their literary fortunes.

Betton discovers that Vyse is quite adept at writing replies that will be polite, but will not encourage more correspondence, yet after only about a week of 'freedom' from reading and answering his correspondence, Betton has 'a shame-faced desire to see his letters' (80). He 'carelessly' asks Vyse to submit them to him *first*, pretending it's not important after he's made such a great show of their burden. When the letters begin to diminish in number, he is embarrassed to discuss the change, and has a paranoid fear that Vyse is keeping some back. He is even more embarrassed to find out that he's wrong. The letters (and reviews) have at any rate been mostly critical of the second book, comparing it invidiously to *Diadems and Faggots*. What can Betton do? Keep the most offensive letters from Vyse? Then there would hardly be *any* for the secretary to answer, which would be 'more embarrassing,' given how Betton had predicted a flood of mail (81).

Angling to fire Vyse doesn't work because Vyse has been such a complete failure he'd take less money, an offer that makes Betton flush. But Vyse is beyond that: 'Oh, hang shame,' he says, and Betton, still guilty about not having sent Vyse's novel to his publisher friend, can't fire him (82). As the letters subside to a trickle, Betton is even more ashamed – surely Vyse is triumphing now, and being fired would prove that Betton is a failure! A sudden resurgence of letters (including a love letter) leaves Betton pleased, but after examining the handwriting, Vyse is suspicious that the same person is writing a number of them – possibly Betton's manservant. Betton is annoyingly sure Vyse thinks it is Betton himself who is behind the sudden increase in correspondence. 'The sense of being held under the lens of Vyse's mute scrutiny became more and more exasperating.' The public and 'glaring failure' of his book is made worse by 'Vyse's knowing it. That remained the central twinge in his diffused discomfort' (85). Still, he cannot fire Vyse, because his secretary will no doubt think Betton is 'ashamed to have him see that [he's] not getting any more letters' (85).

Letters resume after another pause, but this time with a difference; two correspondents dazzle Betton: a voluble intelligent girl from Florida and a Western college professor write 'remarkable' letters Betton blushingly wants to reply to himself. He has never had letters 'so personal, so exceptional.' Both praise his new novel with clarity and intelligence, especially the professor, and Betton 'blushed to think that his opinion of his work had been swayed by the shallow judgments of a public whose taste he despised. . . it was ridiculous to try to do conscientious work if one's self-esteem were at the mercy of popular judgments' (87-8). What a triumph to be understood; before, he 'had gulped the praise of *Diadems and Faggots* as indiscriminately as it was offered; now he knew for the first time the subtler pleasures of the palate' (87). Betton writes asking to meet the girl from Florida. When his letter returns from a Dead Letter Office Betton, unable to look at himself in a mirror, realizes that the author of his new fan letters has been Vyse. Betton admits to Vyse that *he* wrote the very first love letter before this recent series himself. In escalating embarrassment he accuses Vyse of writing the letters because Betton hated him seeing the book was a failure. Then he goes further, confessing his shame about the book he failed to help Vyse get published, but assuming now that Vyse sympathized with his disappointment. Or why else would he write the letters? In the story's last line, Vyse wearily replies that he only wanted to keep his job, because he's broke.

Betton was more burdened by the success of his first novel than he realized. It set up unrealistic expectations for the fate of his second book, and it hooked him on public praise. Relying on the opinions of strangers is perilous, given that Betton seems to have no internal sense of the value of his work, and no satisfaction that isn't based on the tangible, on the comforts his success has brought him. At his 'interview' with Vyse, Betton is uncomfortably aware 'that his high-colored well-fed person presented the image of commercial rather than of intellectual achievement' (78). But he has no idea why this should be so. Betton can only look outside, which partly explains why he feels so embarrassed around Vyse, who he is sure thinks his work is not literature but *business*. The story suggests that Vyse, who Betton admitted was brilliantly effective in faking the letters, has far more talent than Betton (in 'Her Father's Son' the husband wrote fan letters to a famous pianist 'from' his inexpressive wife, and they are so convincing that when his son reads them he assumes he is the pianist's son). Perhaps Vyse's talent explains why Betton never helped him. Betton's reliance on and vulnerability to the opinions of others reminds one of George Darrow in *The Reef*; the lack of deeply-based self-esteem can be the source of a good deal of unintentional cruelty. Wharton's notable achievement in 'Full Circle' is to make us sympathize with the comic problems of a successful novelist at the same time that we find Betton's self-awareness so limited and his treatment of Vyse, and his hunger for praise almost distasteful.

The novelist Mrs Dale in 'Copy' is even more exhausted by success than Betton, and a sign of her status is her secretary, who is blushingly keeping a diary about Mrs Dale that four publishers are already after! The mood in this fable-like tale is nostalgic. Mrs Dale and a former love, Ventnor, 'the great, great poet,'[35] reminisce about the old days before their fame. Days when they 'didn't prepare. . . impromptu effects beforehand and copyright. . . remarks about the weather!' Back then, epigrams didn't have to be kept 'in cold storage' and 'a signature wasn't an autograph' (285). Now, however, Mrs Dale is all too aware of the value of her autographs, just as Ventnor is hyperconscious of the value of his first, hard-to-find volume of poems. And each wants to use the other's love letters in their memoirs, though Ventnor is far more embarrassed about the plan than she is.

Mrs Dale, the more sensitive of the two (compare her romantic last name to his, which is close to 'vendor'), no longer feels like a real person, because of her fame. She tells Ventnor: 'I died years ago. What you see before you is a figment of the reporter's brain – a monster manufactured out of newspaper paragraphs, with ink in its veins. A keen sense of copyright is *my* nearest approach to an emotion' (278). She has, of course, contributed to her sense of unreality: her study is described as full of autographed books and its most salient feature is a portrait of her at her desk, working. The story seems a cautionary tale warning against the loss of self to one's public, especially through the embarrassing, revealing private papers, which Ventnor and Mrs Dale agree to burn here. They thus deprive their publics – and ironically themselves – of 'copy.'

What does it take to succeed as a novelist? The delightful answer in the Wildean 'Expiation' is public scandal that will actually not be humiliating but *remunerative*. Paula Fetherel, new to being an author, awaits the reviews of her novel *Fast and Loose*, brightly blushing, afraid that it will be a *succès de scandale*. She is anxious about dragging her husband's name 'through the mire,' because she didn't publish the book under a pseudonym:

> 'There would have been no merit in publishing such a book under an assumed name; it would have been an act of moral cowardice. *Fast and Loose* is not an ordinary novel. A writer who dares to show up the hollowness of social conventions must have the courage of her convictions and be willing to accept the consequences of defying society. Can you imagine Ibsen or Tolstoi writing under a false name?'[36]

Her cousin Mrs Clinch, the author of natural science books, vows that *she* would love to be denounced – it would certainly boost her sales. But Mrs Fetherel takes this for bad taste until her uncle, the

Bishop of Ossining, tells her the only way for a novel to succeed is through being 'denounced by the press' (443). He himself has authored 'Through a Glass Brightly,' or 'How to Raise Funds for a Memorial Window,' to raise money for a chantry window, and the book is not selling. His publisher has told him that

> 'if a critic were to be found, who called in question the morality of my heroine in sacrificing her own health and that of her idiot sisters in order to put up a memorial window to her grandfather, it would probably raise a general controversy in the newspapers, and I might count on a sale of ten or fifteen thousand within the next year' (443).

A charge of morbidity or decadence would add five thousand more copies sold! All this enlightening talk of sales and pulpit denunciation leads to a serious setback for Paula, however. Though she now understands that the critical condemnation she expects about her book will actually help it sell, *Fast and Loose* is uniformly found to be 'sweetly inoffensive' and 'a distinctly pretty story' (447). She is crushed.

The Bishop then denounces Paula's book, which soars in popularity, and she is 'blushing, embarrassed and happy' to be recognized in public (452), and blushes when she runs into a novelist who praised her novel. Attending the unveiling of the chantry window at her uncle's cathedral, she is deeply thrilled to be recognized and stared at. The Bishop refers to a woman's generosity in connection with the 'anonymous gift' that made the window possible and amid stirring and staring in the church, Paula pulls 'down her veil to conceal an uncontrollable blush' (454). But after much grandiloquent pussy-footing, the Bishop credits his *own* novel as having inspired the gift. Paula is left relieved, angry, blushing. The Bishop's artistic jealousy – which leads him to ignore Mrs Clinch, whose books tend to be reprinted – has saved Paula from exposure, yet she is ironically outraged to have him steal the credit. She is ashamed, but silenced. Her next book, however, will be clearer, and will not need a public denunciation to make its public understand. The title of Paula's book is that of Wharton's own adolescent novel, and Wharton pokes more fun at herself, when Paula proclaims that her novel exposes 'the hollowness of our social shams' (441) – which *The House of Mirth* would certainly do a year later.

Wharton's satire of the publishing industry and the reading public in this story appears in a number of stories. In 'The Legend' Pellerin's work had been turned into a giddy fad; Willis French in 'The Temperate Zone' realizes that he has gotten to write a book about 'his idol,' the painter Horace Fingall, only 'because the vulgar herd at last wanted to know what to say, when it heard Fingall mentioned. . . such was the base rubble the Temple of Fame was built of!'[37] The editor in 'The Angel at the Grave' explains to Paulina Anson what audiences are really like:

> 'Literature's like a big railway-station now, you know: there's a train starting every minute. People are not going to hang around the waiting-room. If they can't get to a place when they want to they go somewhere else.'[38]

The scientist author of a pastiche of current pseudo-science writing in 'The Descent of Man' discovers that his editor and the public *adore* his book, find it deep and moving and spiritual, and he is swayed by the money he earns to consider a sequel. In the justifiably classic 'Xingu,' with its 'women who pursue Culture in bands, as though it were dangerous to meet alone,'[39] learning is merely one-upmanship, and the story is all about shame. Unwilling to be exposed, one character after another pretends to more knowledge than she has, including the sullen, abrasive, taciturn authoress, 'Osric Dane,' who cannot admit that she has never heard of 'Xingu.' In the stories about painters, their public is likewise ignorant, admiring the false and shabby. As an art dealer explains in 'The Potboiler,' the buying public wants what is different from their friends' paintings, but just the same, in the same style. It is a practical, but gloomy assessment.

In 'Expiation,' Paula Fetherel is cursed, as she sometimes sees it, with a loving understanding husband, who makes it hard to be misunderstood, and who fatuously approves of *everything* she does, and is ready to shout her reviews from the rooftops. This is Wharton's most comic view of the emotional relationship (whether friendship, marriage or an affair) with an artist or writer. Another light examination of being married or in love with a great artist is the focus of Wharton's entertaining 'The Temperate Zone,' in which the widow of the painter Horace Fingall and the fiancé of Emily Morland (who died before she could gain happiness) marry each other. Willis French, a biographer, thinks that for both, 'any other marriage would have been a derogation,' and they have thus 'found the one way of remaining on the heights.' This union of 'two custodians of great memories' is thus a doubling of status – anything else would be shameful.[40] And Mrs Fingall gains *new* heights, as a celebrated fashion plate, even though she sees her late husband's work 'in terms of the auction room and the stock exchange!' (462)

Willis French is deeply disappointed because he had been seeking to understand the connection between Fingall's work and his private life. Meeting Fingall's widow shows him nothing – she is merely beautiful and empty. In explanation of her addiction to comfort and dressmakers, her new husband, Donald Paul, blushingly explains that the Fingalls lived a bare and desolate life, and Fingall would have done better had he allowed Mrs Fingall to manage his business affairs – but he admits that living with a great artist is 'different.' Donald Paul is protective of Emily Morland's memory, and gently entreats French to help him with her papers and write a biography. He even gives French, by way of thanks, a sketch of Morland done by Fingall that they unexpectedly find – the only one in existence. The former Mrs Fingall is not so generous and pressures French to use his influence to get the international portraitist, Jolyesse, to do her portrait (Fingall despised the man's work). The joke is that French knows Jolyesse would be happy to paint her, and for free. While both she and Donald seem somewhat unworthy of the great artists they were involved with, the former Mrs Fingall tackles her new role without shame and without insight, whereas Donald is more hesitant and embarrassed. He seems aware of his relative insignificance, while Fingall's widow can only glory in her importance. It is deeply embarrassing for French to watch her and listen to the glib generalities she uses to discuss Fingall's work. Donald Paul is more human, and commendable in his tact.

Wharton tends to depict her artists and writers as alone, like Pellerin in 'The Legend' and Granice in 'The Bolted Door,' or unloved, like Margaret Aubyn in *The Touchstone*. Those wives, lovers or relatives of artists she does treat are made unhappy by their deeper insight into the artists' work or personalities: Lizzie West in 'The Letters,' Claudia Day in 'The Recovery,'; or are wasted by their devotion, like Paulina Anson, who has never even met her grandfather.

Two stories in Wharton's first collection, *The Greater Inclination*, consider the nature of a relationship with an artist or writer in far darker terms than 'The Temperate Zone.' 'The Muse's Tragedy' turns on the opposite of scandalous revelation, and seems almost a sort of refraction of a novel like *The Aspern Papers*. The young poet and writer Danyers, who reveres the poetry of the late Vincent Rendle, meets the great man's muse, Mrs Anerton, and discovers her relationship to Rendle was not what the world thought. Mrs Anerton's name 'was enshrined in some of the noblest English verse of the nineteenth century,'[41] and appears to have inspired Rendle's sonnets as well as 'playful, tender, incomparable prose' (68). Danyers first heard that she is alive through a friend, Mrs Memorall, who pictures Mrs Anerton as a very isolated woman: 'The fact is, she cared only about [Rendle's] friends – she separated herself gradually from all her own people. . . she was always so engrossed, so preoccupied, that one felt one wasn't wanted' (68). Even staying with her one time, Mrs Memorall didn't see Rendle, zealously guarded by the 'ridiculous' Mr Anerton (now dead), who seemed to think of the poet as a family possession.

Mrs Memorall sends her friend Mary Anerton Danyers' volume of sketches which includes an 'appreciation' of Rendle, but the young writer is disappointed by her note of thanks, in terms that recall Betton's disappointment in 'Full Circle' about his fans; she has clearly written such acknowledgements before. On vacation in Europe, Danyers runs into Mrs Anerton, who is far more complimentary about his work in person, even though she reminds him he is very young. His feeling for Rendle over the course of a month together with Mrs Anerton becomes more personal, and he is struck by her perfect balance in speaking of Rendle's books, his critics, his 'intellectual life. . . habits of thought and work.' However, Mrs Anerton never shares anything intimate about the great poet.

She begins to emerge as *Danyers'* muse: ' "You must write," she said, administering the most exquisite flattery that human lips could give' (72). Inspired (and who wouldn't be?), Danyers decides to do a *great* book about Rendle – with Mrs Anerton's help. We later learn in a letter from Mrs Anerton to Danyers that the book was never written, that both were glad of it because they fell in love, and that Mrs Anerton was not Rendle's inspiration because he did not ever love her. Finally she can confess, can open herself up to someone. Victor Rendle sought relief from boredom with Mrs Anerton – she was 'part of his intellectual life,' but nothing more (74). Gossip led to her being invited where he was, and considered his lover; it also made her popular, influential and aggressively sought after. Mrs Anerton understandably never disabused anyone, and to hide the shame of being unloved, when she edited his letters, she inserted ellipses, to make it seem that the more personal passages had been excised for reasons of privacy and good taste! After his death, a flurry of articles and books brought Rendle back to her in 'a kind of mirage of love' (76), but that faded, and she was left with the bitter knowledge that 'he had never cared' (75).

Did Rendle comprehend how cruel his relationship with her was, even though he never pretended anything but friendship? Mrs Anerton cannot know, but she doubts her own attractiveness so much that out of shame, she makes Danyers fall in love with her, in an 'experiment' she claims is crueler to herself than to him. She has discovered that Danyers can love her for herself, and not for her relationship to Rendle – she thus has an identity that transcends her role as muse. But having made Danyers fall in love has taught her how much she has missed.

Readers of Wharton's letters and fiction will be struck by the parallels with this early story: the struggle to understand being profoundly rejected by a man that is a theme of her letters to Fullerton, and Margaret Aubyn's letters to Stephen Glennard in *The Touchstone*. A phrase Mrs Anerton quotes from Pascal in explaining herself to Danyers – *il faut de l'adresse pour aimer* – occurs in Wharton's writing to Fullerton years later. She uses the line – 'one needs skill to love' – in a long letter from the Mount that R.W.B. Lewis calls 'brilliant' and almost 'a masterpiece.'[42] Wharton labels the quotation 'terrible' because she suspects it may not simply mean that one should be tactful in love, but dissembling, dishonest. Mrs Anerton uses it to illustrate how she never bored or troubled Rendle, and yet her own life was in many ways dishonest, built on a public assumption that was untrue and a private hope that was vain. It is deeply ironic that Wharton could not be, like her character, 'so quiet, so cheerful, so frankly affectionate' (76) in her letters to Fullerton, but her rage and shame burst through.

What is most intriguing, however, is the sense of waste and cruelty in this story – Mrs Anerton made Rendle's life comfortable, but lost all sense of herself and her self-respect. Yet when she befriended Danyers and made him fall in love with her, she became as unloving and cruel in her own way as Rendle was to her. She re-enacts this governing scene of being unloved by actually taking the other role, and indeed reversing roles, turning Danyers into herself. One way of responding to shame in an effort to control it is by recasting scenes in just this manner. It is a story almost as bleak as another in the same volume, 'Souls Belated.'

Lydia Tillotson in that story has fled a New York marriage and life of 'purely automatic acts'[43] for wandering in Europe with her lover Gannett, but she detests the sense of obligation that her flight entails: society will expect Gannett to 'do the decent thing' (107) as a gentleman and marry her, and she feels as if her husband has thrown her at Gannett. During their 'wanderings. . . like the flight of outlaws' through Europe, with 'tacit avoidance of their kind' (111) Lydia has 'the exasperated sense of having walked into the trap of some stupid practical joke' (107). She does not want him to marry her just because anything else is shameful: she makes very clear to him that it would be humiliating, a 'vulgar fraud upon. . . a society [they] despised and laughed at. . . sneaking back into a position that [they'd] voluntarily forfeited' (110).

The situation is complicated by his writing, Gannett having 'made himself known as a successful writer of short stories and of a novel which had achieved the distinction of being widely discussed' (112–13). But this promising young writer, who said 'her companionship could bring out his latent faculty' (113) has written nothing since they left America. Lydia blushes when she realizes that, and at not having even thought about his work recently; she feels guilty about the possibility of assuming 'before posterity, the responsibility of thwarting his career' (113). Neither can look at the other when Gannett suggests settling down somewhere out of the way, even though his best work 'has been done in a crowd – in big cities.' Gannett lamely says 'It might be different now; I can't tell, of course, till I try. A writer ought not to be dependent on his *milieu*; it's a mistake to humor oneself in that way' (109). They have been in each other's company, alone, for too long.

Their stay at an Anglo–American hotel is pleasant (not least for breaking up their isolation), and Gannett at first seems embarrassed to be bursting with ideas. Their incognito is threatened, however, when an Englishwoman in the same position as Lydia threatens to unmask her in the hotel's stuffy little social world if she doesn't get Gannett to find out what *her* lover's plans are. Even though the exposure doesn't come, both Lydia and Gannett are ashamed, and feel that they have 'behaved basely, abominably' in pretending to be married (121).

The story ends with a stalemate of sorts: Lydia tries to leave, but fails, and they are stuck with each other, heading, it seems, for Paris to get married. After 'having seen the nakedness of each other's souls' (123), they must settle for – ironically – the distance that marriage can provide. They are bound by shame, by 'a hundred ties of pity and self-reproach' (125). It is a desolate story. Lydia sought to be his muse, saw that as her one excuse for leaving her husband, but she seems to have failed, and it is not clear what the impact will be on his writing. If he is able to write again, and is successful, then that makes a mockery of her feeling they can live fruitfully outside of society.

The story is, like so many others of Wharton's, replete with blushing, looking down or away, and clear references to shame and humiliation. It is in a way a light sketch of the relationship between Vance Weston and Halo Tarrant that Wharton would write some thirty years later in *Hudson River Bracketed* and *The Gods Arrive*, and as inconclusive. Those two novels bring together all of Wharton's themes about writers and artists: the satire of publishers and the reading public, the difficulties of a relationship with an artist, the exigencies of popularity, the conflict between writing for oneself and for others, the pain of artistic failure, and add something even more significant – the search for one's authentic voice.

II

The failures of *Hudson River Bracketed* and *The Gods Arrive* have certainly been much discussed and analyzed. The first volume is damned for its sprawling unruly canvas, its overly broad satire of the Midwest and the New York literary scene. Marilyn French (among others) has noted the surprising change in the second volume from the first: Vance is far more egotistical and Halo far more dependent and subservient in *The Gods Arrive*.[44] For me, the books are a diptych of shame: in the first Vance is battered by experiences of shame in his personal, social and professional life. In the second novel the situation is for the most part reversed – it is Halo who consistently experiences shame at Vance's hands through belittling, rejection and his desire for another woman, and in her role as a woman outside society. In her very last completed novel, Wharton thus returns to the same familiar territory as 'Souls Belated' and many other stories and novels: she cannot conceive of a relationship between a man and woman in which shame does not wound one or the other – or both. Being in intimate relationships, for Wharton, is inevitably an experience that triggers shame.

Hudson River Bracketed is a somewhat sprawling novel, no doubt because its writing was interrupted by Wharton's pneumonia, and she felt harassed by its serial publication starting sooner than planned. It is the story of a young Midwestern man who comes to New York to be a writer. Struggling in the publishing and literary world there, Vance Weston ends up trapped not only in a restricting contract that limits his options as a writer, but in a stultifying marriage to a sweet but unintellectual young cousin – Laura Lou Tracey – who eventually dies of pneumonia. Vance discovers a sense of the past back East, partly through the help of a cousin of the Traceys, sophisticated Halo Tarrant, who becomes his muse. The novel shows him overcoming the limitations of his background, dealing with unexpected success and failure, trying to reconcile his drive and devotion to writing with the demands of the world he has to live in, and searching for the right artistic form that will best use his talents. While critics usually start with Vance in discussing the novel, analyzing how he represents Wharton's ideas about creativity, the artist, and The Novel, I want to first focus on Halo Tarrant's husband, a publisher and would-be writer who is the first man to hire Vance in New York, and becomes in a way his judge and jailer. Lewis Tarrant is a familiar figure in Wharton's writing about artists and writers – an egotist and a failure – only here he has much greater play and his story works antiphonally with Vance's, showing what artists should not be and should not do.

We see Lewis Tarrant almost entirely through his wife Halo's perspective and it is important to note *her* link with Wharton's gallery of failed artists and writers as we consider his. Halo's 'eager interest in life' has been unmatched by real talent. 'She could half paint, she could half write. . . Even had discipline and industry fostered her slender talents, they would hardly have brought her a living.' Thus, convinced that 'her real gift. . . was for appreciating [and, perhaps, appropriating?] the gifts of others,'[45] she marries a man who in many ways confirms this somewhat low opinion of herself. Tarrant's arrogance appeals to her at first. Just as Anna was impressed by Fraser Leath in *The Reef*, Halo is impressed 'by the critical aloofness of mind, which unbent *only for her'* (478) [my emphasis]. Like Anna Leath, she is strongly motivated by shame, marrying someone critical and cold because his attention to her is flattering: if someone with such high standards, someone so discriminating finds her attractive – then surely she has value in the world?

But Halo has married a man who is jealous of her potential (however minor) and clearly afraid of competition with his wife. Lewis Tarrant 'always encouraged Halo in the practice of the arts he had himself abandoned, and while gently disparaging her writing was increasingly disposed to think there was "something in" her experiments with paint and clay' (212). In Tarrant's 'workshop-study,' Halo has 'a *corner* for her modelling and painting [my emphasis],' and as Mary Suzanne Schrieber notes, 'Halo infrequently tries her hand at the arts.'[46] Lewis wants to be a novelist, and comes to this goal after far more significant failures than Halo's: 'various unsuccessful experiments, first in architecture, then in painting' (181). Like so many of Wharton's artists or writers, Lewis's 'appetite for praise [grows] coarser' as his worth seems to go unrecognized by the world at large (461).

Halo wonders if Lewis' wealth isn't an impediment to the budding of his talent, but she is aware of a deeper problem – he is almost completely at the mercy of other people's opinions. Though outwardly cool and calm, inside of him there burns 'such a hunger for approbation' (181). When Tarrant buys the ailing literary journal *Hour*, we see how his egotism demands constant propitiation, as in the following typical exchange between Tarrant and his wife:

'Funny – perhaps what I was really meant for was to be an editor,' he said to his wife, with the depreciatory smile which disguised such a fervour of self-esteem. 'Not a very dazzling career – I suppose I might have looked rather higher; but it may give me the chance to make myself known. . .' [Wharton's ellipsis].

'Of course, Lewis; it's what I've always wanted for you.'

'It is? You've thought –?' he began with his look of carefully suppressed avidity (180).

Halo also needs to help put Lewis together after an emotional scene with anyone – during it, he can control himself, but afterwards he is a nervous wreck. It is Halo's role to help 'him back to self-esteem after one of his collapses; to do so was almost as necessary to her pride as to his' (469). This pattern is strikingly reminiscent of contemporary descriptions of 'co-dependency' in families and relationships where addiction plays a major role. Co-dependents identify with an addicted person, helping maintain balance in the family or relationship by 'denial, control, protection, and minimizing.' Throughout this novel and its sequel, we often see Halo smiling when she is angry, placating, soothing, hiding her own feelings. Like one kind of co-dependent, her desire to be 'accepted and liked' leads her to try pleasing others 'by agreeing with their thoughts, feelings and behaviors.'[47] Her marriage is 'a world of suffocating dissimulations' (174). Despite what she knows to be true, she often agrees with Lewis, and such dishonesty is a further source of shame. One defense against revealing the pain of such dishonest interactions is 'exaggerated helpfulness.' We see how she offers herself to Lewis as well as to Vance, deriving her 'sense of self-worth from taking care of others.'[48] That Wharton so clearly delineated aspects of this dynamic decades before it reached clinical salience, only attests once again to her intimate knowledge of shame.

Lewis Tarrant is utterly bound by shame: 'Every form of external recognition, even the most casual and unimportant, was needed to fortify his self-confidence' (205). Moment to moment, Lewis' perilous internal balance has to be protected. Halo understands her husband's 'exaggerated craving for recognition' as connected to 'a morbid modesty.' And she can no longer laugh at Lewis' need for everyone including the milkman to know how clever he is (205). He experiences no coherent self, no self-esteem, in the absence of reflected appraisals of others. How can such a man be truly creative, when there seems to be no core from which he can create?

Tarrant cannot think for himself, though 'the myth of his intellectual isolation was necessary to Tarrant's pride' (208). He relies on Halo to supply him with opinions that he gradually appropriates and propounds with so much authority that people admire him for knowing 'his own mind' (220). Newness and change leave him 'exhilarated. . . buoyant and masterful' (329), offering as they do splendid possibilities for self-aggrandizement. But for someone who is so completely tied to what other people think, and seems to have no internal standard of achievement, buying a journal is a big mistake. He is linked too closely with its success, as opposed to its quality, though both suffer after initial acclaim. As the magazine (which prints two of Vance Weston's stories) goes into a slump, its rather ordinary performance is both 'mortifying' and 'humiliating' to Tarrant. While such a slide is to be expected, given the difficulty of making *any* journal successful, Tarrant needs to be special, different, *better*, not have 'somebody else's failure. . . become *his*' (329). Tarrant may annex all success as his own, but 'as soon as an enterprise gave the least sign of failure it was Tarrant's instinct to disclaim all responsibility for it' (450). This is a clear example of the transfer of blame strategy that emerges as one prominent defending strategy in response to shame internalization. By transferring blame elsewhere, Lewis also transfers shame away from himself.

It is not surprising that Tarrant's predominant affect interpersonally is contempt, another strategy for controlling shame, which we have seen operating in *The Mother's Recompense* in Kate Clephane, among others. He may rely on Halo's opinions and literary judgments, but he cannot accept the reality of his debt to her, and therefore needs to diminish her in order to keep feeling superior. Halo sees all that, and tingles 'with shame at her lucidity' (184). She has to be careful in what she praises and how, because she has learned how much her husband enjoys 'the satisfaction of asserting his superiority by depreciating what she had praised' (209). We will see below how his contempt affects Vance, but for Halo it has been savage, 'his cool incisiveness cutting into the soul like a white-hot blade into flesh' (467). The ultimate humiliation for Halo, however, and the one that leads to her feeling little more than 'indifference' in their marriage is related to money.

Just when she had decided not to marry Lewis, she discovered that 'all through his courtship, her family had been secretly and *shamelessly* borrowing from him' (462) [my emphasis]. The reverse is true as well – Tarrant had been shamelessly *lending* money, creating a claim on Halo (because he doubted he could win her otherwise?) which she felt bound to honor, though he never mentioned the loans. Yet he clearly resented them, as he reveals during an argument about lending money to Vance Weston when Vance's wife is sick, and thus lays 'bare to [Halo] the corner of his mind where old grudges and rancours were stored' (335). It is a moment that is deeply humiliating to them both, she believes, though Lewis hardly seems to feel it. Lewis' great show of tact all this time has been a deeper assertion of power and superiority over her – to have talked about the loans openly, and about how he currently supports her family, would have diminished the shame. But the issue has been lurking all along.

Discouraged by the *Hour*'s impending failure, Lewis takes to writing a novel, under the encouragement of Jet Pulsifer (creator of a literary prize Wharton modeled after the Pulitzer), a woman one might call more egotistical than Tarrant if she weren't such a wraithlike, scatterbrained dim-wit. Tarrant's desire to write, like his other artistic endeavors, does not seem to stem from having anything to say, or from honest creativity or even honest pain, but from a hunger for praise, for recognition, a hunger that can never be satisfied because it is so terribly remorseless. In that way, Tarrant is the very opposite of Vance Weston, whose writing is first stimulated by sorrow and shame, and is always an attempt to express what is inside of him first and foremost – his *vision*, not his plea for fame. Vance struggles for a voice, Tarrant merely struggles for recognition, and Wharton shows unerring insight into his pettiness, his cruelty, and the dominating role of shame and contempt in his personality.

In choosing Vance Weston's Midwestern background and showing how he overcame it, I do not believe that Wharton was merely indulging in shrill and derivative criticism of her own country – though that has long been the critical consensus. Rather, it seems that she was attempting to find an environment that would be as indifferent and even inimical to literature as her own was, and thus as powerful a source of shame. She needed something emotionally analogous, yet outwardly different enough from her own background, especially because, as Louis Auchincloss remarks, Vance is 'an extension of Mrs Wharton's vision of herself.'[49] At any rate, I think it is a mistake to dismiss Vance's background as crudely done, second-hand Sinclair Lewis, or mere vicious animosity towards a country she didn't really know. James Tuttleton has observed that Wharton's aim in *Hudson River Bracketed* was dramatizing 'the disastrous consequences of cultural deprivation for the American who aspires to be an artist.'[50] But the deprivation goes beyond Vance's specific location to the *emotional* realities. What is crucial here is Wharton's conception of *this* writer's background as both limiting and shame-inducing.

If Wharton grew up in an environment where she lacked intelligent conversation and intellectual stimulus, and in which a life of letters was considered suspect, Vance Weston's home and milieu are just as restrictive in their own way. A real estate broker, Vance's father 'could not conceive of any other career for' (25) his son in an atmosphere where business was king and 'success was the only criterion of beauty' (9). Though people in Euphoria pay lip service to good breeding and social knowledge, they know that 'the real business of life was to keep going, to get there – and "There" was where money was, always and exclusively' (15). Along with an exaggerated reverence for newness, these are the sole values Vance has grown up with. Vance wants to be a writer or poet, but even that desire is shaped by his narrow perspective. He thinks that he should work as a journalist because 'he had never heard of any way to Parnassus save that which led through the columns of the daily press, and ranged from baseball reports to the exposure of business scandals' (24–25). George Frenside, a critic and friend of Halo Tarrant, will later tell Vance in New York that journalism cannot lead to a career as a writer.

But Vance's sense of values is not as immediate a source of shame as is his lack of education. Wharton perhaps overdoes Vance's deficits, making him claim that he never read Coleridge's 'Kubla Khan,' for instance (though he knows 'The Ancient Mariner'), a poem that startles and profoundly awakens him. What she seems to be driving at is his hunger, like the hunger *she* experienced as a child. Throughout the book, Vance to his embarrassment keeps discovering what he doesn't know about literature (which makes him at times seem less like a hick and more like a frantic graduate student). For instance, when he is on the staff of the *Hour* in New York he will discover that he has no idea who 'The Russians' are. Living on slender means in New York before he gets that job at the *Hour*, he becomes terribly conscious of looking like 'a hayseed and an ignoramus.' In the New York Public Library at 42nd Street, Vance will read voraciously because 'his ignorance. . . revealed itself on a scale. . . unsuspected and overwhelming' (159). But the first and most important setting in which his ignorance is thrown into high relief is at The Willows, the book-rich house his cousins the Traceys are caretakers for. It is an evocative, romantic example of mid-nineteenth century Hudson River Bracketed architecture (owned by a cousin of the Traceys' and of Halo's), with a library full of classics Vance seems to have never heard of. And indeed he has 'never been in a private library before' (59). The appeal of the house both shows his sensitivities and his ignorance. Its glimpsed façade suggests 'vastness, fantasy, secrecy' (55), and the house itself represents 'a past so remote from anything in [his] experience it took its place in the pages of history anywhere in the dark Unknown before Euphoria' (59). In R. W. B. Lewis's trenchant observation, for Vance The Willows becomes 'an imperfectly perceived symbol of the rich American past which he now confusedly longs to attach himself to.'[51]

This ignorance of literature and lack of sophistication is not entirely negative. Vance certainly feels ashamed of what he doesn't know about books and life (especially *New York* life), but he attempts to overcome his deficits and those attempts are sources of information, insight, and growth. Here is a crucial difference between Vance and Lewis Tarrant. Imagine Tarrant finding out that there is a writer he doesn't know about, but *should*. He would hide that, or somehow implicate Halo in his ignorance or find out what *she* knows and appropriate her opinions. When pressed, he might act like the women in 'Xingu' too mortified to admit they have never heard of 'Xingu,' in turn believing it to be a philosophy, a set of rites, a language, a religion, a book. Vance has no compunction in asking Halo in New York who the Russians are, if she has them, and if he can borrow the books. His forthrightness in this instance is of a piece with his emotional directness (and part of what she most admires in him). Thus Vance is not entirely crippled by his dismaying lack of information – he actively seeks a remedy. If this shame about being 'uneducated' thus becomes transformed in a way, an even deeper source of shame becomes transformed by his creativity.

The event that precipitates Vance's visit to his Tracey cousins in New York State – and thus eventually leads to his meeting Halo, moving to New York and becoming known as a writer – is a shameful discovery. Vance finds out that his reprobate grandfather is sleeping with Vance's first love, Floss Delaney, who will reappear in *The Gods Arrive* as a lustrous vamp. Here she is 'the somewhat blown-upon daughter of an unsuccessful real estate man' (3), but 'his body and soul still glowed with the memory' (15) of their former relationship. Right after seeing his grandfather jauntily headed for *his* own old trysting place with Floss, Vance is on the point of announcing to his family that he wants to be a writer, but is overcome by the shame and disgust of his discovery: 'something hot and choking welled up in his throat' (26). Vance recovers from subsequent weeks of illness to feel himself 'gorged with disgust.' 'The fair face of the world had been besmirched'

(30). The language is strikingly similar to Kate Orme's painful musings in *Sanctuary*, when she realizes moral ugliness is inescapable in life. Vance feels his life has been ruined, that he 'was like a captive walled into a dark airless cell. . .' (30). But 'he was resolved not to be beaten' and finds relief in writing a story:

> He began hastily, feverishly, the words rushing from his pen like water from a long-obstructed spring, and as the paragraphs grew it seemed to him at last he had found out a way of reconciling his soul to his experiences. He would set them down just as they had befallen him in all their cruel veracity, but as if he were relating the tragedy of someone else (31).

Thus Vance, as a writer, has what so many of Wharton's prisoners of shame do not: a way of distancing himself from his inner and outer experience, of shaping and controlling it in some measure. In *The Gods Arrive*, a now-successful Vance will reflect that artists 'were the happy people – the only happy people perhaps – these through whom the human turmoil swept not to ravage but to fertilize.'[52]

Vance's story – 'One Day' – will not only be printed by *Hour* once but twice, the second time when Lewis Tarrant takes over the journal and discovers it in a back issue. And the story will even be up for consideration for the Pulsifer Prize, establishing a small foothold for Vance on the rocky cliffs of literary New York. Though Vance has no regrets about having written the story or sold it, when it appears in print he is *ashamed*: 'he would have been glad to wipe those pages out of existence, and still more glad to blot from his memory the money they had brought him. . .' (188) [Wharton's ellipsis]. Like Ivy Spang in 'Writing a War Story,' publication makes him feel exposed, but Vance has a great deal more to feel exposed about than she did: the story is deeply autobiographical and full of his 'youthful indignation' (188). Like Wharton's own early tales, it seems to have been written at the 'top of [his] voice,'[53] and given that he too found early publication in the first writing he submitted, it seems likely that Wharton also felt exposed by some of her early publications, which so nakedly treat the dissatisfactions and disappointment of her married life. Unlike Vance, there was a good chance that people she knew would read her published work.

Vance undergoes a number of significant shaming experiences after leaving Euphoria for New York State and then New York City. Because he was raised in an environment that urges progress and renovation (his grandmother wants to reform 'everything'), the drowsy shabby town of Paul's Landing where his cousins live strikes Vance with 'a shock of something like humiliation' (37). His cousins do not at all have the life he expected, are less privileged and comfortable than he was back home. This is his first great disappointment on his quest to be a writer. When Halo Tarrant's shiftless brother Lorry steals some valuable books from the library at The Willows, Vance – as the outsider who has spent a good deal of time going through the books – is blamed as the obvious suspect. At Halo's mute urging, he ends up hiding his knowledge that it must have been Lorry. This humiliation is heightened by his being accused by his landlady, Mrs Tracey, of having led her son Upton on a drunken debauch in New York, when it is really the brother who initiated the whole adventure. There is of course much blushing and rage in Vance, and he leaves, 'diminished and ashamed' (151). By way of apology, he sends Mrs Tracey a silly, elaborate floral arrangement from New York which leaves him 'ashamed of his stupidity' (155). He really couldn't afford the gift, but bought it out of shame, to show the New York florist that he had the money. This gathering storm of shame seems to assault and propel him at that point in the book in the way that Lily Bart seems overcome in *The House Of Mirth* when she is cut by Bertha Dorset and then disinherited. Everything seems to be conspiring against Vance's peace of mind and self-esteem at this point.

A key scene following this sequence in the novel is Vance's seeking out of George Frenside in New York to show him his poetry. Up until his funds were fading, Vance felt that 'he would rather have starved than appeal' to the critic and editor (157); though Halo had given Frenside Vance's poetry, Frenside never remarked on it. Now, however, Vance is desperate, and an interaction with the potential of shaming him turns into something else. Mortified that he hasn't been able to type his poetry, Vance has to listen to Frenside dismiss it as 'Poet's Corner Stuff. Try it on your hometown paper' (165). He is less tactful than Wharton was in writing to the soldier mentioned above, but Wharton shows here *her* recognition of the initial impact her remarks might well have had. Discouraged, weary, Vance feels utterly isolated, descending 'the steep stairs of failure' (166). But what takes hold inside of him is Frenside's advice that Vance not try for a news-paper job because it won't be helpful to him as a writer. He may have felt disparaged, dismissed, and treated like 'any other young fool who presented himself to an editor with a first bundle of manuscript' (167) – but he feels *liberated* now. Of *course* journalism isn't the way – hadn't he always suspected that? This insight leads him to send off 'One Day' to Frenside, who publishes it in *Hour*, and later realize that out of his terrible experience came 'the means of deliverance' (189). This dynamic of disappointment or discour-agement leading to a *reversal* of feeling, and a burst of creativity, seems to me a telling insight into how many writers function. Other characters of Wharton's have no such recourse, and are more deeply enmeshed in their shame, unable to escape even temporarily. At one point in *The Gods Arrive*, for example, compar-ing herself to Vance, Halo Spear will bitterly reflect that Vance will get over his pain and the pain he is causing her: 'He'll use it up in a story, and it will go on living in me and feeding on me.'[54]

Much later in *Hudson River Bracketed*, Vance will be embarrassed to have his 'hick' background brought to the attention of the fashionable literary set he has become a part of when his grand-mother preaches in New York. A religious woman whose fuzzy rhetoric makes her sound like an early Leo Buscaglia, Grandma Scrimser makes no impression in New York, and Vance is both ashamed of her public embarrassment and naturally angry – at those who mocked her, and at her failure to move them, 'torn between his disillusionment and his wrath against those who had shared it' (438). He of course identifies with his beloved grand-mother despite deploring 'the national tolerance of ignorance' her success elsewhere represents: 'He too was the raw product of a Middle-Western town, trying to do something beyond his powers, to tell the world about things he wasn't really familiar with; his pride winced at the exactness of the analogy. . .' (439). Though poor, and needing money for his wife's illnesses, Vance can't take money from his grandmother because it feels like the product of an intellectual fraud.

Louis Auchincloss finds the disintegrating marriage of Vance and Laura Lou as absorbing as the story of Vance's career as an artist, and it certainly is a compelling portrait of a hopelessly mismatched couple.[55] As Carol Wershoven notes, what attracted Vance to Laura Lou was her greater ignorance and helplessness:

'her uncritical adoration of Vance seems a refreshing contrast to Halo's high standards.'[56] But when the marriage is a failure he will of course compare his wife to Halo and find Laura Lou deficient because she does not satisfy his intelligence:

> Into the world of his mind, with its consuming curiosities, its fervid joys, [Laura Lou] would never enter – would never even discover that it existed. Sometimes, when a new idea grew in him like a passion, he ached to share it with her, but not for long. He had never known that kind of companionship, had just guessed at it through the groping wonder of his first talks with Halo Spear, when every word she spoke was a clue to new discoveries. He knew now that he and she might have walked those flaming ramparts together; but the path he had chosen was on a lower level (322).

Vance's simple wife is completely out of her depth in a marriage with a struggling writer. Rushed into, the marriage becomes a drag on Vance's life, and a source of shame. He becomes more and more impatient with Laura Lou, and 'always ashamed of himself' for that (384). The marriage itself was a great disappointment – like so many others in Wharton's fiction – a plunge from a wonderful dream to a dreary reality: 'He had imagined that [Laura Lou] shared all his ideas, whereas she was merely the sounding board of his young exuberance' (411). Sadly, Vance is never himself with her, but rather

> a nervous, *self-conscious*, and sometimes defiant young man, whereas the other, the real one, was disposed to take things easily, to meet people halfway, and to forget himself completely in the pursuit of any subject that interested him (399) [my emphasis].

Vance certainly seems to see himself as far more socially adept and equable than he is; the insight must be weighed against his dissatisfaction with Laura Lou. Vance is perpetually ending up grumbling at his wife, criticizing, and 'half ashamed' of his treatment (414); Laura Lou seems to have 'a genius for putting him into a mood which made work or meditation equally impossible' (415) and she is hardly a wife to bring out into the world he is trying to conquer, as she is socially inept and fearfully ignorant. She, of course, is ashamed of her obvious failings, lamenting to Vance, 'Nothing I ever do is right' (415). Lunching with the Tarrants, she is bewildered and resentful at the range of conversation, the allusions, the manners, the food itself. Auchincloss sagely notes that Laura Lou tenaciously holds onto Vance and that 'her only way to impress him is to make him feel *guilty*, and she can only do this by becoming fatally ill'[57] [my emphasis]. He almost has a chance to get out of the marriage, when Laura Lou's mother thinks he is having romantic meetings with Halo at The Willows (rather than writing a book). It is a scene in which both blush and look down, and Vance is shamed and angered at the role he thinks Bunty Hayes, Laura Lou's ex-fiancé, has played in the confrontation. Hayes has already been a potent source of embarrassment, trying to start a fight with Vance at the *Hour*'s office because he feels Vance stole Laura Lou from him, and will continue to be one. Vance struggles to pay off the money Hayes lent Laura Lou's family (in a fascinating parallel with Tarrant and the Spears), and then Bunty Hayes ends up being Vance's sole hope of earning some money when he asks him for a job writing advertising copy. Wharton thus puts Vance under crushing obligations to the two men who have claims to the women he loves!

Perhaps the most brutal confrontation Vance undergoes in which shame plays a part is an argument with Lewis Tarrant over his contract with the *Hour* and a publisher. Bound for three years, Vance feels he has not earned enough money from his successful first book, *Instead*, and he is seconded in that opinion by George Frenside, and an agent who tries to negotiate with another publisher for Vance. Vance has already suffered under false accusations, as we have seen, and here Tarrant coolly accuses him of dishonesty in seeking a way out of the binding contract, *and* of carelessness and lack of consideration by losing the Pulsifer Prize. (In a masterful evocation of crossed purposes, Wharton had desperate Vance mortify himself and the wealthy, amorous Jet Pulsifer by asking for a loan, which unfortunately happened to be the same amount as the Pulsifer Prize money) Tarrant's 'very quietness increase[s] Vance's sense of inferiority' in their confrontation; Vance 'crimson[s]' and 'tremble[s]' with 'anger and mortification' as Tarrant lectures him dispassionately but insultingly (454). Vance's only initial counterblow is to point out that Tarrant is disappointed in him, which we have already seen is Tarrant's dirty secret, his shame about the general failure of the *Hour*. When

'Tarrant's slow blood [rises] to his cheeks' (456), this master of control and urbanity reveals the power of Vance's strike. Tarrant's escalation of cold contempt then leaves Vance feeling as if he has been struck, 'powerless with wrath and humiliation' (458) – and he tears up his only copy of chapters of a novel-in-progress. The novel Vance destroyed part of does indeed 'belong' to Tarrant. All of Vance's problems seem focused here: his lack of money, his ailing and oppressive wife, his attraction to Halo, his struggle to make his writing career successful.

But by far the most striking source of shame in this novel is Vance's relationship with Halo. She is certainly his guide, his teacher, companion, friend and even champion, but that is only one side of their relationship, the positive one. As Margaret McDowell has recognized, '[c]ondescension and a certain envy mark [Halo's] attitude toward Vance's creative work from the moment when she interrupts his reading at The Willows on his first visit.'[58] Consider this first meeting. Enraptured by 'Kubla Khan' which he finds in an open volume at The Willows, he flushes when Halo is surprised that he likes poetry so much but doesn't know it. Vance curtly admits his ignorance, and then becomes even angrier when he thinks she is criticizing him. Louis Auchincloss notes that '[i]t is difficult for the reader to forget the impression of odious superiority that [Halo] makes [talking about Coleridge]. . . and even after [Vance] explains to her that he knows no German, she insists on reciting Goethe that he may learn to appreciate the sound.'[59]

Vance resents Halo's lack of interest in the old house that he finds so remarkable, her 'taking for granted what to him was the revelation of an unknown world.' But when Halo later suggests taking Vance to a pool in the woods she enjoys, he flushes at her kindness. An engagement to meet her at The Willows leaves Vance 'sore and *humiliated*' [my emphasis] (91) because Halo is very late:

> She had forgotten him; forgotten him because he was too young and insignificant to be remembered; because fellows called for her and carried her off in their cars, because she never stayed anywhere more than five minutes. . . (92) [Wharton's ellipsis].

Note here how he feels not only unimportant and rejected (and he will feel similarly in *The Gods Arrive* when he meets Floss Delaney again), but the sense of not mattering is heightened by invidiously comparing himself to 'fellows' who have more freedom and money than he does, and note too how his shame modulates to criticism of Halo, though muted in this instance.

The first time he reads his work to her, this dynamic will assert itself far more powerfully. He recites a poem from memory, but she asks him to write it down and he is '*mortified* that she thought his reading so bad' (99) [my emphasis]. Exalted by her enthusiasm and her encouragement, Vance is crushed by her criticism, which *feels* harsh. Puzzled, bewildered, he feels dimly aware of 'abysses of error into which he might drop unawares at any moment,. . . brought. . . down like a shot bird.' Then he begins to condemn Halo in his thoughts as 'perverse and arbitrary,' and later thinks she must be 'sound-deaf' since she doesn't think 'dawn' and 'lorn' are rhymes (122). Halo's 'petty patronizing comments' have made him feel like he is 'falling from a mortal height' (101). He has experienced what we have seen other characters of Wharton's experience, plunging from positive affect ('creative exaltation' and 'the wonder of adventure') into the depths of shame. Given what we know of Walter Berry's coldness from Wharton's friends, and what she herself reveals about him in *A Backward Glance*, one wonders if this interaction does not in part describe her working with Berry. There is terrible irony in *The Gods Arrive* when Halo bids Vance to remember their happiness at this occasion; the memory cannot possibly exclude the pain he suffered, yet she seems completely unaware that he was not only joyful then, but suffering.

A dinner at Halo's parents' home in Eaglewood, at which George Frenside is a guest, likewise leaves Vance first feeling insignificant and unremarkable to the critic and then contemptuous of her and Frenside:

> God, to see a tone-deaf woman laying down the law – and all Eaglewood kowtowing! Well, he had to laugh at the thought of those stuffed oracles sitting up there and telling each other what was what. . . What the hell'd he care for their opinion, anyhow – of his poetry, or of himself? Lot of self-opinionated amateurs. . . he had to laugh. . . (122) [Wharton's ellipses].

Summoned by the absentee owner of The Willows when some valuable books have disappeared from the library, Vance feels Halo pleading with him not to implicate her brother Lorry: 'She had bound him fast in a net of unspoken pledges.' Though Vance felt that 'he had failed her shamefully' (144) by not being more careful at the house and making sure all the windows were locked, he now feels 'sick at heart, *diminished* and *ashamed*' (151) [my emphasis] by what she has pushed him to do, that is, lie to protect her brother.

Halo of course does offer him an entrance to a whole new 'world of beauty, poetry, knowledge' (287), and when he reads the opening of his novel inspired by his musings about Elinor Lorburn, the last owner of The Willows, though his 'self-confidence crumble[s],' she thankfully for him is moved and impressed by his work. Halo's 'exquisite participation' is captivating – what a thrill it is for Vance 'watching his vision take shape in another mind' (326). And in this positive glow, Vance can reflect that one thing he likes about Halo is that she does not nag or ask prying, embarrassing questions as Euphoria women (and Laura Lou) tend to do: 'She took things for granted, didn't forever come harping back to them' (341). His personal life, in other words, is not exposed.

It is important to note that Vance was first struck by the melancholy look in Elinor Lorburn's portrait. He sees the heroine of his novel, Elinor Lorburn, as 'watching for what never came' (317) and deeply isolated – 'No one, apparently, had wanted to give her anything, or to receive what she offered' (318). This language is reminiscent of Pellerin's painful confession of having his work utterly ignored in 'The Legend,' and of many Wharton heroines and heroes feeling unwanted, unloved. Though Elinor is not an artist, like Vance himself, 'some inner source of life, had kept her warm. . . instead of withering she had ripened' (318). Thus, shameful loneliness and feeling what so many of Wharton's characters do, that who she is is not valued, does not in this case imagined by Vance lead to *deeper* loneliness. She has been kept warm, in part, by her books, no doubt as Wharton herself was by her father's library, and later by writing. Wharton allows Vance the ability through his art to rise above his shame, and Vance as an artist makes a similar allowance for his 'creation' – Elinor Lorburn – even though she herself cannot create. Halo 'had entered instantly into his idea of evoking the old house and its dwellers, and as he advanced in his task she was there at each turn, her hands full of treasures, like a disciple bringing refreshment to an artist too engrossed to leave his work' (342). And though writing *Instead* is a rich experience for Vance, imagining Elinor Lorburn's life at times leaves him feeling ashamed when he compares her life to his: 'The meagerness of his inherited experience, the way it had been torn off violently from everything which had gone before, again struck him with a pang of impoverishment' (323).

Progress on his book goes very well as Vance and Halo discuss his work at The Willows, Halo supplying many historical details that will add verisimilitude. But Vance falls in love with Halo and when she tells him she has to return to New York because Lewis is coming back from Europe, he is devastated to discover what he feels for her (346). She distances him with a 'meaningless dazzle' of 'banter,' and as Halo keeps talking about the book, he buries his face in his hands, curses himself as a 'fool' (347). Halo speaks to him with 'a voice so cool and measured that every syllable fell with a little hiss on the red-hot surface of his *humiliation*' (349) [my emphasis]:

> She was *teasing* him, *ridiculing* him, condescending to him from the height of all her *superiorities*: age, experience, education, worldly situation; and he, this raw boy, had sat there, forgetting these differences, and imagining that because he had suddenly discovered what she was to him, he could hope to be as much to her! He ached with the blow to his vanity, and a fierce pride forced him to feel no other ache. If she thought of him as a blundering boy, to be pitied and joked with, to hell with dreams and ambitions, and all he had believed himself to be! (348) [my emphases].

After this experience, Vance finds it impossible 'to work out a manner, an attitude, toward Halo Tarrant' and this failure is itself a source of shame; he compares himself invidiously to other people who would, he thinks, know the 'art of social transitions [which] was still a mystery to him' (372). Halo makes him even more ashamed and angry when she comes to his shabby lodgings to see how Laura Lou is (he will also blush when Halo visits his dismal cottage in Westchester after Laura Lou has died). Going to see Halo after her visit to Laura Lou, he feels 'a gnawing anger against the unfairness of life, the cruelty of social conditions,' and a 'blind desire to punish' Halo for humiliating him and his wife (388–89). There can be no common ground between himself and Halo, he feels, divided as they are by such different social positions, but shame and anger stifle him when he sees her again: he is 'bound hand and foot in coils of awkwardness and resentment' (389). He tries to make Halo understand how her visit was so painful, but Halo's kindness and sympathy make him blush, and then he twice hides his face in his hands, finally sobbing, breaking down, and confessing all his pain and disappointment to her, including feeling that she didn't care about him. Vance 'had imagined that pride and loyalty forbade any personal confession' (394), but he ends up rejuvenated, buoyed and focused on his work again. Yet this rapturous release is only temporary. Soon after, Vance reads Halo the opening chapter of his current book – *Loot*, a New York saga – and when he is done, he does 'not dare to lift his eyes' (416). Even though Halo's verdict is that he needs more time to write a novel about New York, he is 'unreasonably' discouraged:

> She always lit instantly on the flaws of which he himself was half conscious, even in the heat of composition, the flaws he hoped she would overlook, but knew in advance that she would detect; and for this reason he lost his critical independence in her presence, and swung uneasily between elation and despondency (416–17).

Halo may be right, here, but she is certainly tactless, and I think in some ways destructive. To instantly focus on flaws may be helpful in the long run, but wouldn't *any* writer be disappointed, and not unreasonably so, by Halo's response? Geoffrey Walton finds her behavior to Vance 'decidedly patronizing.'[60] There is more disappointment in store for Vance now. Vance confesses that he loves her, but Halo will not accept the possibility of an extra-marital relationship. Bitter, crushed, he thinks that Halo is merely feeling sorry for him. Not only has he failed to win her with his writing, but her approval is lacking in a more fundamental way: 'She was the woman his arms longed for, but she was also the goddess, the miracle, the unattainable being who haunted the peaks of his imagination' (421).

When Halo comes to his decrepit suburban bungalow after Laura Lou is dead, she finally opens up about her marital unhappiness, which she had kept to herself even though Vance had told her everything about his own. She has thus made their failed marriages part of a mutual unburdening, and completed the experience of his confession. Yet the joy of their being reunited is overshadowed by a deeper loneliness in Vance that does not presage a happy bond between them: he feels that 'a veil of unreality' has fallen between them (536). Far more significant, I think, is the underside of their relationship. Halo indeed has educated Vance and helped him educate himself, has consistently and fruitfully encouraged him, been a midwife of his fiction, and an ardent supporter of his work and defender of his reputation, but the differences in their background, and more significantly, the ways in which shame keeps cropping up in their interactions, especially around his writing, has been overlooked. It is that anomaly that in part explains the shift in *The Gods Arrive*.

In this livelier and more focused novel, Vance and Halo leave New York, even though Halo is not yet divorced from Lewis Tarrant, and roam from Spain to Paris to the South of France while Vance tries to discover a suitable environment to write in, as well as his own distinctive voice. That quest increasingly alienates the couple and sends him off to England where he meets the now-rich Floss Delaney and discovers he still wants her. Vance is a much sought-after literary star there because his second novel, *A Puritan in Spain*, is a great success. Vance ignores Halo and whatever she may be feeling in his absence, and when he returns they end up deciding to separate because of Floss. Halo languishes in New York, Vance goes back to Euphoria and falls ill on a retreat in the woods of Wisconsin. His third novel is a major flop and he becomes abruptly disillusioned by Floss Delaney's avariciousness; she has also deeply humiliated him. Feeling worthless, Vance heads back to Halo's parents' home at Eaglewood, where he finds her pregnant with his child, preparing to live at The Willows, which she has inherited. Her divorce from Tarrant (who had offered to take her back and raise the child as his) is proceeding, and she forgives Vance.

A scene between Halo and Vance early in the novel highlights some of the deep problems in their relationship which make the positive ending seem completely unrealistic. It occurs in Spain, where Vance has been too overwhelmed, 'benumbed,' to appreciate some of the sights Halo seems to be laying out for him like an attractive buffet.[61] He 'resents her expectant watching for his reactions to new experience,' just as he resents 'her monitoring of his progress as a potential artist.'[62] Halo has been disappointed that Vance does not recognize her greater experience, and she is galled by his sudden friendship with Alders, an American of shallow but fluent learning who seems to impress Vance. Shy but with a 'ravenous sociability' (45), Alders becomes Vance's literary confidant; 'as a comrade and guide [Halo] felt herself superseded' (64). Vance may still see Halo as his 'other brain, his soul and his flesh' (26), and find it 'exquisite to be with a woman who didn't persist and nag' (24) – yet he no longer feels he needs her collaboration. Since that aid has been a large part of what brought them together, and since Halo is in a false position as 'Mrs Weston,' an upheaval is inevitable, and in this first confrontation we see two major themes of the book: Halo's shame, and her dependence.

Their argument comes when Alders invites Vance but not Halo to a local noblewoman's reception. Talking about the reception afterwards, Halo is struck to see Vance blushing, and she realizes that he has told Alders about their not being married. Vance calmly admits that he has. For Halo, 'the discovery that he had been talking her over with a stranger picked up at a café was intolerable to her' (53). Her anger deepens when she realizes that Vance is not at all aware of the social slight to her, or of her sensitivities to her anomalous position, her *shame*, in other words. She feels 'angry and helpless,' as if an 'impenetrable wall seemed to have risen between them' (54). She is absolutely incapable of making Vance feel how insulted she is to have had her privacy invaded in this way by a stranger, and by someone Vance *knows* she doesn't like: 'To discuss things with [Vance] was like arguing with some one [sic] who did not use the same speech' (56). Halo almost threatens to leave Vance, and then breaks off, overcome by a longing 'to be taken into his arms and soothed like a foolish child. Of course that would come in a moment. She felt her whole body drawing her to him; but though she waited he did not move or speak. He seemed remote, out of hearing, behind the barrier that divided them' (56). Sounding 'cold, almost indifferent' Vance walks out, leaving Halo feeling 'powerless' (57).

I have noted in discussing *The Mother's Recompense* Kaufman's discussion of the importance of being held for a child after the 'interpersonal bridge' has been broken, how holding establishes security and reaffirms the relationship. The rupture, the distance, the shame, are replaced by warmth and union. Halo wants all of that, but cannot ask for it by even holding out her hands, and suffers in its absence. Though Vance returns with a gift which he offers her as a 'wedding present' and 'shyly' talks about their getting married, the break is a deep one, not healed by the subsequent 'factitious fervour' of their 'second honeymoon':

> Halo had grown afraid to take her happiness for granted, and afraid lest Vance should detect her fears. The simplest words they exchanged seemed to connote a background of artifice. There were times when the effort to be careless and buoyant made her feel old and weary; others when the perfection of the present filled her with a new dread of the future. There was hardly an hour when she could yield without afterthought to the natural joy she had known during her first weeks with her lover (61–2).

She thus seems in only a few months to have reached a point of falseness and anxiety it took her *years* to get to in her marriage!

Halo of course felt exposed by having been talked about to Alders. She is deeply uncomfortable with her situation, and will be throughout the book. The novel actually opens on a scene of shame on board the ship taking her from New York to Europe, when a steward asks if she is Mrs Weston. Halo blurts out a 'No,' then a 'Yes' and feels incredibly stupid to have made the blunder. While she may consider herself Vance's wife 'before her own conscience and her lover's,' Halo still dislikes 'to masquerade under a name to which she had no right' (3). Not being invited to accompany Vance to the reception in Spain is another painful reminder of how some people view her situation, and how Halo herself does (at least in part), given her upbringing and environment. She has falsely believed that in 'her new existence the meaner prejudices would no longer reach her' (58), that Vance in fact had 'delivered' her from those prejudices, and yet he is the very vehicle for reminding Halo of their hold on her.

Those prejudices explain why she is at first unwilling to go to Paris with Vance; 'their situation [would make] it embarrassing for her to settle down in a city where, at every turn, she was sure to run across friends and acquaintances' (66). And indeed she *does* suffer in Paris as she attempts to fit in with her brother Lorry's bohemian set and only discovers how much she is an outsider. Attempting to belong just heightens her sense of being an alien: 'The audacities she risked, instead of making her new friends feel that she was one of them, only caused them a vague *embarrassment*'

(85) [my emphasis]. What is worse in some ways, is the sting of finding out that a friend of theirs thinks Halo loves Vance too much to realize that his second novel – completed in Spain – is merely clever and not deep (87). Thus the literary acumen Halo prides herself on is not recognized at all; she is further ashamed to find out that Vance has been discussing a new novel with people he's met in Paris when he hasn't even mentioned the book to her. She rightly believes that Vance 'had anticipated her disapproval.' There is cold comfort in recognizing that 'in a certain way it proved her power over him' (101), and Halo 'suffered acutely from the fact that, for the first time, [Vance] had not sought her intellectual collaboration' (102).

The 'meaner prejudices' she had hoped to escape confront her even in a bohemian environment. Her brother Lorry, who has become a somewhat successful stage designer, views her situation as deeply distasteful and shameful for their family. Lorry may not object to the kind of women in his world, but he objects to his sister being ranked among them. He lectures Halo, urges her to marry Vance (because he doesn't know Tarrant is resisting a divorce), and reveals his own shame: he imagines other men saying that 'anybody can have her the day her novelist chucks her out' (91). Blushing at first, Halo tries to laugh Lorry out of his prejudices, but the effort leaves her exhausted and dispirited. Still, when she is cut by an indomitable and dreary New York society woman immediately after Lorry's harangue, she is filled 'with uncontrollable mirth' because Mrs Glaisher – a possible backer of Lorry's next stage production – is so ridiculous (96).

Though she *is* ridiculous and stupid, wealthy Mrs Glaisher helps enlighten Vance about Halo's sensitivity to her 'situation,' but also is the catalyst for the apparent ruin of Halo's chances for a divorce. At a dinner Lorry holds for her, Mrs Glaisher smirkingly wants to know about the 'real people' she is sure are behind Vance's recent novel, and about his romantic experiences, yet she recoils when she discovers Vance is living with the wife of Lewis Tarrant, who is an old friend of hers. Finally beginning to understand Halo's feelings about being outside society (he himself blushed revealing his unmarried state to Mrs Glaisher), Vance seeks Tarrant who he now knows is in Paris, and unsuccessfully tries to convince him to give Halo a divorce. Halo's response when Vance tells her about the sterile confrontation is disappointment and shame: 'It seemed to her that she was gazing at herself *stripped* and *exposed*, between these two men who were disputing for her possession' (156) [my emphasis]. She twice covers her eyes, and blushes, and Vance comes to see what a blunder he made, believing as Halo does that 'Tarrant never forgave any one [sic] who wounded his vanity' (157).

Halo has suffered agonies of apprehension and jealousy when Vance disappears for a few days to write and she wonders if he isn't involved with some other woman. When he returns – and she learns he *has* been working on his book – rather than comforting herself, Halo is *critical*: 'How unworthy, she thought, for the lover and comrade of an artist to yield to such fears. . . Women who cast in their lot with great men. . . should be armed against emotional storms and terrors' (152). Yet such expectations are unrealistic and cruel, and only lead her to further humble herself:

> [S]he swore to herself that never again, by word or glance, would she betray resentment or curiosity concerning [Vance's] comings and goings. Whenever he wanted to get away she would accept his disappearance without surprise. Her yoke should be so light, her nearness so pleasant, that when he came back it should never be because he felt obliged to, but because he was happier with her than elsewhere (152–53).

Their subsequent move to a dim corner of the Riviera, Oubli-sur-mer, only serves to increase Halo's shame in the long run.[63] Taken to be Vance's wife by the local English colony living in reduced circumstances, Halo will eventually be cut, and it is there that she will suffer her deepest pain at Vance's hands. When he leaves for England, he contacts her only twice, briefly, and she feels 'too cruelly shut out from his adventures and experiences' (310). She will learn where he goes there, and whom he meets, only by reading clippings sent by public relations agencies. Her life has become poisoned by 'disenchantment and failure' (311). And when George Frenside abruptly appears bearing Lewis Tarrant's offer of a divorce, she tries to shut him out, but unsuccessfully, because 'he never did notice the screens you hung up in front of things' (315). Halo blushes, lowers her head several times in their conversation, resisting Frenside's probing and his championing of marriage, even though she craves order and continuity. Frenside is 'visibly embarrassed' (316); and she is *ashamed*: 'something deep down in her still resist[ed] this belated charity from either husband or lover' (319). Like Lydia Tillotson in 'Souls Belated', Halo does not want to feel that Vance is *obligated* to marry her.

But Halo is still desolate, still trapped, and soon discovers that Vance is untraceable, having left England without any forwarding address:

> He had vanished into space again, and this time for how long? Had it never occurred to him that in his absence something might happen to her: that she might fall ill, or be suddenly called home by illness in her family, or, for one reason or another, need his presence – or at least require to communicate with him?
> Idle questions! The truth was that he had simply forgotten her. . . it [was] almost unbearable to be forgotten (324–25).

From this depth of unimportance, which resonates with all the pain of Wharton's letters to Fullerton, Halo imagines the shame of returning to America 'without a lover, without a husband, without a child' (325). It is too painful a picture to contemplate, and once again, shame keeps her from leaving an intolerable situation in which she continues to feel shame: 'She, who had given him her life, sat alone, forgotten, as utterly cut off from him as if she had never had any share in his existence' (328). After Vance returns she once again lectures herself on how to behave: 'Be natural, be natural' (338), and even when he starts drinking she cannot mention it because 'Vance would have been humiliated' (339). Her *own* feelings are thus once again shoved aside, counted as inconsequential; what is just as crucial after all this torment, as it was months before, is that she *keep* him no matter what.

When she ran off with Vance, Halo left behind her a husband who may well refuse a divorce because she has not been tactful and conventional by waiting a respectable amount of time as society dictates, and Lewis would find great satisfaction in 'hurting and humiliating her' (5). She also leaves behind a disapproving family which feels strongly about her 'dishonour' – but the rewards seem great: 'Her first chance to be her real self' (34). Yet what *is* that self? Does she even know? Halo seems to have exchanged one prison for another, one temple in which she was the sole bearer of incense for another. Her marriage fell apart because she could no longer fully devote herself to the 'perpetually functioning state' of 'understanding' Tarrant. 'She became first less necessary, then. . . less interesting, finally almost an incumbrance' (9). Yet despite the emptiness of that marriage, Lewis' distance and interest in Jet Pulsifer left Halo feeling isolated and 'unwanted,' unable to leave (10). Only an inheritance gave her the freedom she needed, but Tarrant asked for a divorce before she could.

Though Vance is not as intentionally cruel as her husband was, and is certainly more feeling, Halo has intensified her dependency on a man, and her happiness is 'like a fever. . . going to give her no rest, no peace. . .' (11). Before, she attempted to nurture her husband's meager talents; now she is tied to a *real* artist, and his talent is the very center of her life – yet she has no control over it whatsoever. She is behaving in similar ways in both novels with both men. Here, for instance, reacting to Vance's peremptoriness, she thinks:

> 'I must adapt myself; I must learn to keep step.'
> After all, wasn't it what she had wanted to marry him for? The absorbing interest of seeing his gift unfold under her care had been so interwoven with her love that she could not separate them. But she liked to think that she loved him because she believed in his genius, not that (as a simpler woman might) she believed in his genius because she loved him (29).

Where once she was confident in talking about his writing, early in this novel she feels 'uncertain and *shy*. . . fearful of discouraging or misdirecting him [my emphasis].' Though she worries about becoming 'a blindly admiring wife,' in many ways she has already become that (41).

Halo is completely tied to Vance's success and talent, and to his very presence: 'She had no longer cared to make her life comely for its own sake; she thought of it only in relation to her love for Vance' (104). Halo finds herself *praying* for Vance's next book, 'as lonely wives pray for a child' (88) because it will prove his genius to the world, and thus give her life meaning and value, as well as re-unite them. The material she is working with may be more substantial, but Halo thought in just such terms about Lewis Tarrant, *forcing* herself to believe in him. Her self-esteem is intimately tied to Vance now, and she cares infinitely more about his writing, his being able to write, than about herself.

Halo, not surprisingly, is also deeply fearful that Vance will grow tired of her, and can blush at his too-close examination: 'She felt a sudden shyness when he looked at her with those eyes full of secret visions' (37). How long will it take before Vance no longer sees anything interesting in her and needs another woman? Halo even finds 'an anxious joy' in imagining that she might end up serving as 'a peg to hang a book on[.]' (37) There is something deeply disturbing about her vision of a descent from lover and muse to inspiration of a book as in any way commendable or inviting. That Halo would accept this terrible diminution of her importance in Vance's life and feel at all positive about it shows how desperate and shame-bound she is.

While Halo's confrontation with Vance in Spain over Alders knowing she isn't really Mrs Weston highlights her shame and powerlessness, a crucial scene late in the novel reveals both Halo's power to hurt Vance, however unintentionally, and thus to undermine his self-esteem and their relationship. When he returns to the South of France, Vance tells Halo he'd like to read to her chapters of *Colossus*, the (apparently) stream-of-consciousness novel he has been working on. Halo tries 'to repress her eagerness,' and exults at this sign of a renewed intellectual contact between them (339). But she is too embarrassed at first to speak after he is done reading, and then asks for time to think it over. Vance taunts her as an 'amateur,' she flushes, and he insults her again, pushing her too far: 'If he had to be praised at all costs she felt that he was lost' (341–42). Halo goes on to tell him that she feels the book is too influenced by other people's styles and ideas, even though she knows that such a judgment is 'the most fatal to the artist's self-love, the hardest for wounded vanity to recover from' (342). Hurt and insulted herself, Halo does more here than tell the truth, she retaliates, using it as a weapon. While she may have tried to minimize the impact of such a harsh judgment if she were not angry and hurt, there is no reason to mince words now. Vance, as we might predict, responds childishly and superciliously, and ends up 'embarrassed and half-ashamed of his outburst' (344). However, Halo's 'over-scrupulous sincerity' has led to an 'intellectual divorce,' and then their separation when they end up talking about Floss Delaney (345).

Once before, she was too honest, this time about his second novel, set in 1830s Spain, and the story – suggested by *Alders*, to Halo's dismay – of a New Englander learning the wine business. Halo had been clearly unenthusiastic about Vance writing another historical novel like *Instead*, written at The Willows, and Vance had snapped that 'nobody but a writer can understand' (65). Though the book proved a commercial success, Vance knew it was well done but not written from his depths. Not surprisingly, working on it, he

> had not felt [Halo's] imagination flaming through him as it had when they used to meet at The Willows. The dampening effect of habit seemed to have extinguished that flame. She listened intelligently, but she no longer collaborated; and now that the book was done he knew that she did not care for it. Perhaps that was the real source of his dissatisfaction; he told himself irritably that he was still too subject to her judgments (74–5).

Vance is no struggling writer here but an artist, though an at times insufferably egotistical one. As much as we welcome the truth Halo speaks, it is presented quite ambivalently by the narrator.

After their argument about *Colossus*, Vance tells Halo that 'when a book's growing the merest stupidest hint may deflect its growth, deform it. . . The artist loses confidence, ceases to visualize' (347). He is not whining, but opening himself up to her, helping her see what he needs. That Halo is generally unable to comment on Vance's fiction without leaving him feeling diminished, uncertain, anxious and ashamed points to a deep and unresolved problem in their relationship and in the two novels. She inspires, but she brings down, yet for her to be any less honest would diminish her sense of self even further. She is trapped in a pattern of relating that is unproductive and crippling. Halo is an uncomfortable and unexpected mix of Wharton's lonely shame-bound women like Rose Sellars in *The Children*, who always seem to do the wrong thing, and a critical, destructive figure like Culwin in 'The Eyes.' In *Hudson River Bracketed* we saw how she could quickly light on the faults in Vance's work, and that ability (or curse) has not been affected by her experiences in *The Gods Arrive*, even though Halo feels that 'she had always been too critical, had made her likes and dislikes too evident' (105). At the end we assume that Vance and Halo will live together as man and wife, but their relationship as writer and muse is even more highly problematic than before, given the pain he has experienced. Perhaps we are meant to expect that Vance, who disregarded Halo's literary advice after writing *Instead*, will now value it, especially since his latest book is a failure.

Though Vance longed for Halo so painfully in *Hudson River Bracketed*, the fault lines in their relationship in that book go some way in explaining why they are so unhappy together so much of the time in *The Gods Arrive*. Vance cannot help but associate Halo with his early uncertain days as a writer, and thus though he craves Halo herself, she is a reminder of his floundering, his uncertainty, his shame. It is important for him to feel superior to her, more knowledgeable. Vance needs to feel that he is in charge, that *he* makes the decisions – hence his mortifying contempt for Halo's greater experience in travelling and with languages. Vance rejects, for instance, the books Halo recommends he read about Spain, and even her suggestions about where to go and when. Twice Vance disappoints Halo – and knows it – by not responding to sights as she hoped he would. The first time is in Cordoba, and then more seriously at Chartres, to which they have made a special excursion to see the Cathedral at different times of the day. He feels 'sulky and baffled,' overwhelmed, and what is most important, does not share his reactions with Halo. 'If he had, she would have been full of sympathy and understanding, but he did not want sympathy and understanding' (81). Vance is clearly ashamed of letting her down, of not being suitably responsive, but he closes himself off from her, as she does from him. Neither one of them can reveal the pain inside of them, and such experiences serve to further isolate them from each other, despite their closeness. Indeed, not at all paradoxically, Vance has felt that '[d]uring their first months together he and she had lived in a deep spiritual isolation; at times they seemed too close to each other, seemed to be pressing on each other, pinning each other's souls' (75). The situation is strikingly like that in 'Souls Belated,' and the language of oppression and exposure – also like that story – bodes ill for their future.

It is also important for Vance that he no longer thinks of himself as a 'young ignoramus' (73), as he did in New York. The success and popularity of his second novel fuels his growth away from Halo's tutelage: 'He no longer needed a companion in. . . explorations of the depths' (79), 'the deep workings of his imagination were no longer roused by her presence' (111), and indeed he maintains that Halo 'failed to feel the rhythm of his inner life' (79). Did she ever, we wonder, or did Vance only *think* she did, enraptured to find a sympathetic audience, like Mrs Anerton in 'The

Muse's Tragedy' telling the young man 'You must write.' How can Vance really know what Halo feels when they hide their feelings from each other, or attempt to? When Vance returns from his first and accidental meeting with Floss Delaney, he doesn't say anything. 'It was his vanity that was aching, and his pride; in a sudden craving for self-abasement he longed to cry out his miserable secret' (263), but he is silent about having pursued Floss Delaney and been humiliatingly teased, played with and then dropped. As we have seen, to speak of shame is to risk feeling utterly identified with the affect, that one *is* shameful. Vance's longing and his paralysis here recall Glennard in *The Touchstone* aching to tell his wife that Margaret Aubyn wrote her love letters to him. The scene in which Vance and Halo talk about Floss also has some similarities with the revelation scene in *The Touchstone*. The clippings on his desk, like the mail on Glennard's, become the occasion for an argument, Vance accusing her 'in a hard embarrassed voice' of having deliberately put a clipping about Floss on his desk the night he returned (348). But unlike Glennard's wife, Halo did not know about his relationship with Floss, she merely suspected. Like Glennard, however, Vance continues to be angry – at himself – and he 'burie[s] his face in his hands,' unable to speak or look at her. Though Cynthia Griffin Wolff condemns Wharton for the echoes in these two novels of her previous fiction, R.W.B. Lewis is intrigued, and I would agree with him that the resonances add depth to the novels rather than subtract substance.[64]

In demeaning Halo, and thus making himself superior, Vance is also 'excusing' his attraction to Floss Delaney, just as Darrow in *The Reef* compared Sophy Viner to Anna Leath. That is certainly one way to understand why Vance thinks that only George Frenside and a friend in Paris illuminated his work – but Halo never did. Vance desperately needs a sense of accomplishment, independence and security because in many ways he is still the 'blundering boy' (120) he was before he met Halo, and he is still comparing himself invidiously to other men. A friend they make in Paris jealously strikes him as having '[Lewis] Tarrant's social ease, the cool bantering manner which Vance had long since despaired of acquiring. . . the type of man [Halo] had been used to in her own circle of friends' (123). And for all his feeling that he and Halo have chosen their situation 'freely,' he blushes in humiliation when he has to explain to Mrs Glaisher that he and Halo are not married, not yet. He will also blush revealing this fact to a quite insignificant neighbor in the south of France. So while Vance may be able to see how Tarrant is caught up in 'helpless vanity, *humiliation* and self-deception' (148) [my emphasis] when he tries to convince Halo's husband to divorce her, he is quite incapable of seeing the hold shame has on him.

Falling into Floss Delaney's clutches in England, following her around like a puppy, he is as blushing and immature as he was years before in Euphoria, and as gullible. Floss is even more lustrously sexual after her father made an unexpected killing in real estate. And Vance is so obsessed by her that he is as uncertain about his ability to interest her, and as critical of himself as he was when he was first getting to know Halo. Watching Floss bask in masculine attention at a luxurious Riviera villa one night, he reflects that 'he had been fatuous enough to think that she would exchange that homage for a moonlight ramble with an obscure scribbler'! (243) Spending some time alone with Floss at her rented English estate, he will be put off from lovemaking, and humiliated to be forgotten when she is on the phone, and abandoned when she leaves without him.

Mortified, defeated, Vance does not go straight back to Halo though he suffers a 'blind animal craving for [her] nearness.' What keeps him away? A 'vague sense of shame and unworthiness' (332). Finding out by reading his clippings that Halo must have followed his active social life in London and read about him and Floss in society columns, he is both mortified and resentful: 'He felt a rush of anger at the idea that she knew his *weaknesses* and was concealing her real thoughts about him. He wasn't going to be pitied by anybody, *least of all by her*. . . [Wharton's ellipsis, my emphases]' (335). That 'least of all' shows how vital it is for Vance to be superior to Halo – and in this he seems just like her husband. Of course Halo is sensitive to his feelings, and she is extremely cautious around him now: 'She knew nothing would irritate him more than any sign of exaggerated sympathy' (338). Halo is dimly aware at this point 'of something shy and dependent in [Vance], something that besought her compassion yet would have resented her showing it' (337). She knows no other way of responding to this insight into Vance than behaving 'as if nothing were changed,' and thus maintaining the emotional status quo in their relationship (337).

Returning to Euphoria after his breakup with Halo, Vance suffers 'mortification' (371) in having to dash the family's expectations of a Park Avenue wedding with Halo. There is more humiliation ahead of him: his novel sinks after some initial good sales built only on his reputation, and Vance is painfully aware of its flaws and his own sudden loss of celebrity. He even imagines another, more popular writer damning him with faint praise. Vance blushes mentioning his book, and thinking about having been overly influenced by other writers and their ideas about fiction. Accidentally meeting Frenside in New York, he flushes at the thought of sending Halo a message. He knows that he has 'failed her' (424) far more seriously than when he thought his negligence had left The Willows vulnerable to a thief. We are evidently meant to see Vance as having had an epiphany when he reads *The Confessions of Saint Augustine* in a Wisconsin forest retreat, and understands his grandmother's deathbed words about the importance of facing and feeling pain. Vance thinks about not abandoning hope but rather forging ahead into 'the crowd and the struggle' (422). He is determined to be an adult and not avoid pain. Yet when he goes to Eaglewood, he berates himself:

> It came over him that he was seeking the solace of these old memories as a frightened child runs to *hide its face* in its nurse's lap; and in a rush of *self-contempt* he strode down the hill to the station. What he wanted was to regain his strength and then face life afresh, not to go whining back to a past from which he had cut himself off by his own choice (427) [my emphases].

When Vance repeatedly tells Halo at the novel's end that he isn't fit for her, he seems no more insightful than when he returned to the South of France and professed he wasn't fit to return because he was a 'damned worthless fool' (336). I do not entirely agree with Marilyn French and the many other critics that this novel is a *bildungsroman* in which Vance has developed from 'self-centered ignorance of emotion, art and society to a degree of knowledge, of sensitivity and awareness.'[65] As we shall see below, his final scene with Halo does not show much sensitivity. And have both novels shown Vance *escaping* pain? It seems more accurate to say that he has used his pain, found a means to keep it from overwhelming him. He is somewhat less ignorant, and the rough edges have been worn down, but I think it is a mistake to read the novel too positively. Though Vance may understand that he needs to 'cut a way through the jungle of his conflicting purposes' (411), what is clearest is that Vance has been progressively humbled, not deepened. The fact that Vance is on his knees to Halo at the end is deeply distressing in terms of Wharton's *oeuvre*. Elizabeth Ammons finds the final vision 'saddening' because 'it conceives of women in totally maternal terms, it writes men off once and for all, it reverses rather than equalizes or eradicates the hierarchy of gender.'[66] Thirty years after *Sanctuary* and *The Touchstone*, Wharton still has difficulty picturing a resolution between a man and woman without one of them subservient to the other. The similarity with *Sanctuary* also extends to Halo's vision of the future; what will save her? Her child – just as Kate Orme hoped for a child to heal her shame: 'Housekeeping and homemaking were her escape, she supposed: she must build up a home for her son. . .' [Wharton's ellipsis] (431). Even more saddening, as in those earlier novellas, the final tableau is organically unconnected to the rest of the book. The problems between them will not be resolved by Vance grovelling at her feet, nor can we assume that for Halo, her sense of self will be strengthened by identifying with a man who is even weaker than before. Neither one of them clearly considers their impact on the other, and the suffering they have caused goes unmentioned and unanalyzed. Wharton can limn the problem and its terrible consequences, but she cannot resolve it, just as the contradictions in Halo's character go unresolved. While the two parts of her name may suggest the martyrdom of a saint and even the Crucifixion, they point to the fundamental split in her between beneficent muse and destructive critic. At some level Wharton must have been aware of the split, given how clearly she shows us Vance's two-sided reactions to Halo. But Wharton does not adequately explore the nature of Halo's influence on Vance's writing and how he feels about his writing.

The final scene is not merely one of triumph or forgiveness and reconciliation, rather it is a scene of prolonged shame. Despite her new tranquility, when she first speaks to Vance Halo does so 'shyly' (435). He flushes when she asks if he has really come back just to tell her he intended not to return until he was worthy of her. This is certainly a rather perverse mission. It is as if Vance is so blinded by his own needs, his own pain and problems that he cannot even imagine how they might affect her. Halo's 'pride [meets] his with an equal shock' when she feels the 'unseen barrier between them. . . as impenetrable as ever' (437). Revealing her pregnancy, Halo once again covers up what she is experiencing – here, 'the old tremors in her breast,' and gives 'a little laugh' (439). Having seen Vance 'so powerless and broken made her feel strong, confident, sure of herself.' But if that is what it takes for Halo to feel those things, then surely she is still as outwardly directed as ever? How can we imagine anything positive coming from what Wharton apparently intends as a scene of reconciliation? Though Vance and Halo remark on the writer's ability to use and transcend pain, Vance, like so many of Wharton's characters, is still imprisoned by it, and so is Halo. In their last scene, Wharton seems to have been attempting to 'lift the novel to a higher plane and to say something profound about the relationship between men and women,' but one is unfortunately left wondering 'how clear [she] herself was about the issues raised.'[67]

In depicting Vance's struggles with form, Wharton is also lifting herself up. Vance alternately tries his hand at autobiographical, historical, naturalistic and stream-of-consciousness novels – but none of them ultimately seem satisfying in the book to him or to Halo. James Tuttleton holds that Wharton wished to defend 'the novel of social life, the realistic novel of manners' and that Vance's rejection of those other forms is 'a rationalization of [her] preference and practice.'[68] It is more than that, however, it is a strong defense against the shame of feeling herself dismissed, as she wrote to Sinclair Lewis, by so many younger writers as 'the Mrs Humphrey Ward of the Western Hemisphere.'[69] It is not surprising, then, that *Hudson River Bracketed* and *The Gods Arrive* were among her personal favorites.

Cynthia Griffin Wolff is not alone in decrying the way Wharton depicts the relationship between an artist's life and work in the two novels. She finds Wharton's treatment of this major theme superficial and quite unsuccessful.[70] I disagree, and would argue that Louis Auchincloss's reading of Wharton's success in creating Vance as an artist is both acute and important. Auchincloss notes that:

> The principal thing about Vance is that he is a writer. Everything and everybody are grist to his mill; the world entrances him, but he is never so seized by his trance that he does not immediately try to covert it into words. A proper name, a branch against the spring sky, an old house on the Hudson, a cocktail party, a fatuous hostess, they all have their uses to the would-be novelist. But, also – and this is the darker side of the artist's character –

a kiss, a family scandal, even his own marriage, have their uses for him. The essence of Vance Weston is that he wants to engage passionately in the business of living, but that he can never get away from the inner eye that is always engaged in watching himself in that process and recording data to be used in a work of fiction.[71]

As we have seen, this dedication, or obsession if you will, can be both a release from shame and a source of shame. Writing 'One Day' pulled Vance out of the misery of imagining his first love having sex with his grandfather, yet when the story was published, it made him feel exposed, even though he was proud of having written it. This ambivalence strikes me as something many writers struggle with. And the very art itself, dependent as it is on the judgments of others, opens one up to shame. That in part explains Alders in *Hudson River Bracketed*, and a self-styled journalist, Chris Churley, in *The Gods Arrive*; Vance is partially defined as a real writer by those around him (like Lewis Tarrant) who are phonies or failures. Alders is never quite sure what the subject of the book he is writing is, and Chris Churley adores talking about writing, playing with ideas, and even the idea of himself as a writer – but neither one publishes, neither can buckle down to actually writing. And so they avoid the possibility of failure, of disappointment, and of shame if their work were to be rejected, derided or condemned. Octavius Brant, a famous talker in London, who discourses magnificently on a book he has never written, says as much to Vance in explaining why people should wait for the book that is inside of him: 'How can you expect me to drag it brutally into the air, to throw it at your feet. . .?' (285) Even Vance, who has real talent at more than talking about his work, has 'the artist's quivering sensitiveness to praise, and anguished shrinking from adverse criticism' (175).

He may not be the genius that Halo thinks him, and that Wharton seems to believe he is, but Vance is very much a working and authentic writer both before and after success. We see him, for instance, convinced that his adolescent musings make him a poet, and discovering that he has an unexpected gift for fiction – but after two sales he is blithely overconfident: 'He felt no doubt that he could sell as many [stories] as he chose.'[72] Urged to keep his independence by George Frenside, but desperate for money and prestige, he succumbs to a contract that options *everything* he writes for three years. With only a dim idea of what publishing is like, he is shocked to find how much it is a business, and how important advertising, maneuvering and influence are in creating an impression, winning prizes, getting good reviews. Like many beginning writers he is both overwhelmed by ideas and struck by how little he knows of the world.

Vance also has to produce a monthly column and finds the burden of meeting a deadline *and* being regularly original, fresh, and startling to be too much pressure. His column is a failure, and he feels pushed by the 'dreadful system of forcing talent, trying to squeeze every drop out of it before it was ripe; the principle of the quick turnover applied to brains as it was to real estate [.]'[73] Well-reviewed on his first novel, which builds on the reputation of his two published stories, Vance faces the hazards of early success as George Frenside points out: '. . . one blurb on a book jacket can destroy a man's soul. . . after you've made your first hit, the world is all one vast blurb.'[74] Equally as real is Vance's confusion over what to do next, what kind of book to write, how much he should follow the advice of other writers and critics – and his distaste for many of the books people are reading and praising. The pitfalls and disappointments of success as well as failure are created in these two novels with great authenticity. He may have a well-reviewed first novel, but he makes almost nothing on it (and first novels indeed rarely produce profits), but he also has a popular success and a bomb. The many issues Wharton thus deals with related to his writing are not trivial by any means. Anyone who has spent time with editors, publishers and authors knows, for instance, that being interviewed by an idiotic reporter can indeed be a nightmare, or that being harassed by readers who cannot separate fiction from autobiography can feel as oppressive, embarrassing and offensive as it does to Vance.

Perhaps Wharton's most striking insight, however, is into the deep loneliness that can be both fruitful and terrible in a writer's life, yielding knowledge but also the fear that 'life would never again be bearable. . . except as material,' and the sense that 'the creator of imaginary beings must always feel alone among the real ones.'[75] The writing that is meant to banish that loneliness only turns out to deepen it. Wharton thus powerfully grapples here with a concern that worried her, as Cynthia Griffin Wolff observes, at the very beginning of her career: that 'the life of making and doing might lead to irretrievable isolation.'[76]

7

Wharton's Classics

If shame is a central and compelling force at work in the novels, novellas and short stories considered thus far, the next obvious question is: what about the role of shame in Wharton's 'classic' works, *The House of Mirth, Ethan Frome, Summer, The Custom of the Country,* and *The Age of Innocence*? Is the prevalence of shame perhaps part of what has made the other novels 'minor' – in other words, has Wharton's preoccupation with shame in those books, as in her own life, diminished them artistically? To varying degrees, shame infuses the language, texture and conception of Wharton's classic novels just as it does books like *The Touchstone, The Glimpses of the Moon,* and *The Reef*. In her five classic novels, we find the now familiar landscape of shame: interactions, scenes and patterns of behavior in which shame plays a governing role. The language, and more importantly, the *phenomenology* of shame are no less present in her classic novels than in those generally judged as minor. Even though these books have been much analyzed and discussed, examining them in terms of shame is nevertheless illuminating.

More has been written about *The House of Mirth* than any other of Wharton's books, especially in the last twenty years. But whether one sees Lily Bart as the victim of a deeply sexist society, or of other women, or of her own lack of self-esteem and values, or of a profoundly uncaring universe, capitalism, narcissism, or masochism, it is clear that shame is a dominating force in this novel. *The House of Mirth* is punctuated by pivotal shame scenes involving individuals or groups, and shame also functions as a source of motivation, a social weapon and as a barrier to the expression of genuine emotions.

The first significant shame scene or sequence of scenes occurs in the novel's opening chapter when Lily is leaving Selden's bachelor apartment in New York after having impulsively decided to have tea with him there. Lily had been en route to the Trenors' Bellomont estate, but missed her train and had time to kill. As a single woman, however, she could seldom 'allow herself the luxury of an impulse!'[1] – and she blushed when Selden, who ran into her at Grand Central Station, asked her to his apartment. This blush is significant, because for Selden it is, rather fatuously, an example of Lily's social skills: 'She still had the art of blushing at the right time' (6). As we know, blushing is an *automatic* facial sign of shame, and Selden's sharp misreading of Lily is an immediate example of his rather one-dimensional perception of Lily: 'Her simplest acts seemed the result of far-reaching calculations' (3).

Lily blushes again when Selden asks why she isn't, at twenty-nine, married yet, after she's said that she's 'been about too long – people are getting tired' of her (9). This relative openness on her part has come after some verbal sparring between them, and after Lily's sudden confession that she has imagined Seldem might be a real friend to her, someone who could speak the truth to her, however 'disagreeable.' She has made herself comparatively vulnerable – 'she sat gazing up at him with the troubled gravity of a child' (9) – and goes on to explain that her friends take advantage of her and don't care about her at all. Selden is not remotely sympathetic or interested, and has even misread her seriousness enough to contemplate 'one or two replies calculated to add a momentary zest to the situation' (9). Instead, he asks why indeed she isn't married, but after having hoped that she doesn't have to be on guard with him, and admitting that she feels out of place, how can Lily not perceive this question as implicit criticism? Of course, Lily's response is shame; she 'colours' and then laughs. Kaufman notes that laughter, which recruits positive affect, is an 'effective means of reducing intense negative affect, particularly shame.'[2] The tone shifts and Lily is a little bit less serious, but Selden remains detached and critical: 'It was impossible, even with her lovely eyes imploring him, to take a sentimental view of her case' (12). Later in the novel Selden will feel touched by Lily, and perhaps even in love with her, but will be buffeted by social usages, by misunderstandings and by his own emotional reticence, and he will feel disgust or contempt for Lily, and draw away.

Leaving Selden's apartment, Lily flushes twice when a charwoman stares at her on the staircase. Her attempt to lift herself above this shame is a contemptuous speculation that the woman must be staring because 'the poor thing was probably dazzled by such an unwonted apparition' (14). Lily immediately afterwards lies to the wealthy parvenu Simon Rosedale in front of the building (which he happens to own) about why she was there, and then snubs his offer of a lift to the station. She 'had always snubbed and ignored' (16) the man desperate to climb New York's social heights – hence her abrupt rejection of his offer. But the charwoman's prolonged and unpleasant scrutiny, and Lily's sense of being subjected to 'some odious conjecture' (14) guaranteed that she could not simply and disarmingly tell Rosedale the truth, that she'd been 'taking tea with Selden' (15). The blunder puts her in Rosedale's power to a certain extent, and leaves her subject to the corrosive force of gossip.

Patricia Meyer Spacks has discussed the relation in *The House of Mirth* between gossip, money and power: 'Endless restless talk about human behavior establishes and limits possibility.'[3] As Lily herself says when she has sunk well down the social ladder, 'the truth about any girl is that once she's talked about she's done for; and the more she explains her case the worse it looks' (226). She also is fully aware of how vicious and painful shaming gossip can be: 'Lily knew every turn of the allusive jargon which could flay its victims without the shedding of blood' (110). Had Lily not felt ashamed on the stairs, she would have been poised and controlled as usual and dealt with Rosedale far more tactfully, or at least without shaming him so obviously by escaping into a cab, and exposing herself further. Indeed, through much of the novel, Lily will be at her social worst with Rosedale, 'conscious of marking each step in their acquaintance by a fresh blunder' (113). In a world which Lily has often felt to be inimical, that charwoman's unnerving appraising stare is like the concentrated exposing hostility of all the vague forces seemingly leagued against her.

Lily's somewhat idle flirting with Selden takes on a different perspective when he suddenly arrives at Bellomont, though he had no intention of going. Lily – who is stalking the wealthy Percy Gryce – greets Selden's arrival with 'a blush of wonder' (50) and assumes he has come to see *her*. But at the first sign that perhaps he is there for Bertha Dorset, his ex-lover, Lily is crushed: 'She was only aware of a vague sense of *failure*, of an inner isolation deeper than the loneliness about her' (61) [my emphasis]. Selden does, however, come out after her in the Trenor gardens and they walk and talk on a perfect Fall afternoon. Selden expounds on his notion of success as a 'republic of the spirit' (68) in which one keeps one's freedom, and they enter a prolonged debate about independence versus wealth. Lily twice blushes in response to Selden's questions, the first time when he wonders how rarely she feels free of 'material accidents' and again when he asks if she hasn't seen 'a miserable future' for herself. Lily twice accuses Selden of contempt that leads nowhere:

> 'You despise my ambitions – you think them unworthy of me!' (71)
>   'Why do you do this to me?' she cried. 'Why do you make the things I have chosen seem hateful to me, if you have nothing to give me instead?' (72)

When Selden agrees, Lily *hides her face* and weeps. Selden's response to this abrupt open expression of Lily's feelings is once again critical and distancing: 'He said to himself, somewhat cruelly, that even her weeping was an art,' and his tone is a mixture of 'pity and irony' (72). Lily quite rightly claims, 'But you belittle *me*, don't you. . . in being so sure [that wealth, etc.] are the only things I care for?' (72) Selden insists that Lily *does* care for wealth and all it means and she naturally greets this continued accusation with 'derision': 'For all your fine phrases you're really as great a coward as I am, for you wouldn't have made one of them if you hadn't been so sure of my answer' (72–3). The accusation throws Selden off balance, and he surprises Lily (and the reader) with a measured and serious reply that neither of them can be quite sure about that. Lily asks if Selden wants to marry her, and he fends off her honest question with saying he might want to, if she did.

The blossoming closeness between them is broken, however, when Lily hears a car and feels exposed, remembering that she told the Bellomont guests she was too ill to go out. She blushes when Selden points out the car was headed in a different direction, but the mood continues to deteriorate. It is Selden, now, who seems ashamed of slipping from Lily's attention, and determined to show himself superior, distant; 'he had an almost puerile wish to let his companion see that, their flight over, he had landed on his feet' (74). Shame has separated them, and has unnerved Lily again. When she asks Selden if he had been serious before, her tone seems 'caught up, in haste, from a heap of stock inflections, without [her] having time to select the just note' (74). Selden is cool, distant, aloof. As we will discuss below, their relationship continually ebbs and flows in this way, shame stifling or distorting what they say and feel, limiting their possibilities, but it is almost always Lily who is shamed by Selden and not the reverse. We see here to some degree the emotional dynamic that Wharton herself would live out with Morton Fullerton; despite the intense joy she experienced sexually, she felt inferior to him, and to other women he had known, deeply and irrevocably inadequate.

Lily's obvious interest in Lawrence Selden at Bellomont enrages Bertha Dorset, his unhappy ex-lover, and Bertha gossips about Lily to Percy Gryce, the wealthy bore Lily has hooked and almost landed as a husband. Bertha's momentary revenge helps destroy Lily's chances of marriage to Gryce. But Lily unexpectedly comes into possession of a weapon that would give her power over Bertha, through the approach of Mrs Haffen, the charwoman at Selden's building. The woman offers to sell Lily Bertha's importuning letters to Selden, letters Selden rather carelessly discarded. Lily blushes when she realizes that the woman thinks *she* is the correspondent, and then she angrily wants to throw Mrs Haffen out, but her desire to protect and help Selden outweighs her anger. The possibility of returning the letters to Bertha and 'the opportunities the restitution offered. . . lit up abysses from which [Lily] shrank back *ashamed*' (105) [my emphasis]. Lily will ultimately burn the letters, even when they offer her the means to re-establish herself in society, and *unambivalently* destroying them will be a sign of how very great a change has occurred in her values. Meanwhile, however, Lily bargains hard for the letters, but is unwilling to read them: to do so 'would have seemed degrading' (107). Right afterwards, reminded that Percy Gryce is going to marry a lackluster and rich woman, she is painfully struck by the comparison between her comfortable but dowdy and charmless boudoir and the room of her dreams 'which should surpass the complicated luxury of her friends' surroundings' (110). The invidious comparison between her own surroundings and those she fantasizes about points out her powerlessness to take control of her own life, and is a further source of shame. Kaufman notes that

> Powerlessness is not an affect per se but an *activator* of affect; it is experienced with any of the negative affects or combination thereof. Defeat, failure, rejection, and loss thus guarantee a perpetual vulnerability to shame. . .[4] [my ellipsis].

Lily is indeed powerless throughout the novel, and the words 'disappointment' and 'failure' reappear like the dismal tolling of a bell.

Lily is inordinately sensitive to her surroundings, but even worse than despairing at the ugliness of her room which is symbolic of the bleakness of her hopes, Lily, who 'disliked being ridiculed' (32), imagines Bertha Dorset triumphantly gossiping about her (over the 'loss' of Percy Gryce), and flushes at the picture. Her vulnerability to the opinions of others is a major chink in her social armor, at the same time that it also gives her glimpses of insight into how others might feel. She is, unfortunately, adrift in a society where selfishness reigns; her set's defining attribute is 'a force of negation which eliminated everything beyond their own range of perception' (48).

One of the most striking scenes in the novel is the evening of the *tableaux vivants* at the *arrivistes* Wellington Brys' magnificent New York mansion, in which Lily chooses to 'impersonate' a simple painting by Joshua Reynolds rather than appear in an elaborate costume. She does not herself experience shame in the scene, but her appearance is ultimately shameful and shaming, even though Lily feels that she has triumphed by presenting herself in this way. Lily's decision to be herself is, as Dale Bauer writes, a defiant assertion of self which is shocking because she has misjudged the proper role of single women in her society.[5] I would add that this misjudgment has its roots in shame. Lily is afraid of exposure, afraid of isolation in a universe 'so ready to leave her out of its calculations' (27). Isn't appearing comparatively uncovered and unprotected, then, a strange choice for a woman so conscious of having been 'too long before the public' in her unmarried state? (87) It is shame that motivates her representation of herself at the *tableaux vivants*. By turning one of her fears (exposure) into an apparent triumph, she is at once conquering that fear. Ironically, as Carol Wershoven explains, Lily is 'spared the humiliation' [6] of knowing that while her beauty was admired, people also saw her 'standing there as if she was up at auction' (157). She has thus made herself *more* vulnerable, rather than less, and the next shame scene is in part an outgrowth of Lily's miscalculation in this one.

Almost broke because she has been playing bridge for money with her society friends, Lily had appealed to the sullen Gus Trenor at Bellomont and he offered to invest for her, though the checks she subsequently began receiving were not really the fruit of Wall Street deals on her behalf. Lily blinds herself to the complications of Trenor's 'help': her haziness about money matters has served 'as a veil for her embarrassment' (85) until he threatens to rape her in his mansion. Lily has come there alone in response to Judy Trenor's invitation, but Judy changed her plans and stayed at Bellomont; Gus didn't let Lily know this. Trenor's deep resentment of Lily grows out of his shame: he complains that Lily has let 'a lot of other fellows make up to [her]. . . letting 'em make fun of [him]' (144). Ugly, loutish Trenor, 'who was seldom listened to, either by his wife or her friends' (81), feels ridiculed and used, and crudely demands 'payment'. Lily is trapped: 'She flamed with anger and abasement, and the sickening need of having to conciliate where she longed to humble' (145). The situation may be extreme, but it is also typical of Lily's 'humiliating contingencies' (97) – of always being in situations where she seems to have no choice but to please or placate someone else.

Trenor shocks her even further by alluding to her having visited Selden 'in broad daylight' and she is dizzied by understanding herself to be the victim of gossip: 'This was the way men talked of her' (145). Trenor goes on to humiliate Lily by assuming that she has gotten money from men before this, and then while confessing his love for her, offers as much money as she might want, if she will sleep with him.

Over and over her the sea of *humiliation* broke – wave crashing on wave so close that the *moral shame* was one with the physical dread. It seemed to her that self-esteem would have made her invulnerable – that it was her own *dishonour* which put a *fearful solitude* about her (146) [my emphases].

With Trenor barring the door, Lily 'must fight her way out alone' – anything else would create a scandal, 'a hideous mustering of tongues' (147). But Lily's sang-froid finally leaves him 'chill and *humbled*' (147) [my emphasis]. Outwardly, at any rate, Lily has maintained her dignity, has not showed fear, and she is able to escape. But to what? She feels 'all alone in a place of darkness and pollution' (148) – like Kate Orme in *Sanctuary*. And she soon sees the $9,000 Trenor has given her differently: 'The flimsy pretext on which it had been given and received shrivelled up in the *blaze of her shame*: she knew that not a penny of it was her own, and that to restore her self-respect she must at once repay the whole amount' (169) [my emphasis].

For Trenor, raping Lily would have been, as Kaufman notes in discussing sexual abuse, an act of 'power and revenge, born of impotence and fueled by shame.' In a sense, Lily has become identified with all the sources of shame in Trenor's life; by 'defeating and humiliating' her he would at least momentarily become 'freed of shame.'[7] Understanding the affect dynamics of Trenor's relationship with Lily in no way excuses his action, but it does help explain why Trenor viciously pounds away at her as he does, attempting to bully and frighten her before he even touches her.[8] He is enacting his own shame scene, but recasts it by reversing the roles and this time attempting to be the one who does the shaming. It is social shame, however, that finally stops him, working through [o]ld habits, old restraints, the hand of inherited order' (147). The attempt fails, at least outwardly, but extreme violence *has* been done to Lily nonetheless, and to her conception of herself.

Lily's ill-advised turning to Trenor for financial help has other consequences, once again through gossip. Lily has already made an enemy of her drab and poor cousin Grace Stepney by seeing that this dull woman is not invited to a family dinner that would have thrilled her, and by her indifference, which Grace has construed as Lily's disliking her. Grace draws that conclusion because of shame: 'It is less mortifying to believe one's self unpopular than insignificant, and vanity prefers to assume that indifference is a latent form of unfriendliness' (122). Taking no notice of Grace is an unfortunate mistake, however, because Grace has a mind 'like moral fly-paper, to which the buzzing items of gossip were drawn by a fatal attraction, and where they hung fast in the toils of an inexorable memory' (121–22). Grace relays the gossip that Lily must be Gus's lover to Lily's aunt and protector, Mrs Peniston. After all, since Lily and Gus are seen together, and she is spending money on clothes rather conspicuously, what other connection can be made? This unpleasant insinuation lays a foundation of distrust for Lily's aunt, who believes that it 'was horrible of a young girl to let herself be talked about; however unfounded the charges against her, she must be to blame for their having been made' (127).

Thus Lily's aunt is not at all sympathetic when Lily asks for more money so that she can wipe out her debt to Gus Trenor – though Lily claims to be burdened by dressmaker's bills. This scene is another humiliating episode in a relationship which at its core is demeaning for Lily. Lily's wealthy relatives always suspected that Lily held them in contempt for living 'like pigs' (36), and so her Aunt Peniston was the only one who offered to take care of her after her father and then her mother died. Her motives were rooted, in fact, in shame. Mrs Peniston had the kind of *mauvaise honte* [bashfulness] which makes the public display of selfishness difficult, though it does not interfere with its private indulgence. It would have been impossible for Mrs Peniston to be heroic on a desert island, but with the eyes of her little world upon her she took a certain pleasure in her act (36).

Though Lily does have a life of 'good food and expensive clothing' (37) with her aunt, Mrs Peniston restricts Lily's freedom by not making her a 'fixed allowance': 'Mrs Peniston liked the periodical recurrence of gratitude evoked by unexpected cheques [*sic*], and was perhaps shrewd enough to perceive that such a method of giving kept alive in her niece a salutary sense of dependence' (38). She has made Lily determined 'at all costs [to] keep Mrs Peniston's favour' (38).

That favor is pretty much withdrawn because of the staining gossip Mrs Peniston has heard, but doesn't mention to Lily when she asks for money, thus depriving her of the chance to tell the truth. When Lily, after a long and painful inquisition about her dressmaker's bills (which is doubly mortifying since the story is just a pretext), Lily flushingly 'confesses' that she has gambling debts, and has even played cards on Sunday. Mrs Peniston is outraged. All Lily's conversational shifts and maneuvering to get money from her aunt have failed, and she has had to damn herself in her aunt's eyes.

> Pride stormed in her, but *humiliation* forced the cry from her lips: 'Aunt Julia, I shall be *disgraced* – I – ' But she could go no farther. If her aunt turned such a stony ear to the fiction of the gambling debts, in what spirit would she receive the terrible avowal of the truth? (172–73) [my emphases].

Of course, Lily's aunt says that she is *already* disgraced. Indeed, Lily feels utterly trapped, 'shut in with her dishonour – ' (173). Lily waits for Selden's arrival, hoping his love can save her, not knowing, however, that he is disgusted after having coincidentally seen her leave Gus Trenor's house, and will not come. She has to submit to Simon Rosedale's crude proposal of marriage, once again ashamed – 'the colour burned in Lily's face as he ended' – but unable to risk 'offending him at a perilous moment' (177). Into this terrible straitening of her life comes an invitation from – of all people – Bertha Dorset to a Mediterranean yacht cruise which will lead to the novel's shame scene with the greatest consequences for Lily. Because she is desperate enough to consider marrying Rosedale, the invitation offers Lily a miraculous escape.

Bertha, dallying with young Ned Silverton, has invited Lily to keep her husband George busy, which Lily can do quite well since he is so smitten with her. Lily is nearly broke, as usual, but she cannot share 'this vulgar embarrassment' (197) with the Dorsets, though she luxuriates in their comforts. Even more seductive than having escaped from New York is Lily's great success in the South of France; written about in the local social gazette, she is admired again and able to brush aside inconvenient worries. It is a dangerous situation, however, and through three months 'her fears had always been on the alert for an upheaval' (203). Given Bertha Dorset's past envy of Lily, it is not surprising that she is jealous of Lily's success, and even hints to Selden, who discovers them in Monte Carlo, that Lily has been after George Dorset.

The balancing act between the Dorsets cannot last, and when George has incontrovertible evidence that Bertha is cuckolding him, it is Lily, hoping to reconcile the couple, who is sacrificed. Though George's confession of outrage and self-contempt leaves Lily 'shrinking and seared' she finds relief in thinking herself superior and competent, the one person to 'drag him up again to. . . sanity and self-respect' (203). Ashamed, George pleads with Lily to help him: 'You can't want to see me ridiculous' (204). Lily gets him to consult with Selden, who is a lawyer, and then succumbs to a vision of aiding Bertha. Lily *identifies* with her and imagines Bertha feeling as vulnerable as *she* does: 'She pictured the poor creature shivering behind her fallen defenses and awaiting with suspense the moment when she could take refuge in the first shelter that offered' (205). Lily even fears that a desperate Bertha may commit suicide, but Bertha confuses her by implicitly denying everything – and criticizing *Lily*, who flushes, ashamed but uncertain what Bertha is driving at. Lily had hoped for a real human connection between them, but Bertha only distances her with contempt, clearly revealing how Lily's social superiority has made *her* feel ashamed: 'I've positively lived on [your hints] these last months. . . what not to be and to do and to see' (208).

Bertha manages to quash George's rage, and arranges a public humiliation for Lily that will make *her* seem to be the problem. At a showy restaurant where 'conspicuousness passed for distinction' (216) Bertha Dorset announces as the party is breaking up, 'Miss

Bart is not going back to the yacht.' Her implication is utterly clear to everyone:

> A startled look ran from eye to eye; Mrs Bry *crimsoned* to the verge of congestion, Mrs Stepney [a cousin of Lily's] *slipped* nervously *behind* her husband, and Selden, in the general turmoil of his sensations, was mainly conscious of a longing to grip Dabham [the social reporter] by his collar and fling him out onto the street (218) [my emphases].

George Dorset protests, Bertha insists, and Lily responds with contempt: 'The faint disdain of her smile seemed to lift her high above her antagonist's reach, and it was not until she had given Mrs Dorset the full measure of the distance between them that she turned. . .' (218). Cooly claiming other plans, Lily is escorted out by Selden, after she has registered 'incredulity in [the women's] *averted looks*, and in the mute wretchedness of the men behind them. . .' (218) [my emphasis].

Why has Lily stayed on the yacht so long or even gone on the trip at all? Why does she reach out to Bertha (who helped destroy her chances of marrying Percy Gryce), feel sympathy for her, and even compassionately interpret Bertha's initial attack on her as merely 'senseless bitterness' (208) and fear, rather than the calculated onslaught of a vicious hypocrite? Lily seems to be re-enacting the central drama of her family life. Her mother's careless use of her father is echoed in Bertha's cavalier and cruel treatment of her husband. By helping them stay together, she is in a sense healing the breach that 'separated' her parents, and it is significant that she is so upset by George's confession but keeps attempting to reach Bertha. Her father was always a stranger to her, seen through a fog 'of distance and indifference' (33), and even more so when he fell ill, while her mother, at least, approved of her. Lily seems to be seeking this approval from Bertha, seeking to be found competent and admirable in this crisis, even though Selden and Carrie Fisher have warned her to get out before a blow-up.

The scene of Lily's 'dismissal' by Bertha will be reported to Lily's aunt, and considered to be a revelation of truth by Lily's set. All the participants will get back to America before her, guaranteeing that her version will be overwhelmed (as Angelo says in *Measure for Measure*, 'Say what you can, my false o'erweighs your true'[9]). But shame would have kept Lily from defending herself anyway:

'Some obscure disdain and reluctance would have restrained her. . . a feeling that was half pride and half humiliation' (227). She would find the whole matter distasteful, contemptible to have to discuss, and it would be too exposing. After all, she knew from the first that Bertha wanted her on the yacht as a smokescreen: 'The part was not a handsome one at best' (227).

Lily's inheritance will,be drastically cut, with Grace Stepney made Mrs Peniston's major heir. This disgrace will ironically come after Lily had made 'an almost triumphant progress to London' where she was as amusing and charming as she could be (227). At the reading of the will, Lily will be further humiliated, excluded and ignored by her relatives. They greet her entrance with hesitant nods and vague gestures. Lily defiantly does not join them, but sits off by herself, which is where she is left after the will is read:

> Lily *stood apart* from the general movement [to Grace Stepney], feeling herself for the first time *utterly alone*. No one looked at her, no one seemed aware of her presence; she was probing the very *depths of insignificance*. And under her sense of the *collective indifference* came the acuter pang of hopes deceived. Disinherited – she had been disinherited – and for Grace Stepney! (223) [my emphases]

The release from struggle that Mrs Peniston's legacy was supposed to have offered is torn away, and Lily's humiliation is deepened by her being replaced by someone she always saw as her inferior. Lily's relatives now have the late Mrs Peniston's approval as well as a general social permission to cut Lily, as she explains to Gerty Farish, Selden's poor cousin: 'They were afraid to snub me while they thought I was going to get the money – afterward they scuttled off as if I had the plague' (224–25).

The scope of Lily's humiliations narrows from this point on as do her options for survival. Lily eats at lavish restaurants with Gerty Farish, keeping up the pretence of resources, as her mother did when she was plunged into relative penury, and is politely but unmistakably snubbed. As she becomes involved with a social set well below her former empyrean, she is painfully aware of having to 'exact fresh concessions from her pride' (237). She is shamed when Carrie Fisher suggests she has the information to destroy Bertha, humiliated by Rosedale's familiarities, and both embarrassed and contemptuous when George Dorset pleads with her to set him free from his marriage to Bertha. Lily's superiority to him and her contempt for his 'weakness' ensure that he will not be her route to social rehabilitation. Lily then humiliates herself perhaps more completely than at any other time in the book, by telling Rosedale that she is now willing to accept his previous offer of marriage. He turns red because she is – as a victim of gossip – no longer as valuable a match as a year before. Lily 'flushe[s] to her temples' (255) when he alludes to the stories told about her, and ultimately reveals that he knows Mrs Haffen sold her Selden's letters. Rosedale offers a deal: if Lily uses the letters to get Bertha to support her return to society, he will marry her. Lily is somewhat swayed but finally 'disgusted' by the deal's 'essential baseness' (260). The act itself would be more shameful than her expulsion from society has been.

Lily leaves the 'employ' of a vague but rich Mrs Hatch on the fringes of society 'ashamed and penitent' (283), unwilling to help arrange a marriage between her employer and a man from Lily's former social set. Lily ends up working in a hat shop, but her inability after two months is 'humiliating' – 'it was bitter to acknowledge her inferiority even to herself' (297). The scenes of her roaming hungry life after her father's death are taking over: 'Something of her mother's fierce *shrinking from observation* and sympathy was beginning to develop in her. . .' (287) [my emphasis]. In another chance meeting with Rosedale, they both suffer embarrassment and Lily confesses how she really got money from Trenor. The confession leaves her 'with a deep blush of misery' (292) and is *not* a relief. Lily feels further 'humiliation' when Rosedale offers to lend her the money to repay Trenor. He still wants her to reclaim her old status, and using Bertha's letters to Selden would be the only path. The idea of 'trading on [Selden's] name, and profiting by a secret of his past, chilled her blood with shame' (304). In Lily's final meeting with Selden she is struck by how deeply embarrassed he is at her presence, and though she is beyond being bothered by that now, it is chilling to feel herself 'shut out from Selden's inmost self' (307). Cool, distant, Selden can only himself blush and vaguely offer to help her. His words, his gestures are from another life, another time.

Though Selden had tried to save her from being involved in the embarrassing 'public washing of the Dorset linen' (209), his attitude towards her is a major source of shame in her life, and Lily's relationship with Selden is one in which shame continually interferes with the complete and open expression of their feelings. Even more importantly, their relationship is one in which Lily is made to feel ashamed for the way she lives her life, but without anything really positive offered to her by Selden, whose 'presence always [has] the effect of cheapening her aspirations, of throwing her whole world out of focus' (88). Yet the goal she has in mind, 'the life of fastidious aloofness' (90) is oddly in tune with Selden, who is both aloof and fastidious, like Fraser Leath in *The Reef* and Lewis Tarrant in *Hudson River Bracketed*. Like so many other Wharton heroines, Lily Bart is attracted to Selden's superiority and contempt, though she suffers its effects. She admires his 'social *detachment*' (54) and 'friendly *aloofness*': 'Everything about him accorded with the *fastidious* elements in her taste. . . She admired him most of all, perhaps, for being able to convey as distinct a sense of *superiority* as the richest man she had ever met' (65) [my emphases]. Though she enjoys and welcomes Selden's 'complete understanding' (94), his making her 'feel that she was worthy of better things' (174) is as much a consistent source of shame through the very superiority she admires, as it is a revelation of nobler possibilities.

Time and again when she is with Selden, Lily blushes, looks down or away because he makes the values she has come to pursue seem 'unworthy' of her. A good example of shame operating in their relationship is the scene in Book Two in which Selden comes to urge her to leave her somewhat ill-defined role as social advisor to the parvenu Mrs Hatch, whose friends are arranging a match between the young socialite Freddie Van Osburgh and Mrs Hatch. Selden's arrival causes Lily 'an inward start of embarrassment,' but his constraint restores 'her self-possession' (277). Between them lie two lifetimes of dissimulation and their own particular history of crossed purposes: 'The situation between them was one which could have been cleared up only by a sudden explosion of feeling' (278) – but habit, society, and personal inclination make that impossible. Intense feeling is there, but unexpressed, at least in words. Lily flushes and declares she is *not* ashamed of being where she is, and lifts her head pridefully; Selden cannot express any 'personal sympathy' and so 'her hurt pride' turns to 'blind resentment of his interference' (281). We have seen anger follow shame in many of Wharton's characters. Lily is of course aware of her false position, but Selden's visit made her resist his help.

Ironically, however, given that Lily is so vulnerable to shame, one of her great social gifts is *neutralizing* shame; she has 'the art of giving self confidence to the *embarrassed'* (18) [my emphasis]. On the train to Bellomont at the novel's opening, for instance, Lily is aware that the wealthy Percy Gryce is too shy to approach her, and her smoothness overcomes his furious blushing and self-consciousness. Even more important, she is aware that though Gryce is deeply shy, like many timid people he has a 'secret compensation' (21). Gryce glories in seeing his name in print as owner of a fabulous collection of Americana and he revels in dilating about this collection. 'It was the one subject which enabled him to. . . assert a superiority that there were few to dispute' (20). Later in the book, when Selden meets Lily in Monte Carlo after a number of embarrassing scenes, Selden is conscious of how able Lily is to bridge the gap between them so that 'no inconvenient glimpses of the past were visible' (192). She is a practitioner of what Castiglione praised in *The Book of the Courtier*: *sprezzatura* (nonchalance), the art that conceals all art.[10] Her great skill is to appear effortless in everything that she does.

We have already seen how Wharton's characters use contempt as a defense against shame, a defense that lifts them above potential and actual sources of shame, distancing those people, making them inferior. Not surprisingly, Lily often manifests contempt in the book – though less so as she sinks lower socially and seems to develop a sense of values that is less superficial than the one she has operated under. At the Van Osburgh wedding, for instance, 'in the consciousness of her own power to look and to be so exactly what the occasion required, she almost felt that other girls were plain and inferior from choice' (89). After the Gryce débâcle, she accepts an invitation to spend Thanksgiving in the Adirondacks with the Wellington Brys, who she would have previously been hesitant to associate with. Now, however, Mrs Bry, a woman of 'obscure origin and indomitable social ambitions' (112), buoys Lily's need to be in luxurious surroundings and to feel superior. Lily gratifies the Brys because her status helps them appear in society columns:

> The young lady was treated by her hosts with corresponding deference; and she was in the mood when such attentions are acceptable, whatever their source. Mrs Bry's admiration was a mirror in which Lily's self-complacency recovered its lost outline. . . If these people paid court to her it proved that she

was still conspicuous in the world to which they aspired; and she was not above a certain enjoyment in dazzling them by her fineness, in developing their puzzled perception of her superiorities (113).

Her feelings about being in Mrs Hatch's employ later in the book will be rather similar: 'Mrs Hatch showed from the first an almost touching desire for Lily's approval. Far from asserting the superiority of wealth, her beautiful eyes seemed to urge the plea of inexperience' (276).

Because Lily has become increasingly dependent on her rich friends as she continues to stay unmarried, and ever more in social bondage to their whims, Lily's fantasies of success and wealth always involve creating settings that would outshine theirs, because of the 'artistic sensibility which made her feel herself their superior' (110). Her success will in part be a triumph over the prolonged shame of her unmarried state, and over what is merely 'servitude to the whims of others' that precludes 'asserting her own eager individuality' (101):

> She would have smarter gowns than Judy Trenor, and far, far more jewels than Bertha Dorset. She would be free forever from the shifts, the expedients, the *humiliations* of the relatively poor. Instead of having to flatter, she would be flattered; instead of being grateful, she would receive thanks (49) [my emphasis].

Carol Wershoven notes that Lily's ability to please becomes an ability to *feel* as the book progresses.[11] An 'insatiable desire to please' (151) is indeed the center of Lily's life, and she wants to be looked at, admired, affirmed. The intensity of that need for affirmation reveals the poverty of her inner resources, and the isolation and loneliness of her early years. Affirmation is a source of power, a reversal of the powerlessness she feels as a woman, and as a woman without substantial means. But Lily needs not just to be admired (and the quality of admiration at such times is less important to her than the quantity), she needs to be *superior*. Her triumph at the *tableaux vivants* is heightened not merely by her sense of her own beauty, but at feeling 'lifted to a height apart by that incommunicable grace which is the bodily counterpart of genius!' (116) Like Gryce wallowing in his Americana, Lily has an inflated sense of her own worth which is the counterpart of her shame-ridden self, but she is not without insight. After Gus Trenor threatens to rape her, she wonders to Gerty Farish how Selden would respond if she said to him

> 'I am bad through and through – I want admiration, I want excitement, I want money – yes, *money*! That's my shame, Gerty – and it's known, it's said of me, it's what men think of me –' (166).

Lily has often had wonderful opportunities to snag wealthy husbands, but they have all failed, and not through laziness. As her friend Carrie Fisher notes, 'she works like a slave preparing the ground and sowing her seed; but the day she ought to be reaping the harvest she oversleeps herself or goes off on a picnic.' Mrs Fisher, a glamorous divorcee who is a sort of social advisor and equerry for the *nouveaux riches*, reflects that Lily perhaps 'despises the things she's trying for' (189). Exactly. Selden's contempt for everything Lily strives after is matched by her own dim awareness of the shabby standards her search for wealth and power exhibit. Here is where we see the ambivalence of shame played out. Lily can manipulate circumstances and men so that marriage is imminent, yet having almost claimed the dreary and dispiriting Percy Gryce, for instance, she is all too aware that gaining him is not an unalloyed pleasure: marrying Gryce is insuring the possibility of being bored for life. Even the process of 'seducing' him, one she can revel in because it reveals her grace, her charm, her subtlety, is a process she cannot help but see as beneath her, contemptible. Having made a success of their impromptu tea on the train to Bellomont, Lily knows she 'must *submit* to more boredom, be ready with fresh *compliances* and adaptabilities' (25) [my emphases]. The trap is obvious. To escape shame, she can see only a marriage that will lift her above the sources of shame, but the means of accomplishing that marriage are themselves shameful, and she, the proud, beautiful, talented, exquisite Lily Bart, must sink herself to the level of a dim and depressing man, too 'horribly shy' (45) to order tea for himself on a train! The very weapons she has been trained to use inspire her with contempt for the intended victims of those weapons. A clod like Percy Gryce would have absolutely no real appreciation of Lily's talents, though he would be dazzled and enticed.

What then are the sources of Lily's shame-based identity? At the end of the novel, exhausted, beaten down, Lily Bart reflects on the legacy of her family. Because of their rootlessness, she had grown up with 'no centre of early pieties, of grave endearing traditions, to which her heart could revert and from which it could draw strength and tenderness for others' (319). She has thus always been 'rootless and ephemeral' (319). But the inheritance is even darker than that. Dale Bauer sees Lily, an 'overdetermined subject,' as desiring 'escape from the family by which she is cloistered, controlled, and ultimately silenced.'[12] What controls her, I think, is shame; it is the instrument of social and personal subjugation. Bauer notes that 'Lily has not learned or been encouraged to separate her identity from her mother's,' but Mrs Bart's vision of Lily as saving the family's honor and fortunes does more than just 'infiltrate Lily's consciousness.'[13] Her mother's and her family's financial disgrace is the key to understanding Lily's successes and her ultimate failures.

Lily has grown up in a chaotic, 'turbulent' family environment without much direction or emotional attachment anywhere. Gerty Farish will tell Selden of rushing up to Lily as a child, hugging her and being remonstrated with: 'Please don't kiss me unless I ask you to' (271). Lily's 'vigorous and determined' mother sees Lily's 'effaced and silent' (29) father as nothing more than a supply of money, of which there was never enough, 'and in some vague way her father seemed always to blame for the deficiency' (30). Thus financial doom always lurks in the wings for the Barts. Though on shaky ground, the Barts put up a bold and dishonest front – it is of course shame that makes them attempt to live 'as though one were much richer than one's bankbook denoted' (30). Lily's mother even finds this masquerade 'heroic' and Lily is 'naturally proud of her mother's aptitude' (30). What are the alternatives? Living 'like a pig' – which the Barts' rich relatives do: that is, living without grace, style, or 'any proper standard of conduct' (30). Such a life is 'disgusting,' and the disgust reaction occurs over and over throughout the book, characters disgusted by their surroundings or someone's behavior. Finding their relatives disgusting gives Lily 'a sense of reflected superiority' and also a determination not to be disgusting, but to indulge her 'lively taste for splendour' (30).

When Mr Bart's fortunes collapse, Lily is unable to do more than pity him from a distance, while her mother seethes with resentment at the plunge into uncertainty. After his death, Lily and her mother are thrown on the mercy of their rich relatives (a humiliating turn of events). They also 'vegetate' in 'cheap continental refuges'

> where Mrs Bart held herself *fiercely aloof* from the frugal tea-tables of her companions in misfortune. She was especially *careful to avoid* her old friends and the scenes of her former successes. To be poor seemed to her such a *confession of failure* that it amounted to *disgrace*; and she detected a note of *condescension* in the friendliest advances (34) [my emphases].

Two years of 'hungry roaming' follow, and Mrs Bart dies 'of deep disgust' at her own failure: 'She had hated dinginess, and it was her fate to be dingy' (35). Lily's mother urges her 'to escape from dinginess if she could' and to use her beauty, which Mrs Bart passionately studied 'as though it were some weapon she had slowly fashioned for her vengeance' (34). Lily will save the family's honor, redeeming Mr Bart's financial disgrace: 'It was the last asset in their fortunes, the nucleus around which their life was to be rebuilt.' Such adjurations leave Lily 'impressed by the magnitude of her opportunities' and longing for 'the existence to which she felt herself entitled' (34). For all Lily's awareness that she must not 'betray any sense of superiority,' as we have seen, she craves that superiority in the moment and in the scenes she imagines off in the future. Yet these ambitions are not unambivalent: 'She was secretly ashamed of her mother's crude passion for money' (35). Thus, the intensity of her mother's desire for revenge in the form of a brilliant marriage for Lily is in reality an attempt to triumph over shame. But the very intensity of that desire is *itself* shameful – and Lily is split between wanting to succeed, and feeling contempt for the path to success. The superiority endemic in her mother's attitudes has molded Lily – so that she is deeply contemptuous of the very men she sets out to win. How can she not be, when she has been taught to think less of them? Yet each and every time she fails, the family failure – so large and public – must seem like an inescapable curse.

Cynthia Griffin Wolff notes that *The Custom of the Country* 'is in many ways a companion-piece' to *The House of Mirth*.[14] And indeed, though the former book spans more years and includes a wider range of characters and settings, there are some deep and striking similarities, especially between the two heroines. Both are beautiful, restless, and addicted to being admired. And even though Undine Spragg is never as sophisticated as Lily, and is far less human and emotional, for both women their looks are the passport to freedom, wealth and power – though limited. Many critics note the angry sometimes blistering satire of this book, and in large part, it is aimed at a shameful reality of American life, the 'custom of the country' which confines women to a position of perpetual inferiority and indignity. In an environment which reduces 'human beings to things and measures them solely in material terms,' Lily Bart was finally helpless, but Undine somewhat more successfully 'exploits these materialistic values to her advantage.'[15]

The situation is clearly enunciated in the novel by Charles Bowen, a representative of the old New York that is crumbling under the relentless assault of new-money Barbarians. Bowen charges that 'the average American man looks down on his wife.'[16] He assesses the problem as an unwillingness in American men (unlike their European counterparts) to let their wives share in what is most real and important in their lives – that is, business, which is the 'emotional centre of gravity' in America. Despite the apparent 'slaving, self-effacing, self-sacrificing' they do for their wives, American men are really 'the most *indifferent*. . . The "slaving's" no argument against the *indifference*' (119) [my emphases].

We have seen in Chapter 1 and in a number of the works already discussed that indifference often has a very personal and poisonous resonance for Wharton as a deep source of shame because it seems to render the object of indifference unimportant, unvaluable, even non-existent. Undine Spragg struggles throughout *The Custom of the Country* against indifference – it is her chief nemesis. For instance, for her to 'know that others were indifferent to what she had thought important was to cheapen all present pleasure and turn the whole force of her desires in a new direction' (164). Later in the book, when the Marquis de Chelles is interested in her (their marriage will end 'her bitter two years of loneliness and humiliation' [270]), but his family has cooled, she experiences indifference on a social call where she is completely ignored by them. 'The sense of having been thus rendered invisible filled Undine with a vehement desire to make herself seen' (231). The most significant shame scene in the book – which recalls Lily's being publicly cut after her aunt's will is read – revolves around indifference. Showing herself at New York's opera house after her divorce from Ralph Marvell (and her affair with Peter Van Degen),

Undine is devastated 'that no one noticed her' (211) and once again 'felt a defiant desire to make herself seen' (212). Her former society friends blush and ignore her, her father humiliates her afterwards by ordering her to return a magnificent pearl necklace her lover Van Degen gave her – and worse, 'the humiliation. . . in going to the opera' was one she brought on herself. Undine at this nadir in her fortunes feels unequipped 'to fight the forces of indifference leagued against her,' and stung by the 'humiliation of carrying about with her the price of her shame' (213).

Undine's need to be important, to be valuable, to exist is unfortunate because the terms in which she can gain that significance and sense of power make her perpetually vulnerable to shame. For Undine, as for Lily, being *seen* is absolutely essential to her sense of self, and being seen as admirable, beautiful, special. This dependence on others for internal valuation places her at the mercy both of other people and her own dissatisfaction; as Carol Wershoven observes, Undine 'can define herself only through other people's eyes.'[17] Her basic interpersonal need for affirmation is also unfortunately bound up with her drive to have power over others, and Kaufman lists striving for power as one key way to defend against shame. 'Gaining power over others and in interpersonal situations, jockeying for position in social groups and keeping control in relationships are particular manifestations' of this striving.[18]

Just as Lily Bart does, Undine has an excellent sense of her physical charms, partly because of her shame, because they both 'crave the reflecting reassurance of the mirror to assuage an otherwise intolerable inner loneliness.'[19] One of the most vivid images in the entire book is Undine in front of the mirror, pretending that she is being observed, 'fanning, fidgeting, twitching at her draperies, as she did in real life when people were noticing her' (16). It is a great joy for Undine to imagine the effect she will have on others, and even when she is still relatively untutored in social niceties after only a few years in New York, she has an intuitive sense of herself as a picture – just as Lily Bart had. After her marriage to Marvell, when she meets Elmer Moffatt (a Rosedale figure who is her first and then fourth husband) with her child, Undine knows that she is 'present[ing] a not unpleasing image of young motherhood' and she is highly conscious of 'the picture she and her son composed' and its effect on Moffatt (153). Undine's physical beauty is not enough, however, to help her rise in society, though she skillfully uses her sexual attractiveness as a weapon 'to achieve power and material pleasures,' and she is able to be cold and calculating, *business-like*, because of her 'sexual indifference.'[20] She is aided by being 'passionately imitative' and 'could not help modelling herself on the last person she met' (14). Late in the novel, for example, she is keenly aware of having surpassed some of her old friends in tact and demeanor, having learned 'shades of conduct, turns of speech, tricks of attitude' (314) through her contacts with old New York and French aristocracy. Though in French society, she will be humiliated to learn that her looks and clothes are not enough to make her successful. Another American who has married a French noble explains that in addition to looks, a woman has 'to know what's being said about things' (305), and of course Undine blushes to be considered a bore: '[a]ny sense of insufficiency exasperated her' (305).

Undine is used to being 'wanted' by those who have seen her. But without being the center of attention, she is crushed; and her mother early on fears what will happen when Undine – with her indomitable will and bad temper – realizes she is 'too small' for New York and virtually invisible there, despite being perched in an ostentatious hotel with a treasury of beautiful clothes (10). Undine's need to be admired and regarded is a constant throughout the novel, whereas of course for Lily Bart, the need diminishes in intensity as her values undergo a transformation. Undine's husband Ralph Marvell, the weary old New Yorker, quickly comes to understand that 'what Undine really enjoyed was the image of her own charm mirrored in the general admiration' (91), but he unfortunately misjudges the power of this need, and imagines she will change and become more thoughtful and mature. Before they are married, Undine wants Ralph to see her talking to the wealthy Peter Van Degen; she enjoys Van Degen's stares because they make up for his wife's indifference to her. After her marriage, Undine 'thrilled agreeably under the glance' of Claude Popple, the society painter doing her portrait (109). She especially enjoys having people overhear Popple talking to her, another example of her being perpetually on stage *and* in her own audience. The unveiling of Popple's portrait of her is another welcome occasion for self-regard:

> Any triumph in which she shared left a glow in her veins, and the success of her picture obscured all other impressions. She saw herself throning in a central panel at the spring exhibition,

with the crowd pushing against the picture, repeating her name. . . (114).

A magnificent ball is yet another opportunity for her to be seen: 'What could be more delightful than to feel that, while all the women envied her dress, the men did not so much as look at it? Their admiration was all for herself. . .' (131). Thus being admired is not enough for her, she also wants to be *envied*: 'Undine always liked to know that what belonged to her was coveted by others' (130). Undine is in many ways similar to Lily, who imagines future glorious settings for herself in which she can triumph over her friends who have abused her or gossiped about her. Undine's fantasies are somewhat cruder and involve more publicity, but revenge over those who have been indifferent or hostile is as much a part of her character as it is of Lily's. Imagining the reversal of roles with one's humiliators is a prominent strategy for counteracting shame. It combines elements of rage, contempt and power strategies with the aim of at last vanquishing or triumphing over those who previously caused one to suffer shame. Undine 'remembered her failures as keenly as her triumphs, and. . . the passionate desire to obliterate, to "get even" with them, was always among' the latent incentives of her conduct' (58–9). In this sense, she is something of a perfectionist, wanting always the best, but wiping away shameful failure. This element of her personality – feeling for instance that despite the pinnacle of success she has reached at the novel's end, 'there were other things she might want if she knew about them' (333) – is clearly an aspect of the way shame shapes her desires. Kaufman writes that perfectionism

> is an attempt to compensate for feeling inherently defective, never quite good enough as a person. Hence, the perception that nothing done is ever good enough – it could always have been better. The inevitable result is that one is plunged back into shame.[21]

Indeed, Undine will realize 'that it was always her fate to find out just too late about the "something beyond". . . [something] more luxurious, more exciting, more worthy of her!' (34) Her life is the American treadmill – a perpetual search for *more*, for something better, a search that makes satisfaction impossible because there is no such thing as 'enough' in America. Undine's psychic trap is even more recognizable today than when the book was first written. Undine's first important social event, a dinner with old New York aristocracy – Fairfields, Dagonets, Marvells where she meets her future husband Ralph Marvell – is a humiliating one, and a perfect example of the ways in which shame shapes her behavior. Though 'she wanted to be noticed. . . she dreaded to be patronized' (24), reminding us in a way of Vance Weston's early fears in *Hudson River Bracketed* of being ridiculed and his intense hunger to be paid attention to. The evening's literate and genteel talk confuses Undine, leaving her angry and ashamed: 'She felt a violent longing to brush away the cobwebs and assert herself as the dominant figure of the scene' (24). Even worse, she misreads being talked to by a married man after dinner; such social usage is unheard of where she comes from, and she assumes it as a public acknowledgement of her unimportance: 'She inferred that the others didn't care to talk to her' (25). She counters her shame by resisting conversational overtures, and by the gesture we are already familiar with as an anti-shame facial response, 'holding her vivid head very high' (25). As the dinner party is breaking up, Undine quite unreasonably expects an invitation from Clare Van Degen to dinner, and she plummets into shame when she is merely invited to call 'some afternoon' – the disappointment leaves her with her face burning. Yet once again her spirits rise as she – even more unreasonably – expects Ralph Marvell to escort her back home because he 'had really no eyes for any one but herself.' When he simply says goodbye she cannot 'help the break of pride in her voice' (24).

Undine is just as vulnerable to shame, two marriages, one child, one affair and several years later, despite her wealth, her travel, her experience, her jewels and clothes. Married to a French count, she is more and more aware that she is a disappointment to him as much as he is to her. Their life is not one of luxurious delights in Paris, but mainly of stultifying family boredom at his chateau. She has – humiliatingly – not borne him a child, and her struggles to get more freedom and more time in Paris are futile. Her rage that his brother will have the more spacious apartments in the family's Paris hôtel leaves her 'half-ashamed' (284), but she is even more 'mortified by the discovery that there were regions of [her husband's] life she could not enter' (285) – business, current affairs, books all leave her with a 'sense of inadequacy' which Charity

Royall will experience similarly with Lucius Harney in *Summer*. Attempting to make up the differences between them by luring him back to her bed, she is politely rebuffed, and understandably can't confess her 'wounded pride' to even her closest friend, another American married into the French aristocracy. In language that is by now completely familiar to us, 'her impulses of retaliation spent themselves against the blank surface of [her husband's] indifference' (293) and 'she was humiliated by his indifference, and it was easier to ascribe it to the arts of a rival than to any deficiency in herself' (295).

There are many other scenes and moments in which Undine experiences shame, though she continually, and unsuccessfully, attempts to rise above it, because '[n]othing was bitterer to her than to confess to herself the failure of her power' (135). When she is thinking, for instance, of selling the chateau's fabulous tapestries, Elmer Moffatt turns out to be the potential buyer, and Undine is '*humiliated* that he should suspect her of being in financial straits. She never wanted to see Moffatt except when she was happy and triumphant' (300) [my emphasis]. She is unable to be seen to such advantage at this point, however, blushing when he appears, embarrassed when she has to explain away not getting to Paris much, flushing when she asks why he had lent her money once, and finally confessing her loneliness and ending up '*ashamed* of her tame acceptance of her fate' (302) [my emphasis].

R.W.B. Lewis notes the ways in which Undine is surprisingly a reflection of minor and major aspects of Wharton herself: both she and Undine liked dressing up in front of mirrors as children; one of Undine's nicknames – Puss – is the same as Wharton's; Undine's struggle against stifling social constraints reminds us of Wharton's, as does her sense of marriage as 'no more than another mode of imprisonment.' Lewis finds the strongest connection in their fierce energy and strength, and I would add that the ways in which shame is an element of their personality and motivates them are just as significant.[22]

Shame does not finally vanquish Undine; it merely haunts her and helps make her perpetually dissatisfied, but shame *does* destroy her husband Ralph Marvell, one of the best portraits of the dilettante artist in Wharton's fiction. In fact, as Cynthia Griffin Wolff points out, Ralph's 'affection for Undine is the lust of a creator to shape and give symmetry.'[23] But Ralph is unable to see Undine for who she really is, and so their marriage ends in disappointment and divorce, the ultimate scandal in his family. A dreamy and gentle gentleman, Ralph is first stirred by Undine to a surprisingly martial sentiment, which makes him abandon his detachment to become part of what was happening 'to the American and French aristocracies in the first decade of the twentieth century. Both were giving way before the major forces of the historic moment – sexual power and financial aggressiveness.'[24] Ralph is initially appalled that Undine has attracted Peter van Degen, 'the gross millionaire playboy,'[25] who has married into old New York by marrying Clare Dagonet, Ralph's cousin. He considers Van Degen 'unspeakable. . . cheaply fashionable' and pictures Undine as vulnerable, a 'flexible soul [offering] itself to the first grasp.'

> That the grasp should chance to be Van Degen's – that was what made Ralph's temples buzz, and swept away all his plans for his own future like a beaver's dam in a spring flood. To save her from Van Degen and Van Degenism: was that really to be his mission – the 'call' for which his life had obscurely waited? (49)

He imagines himself rescuing her as if she were 'lovely rock-bound Andromeda' (50) and all his previous dreams and ambitions (however tenuous) 'sank into insignificance under the pressure of Undine's claims' (49). Ralph is certainly intoxicated by Undine's very presence, but despite his sense of irony about the fading of his class, shame snares him here. Winning Undine is not something to do for herself, but a tribute to his vigor and strength. Given the fantasy, it is no wonder that he will be even more profoundly disappointed in his wife than Anna Leath was by her husband in *The Reef*.

He notes the crudeness of Undine's perceptions, her love of noise and crowds, the fact that her 'mind was as destitute of beauty and mystery as the prairie school-house in which she had been educated; and her ideals. . . pathetic' (86), yet for a long time he persists in imagining that 'as she acquired a finer sense of values the depths in her would find a voice' (105). Sadly, their marriage becomes for him 'marked by one disillusionment after another' (123), leaving him with 'the miserable ghost of his illusion' (127–28). Where are her depths? She is merely a wilful, insensitive creature who is frightening, almost, in her inability to empathize with his feelings (which deficiency makes her quite unlike Lily Bart). The marriage itself becomes a source of humiliation as Ralph gives up his vague dreams of writing, and takes a dreary real estate job to make money. He is left with 'an unquenchable ache for her nearness, her smile, her touch. His life had come to be nothing but a long effort to win these mercies by one concession after another. . . [he is reduced to] the incessant struggle to make enough money to satisfy her increasing exactions' (125). This contemplative man who imagines that a honeymoon in the hill towns of Tuscany is heaven, winds up with a wife who enjoys 'publicity, promiscuity' more than anything else (129). One of the great achievements of the book is the power with which Wharton creates Ralph's 'dull daily ache of feeling her so near and yet so inaccessible' (152).

With Undine ensconced in Paris while Ralph slaves away at miserably uncongenial work, he suffers the embarrassment of not hearing from her, and having to talk about the absence of letters to her parents. Utterly unhappy, Ralph, like so many of Wharton's characters, cannot reveal how he feels because it would be too shameful. He isn't even completely honest with Clare Van Degen, the gentle if not entirely perceptive cousin whom he still seems to love, about how Undine has made him miserable. 'He would not for the world have confessed his discouragement, his consciousness of incapacity' – he can complain about the dreary, stifling work he's doing, but he goes no further than that. Alone at home, waking up after a crying jag, he is ashamed of himself, wondering how he could have been 'such a fool,' criticizing himself for having let go (184–85).

But all the shame of his disappointing marriage, his shipwrecked hopes of artistic creativity, and the heavy weight of a job he is unfit for are nothing compared to the public humiliation that awaits him when Undine files for divorce – which old New York sees 'as a vulgar and unnecessary way of taking the public into one's confidence' (182). This fierce taboo will have devastating effects on his life and ultimately make him commit suicide. He is completely isolated, with 'no one with whom he could speak of Undine. His family had thrown over the whole subject a pall of silence' (190). The scandal is something his family refuses to acknowledge; divorce is a disgrace and even though he is Undine's 'victim' in this case, he is 'inevitably contaminated' (191). There is something horrifying yet comic in their reaction to a divorce:

the time involved in the 'proceedings' was viewed as a penitential season during which it behoved the family of the person
concerned to behave as if they were dead; yet any open allusion
to the reason for adopting such an attitude would have been
regarded as the height of indelicacy (191).

Against this wall of silence and shame, Ralph at first 'passionately
longed to cry out his humiliation, his rebellion, his despair' (192).
Subtle family attempts to help him forget Undine leave him 'angry,
sore, ashamed' (193) and it is shame that ultimately defeats him
because he allows Undine to keep custody of their little boy, whom
Undine will use as a way of prying money out of Ralph (she will
need it to get a Papal annulment from de Chelles). Ralph does not
contest the divorce, has almost nothing to do with it. 'The idea of
touching publicly on anything that had passed between himself
and Undine had become unthinkable' (193). The whole business is
'grotesque' and 'degrading' and his family unfortunately conspires
against his future happiness, using 'the full and elaborate vocabulary of evasion':

> 'delicacy,' 'pride,' 'personal dignity,' 'preferring not to know
> about such things'; Mrs Marvell's: 'All I ask is that you won't
> mention the subject to your grandfather,' Mr Dagonet's 'Spare
> your mother, Ralph, whatever happens,' and even Laura's terri-
> fied: 'Of course, for Paul's sake, there must be no scandal' (246).

Worse is to come. Though Ralph has locked the divorce decree in
his desk, hoping to put 'the whole subject out of sight,' he cannot
escape the painful reality (194). Like Glennard ashamed in *The
Touchstone* to see advertisements of Aubyn's *Letters* seemingly
everywhere he looks, Ralph reads about Undine's divorce in someone's newspaper in the subway on the way to work. The article
refers to him as too busy to pay attention to his wife, and Ralph
blushes. 'For weeks afterwards, wherever he went, he felt that
blush upon his forehead. For the first time in his life the coarse
fingering of public curiosity had touched the secret places of his
soul, and nothing that had gone before seemed as humiliating as
this trivial comment on his tragedy' (194–95). The article even
seems to have a bizarre life of its own, cropping up in different
forms: 'Whenever he took up a newspaper he seemed to come
upon it' (195).

Not fighting for custody of his son Paul plays right into Undine's hands. Ralph subsequently feels trapped into buying Undine off when she demands her son back (for appearances, as Clare Van Degen astutely notes). Feeling 'miserably diminished by the smallness of what had filled his world' (253), he attempts to raise the money Undine wants for her annulment, and gets involved in a deal with Elmer Moffatt which does not pan out. The quick turnover he desperately needed doesn't materialize, and in his anger he insults Moffatt, who reveals that he too was married to Undine at one time. If Ralph had hoped to save Undine from 'Van Degenism,' that hope is revealed to have been an impossible dream from the very beginning because Undine had 'lied to him from the first' (266). Moffatt is even grosser and cruder than Van Degen, more an object of disgust and contempt. Ralph is trapped, completely defeated – his son will have to be delivered up to Undine, and he has reached his final humiliation. He can stand no more exposure: 'It seemed to him intolerable that anyone should ever cross the threshold of [his] room again' (268).

One terrible irony is that before this very last disaster that makes him blow his brains out, Ralph's life had seemed to be improving. He has been enjoying the sweet and uncomplicated company of Clare, his son, and the work on his novel, which had been pressed on him as therapy after the divorce, and which he had resisted at first. Informed by Ralph's new vision of men as insects where before he had seen life on the heroic scale (241), the book had begun to take shape; it gave him some distance from his pain and even made social life easier. Among people who ignored his sorrow, he could feel more assured and less ashamed. He 'shrank less from meeting his friends, and even began to dine out again, and to laugh at some of the jokes he heard' (241). All this tentative recovery is undone, of course, by his failure to raise the money Undine wants, and his sexual humiliation by Moffatt.

In pairing this old New Yorker, whose fantasies of writing something great often seem just that, with a woman who can only read popular romances on the rare occasions when she *does* read, Wharton brings together perhaps the most mismatched couple of her fiction. Everything that is positive in them – Undine's enthusiasm, Ralph's delicacy – clashes, and everything that is negative in them – Undine's insensitivity, Ralph's fecklessness – quickly breeds domestic tragedy. In Undine, shame functions as an individual's source of motivation, whereas in Ralph, shame is part of his cultural inheritance. He sees that 'weakness was innate in him,' shame in the form of 'the conventions of his class' has 'mysteriously mastered him, deflecting his course like some hidden hereditary failing' (247). I would argue that the 'most malignant heritage of old New York' is not apathy, as Cynthia Griffin observes in her reading of this novel, but *shame*.[26] It gives him an exaggerated sense of his possibilities, blinds him to reality, and then subdues his natural feelings.

Watching Lily make tea early in *The House of Mirth*, Lawrence Selden thinks 'that the links of her bracelet seemed like manacles chaining her to her fate.'[27] The narrator of *Ethan Frome*, on first observing Frome at Starkfield, is struck by Frome's 'lameness checking each step like the jerk of a chain.'[28] Ethan Frome is chained to an even darker fate than Lily's, because he doesn't escape into death, yet his story too is one of disappointment, failure, powerlessness and shame – for him and in lesser ways for Mattie Silver and even his wife Zeena. The physical burden is matched by an emotional chain that constantly pulls Ethan short, that silences him, that constricts his life: shame over a lifetime of disappointments, culminating in being trapped ('most of the smart ones get away' [6] from Starkfield), and over his deep inadequacies as a man. In *Ethan Frome*, shame becomes more and more potent a force as the novella progresses and its conflicts intensify.

Kaufman notes that 'the affective source of silence is shame, which is the affect that causes the self to hide. Shame itself is an impediment to speech.'[29] In the narrator's first extended contact with Frome, he reflects that Frome 'seemed a part of the mute melancholy landscape, an incarnation of its frozen woe, with all that was warm and sentient in him fast bound below the surface. . .' (14). Living in Starkfield, 'silence had deepened about him year by year' (69). We gain our first glimpses below that surface of silence watching Frome interact with the narrator, who is visiting Starkfield on an engineering job. Frome finds 'a volume of popular science' that the narrator left behind, and with 'a queer note of resentment in his voice' (16) says the book is full of things he knows nothing about: 'He was evidently surprised and slightly aggrieved at his own ignorance' (16). For the narrator, these comments point up 'the contrast. . . between his outer situation and his inner needs' (17). Frome's 'old veil of reticence' (22) is a mask for the bitter life of disappointment. And even in a town where people have suffered enough to feel 'indifferent' to other's troubles, Frome is seen as having 'had his plate full up with [sickness and trouble] ever since the very first helping' (13). In the narrative built up about Frome, we learn of the early roots of his shame in disappointment. Though he had gone to a technical college for a year and been interested in physics, the death of his father 'and the misfortunes following it' (27) ended the possibility of study, and through that, escape from the constricting life of Starkfield. Unlike Lily Bart, Ethan Frome has no personal gifts or talents that can offer even the fantasy of a better life. His life of isolation changes, however, when Mattie Silver comes to stay with him and his wife.

Mattie's circumstances recall Lily's in some ways (she too can 'trim a hat' [59]). She is the daughter of a cousin of Zeena's, whose misfortune has 'indentured her' to the Fromes. Mattie's father 'had inflamed his clan with mingled sentiments of envy and admiration' (58) by a successful move to Connecticut, marriage and business ventures. But he mishandled money that relatives had given him, all of which was revealed after his death. The shameful disclosure killed his wife, and left Mattie a victim. 'Her nearest relations. . . ungrudgingly acquitted themselves of the Christian duty of returning good for evil by giving [her] all the advice at their disposal' (59). Zeena only took Mattie in because her doctor said she needed help around the house: 'The clan instantly saw the chance of exacting a compensation from Mattie' (59). Like Lily, Mattie is proof of someone else's beneficence, and her 'liberation' is a kind of imprisonment, since she has to 'pay' for her father's success *and* his failure.

For Frome, Mattie's youth and enthusiasm offer him a pathway out of isolation. She is someone he can share his observations and thoughts with: 'He could show her things and tell her things. . .' (33). He also enjoys her 'admiration for his learning' (34) – she can make him feel happy and proud. Yet because of her new importance in his life, she is also a source of shame. Waiting to take her home from a squaredance in town, he is struck by not feeling special. Through a window he sees 'two or three gestures, which, in his fatuity, he had thought she kept for him. . . the sight made him unhappy' (35). Even more painfully, he wonders 'how he could ever have thought his dull talk interested her. To him, who was never gay but in her presence, her gaiety seemed plain proof of *indifference*' (35) [my emphasis]. When she is leaving the dance,

[a] wave of *shyness* pulled him back into the dark angle of the wall, and he stood there *in silence* instead of making his presence known to her. It had been one of the wonders of their intercourse that from the first, she, the quicker, finer, more expressive, *instead of crushing him by the contrast, had given him something of her own ease and freedom*; but now he felt as *heavy* and *loutish* as in his student days, when he had tried to 'jolly' the Worcester girls at a picnic (41) [my emphases].

Frome is 'by nature grave and inarticulate [and] admired recklessness and gaiety in others' (68); one of Mattie's great gifts is to ease Frome's shame. Mattie's impact on Frome recalls Lily's skillful easing of Percy Gryce's profound embarrassment on the train to Bellomont. But Mattie is naturally capable of doing what in Lily is planned and reasoned. Wharton's intuitive understanding of shame is clear here; of course someone stiff and shy like Ethan would be struck by the contrast between himself and someone natural and free, and that invidious comparison would potentially be the source of shame. So much depends on her – and Frome attaches 'a fantastic importance to every change in her look and tone' (46). Doesn't this terrible dependence on others for one's own self-esteem remind us of characters throughout Wharton's fiction?

The night Ethan picks Mattie up at the dance, he is jealous of young, well-off Denis Eady, who had danced with Mattie. Later, thinking about Mattie and Denis, he will feel 'ashamed of the storm of jealousy in his breast. It seemed unworthy of the girl that his thoughts of her should be so violent' (78). Now, he is relieved when Mattie resists riding with Denis, but then Mattie's 'indifference was the more chilling after the flush of joy into which she had plunged him by dismissing Denis Eady' (46–47). Their idyllic walk home, 'as if they were floating on a summer stream,' ends with a grim reality: withered, censorious Zeena is waiting for him, and he goes up to their bedroom 'with *lowered head*' (55) [my emphasis]. Shame is certainly a key element of his relationship with Zeena, the cousin who came to nurse his mother, and who stayed after Mrs Frome died. Unlike Mattie, she arouses little that is positive in Ethan. Zeena's 'efficiency shamed and dazzled him' and he keenly felt a 'magnified. . . sense of what he owed her' (70). Zeena's own shame helps trap him in Starkfield, which they had originally agreed to leave:

she had let her husband see from the first that life on an isolated farm was not what she had expected when she married. . . . She chose to look down on Starkfield, but she could not have lived in a place which looked down on her. Even Bettsbridge or Shadd's Falls would not have been sufficiently aware of her, and in the greater cities which attracted Ethan she would have suffered a complete loss of identity (71–72).

Her feelings are thus clearly much more than what Richard Lawson describes as a 'disinclination to accept any change.'[30] Her power over Ethan manifests itself in a critical silence, hinting at 'suspicions and resentments impossible to guess' (73). Still, though vaguely threatened by Zeena, he is not reduced to *complete* powerlessness: 'There had never been anything in her that one could appeal to; but as long as he could ignore and command he had remained indifferent' (118).

The balance between them changes when Zeena goes off for more doctor's advice and Ethan and Mattie spend some time together alone – their first such occasion, which is both festive and furtive. Ethan is 'suffocated with the sense of well-being' (82) coming in from his hard day's work for dinner, but when Zeena comes up in their conversation, Mattie feels 'the contagion of his embarrassment' and she flushes (84). The next day he feels intoxicated 'to find. . . magic in his clumsy words' (91), but he makes Mattie blush when he mentions having seen engaged friends of hers kissing: 'now he felt as if her blush had set a flaming guard about her. He supposed it was his natural awkwardness that made him feel so' (92).

Zeena's return with the diagnosis of 'complications' – which confers morbid 'distinction. . . in the neighbourhood' [108] – precipitates the first fight between Ethan and herself 'in their seven sad years together' (112). Zeena claims that she will need full-time help around the house that Mattie cannot supply, and bursts out that she would have been ashamed to admit to the doctor that her husband begrudged her the help, that she lost her health nursing his mother, and her family said he 'couldn't do no less than marry' Zeena in the circumstances (111). Ethan explodes, and is 'seized with horror at the scene and shame at his own share in it' (112). Zeena taunts him with the possibility she might end up in a poorhouse, as other Fromes have done, and then Ethan's big lie is exposed. He had clumsily said he couldn't drive her to her train because he was going to get a payment for lumber from Andrew Hale. When he tried to get that unprecedented advance from Hale, Hale flushed, leaving Ethan 'embarrassed.' Shame kept him from pleading an emergency: since he had struggled to become solvent after his father's death, 'he did not want Andrew Hale, or any one else in Starkfield, to think he was going under again' (75). Frome naturally responds with anger when Hale asks if he is in financial trouble, because he of course feels further exposed.

Now, facing Zeena, Ethan blushes and stammers, trying to explain that there was no money coming in, and he is devastated when his wife announces she has hired a girl and that Mattie *must* go: he is 'seized with the despairing sense of his helplessness' (116). Ethan tries to shame Zeena into keeping Mattie, pointing out that people will frown on her kicking out a poor, friendless girl, but Zeena is adamant, leaving Ethan 'suddenly weak and power-less' (117) – and enraged:

> All the long misery of his baffled past, of his youth of failure, hardship and vain effort, rose up in his soul in bitterness and seemed to take shape before him in the woman who at every turn had barred his way. She had taken everything else from him; and now she meant to take the one thing that made up for all the others (118).

Ethan is so distraught that he blurts out to Mattie that she has to leave, and then feels 'overcome with shame at his lack of self-control in flinging the news at her so brutally' (120). The grim evening ends witn Zeena's discovery that her prized pickle dish, a never-used wedding present, was broken during her absence when Mattie and Ethan were having dinner, and that Ethan had tried to hide the breakage. Glad that Mattie – with whom she compares so poorly – is leaving, Zeena's joy turns to profound sorrow at the destruction of the one treasure in her miserable life.

Ethan longs for escape with Mattie to the West – but he hasn't enough money: 'The inexorable facts closed in on him like prison-warders handcuffing a convict. There was no way out – none. He was a prisoner for life, and now his one ray of light was to be extinguished' (134). In a way like Lily, 'the passion of rebellion' (139) breaks out in him and he plans to ask Andrew Hale for money to pay for Zeena's new hired girl (though the money would really be for his 'escape'). After all, Hale knows Ethan's money troubles well enough for Ethan 'to renew his appeal *without too much loss of pride'* (140) [my emphasis]. On the brink of making this request, however, unexpected sympathy from Mrs Hale turns Ethan away, with 'the blood in his face' (143). Having been accustomed to think people 'were either indifferent to his troubles, or disposed to think [them] natural,' he is warmed by her compassionate 'You've had an awful mean time, Ethan Frome' (142). Like Lily, unable to use Selden's letters despite Rosedale's seductive offer, he is 'pulled up sharply' (143). How can he dishonestly take money from the Hales when they sympathize with the way life has cheated him?

Still, Ethan's 'manhood was humbled by the part he was compelled to play. . . as a helpless spectator at Mattie's banishment' (139). When she later weepingly wishes she were dead, Ethan will feel ashamed too (159). Taking Mattie away, they stop at the pond where they first realized at a picnic that they loved each other; it is a 'shy secret spot, full of the same *dumb melancholy* that Ethan felt in his heart' (153) [my emphasis]. Their blissful reprieve of sledding turns into an attempted mutual suicide, but as in so many other things, Ethan fails to pull it off, and he and Mattie are left crippled and even more dependent on Zeena. Ethan is so ashamed of what his life has come to that no stranger sets 'foot in [his] house for over twenty years' (176).

All this, of course, is the *vision* of the narrator, and Frome is 'the man he might become if the reassuring appurtenances of busy, active, professional, adult mobility were taken from him.'[31] The life of silence and constriction Ethan Frome leads is indeed a nightmare, as Cynthia Griffin Wolff has eloquently shown, but I see this as a nightmare in which shame has reduced human possibilities and even human speech to an almost unbearable minimum. Ethan's fantasies of being buried next to Mattie, his 'warm sense of continuance and stability' (50) at the sight of the family graveyard, is a longing not for passivity but for *release* from the crushing weight of a lifetime of humiliating failure and disappointment. Wolff makes a compelling case for echoes in *Ethan Frome* of Wharton's complex involvement with the aging Henry James, querulous and unpredictable Teddy Wharton. Certainly a marriage like hers, especially as it blundered towards dissolution, was a source of intense shame.[32]

The mortal isolation at the heart of *Ethan Frome*, that 'chill little masterpiece,'[33] is also at the heart of *Summer* in which Charity

Royall, ward of Lawyer Royall, has a blissful affair with the architect Lucius Harney, who is studying and drawing Colonial houses
in the area of her dreary village. Later, pregnant and abandoned by
Harney, she will return to the Mountain (whence Royall brought
her as a child), home of a lawless band of men and women, hoping
to find her mother. On the way there, however, she learns that her
mother is dead, and she decides she cannot stay. 'Rescued' again
by her guardian, Lawyer Royall, who has twice pressed to marry
her, she finally submits in a daze to becoming his wife and they
return to his house in North Dormer.

Charity lives with the reality of shame in a way more intense
than Wharton's previous heroines: it is embedded in her very
name, which urges her to 'remember that she had been brought
down from [the Mountain], and hold her tongue and be
thankful.'³⁴ 'She knew that she had been christened Charity. . . to
commemorate Mr Royall's disinterestedness in "bringing her
down," and to keep alive in her a becoming sense of dependence'
(16). No wonder, then, that she feels 'no particular affection for
[Royall], and not the slightest gratitude.' Such feelings have to be
earned, not demanded. The name she was given is not just a
reminder to her, it is a prideful swaggering brand that marks her as
belonging to him forever, a name that reduces her to an exhibit in a
museum of benevolence. Her comfort is thus as precarious as Lily
Bart's and Mattie's.

In a town that 'lies high and in the open,' lacks shade (3), and 'is
at all times an empty place,' Charity is the most exposed resident
in this exposed and backward spot, which Charity dismisses without pity:

> She knew that, compared to the place she had come from, North
> Dormer represented all the blessings of the most refined civiliz-
> ation. Everyone in the village had told her so ever since she had
> been brought there as a child. . . Charity was not very clear
> about the Mountain; but *she knew it was a bad place, and a shame to*
> *have come from*. . . (6) [my emphasis].

Charity 'knew herself to be – humblest of the humble even in
North Dormer, where to come from the Mountain was the worst
disgrace' (15). Not surprisingly, then, Charity, if she can help it,
'did not care to have it known that she was of the Mountain' (40)
and she feels a 'fierce impulse of resistance which she instinctively

opposed to every imagined slight' (46). Lawyer Royall, her guardian, comments on the effect of this stigmatization: 'you're the proudest girl I know, and the last to want people to talk against you' (84). Marilyn French observes that Charity 'is shy, but covers her shyness with bravado and indifference.'[35] Charity has always 'kept to herself' and stayed *'contemptuously aloof* from village love-making, without exactly knowing whether her *fierce pride* was due to the sense of her tainted origin, or whether she was reserving herself for a more brilliant fate' (44) [my emphases]. At any rate, contempt has served to insulate her from an environment that offers admonitions rather than affection or even support.

Charity's shameful background initially beclouds her relationship with Lucius Harney, and significantly, before Charity even knows who he is, he makes her feel ashamed and angry. The unknown young man, a stranger, brings with him the implicit invidious comparisons of larger, more sophisticated and exciting places, putting even her one experience with a real town, Nettleton, to shame. Seeing Harney laughingly chase his hat in the wind down North Dormer's only street, she retreats into her house, because 'the *shrinking* that sometimes came over her when she saw people with holiday faces made her *draw back*. . .' [my emphases]. Looking 'critically at her reflection [she] wished for the thousandth time she had blue eyes like Annabel Balch' (4). Charity falls into musing about her shameful background, and ends up feeling 'ashamed of her old sun-hat, and sick of North Dormer, and jealously aware of Annabel Balch of Springfield, opening her blue eyes somewhere far off on glories greater than the glories of Nettleton' (7). This Annabel, who will later turn out to be Harney's fiancée, 'represented all the things that Charity felt herself most *incapable of* understanding or achieving' (163) [my emphasis]. These very few moments of observing Harney throw her shame, her jealousy, her contempt into bold relief.

Charity's first meeting with Harney is likewise partially marred by her shame. Harney has come to the memorial Hatchard library she is dispirited custodian of, looking for a book of local history. She is sharp with Harney, thinking there is 'a slight condescension in his tone,' and then when he seems to have forgotten her, his 'indifference nettled her, and. . . she resolved not to offer him the least assistance' (9). Even though he is a cousin of Miss Hatchard, the village's dim equivalent of a grande dame, that bond does not serve to make him understandable to Charity. His conversation frustrates her; 'Her bewilderment was complete: the more she wished to appear to understand him the more unintelligible his remarks became' (10–11).

Harney's subsequent advice to his cousin Miss Hatchard that the library needs better care and better ventilation unfortunately gets misinterpreted as an accusation that Charity has been heedless in her duties (when she has merely been lackadaisical). Charity flares out in anger and disappointment at Harney, thinking she is going to lose the job that yields her some status and money in that grim little community. When Harney offers to set things right with Miss Hatchard, Charity's boss, Charity's 'pride flamed into her cheeks at the suggestion of his intervening' (37). Harney blushes too, but the contretemps is soon settled and Charity begins to serve as his guide to local houses that might interest him.

On these sketching trips of Harney's, Charity wanders off from him while he is working:

> It was partly from *shyness* that she did so: from a sense of *inadequacy* that came to her most painfully when her companion, absorbed in his job, forgot her *ignorance* and her *inability* to follow his least allusion, and plunged into a monologue on art and life (43–44) [my emphases].

While Charity certainly doesn't mind people thinking that she is '"going with" a young man from the city,' (45) a new kind of '*shyness* had been born in her: a terror of *exposing* to vulgar perils the sacred treasure of her happiness' (44) [my emphases]. Just as Lily Bart is aware of the power of gossip in her social world, Charity knows all too well that her little town is full of watchful eyes and spiteful tongues: 'Where there is so little to go around, any good fortune is bitterly resented.'[36] As Charity angrily tells Harney, when you have to live in North Dormer, 'it's enough to make people hate each other just to have to walk down the same street every day' (34).

It is important to note that though Harney is a sophisticated, handsome and intelligent young man who 'had the air of power that the experience of cities probably gave' (37), he is also somewhat shy, which seems to make him less imposing for Charity. At their first meeting in the library he hesitates when he realizes how pretty she is. His hesitation is deeply revealing for Charity: 'She had learned what she was worth when [he], looking at her for the first time, had lost the thread of his speech, and leaned *reddening* on the edge of her desk' (44) [my emphasis]. During their first meeting, Harney also blushes at his own strong interest in Colonial houses: 'He stopped short, with the blush of a shy man who overhears himself, and fears he has been voluble' (11). His smile may be confident, but it is also shy, and though he seems to 'know lots of things she had never dreamed of, [he] wouldn't for the world have had her feel his superiority' (15). Harney's appealing shyness makes his superiority not only attractive to Charity, but stimulating – the key point, however, is that he doesn't ever *deliberately* shame her for knowing so much less than he does. It is thus not merely his youth, vigor and newness that make him become so important in her life. How could Lawyer Royall possibly appeal to her sexually or emotionally when he has branded her as an object of pity, called everyone's attention to his generosity and her unfortunate origins?

Charity's deepening fondness for Harney, who is taking his meals at Lawyer Royall's, is temporarily overcome by her shame when she hears Royall telling Harney about her background, even though she has already said to him that she's from the Mountain, and he was intrigued, not shocked. Royall tells Harney that Charity was born to a Mountain criminal and a woman who would 'have given her to anybody' (53). Charity's shame at hearing the worst about herself is compounded by feeling exposed to Harney:

> choking with humiliation. . . She knew at last: knew that she was the child of a drunken convict and of a mother who wasn't 'half human,' and was glad to have her go; and she had heard this history of her origin related to the one being in whose eyes she longed to appear superior to the people about her! (53)

Charity has already been deeply aware of 'the gulf' of '[e]ducation and opportunity' dividing herself and Harney (55), and so now she believes that this terrible story undoubtedly 'must widen the distance between them' (53). Of course, she longs 'that she might never see young Harney again' (55). But she doesn't have that choice, and the next day brings a confrontation with her shame. They drive off to see a house partway up the Mountain, and she thinks of suggesting a different house because 'she did not want him to see the people she came from while the story of her birth was fresh in his mind' (58). Yet she can't make the suggestion: 'shyness and pride held her back' and she defiantly thinks 'he'd better know what kind of folks I belong to.' As the narrative notes – this is 'a somewhat forced defiance; for in reality it was shame that kept her silent' (58). Wharton thus shows her intuitive understanding that anger is a common response to shame which thereby masks it.

Taking refuge from the rain in the now-squalid 'bare and miserable' (60) home with only a few traces of its former beauty, Charity is ashamed and disgusted by the family, whom she cannot convince herself are her kind of people, the folks she belongs to. Harney almost leaves them money before he and Charity go and he blushes when Charity probes his hesitation. Did he, she asks, think that she would 'be ashamed to see [him] give them money' – when he can barely reply, she sobs: 'I ain't – I ain't ashamed. They're my people, and I ain't ashamed of them' (64). Her emotion obviously belies her claim. But almost miraculously, Harney offers to her what Fraser Leath seems to offer Anna in *The Reef*: *release* from shame. Instead of drawing away from Charity after knowing her squalid background and seeing the kind of impoverished, drunken and ignorant people she 'comes from,' he is warm and sympathetic: 'He made her feel that the fact of her being a waif from the Mountain was only another reason for holding her close and soothing her with consolatory murmurs' (70). He even leaves her feeling *exhilarated* – for the source of her deepest isolation, anger and shame has become, at least momentarily, something attractive. Charity has been stigmatized since she became Royall's ward, and for the first time, it seems, she is treated with real kindness and concern.

Lawyer Royall has been growing jealous of Charity's obvious interest in Harney and banishes him from the house; he and Charity have a bruising confrontation over Harney after a dirty wave of scandal washes ashore at Charity's feet. Drawn from home one evening, she ends up outside of Miss Hatchard's house, and simply watches Harney, knowing what would happen if she went in to him, and knowing how she would feel. This 'vigil lengthens into a vivid sensual indulgence' as she takes in the details of his masculinity, luxuriating 'in the warm nearness of his body.'[37] But Charity's coming and going has been observed, and the town is abuzz with the news that she spent at least part of the night alone with Harney. Desperate to take care of her, and to protect her from scandal, Royall proposes marriage to her, bringing up a crucial incident in their past. Once, when she was seventeen, a drunk Royall had tried to force his way into Charity's room to sleep with her. Now, apologizing for that 'shameful thought,' as he calls it, he offers her a new life 'in some big town, where there's men, and business, and things doing' (85). The 'lost years and wasted passion in his voice' (86) leave her unmoved and scornful, and in 'the extremity of his humiliation' which seems to have given him 'new vigor' he surprisingly offers to force Harney to marry her – if that is what she wants (86). All of this 'fingering of her dreams' (83) has a devastating effect:

> She was still *trembling* with the *humiliation* of his last words, which rang so loud in her ears that it seemed as though they must echo through the village, proclaiming her a creature to lend herself to such vile suggestions. *Her shame weighed on her* like a physical oppression: the roof and walls seemed to be closing in on her, and she was seized by the impulse to get away. . . (87) [my emphases].

Though Harney moves away, they begin meeting clandestinely, with Charity 'so full of mortification and anger' the first time she sees him again (94). Their entrancing Fourth of July trip to Nettleton leads to her agonizing public humiliation. In the crowds there she runs across Julia Hawes, a North Dormer girl who had gotten pregnant and had an abortion and is now apparently a prostitute. Charity had lied to Royall about where she was going, of course, and in any event, whenever 'she was with Lucius Harney she would have liked some impenetrable mountain mist to hide her' (93). Understandably then, Julia's 'cold mocking smile' gets under her skin: 'Charity flushed to the forehead and looked away. She felt herself humiliated by Julia's sneer, and vexed that the mockery of such a creature should affect her' (107). Kaufman notes that there is often secondary shame about shame, as we see here.[38]

After a full and exciting day, capped by glorious fireworks, and an intoxicating passionate kiss from Harney, Charity sees Lawyer Royall in a rowdy drunken bunch of men and women that includes Julia. Royall denounces Charity as a 'bare-headed whore' (111):

> . . . suddenly she had a vision of herself, hatless, dishevelled, with a man's arm about her, confronting that drunken crew,

headed by her guardian's pitiable figure. The picture filled her with shame (11).

Just before, she had been on top of the world, clinging to Harney 'speechless, exultant. . . isolated in ecstacy,' and now she plunges from those heights into the depths of shame. The mortifying incident drags on because Charity tries to extricate Royall from his companions and is rebuffed by him and mocked by his laughing jeering mates. Charity is afterwards so pained that she is relieved to be driven the last part of the way home alone after Lucius has gotten off at another hamlet. Back at North Dormer, however, she feels trapped and exposed by the town 'with all its mean curiosities, its furtive malice, its sham unconsciousness of evil.' She cannot bear the thought of seeing her friend Ally, 'having to meet her eyes and answer or evade her questions' about the previous day's jaunt. What can she do? 'Suddenly it became clear that flight, and instant flight, was the only thing conceivable' (115). Kaufman notes that rage, fear and distress are the most common immediate affective responses that follow shame, and not surprisingly, in the past, Charity's 'moments of distress' had sparked in her the 'longing to escape' (115–116). Now, however, that longing is more intense than even before because of her public humiliation by Royall, whose 'words had *stripped her bare* in the face of the grinning crowd' (117) [my emphasis]:

> She felt she could not remain an hour longer under the roof of the man who had publicly dishonoured her, and face to face with the people who would presently be gloating over all the details of her humiliation (116).

The 'blind propulsion of her wretchedness' (117) leads her to feel that she must never again 'see anyone she had known; above all, she did not want to see Harney. . .' (117) [Wharton's ellipsis]. Cynthia Griffin Wolff makes the intriguing point that Charity has been struggling to see her burgeoning sexuality as quite different from what Royall feels, to see herself as innocent and not animalistic.[39] Affectively, I would add, sexuality for her has been something shameful – what 'North Dormer ignored in public and snickered over on the sly' (77). The scene with Royall at her door has overlaid sexuality with fear and disgust as well – and she also comes from the Mountain, where sexuality is unlicensed. The confrontation with Royall brands her as the disgusting creature she does not want to be.

Fleeing to the Mountain, she intends to stop partway there at a deserted little house because the trek is too long for a day, but Harney finds her and his obvious strong delight in her presence quiets her a bit. More powerful, though, is his manner; he talks to her 'as if nothing had happened that could shame or embarrass them' (121), and they head up to the house together. Harney attempts to excuse Royall, but blushes when Charity says that she knows what men are like, and he is outraged after she tells him, 'look[ing] away from him', that Royall had wanted to sleep with her. When she feels Harney examining her 'for more light on what she had revealed to him. . . a flush of shame swept over her' (123). Charity fumbles out her fear that Harney must think less of her for talking about such things, but the scene ends with their second kiss, and their affair begins.

The rapture of feeling 'the wondrous unfolding of her new self' (132) is undercut by her sense of Harney's belonging to an alien and seductive world she has no power to challenge, and it is ultimately spoiled by Lawyer Royall. He eventually finds her in the abandoned house they have turned into a pretty trysting place, and he challenges Harney to marry Charity. Both of them are ashamed, 'Charity too humbled for speech'; Harney's eyes lowered 'under the old man's gaze' (153). Sounding almost like Gus Trenor accusing Lily of having yielded her favors to other men, Royall says nobody will marry her now because no one needs to; *he's* the only fool who bothered proposing. In the depths of his own shame, he abuses Charity further by telling them her mother was a Nettleton prostitute. The tirade ends with him sitting down and burying his face in his hands, Harney looking away from the shameful sight of Royall's despair as well as from Charity, to whom *he* has been exposed by Royall's denunciation. After Royall is gone, Harney doesn't embrace her but looks away again, and Charity holds her head up (an anti-shame facial response), declaring she isn't sorry for *anything*. He weakly promises to return from vague 'things' that need 'arranging,' and marry her. But Charity is not overjoyed. After the terrible scene with Royall, a 'leaden weight of shame' hung on her, benumbing every other sensation' (157) [my emphasis]. The prospect of marriage to Harney is shame-inducing because Charity is certain 'she would be compared with other people, and unknown things would be expected of her' (157-58), a girl who knows nothing of the world.

Her efforts to write to Harney only strike her as revelations of her inadequacy at putting her feelings in words, at reaching into the alien world he inhabits and penetrating the 'inscrutable mystery of his life' (145). As Judith Fryer notes, Charity's 'inability to enter this world of words – Wharton's salvation – makes her unable to control her fate in a world that excludes her. . .'[40] When Charity learns that Harney is engaged to her nemesis, Annabel Balch, she writes to tell him to honor that engagement and he replies beautifully but vaguely. This crushing blow leaves her aware that 'she had needed him more than he had wanted her' (170), and reminiscing about their affair, brings back – significantly – first the '[f]oolish things she had said' (171).

Pregnant, Charity is faced with the knowledge that there is no 'hope that those signs would escape the watchful village; even before her figure lost its shape she knew her face would betray her' to the 'derision' of her neighbors (174). Once again Charity decides to head for the Mountain, 'desperate. . . to defend her secret from irreverent eyes. . . and hide herself' (176–177). Her hope of finding her mother is doomed, though, before she even ascends to the mountain, because a minister going to officiate at her mother's funeral meets Charity on the way up, and she is once more faced with her terrible isolation.

The savage poverty and ignorance she finds on the Mountain, where her mother lies uncared for and unmourned, 'like a dead dog in a ditch' (186), cannot keep her there. She does not belong, and is unable to even stay the night after her mother's grotesque funeral. Charity meets Royall coming up to find her. Knowing everything, he wants to marry and protect her. Passive, dazed, blushing and flushed, Charity alternately feels a relieving sense of being taken care of 'through her own immeasurable desolation' (205) and a 'sick sense of coming doom' (209). Like a zombie, she goes through her wedding and her wedding night at a fancy hotel (where Royall sleeps in a chair), and at the novel's end she feels 'ashamed and yet secure' when Royall looks at her (216).

As Judith Fryer points out, 'despite [Royall's] considerate protectiveness at the end of the novel, [w]e remember him. . . confronting her on the Fourth of July in Nettleton. . .'[41] I would add, we remember him humiliating her at the house halfway up the mountain, humiliating her by telling Harney the story of her parents, humiliating her by offering to force Harney to marry her. The auguries for such a marriage are dim indeed, given that Royall, for all he makes her feel 'secure,' has been a source of great shame in her life, exposing her to others. In a diminished way, their new bond is as claustrophobic as that between Ethan Frome, Zenobia and crippled Mattie – a source of constriction and not fulfillment.

It is not only Royall who has shamed Charity, however; she has humiliated him as well, consistently and deliberately. As Margaret McDowell notes, while Charity 'feels hatred and sexual revulsion for him, she enjoys dominating him.'[42] What other ways are there for Charity to feel powerful and superior? She is contemptuous and aloof with the village's young men, and she thinks of her job as library custodian as a type of imprisonment. After Royall tried to sleep with her, he proposed, and she was merciless, scornful, contemptuous (though she is aware he is superior to most of North Dormer). Indeed, her contempt and anger in response to her general situation are obvious from her very first line in the book: 'How I hate everything!' (4) After Royall's nocturnal prowling, Charity soon arranged to have a cook at the house so that she would never be the only woman there, but

> it was far less for her own defense than for [Royall's] *humiliation*. She needed no one to defend her: his *humbled pride* was her surest protection. He had never spoken a word of excuse or extenuation; the incident was as if it had never been. Yet its consequences were latent in every word that he and she exchanged, in every *glance they instinctively turned from each other* (26–7) [my emphases].

Charity may be in command of the Royall household, but the circumstances that gave rise to her control in the most important house in North Dormer are deeply unpleasant: '. . . she knew her power, knew what it was made of, and hated it' (15). Why *shouldn't* Royall be gentle, understanding and calm at the end of the book? All along 'determined to have her,'[43] he has brought an utterly subdued Charity down from the Mountain and finally gained sexual control over her; he has also triumphed over Lucius Harney, the younger, handsomer, more talented man. And Charity will be more proof in the village of his superiority. He has achieved a vindictive triumph, as Karen Horney describes them, and its roots are in 'the desire to humiliate others, to make them feel the shame, envy and self-contempt that plague the vindictive one.'[44]

Just as Rosedale wanted Lily to marry him so he could make her outshine all the women in her set, Royall tells Charity, 'I always wanted you to beat all the other girls. . . I want you to beat 'em all hollow' (211–212). As with George Darrow and Anna Leath in *The Reef*, the prospects for such a union seem dismal. He, a failure, has scored a vindictive triumph; she, a perpetual outcast, has submitted to being married, as 'someone to whom something irreparable and overwhelming had happened' (204).

Charity's sexuality – though thrilling and movingly intimated throughout the book – has led to this terrible cul de sac. As we have seen in Chapter 1, sexuality was for Wharton a deeply shameful subject never to be discussed, and when it was brought up, she was humiliated for the ignorance she had not struggled against. Her sexual liberation through the sensual offices of Morton Fullerton not only made her see what she had missed, but was also inextricably bound with shame, as her letters to him clearly show. In connecting the erotic fragment 'Beatrice Palmato' with *Summer* both in terms of its language and the relationship of older man with younger woman (incestuous in the fragment), Cynthia Wolff concludes that the fragment yields 'striking insight into the way Edith Wharton *conceptualized* love and sexuality.'[45] That fragment is worth looking at here for that very reason, though my reading of it leads in a direction different from Wolff's because my starting point is affect.

Both R.W.B. Lewis and Wolff have interpreted this fragment as a positive imagining of sexuality, focusing on the undeniably pleasant physical sensations, the sensuous descriptive language. But there is an element of the fragment which they have overlooked: the fragment emphasizes *looking* without turning away, *exposure* without shame. Not only is the movement of the piece towards a vindictive triumph over Beatrice's husband, but the whole episode reads like a willed triumph over shame.[46] The taboo against incest is not the only one broken here; Wharton breaks the taboo against looking. The episode takes place not in darkness, as their previous encounters, but in the light. She is uncovered, and Palmato says, 'let me *show you* what only you and I have the right *to show* each other.' Uncovering her, he wants his eyes '*to see* all that [his] lips can't cover.' When she fellates him, 'it was the first time she had ever seen [his penis] actually *exposed to her eyes*'[47] [my emphases].

This fragment certainly demonstrates that Wharton experienced sexual pleasure, or at least could convincingly imagine it, albeit in rather stereotypic ways. But its arc is negative; the fuel is sexual bravado, an overturning of civilized constraints, a victory over internalized shame that makes one see Wharton less as free and sexually released, than still imprisoned. As D.H. Lawrence pithily observes in his *Studies in Classic American Literature*, 'the most unfree souls. . . shout of freedom. . . The shout is a rattling of chains. . .'[48] Seeing into the heart of 'Beatrice Palmato,' one understands even more why Charity's passion leads to disaster, why Charity's early despair over Harney's effect on her – 'the first creature who had come toward her out of the wilderness had brought her anguish instead of joy' (31) – is also her epitaph, for she too, is buried alive.

Carol Wershoven astutely points out that 'images of entrapment, of suffocation, of a kind of death-in-life' pervade *The Age of Innocence*.[49] I would add that this novel movingly dramatizes 'the losing struggle between individual aspiration and the silent, forbidding authority of the social tribe'[50] in part by demonstrating the terrible power of shame over individuals like Newland Archer, and over a group: the 'tight little citadel of New York' (31). We have already seen that world avoiding the scandal of public exposure in *The Custom of the Country* where Ralph's family will not even *discuss* the failure of his marriage. In Wharton's Pulitzer prize-winning masterpiece, she explores the outlines of that unwillingness to deal with anything that might arouse shame. Old New York in the 1870s is a world permeated by 'the chill of minds rigorously averted from the "unpleasant"' (98). That very term itself is a muffling of experience – so vague, so pallid. Yet the strength of the desire to avoid the unpleasant is all-consuming, as Wharton lets us know. Newland Archer and his young wife May Welland have been raised with 'the resolute determination to carry to its utmost limit that ritual of ignoring the "unpleasant"' (26) in a society 'wholly absorbed in barricading itself against the unpleasant' (99) – that catch-all term for everything it fears, loathes or does not understand. Not surprisingly, then, it is a society ruled by the tyrannical notion of Good Form and doing things the right way. This society is thus fearful of being 'different' in any way, of exposing itself to potentially embarrassing public scrutiny. Crusty old Mrs Manson Mingott tartly observes that '[n]ot one of them wants to be different; they're as scared of it as the smallpox' (154). Newland Archer may think himself more intelligent and inquiring, and better read than his friends and acquaintances, but he is keenly aware that 'it would be troublesome – and rather bad form – to strike out for himself' (8). In a world where doing the right thing has the power of ancient taboos, conformity 'to the discipline of a small society had become almost his second nature. It was deeply distasteful to him to do anything melodramatic and conspicuous' (321).

These people are so afraid of being embarrassed that when they travel abroad, they scrupulously keep to themselves (which modern gregarious Americans abroad may find quite curious). Why? Because of 'the old New York tradition that it was not "dignified" to force one's self on the notice of one's acquaintances in foreign countries' (191). One is supposed to affect 'a haughty unconsciousness' (196) of others – and of course we know that such haughtiness is a defense against being exposed in some way. Afraid to 'risk its dignity in foreign lands,' (202) old New York is terrified to 'appear pushing and snobbish' (197).

Their fear of the unpleasant has even wider implications. This world is 'inexorable in its condemnation of business irregularities,' and it shuns those connected with them. Though 'unblemished honesty was the *noblesse oblige* of old financial New York' (273), it has enjoyed the balls thrown by the wealthy, vulgar and somewhat shady Julius Beaufort, whose wife, at least, is one of their own. But when his speculations cause the failure of his bank, which he has dishonestly kept afloat through rumors and the ostentatious public display of more jewels on his wife, New York attempts to ostracize him. Regina Beaufort appeals to her cousin Mrs Manson Mingott for the 'whole family to cover and condone their monstrous dishonor,' but the old woman's response is that Regina has no choice but to sink along with her husband, since they are both 'covered. . . with shame' (272). The family would be much happier if Regina would act appropriately under the circumstances, the way New York women used to: 'The wife of a man who had done anything disgraceful in business had only one idea: to efface herself, to disappear with him' (273). 'The mere idea of a woman's appealing to her family to screen her husband's business dishonor was inadmissible, since it was the one thing that the Family, as an institution, could not do' (274). As Carol Wershoven notes, in this situation, even 'family members must be sacrificed so that New York will not have to look upon, or deal with, pain or dishonor,'[51] – and thus they avoid feeling shame.

The scandal makes the private and ugly unbearably public (as with Ralph's divorce in *The Custom of the Country*), and such publicity is abhorrent to old New York. The possibility of photographers getting pictures of a young bride into the newspapers, for instance, is an 'unthinkable indecency' from which New York recoils 'with a collective shudder' (183–84). But it takes Ellen Olenska, the glamorous old New Yorker who made a disastrous marriage to a Polish count and has fled him to return to her home, to point out a central irony in the shame-bound life of her native but very foreign-seeming city: 'You're so shy, and yet you're so public' (133–34). There is indeed a sense throughout the book that the characters are living in a fishbowl, painfully aware of one another's movements, dinner engagements, jewels and entertainments. For instance, walking up Fifth Avenue one night, Newland Archer sees the wealthy and somewhat mysterious Julius Beaufort stepping into his carriage. The implications are nakedly obvious to Archer: 'It was not an Opera night, and no one was giving a party, so that Beaufort's outing was undoubtedly of a clandestine nature' (101). Beaufort is exposed here, and Archer will be at various points in the novel, as when he is speaking to Ellen on the street and two of his friends cross the street to pretend he hasn't been seen with her. Early in the novel, when Archer makes his ritual and boring round of engagement visits to relatives, he feels 'that he had been shown off like a wild animal cunningly trapped' (69) – and here the image is equally divided between entrapment and exposure. Late in the novel, when Ellen has been called back to New York because her grandmother is sick, Newland comes with a family carriage to meet her, because 'it might appear inhospitable' (280) if no one did so. But Newland does something quite inhospitable: he gets out before they have reached their destination, letting her go on alone. On their ride uptown he tells her that he longs for her without sanctions, but is distressed when Ellen reveals the depth of her sad knowledge of the world. Sighing and then laughing, she asks what R.W.B. Lewis calls one of Wharton's 'most poignant but unsentimental questions': 'Oh, my dear – where is that country? Have you ever been there?' (290) Leaving her unattended in the carriage is an anomaly that is soon after called to his attention by the sympathetic Mrs Manson Mingott – so we can imagine that others, less sympathetic, have also observed this lapse in form, and have drawn their own conclusions.

Archer does not, however, seem to realize the all-pervasiveness of public scrutiny, perhaps because he feels, as a man, less vulnerable in society than Lily Bart does. It is not until Ellen Olenska is being shipped back to Europe near the novel's end that he realizes his wife, his relatives, in fact all of New York have wrongly assumed that he and Ellen were having an affair. His persistent and somewhat irate championing of her cause had apparently begun to seem excessive (especially when the family decided she should return to Europe and her husband), and the moments he stole to be with her could not have gone entirely unobserved. Archer compounded the possibility of such an interpretation by a tangled lie to his wife about going to Washington on business, when he simply wanted to see Ellen there. He makes such a mess of his explanations – and he ends up never going because Ellen has returned – that his wife leaves him blushing with her unexpectedly determined attempt to understand him: 'He felt the blood rising to his face, as if he were blushing for her unwonted lapse from all the traditional delicacies' (282). Yet no scandal breaks out, nothing ripples the serene lake of factitious harmony on which New York sails. Archer and Ellen are skillfully kept apart at the farewell dinner, as everyone is 'resolutely engaged in pretending to each other that they had never heard of, suspected, or even conceived possible' any questions about 'the propriety of Madame Olenska's conduct, or the completeness of Archer's domestic felicity' (339).

> It was the old New York way of taking life 'without diffusion of blood': the way of people who dreaded scandal more than disease, who placed decency above courage, and who considered that nothing was more ill-bred than 'scenes,' except the behavior of those who gave rise to them (335).

Because of the terrible fear of shame in this society, honesty (though absolutely essential in business affairs), is not quite as evident in private life, but in a very specific way. In Archer's New York, 'hypocrisy in private relations' (258) *is* tolerated, but when single, a man has to make sure he protects the woman's honor, and after marriage, 'no one laughed at a wife deceived' (305). Indeed, womanizing married men are generally objects of contempt. These old New Yorkers 'lived in a kind of hieroglyphic world, where the real thing was never said or done or even thought, but only represented by a set of signs' (45). We have seen the products of such a world throughout Wharton's fiction –

consider Kate Orme in *Sanctuary* unable to honestly tell her son what she feels, Anna Leath in *The Reef* stifled as a girl by what she wants to say to the man she loves, or Rose Sellars gamely pretending that nothing is wrong in her relationship with Martin Boyne in *The Children*. It is shame that binds speech, enforces silence about whatever is closest to the heart. John Halperin rightly calls such silence in Wharton's fiction tragic: 'Stories which describe, as hers do, the muffling of honest feeling must be tragedies. Few of her characters learn from their mistakes or overcome their early training in time to carve out happy lives for themselves. That is what tragedy means.'[52] Perhaps here more than in most other Wharton novels, the terrible sense of waste created by this inability to break through into free and honest expression is heaviest, though Newland's son Dallas will years later comically call his father's world a 'deaf-and-dumb asylum': 'You never did ask each other anything, did you? And you never told each other anything. You just sat and watched each other, and guessed at what was going on underneath' (356).

When Ellen Olenska returns to New York from her failed marriage, she is as trapped at first by the prohibitions on honesty that we see Kate Clephane facing in *The Mother's Recompense* on *her* return. As Wershoven notes, it is Ellen's intrusion as an unpleasant reality that 'exposes New York as a fortress of evasion.'[53] When Newland tells Ellen that her relatives want to help her, Ellen points out the price she has to pay for this help:

> She shook her head and sighed. 'Oh, I know – I know! But on condition that they don't hear anything unpleasant. Aunt Welland put it in those very words when I tried. . . Does no one want to know the truth here, Mr Archer? The real loneliness is living among all these kind people who only ask one to pretend!' She lifted her hands to her face, and he saw her thin shoulders shaken by a sob (78).

As Fred Landers does for Kate Clephane in *The Mother's Recompense*, Archer attempts to stop her from crying; while this may seem a natural response of offering comfort, it also serves to stifle her feelings, and she not surprisingly pulls away, wondering, 'Does no one cry here, either?' (78) Such expression of feeling clearly must be quashed by this society – it reveals too much and is too embarrassing.

Ellen represents a threat to harmony and stability from her very first appearance in the book. Having fled her husband in somewhat dubious circumstances (with the help of his secretary), she is a fire of potential scandal and embarrassment her relatives keep trying to put out all the way through the novel. And Newland Archer unexpectedly becomes her champion even though he is, initially, as concerned with appearances as anyone else. When Ellen enters the opera box her New York relatives are in, she creates a commotion in society, one of its arbiters wondering how her family could have 'tried it on' (11). And as if her past isn't problematic enough, she is wearing a dress that reveals 'a little more shoulder and bosom than New York was accustomed to seeing, at least in ladies who had reasons for wishing to pass unnoticed.' This dress 'shocked and troubled' Archer, despite the qualifying 'a little.'

> Few things seemed to Newland Archer more awful than an offense against 'Taste,' that far-off divinity of whom 'Form' was the mere visible representative and viceregent. . . He hated to think of May Welland's being exposed to the influence of a young woman so careless of the dictates of Taste (15).

The publicity and exposure is a key point here – it is assumed that because of her troubles, Ellen will slip into society and take a quiet and unobtrusive part, as if she has become a member of some lay order – Sisters of Shame, perhaps – sworn to silence and inconspicuousness. Though her grandmother, the wealthy and important Mrs Manson Mingott, showily married *her* daughters off to foreigners, and is heartier and more honest than the norm, her granddaughter Ellen is not expected or allowed to follow such an example. Besides, Mrs Manson Mingott is rich, which gives her power and a certain immunity from criticism. Ellen, however, has no such influence, nor does she have beauty, 'a gift which, in the eyes of New York, justified every success, and excused a certain number of failings' (14).

What she does have is her foreignness, and a 'mysterious faculty of suggesting tragic and moving possibilities outside the daily run of experience' (115). Like the Europe she has known intimately, she seems to have produced a good deal more history than she can absorb, and certainly more than her staid and nervous relatives can accommodate in their narrow world. Ellen's unconsciously calling attention to herself at the Opera is distinctly unnerving to Archer (his sister will blush after likening Ellen's dress to a nightgown), and he feels thrown 'into a strange state of embarrassment': 'It was annoying that the box which was thus attracting the undivided attention of masculine New York should be that in which his betrothed was seated between her mother and aunt' (12). Archer certainly approves of the Mingott family demonstrating 'family solidarity' by 'resolute championship' of Ellen Olenska, one of their rare black sheep, but surely such solidarity should be offered *in private*. To produce Ellen 'in public, at the Opera of all places, and in the very box with the young girl whose engagement to him, was to be announced within a few weeks' is wildly inappropriate (13). It casts shame on him, on May and the entire family by drawing all eyes to the box, even though most of the Mingotts are passing the event off with perfect aplomb. However, 'May betrayed, by a heightened color. . . a sense of the gravity of the situation' (15).

In a show of support, Newland joins his fiancée in the Mingott box, earns her unspoken thanks, and he urges that they announce their engagement that very evening – so as to take attention away from Ellen Olenska, and deal with the public embarrassment. Newland's reasons for being there, however, cannot be discussed because of 'the family dignity which both considered so high a virtue' (17). Archer goes an important step further by sitting next to Ellen 'a little ostentatiously, with the desire that the whole house should see what he was doing' (18). But despite this outward display of 'solidarity,' Newland is afraid that Ellen will afterward be brought to the Opera ball. None of this can be forthrightly discussed, of course, and when May and Archer discuss Ellen's absence at the ball, Archer is determined to never let her know he has heard anything scandalous about her cousin. Nor can Archer mention to her his fear that Ellen would be at the ball.

New York feels that Ellen makes herself even more conspicuous by being seen 'parading up Fifth Avenue,' with the womanizing Julius Beaufort 'the very day after her arrival' (32). Even more embarrassing, she has gone out in 'glaring sunlight,' with many people about – 'an indelicate thing for a compromised woman to do' (29). There is a strange irony in her going out, because she is absent when Archer and May make their wedding visit, which thus 'spared them the embarrassment of her presence, and the faint shadow that her unhappy past might seem to shed on their radiant future' (29). Ellen also begins to frequent 'bohemian' Sunday gatherings where the Sabbath is broken by champagne – acceptable in Europe, but distasteful to New York.

Archer finds such behavior in Ellen understandable, given her foreign ties and interests, but still strongly disapproves. Of course, since he is marrying Ellen's cousin May, he is now related to Ellen, or at least allied to her family, and so Ellen's behavior cannot help but affect him. Though Archer has hypocritically inveighed in the past against society's double standard for moral behavior, when faced with a woman who may have violated his society's rules, he is at the beginning censorious and uncomfortable. But the book will chart his painful shift to sympathy and then love for Ellen, who seems to offer an escape from a life he more and more understands as empty and meaningless – all form and no substance.

· In the initial stages of his relationship with the glamorous and disturbing Ellen, Newland is concerned with saving her – and thus his fiancée, her family, and himself – from embarrassment. Feeling 'pitchforked into a coil of scandal' (47), Archer blushes defending Ellen at a family dinner, the first time when it is implied that the Mingotts have control over his actions. Archer had protested: 'Why should she have to slink about as if it were she who had ·disgraced herself?' (41) Having thus defended Ellen, he blushes after dinner hearing that it is rumored Ellen lived together with her husband's secretary after her flight from the Count. It certainly would be more convenient defending a woman about whom the accusations were less specific and less damning! Even when he is already in love with her, a casual implicit reference to the Count's secretary will make him blush, and deeply (232). When he accidentally meets the man, who has been sent to America to persuade Ellen to go back, the conversation will be punctuated by blushing.

Archer is drawn into a more active role defending Ellen when old New York deliberately, pointedly insults Ellen; most of the guests refuse an invitation to a Mingott dinner arranged in her honor, and the refusal notes are all identically worded 'without the mitigating plea of a "previous engagement" that ordinary courtesy prescribed' (48). Because the social world these people inhabit is so very small, everyone knows for certain that the refusals are deliberate insults. Outraged, Archer gets his mother to appeal to the ultimate social arbiters, their cousins the reclusive and remote van der Luydens, who enter the lists on Ellen's side with the aim of asserting their authority in society, and smacking down those they consider to be upstarts. But the magnificent dinner arranged to show that Ellen is indeed welcome (it includes a duke) does not really impress her, and she even enters late, without one glove on, fastening her bracelet, but 'without. . . embarrassment' (61). Later we will learn (and Archer will be both shocked and delighted) that Ellen thought the august New Yorkers rather dull. Yet she will be ambivalent about the dullness, attracted to it, soothed, it seems, telling Archer, 'If you knew how I hate to be different!' (108) Much later, when propinquity has worked its spell and they have been precariously drawn to one another, Ellen will almost champion that dullness. At her most impassioned, while she and Archer are alone in Boston after his marriage, spending a blissful but tormenting day together, she will explain to Archer 'that under the dullness there are things so fine and sensitive and delicate that even those I most cared for in my other life look cheap in comparison' (241). She will continue to cherish New York's ideals, or at least her interpretation of them, for *her* kindness is real. Carol Wershoven notes the irony here; Ellen believes that 'New York's inner goodness has made her a better person [but] the result of society's passion for avoiding the unpleasant is a world filled with hypocrisy and cruelty, devoid of intellectual development.'[54]

Early in the novel, Archer emerges as a veritable ambassador to Ellen, entrusted by his law firm and the Mingott family with the mission of saving Ellen; it is a mission he undertakes feeling 'the blood in his temples' (93). He must convince Ellen that the divorce she is contemplating from her monster of a husband is simply impossible. Archer takes on the mission 'rather than let her secrets be bared to other eyes':

A great wave of compassion had swept away his indifference and impatience; she stood before him as an exposed and pitiful figure, to be saved at all costs from farther wounding herself in her mad plunges against fate (96).

Up until reading the papers related to her case, Archer has not been entirely sympathetic, indeed he has had contempt for her openness in discussing her marital difficulties, comparing her to his bride-to-be who no matter *what* the circumstances, would surely never be seen 'hawking about her private difficulties and lavishing her confidences on strange men' (95). But even given his growing interest in helping Ellen (which is in part a sort of paternalistic and chauvinistic sentiment like that of the van der Luydens' 'gentle and obstinate determination to go on rescuing her' [129]), dissuading her from divorce is not as easy as he thinks, because he is so ambivalent, even though he is sure that 'she was risking her reputation' (107).

Archer was not surprisingly subject to an 'excess of discretion' (105) when he wrote asking to see her – so he didn't request a private talk. He thus arrives to find her talking to the egregious Julius Beaufort, and is almost angry enough to leave. Outstaying Beaufort makes him feel superior, and yet he blushes when Ellen declares she wants to 'cast off [her] old life,' and he feels 'as awkward and embarrassed as a boy' (109). 'How little practice he had in dealing with unusual situations!' (109) Archer's conversation with her is a series of circumlocutions about the possibility of her husband's charge of her own adultery being true: he brings out equivocations like 'offensive insinuations,' 'beastly talk' the 'vileness' of newspapers (111, 112) and takes Ellen's silence to be the admission of an affair with her husband's secretary. He is so embarrassed by what he assumes to be her admission of guilt that he becomes suddenly voluble, spouting clichés about the family versus the individual. Even though he is there as a lawyer, as a family member, he is determined to 'keep on the surface, in the prudent old New York way [rather] than risk uncovering a wound he could not heal' (112). Unexpectedly, Ellen yields to his clichés about family and social harmony being predicated on the indissolubility of marriage, leaving him blushing and surprised.

It is a very odd mission he has been on – to persuade by indirection, to seek out the truth without an honest question, and the whole experience is 'intolerably painful to him.' But there *is* the consolation of feeling 'glad it was to him she had revealed her secret, rather than the cold scrutiny of [his boss], or the embarrassed gaze of her family' (116–17). Their strained and indirect conversation has unexpectedly connected them: 'He felt himself drawn to her by obscure feelings of jealousy and pity, as if her dumbly-confessed error had put her at his mercy, humbling yet endearing her' (116). Her shameful past thus operates to make him feel superior to her, and yet not entirely, for it is Archer more than Ellen who will have a 'wound that can not heal,' and make a 'mad plunge' against his fate – or attempt to. It is Ellen who will be far more aware of their limitations.

Shame stalks their relationship from the very beginning until its snuffing out in public. Before they know each other at all well, Ellen makes the mistake of asking if he is 'very much in love' with May, and her too-honest inquiry makes him blush, then laugh off the embarrassment, and respond with a cliché (64). In response to another question, Archer points out that American marriages are never arranged ones, and when she blushes he regrets his response (65). First summoned to her little house in a bohemian quarter of New York, Archer is surprised not to find her at home, but feels 'more curious than *mortified*': 'The atmosphere of the room was so different from any he had ever breathed that *self-consciousness* vanished in the sense of adventure' (71) [my emphases]. We see here the potential for shame clearly recognized in his anomalous position. Continuing to wait for her, he feels 'rather foolish' and despite his 'consuming desire to be simple and striking', he is struck that his comments about her home come from someone 'imprisoned in the conventional' (73), and he turns red when Ellen mentions the van der Luydens without reverence.

Soon afterwards, at a play with a deeply touching and romantic scene of parting, Ellen makes him blush by mentioning the yellow roses he has sent her after visiting. Archer is surprised by her reaction to his feelings about the scene: 'Her color rose, reluctantly and duskily. She looked down. . . ' (118). Mentioning that she has told her family that she has abandoned the idea of divorce leaves him 'embarrassed' and when he hopes to hear from her afterwards, her 'unexpected silence mortified him beyond reason' (127). She already has tremendous power over his feelings, though he does not quite recognize it. Through Ellen, he is 'exposed to a whole new world of perception.'[55] Not long after meeting her and beginning to consider her past, he is plunged into wondering about a social system that has decreed his wife would be a 'creation of factitious purity. . . because [that] was supposed to be what he wanted, what he had a right to, in order that he might exercise his lordly pleasure in smashing it like an image made of snow' (46). Ellen's disturbing presence throws everything into a different light. She makes him both value May's simplicity and tact in comparison to her foreign showiness, and begin to chafe against conventional niceness and the preconceptions about men and women that undergird his life. 'For the first time he perceived how elementary his own principles had always been' (96). Ellen is indeed the 'intruder figure' Carol Wershoven has identified as a 'recurring motif' in Wharton's fiction: 'The woman who is at once more vital, brave, and more receptive to all of life than the society she must confront and challenge. . . [she is the] living alternative to the suffocation around her.'[56]

Though Archer will follow Ellen up to the van der Luydens' home where she is weekending, he blushes after she says he can protect her. The unwelcome arrival of Julius Beaufort, who seems to be pursuing Ellen as his mistress (for what else can such a man be after?) is deeply annoying, because Archer is already beginning to fall in love with her. Throughout the book, he has contempt for Beaufort; he will act as if Beaufort is his rival, or that Beaufort's crude attentions to Ellen somehow degrade her, and himself. Lunching with Ellen long after he is married, Beaufort's name comes up even though Archer has just been soothed to feel 'that she was beside him, and they were drifting forth into this unknown world, they seemed to have reached the kind of deeper nearness that a touch may sunder' (237). Ellen brings up 'the blind conformity to tradition' that she sees in their friends and Archer blushes: 'And Beaufort – do you say those things to Beaufort?' He clearly feels inferior to the vulgarian who is not like himself, not 'damnably dull. . . [with] no character, no color, no variety' (240). Like Selden's ambivalence about Lily, Archer wonders whether Ellen is actually having an affair with Beaufort: 'If she had done that, she ceased to be an object of interest, she threw in her lot with the vulgarest of dissemblers: a woman engaged in a love affair with Beaufort "classed" herself irretrievably' (138). This is the voice of New York talking, with its unambiguous judgment of human behavior, the voice that Archer struggles against as he tries to see Ellen for the individual woman she is.

At the van der Luydens', Beaufort's booming personality makes Archer feel invisible – and this is 'humbling to his vanity.' Though Beaufort is intensely vulgar, he speaks the same language as Ellen, who comes from 'a wider world' than that 'bounded by the Battery and Central Park' (138). Archer of course compares his limited range invidiously to Beaufort's, and though invited to see Ellen again, he flees to Florida where May and her family are vacationing. While there, mentioning Ellen's name for the first time, 'he felt the color rise to his cheek' (145). But even more significant is his response to feeling deeply jealous of Beaufort's hold on Ellen, and the scenes his jealousy precipitates between himself and May. Beaufort's 'life, and a certain native shrewdness, made him better worth talking to than many men, morally and socially his betters' (138) – like Archer, who feels 'buried alive under his future,' with the 'taste of the usual. . . like cinders in his mouth' (140). Strained, uncertain, when he sees May in Florida after precipitously leaving New York and his thoughts of Ellen, he kisses her far too vehemently: 'The blood rose to her face and she drew back as if he had startled her. . . A slight embarrassment fell on them, and her hand slipped out of his' (142). He later presses her for an early marriage, and after bowing her head, she asks if he might be worried that he no longer loves her. Like Martin Boyne in *The Children* feeling exposed by Rose Sellars, he responds angrily, jumping up. But May urges him to be honest; Archer looks down, as does May, and she warns him not to betray a former mistress, if that is still who he feels tied to. Amazed at her 'courage and initiative,' he is also 'dizzy with the precipice they had skirted' (150), and finally disappointed that after such a remarkably generous and un-New York offer, May is merely herself, unchanged.

The next time Archer sees Ellen, at her grandmother's house, he is 'stung by her manner'; her friendliness 'might have been a studied assumption of indifference' (155) and when he meets her bedraggled and eccentric mother, *her* gratitude for having convinced Ellen not to sue for her divorce leaves Archer 'with considerable embarrassment.' Annoyed, he wonders, 'was there anyone. . . to whom Madame Olenska had not proclaimed his intervention in her private affairs?' (160) It is that very evening that the noose around Archer begins to tighten because he realizes the depth of his love for Ellen only hours before receiving a telegram from May that her family had agreed to move up the date of their wedding, as he had previously urged.

Ellen's mother has come to New York bearing a message from the Count asking for her to return and when Archer says her mother believes she will, this is the intensely dramatic result: 'A deep blush rose to her face and spread over her neck and shoulders. She blushed seldom and painfully, as if it hurt like a burn' (166). Indeed it *does* hurt for Ellen at this point to feel that *anyone* could believe something so cruel about her. While aware that Ellen begins talking about his upcoming marriage to change the subject 'from her own affairs,' Archer is desperate to keep 'a barrier of words' from dividing them as it did when they 'talked' about her divorce (167). He blushes when Ellen asks what might be wrong with his getting married sooner than conventions dictate, and when he implies that he is in love with her, and willing to give up May, Ellen pulls away from him, urging him not to make love to her: 'Too many people have done that.' He turns red again at 'the bitterest rebuke she could have given him' (169). Once again, he is left feeling trapped in the conventional and the ordinary. But the trap is deeper and more ironic than he could have imagined. Angrily, Ellen confesses that she gave up the idea of divorce only because of his persuasion, and as he watches 'the same burning flush creep up her neck to her face' she demands to know why he convinced her (170). Understanding now that he suspected that her husband's accusation was true, Ellen says she only feared 'to bring notoriety, scandal, on the family – on you and May. . . I had nothing to fear. . . absolutely nothing!' Crushed, Archer *lowers his head* and *covers his face*, and is unable through the subsequent heavy silence to 'raise his head from his hands' – he continues 'staring into utter darkness' (170). Ellen passionately explains that it is Archer's kindness, his hating 'happiness brought by disloyalty and cruelty and indifference' that swayed and reassured her, grounding her in a different reality (172). Ellen is immune to his pleading, and makes him blush when he says he doesn't understand her. Like so many other Wharton characters who imagine a scene of happiness only to be disappointed, Archer is face to face with an entirely unexpected reality:

> He turned away with a sense of utter weariness. He felt as though he had been struggling for hours up the face of a steep precipice, and now, just as he had fought his way to the top, his hold had given way and he was pitching down headlong into darkness.
> If he could have got her in his arms again he might have swept away her arguments, but she still held him at a distance by something inscrutably aloof in her look and attitude. . . At length he began to plead again (174).

Their conversation is cut short by a happy telegram from May to Ellen, announcing the moved-up date of the wedding, and the second half of the book will show us Archer's further plunge into the darkness he is just beginning to enter here.

The drama and importance of Ellen's blushing in this scene is not isolated. May's blushing is a highly significant aspect of her personality, and in fact we are first introduced to her in the novel in the act of blushing. During the Flower Song of *Faust*, when Marguerite sings 'M'ama!' (I am loved):

> a warm pink mounted to the girl's cheek, mantled her brow to the roots of her fair braids, and suffused the young slope of her breast to the line where it met a modest tulle tucker fastened with a single gardenia. She *dropped her eyes* to the immense bouquet of lilies-of-the-valley on her knee. . . (6) [my emphasis].

Newland quite understandably turns from this vision of innocence with 'satisfied vanity' (6), absolutely sure that May 'doesn't even guess what it's all about' (7). Her color stays high and her face grows 'rosy as the dawn' when Archer 'rescues' her at the opera by going to her family's box. Though married, May will be 'crimson to the eyes' when old Mrs Manson Mingott refers to the naked gods and goddesses on the ceilings of her summer house, and blush at the mention of children. Jaunty Mrs Mingott rather cruelly calls attention to May's embarrassment: 'Well, well, what have I said to make you shake out the red flag? Ain't there going to be any daughters – only boys, eh? Good gracious, look at her blushing again all over her blushes! What – can't I say that either?' (213) Those blushes are far too revealing about what disturbs May, but not everyone is willing to deal with their implications or even call attention to them. When Ellen later comes up at a family dinner, 'a sudden blush rose to young Mrs Archer's face; it surprised her husband as much as the other guests about the table' (259). Even worse, it does not subside at this dinner, but remains 'permanently vivid: it seemed to have a significance beyond that implied by the recognition of Madame Olenska's social bad faith' (259–60). Archer is set to wondering what 'was the meaning of May's blush when the Countess Olenska had been mentioned?' (261) And on the drive home, Archer still feels May 'enveloped in her menacing blush' (265). Nothing of any substance about this can pass between them, of course, and their dynamics recall Glennard and his wife in *The Touchstone* unable to discuss what is eating away at their marriage.

Whenever Ellen comes up, in fact, May seems to blush, and Archer does not openly respond to what she is feeling, but circles around it, or changes the subject. Admitting that she may have been unfair to Ellen, who she says 'seems to like to make herself conspicuous,' May has 'a deep blush on her cheeks' (315) and she twice flushes when the subject comes up of Ellen using Mrs Mingott's carriage to visit the now bankrupt Beauforts, a gesture as conspicuous as Archer's sitting by Ellen at the Opera. May is the one to reveal to Archer that the family has agreed to send Ellen back to Europe (but with an allowance to keep her independent of the count), and flushing, she lowers her eyes in the face of Archer's shocked stare. Near the end of the novel, when May plans a dinner as a send-off for Ellen, she blushes when Archer wonders why, his puzzlement leaving her embarrassed. Her final scene in the book, in which she circumlocutiously tells Archer that she is pregnant, leaves her as we saw her in the first chapter, with 'the blood flushing up to her forehead' (343). Pressed by Archer, she admits that she told Ellen she was pregnant weeks before, when she wasn't entirely certain, but she does not look away now, even though her 'color burned deeper' (343).

May, this creature of 'abysmal purity' (7) was hardly an individual for Archer – she is a perfect match, the best and most suitable (which he is sure he deserves), and her beauty is as much a reflection on him as it is something to admire in her: 'Archer was proud of the glances turned on her, and the simple joy of possessorship cleared away his underlying perplexities' (81). Even after his marriage when he longs for Ellen Olenska, May's beauty will kindle in him 'the glow of proprietorship that so often cheated him into momentary well-being' (210). Like George Darrow in *The Reef* imagining Anna Leath as his wife, and the public notice she will bring him, Archer feels that it 'was undoubtedly gratifying to be the husband of one of the handsomest and most popular married women in New York, especially when she was also one of the sweetest-tempered and most reasonable of wives' (207). New York, and his sinking into 'the whole chain of tyrannical trifles binding one hour to the next' (217), have made it impossible for Archer to allow May the freedom to become something different. She, too, is trapped, though she was apparently spared knowing what her husband does, that 'he had missed. . . the flower of life' (347). Musing over his wife's 'hard bright blindness, 'he realizes that as the perfect product of New York, she was 'so lacking in imagination, so incapable of growth, that the world of her youth had fallen into pieces and rebuilt itself without her ever being conscious of the change' (348).

After her death, Archer learns from his son Dallas that May had always trusted Archer because when she made the unspoken request that he give up Ellen, he did. It is important to note that even talking to his son, Archer is embarrassed discussing Ellen, and he feels that listening to confident strong Dallas, 'his sense of inadequacy and inexpressiveness increased' (358). It makes perfect sense that when he and Dallas are in Paris, he will not go up to Ellen's apartment, thinking 'it's more real to me here than if I went up' (361). The spirit of Napoleon pervades the final scenes – his statue tops the column at the Place Vendôme where Archer and his son are staying, and of course the Invalides, near which Ellen lives, is where Napoleon is buried. The shadow of that hero seems almost unnecessary – surely we can see how unheroic and limited in imagination Archer is, how chained to the ordinary, without the intrusion of the Emperor? Though Archer never saw Ellen in terms of her effect on his status, she was as unreal to him as May, even though she was not beautiful, not perfect. Ellen served as a fantasy of escape; Archer longing for a world where they could be together and words like 'mistress' didn't count, but Ellen had to sadly explain that such a world does not exist. And while she may have 'freed his thoughts and filled his imagination. . . Ellen could never give Archer the strength to act against his New York upbringing.'[57]

Like so many of Wharton's novels, *The Age of Innocence* has at its center the theme of 'the thwarted exit: the desire but the ultimate impossibility of achieving any real escape from the conditions which have formed one's life and character.'[58] Archer, Ellen and even May are all 'chained to their separate destinies' and concomitant with Wharton's loving recreation of a vanished world, and the delightful social comedy, is a terrible 'sense of waste and ruin' (243), even though Ellen, at least, has escaped New York, and Archer's children seem happier and freer. Waste and ruin are central in all of her classic works: Lily Bart dies, Charity Royall is trapped in a marriage that will forever limit her freedom and her growth; Ethan Frome and Mattie Silver are doomed to despair, Undine Spragg is like a female Tantalus, with food forever out of reach. As Viviane Forrester has pungently observed, these are tragedies of a hell without fire, but that much more infernal.[59]

Conclusion: Scenes of Shame

An understanding of shame in the context of affect theory allows us an entirely new entrance into Edith Wharton's fictional universe, highlighting what has been overlooked and clarifying what has often been misinterpreted or simply ignored. A novel like *The Glimpses of the Moon*, which has been classed as a thin and melodramatic failure, seems less flawed when one examined the ways in which Wharton portrays shame disrupting a marriage. *Sanctuary*, which is often mocked by critics for Kate Orme's decision to save a child she hasn't had, is more substantial when that decision can be seen in the context of an emotional reality hitherto unexplored. When looked at from the perspective of affect theory, *A Son at the Front* emerges in part as a fascinating exploration of shame in the wake of divorce and as it works out in new relationships created by remarriage. Wharton's stories about artists and writers have been considered romantic products of an amateur, but they reveal themselves to be insightful recreations of situations in which shame impacts a creative artist's life. A number of Wharton's portraits of men seem richer and more subtle than has previously been acknowledged or understood: George Darrow is a deeper figure when we consider the role of shame in his life.

We have seen in Chapter 1 that Wharton had limited insight into her own shame in the form of shyness. Was Wharton conscious of shame and the role it played in her fiction? Occasionally her characters reflect on shame, as Lily Bart does, aware of the ways in which she can use Percy Gryce's shyness to her advantage, or as Margaret Ransom does in 'The Pretext,' as when she observes what shame feels like. At other times, Wharton's characters openly address their shame, either denying that they feel it, or saying that they are beyond shame, as Dr Wyant does in *The Fruit of the Tree*, and Duncan Vyse in 'Full Circle.' Though a work like *The Touchstone* refers so consistently to shame and humiliation, and Wharton's fiction is so full of references to various forms of shame and to its physical manifestations, Wharton's understanding of shame as it affected individuals, relationships and society as a whole seems for the most part to have been intuitive. Its presence in her work may show how much a part of her identity it was, rather than her objective understanding of the phenomona she so clearly describes.

Despite changes in Wharton's subjects over the years – for example, the shift in the 1920s towards a concern with intergenerational misunderstandings – shame concerned Wharton throughout her career, and it appears in scenes that occur and reoccur with insistent regularity. Wharton's fictional universe is pervaded by shame and the imagery of exposure: glaring lights and glaring eyes. Exposure is a terrible possibility that haunts this fictional domain, sometimes through the seemingly inhuman nature of newspapers and magazines. Whether reading about themselves, like Ralph Marvell in *The Custom of the Country*, or those they love, like Nick and Susy Lansing in *The Glimpses of the Moon*, the news transmitted is frequently a source of humiliation. Wharton's fictional universe is one where parents often express indifference for their children, mock and deride them, and are unable to see them as distinct persons. Wharton's men and women frequently discover that the world is uglier, more corrupt and disgusting than they had believed, and the discovery leaves them in different ways ashamed.

Wharton's characters find out to their shame that they are far less important in the lives of those they love than they had imagined, like Halo Tarrant in *The Gods Arrive* or Lizzie West in 'The Letters.' Sometimes the disappointment comes with evidence of an actual betrayal, as for Anna Leath in *The Reef*. But if Wharton's men and women are often brought low, plunged into the torment of shame with the awareness of their own apparent and unsuspected insignificance, other equally painful discoveries await them. In most cases, those whom her characters respect, love, even adore, turn out again and again to be profoundly disappointing: flawed, shallow, untrustworthy. This drop from high expectation and hope, or even just contentment, into bitter reality is one of the most frequent trajectories in Wharton's fiction, the disappointment inevitably producing shame.

The specter of financial embarrassment or ruin haunts many of her characters, like Lily in *The House of Mirth*, and others are caught in various shameful struggles to survive, like the Bunner Sisters or Odo Valseca's mother in *The Valley of Decision*, or to succeed, like Hubert Granice in 'The Bolted Door.' A taste for luxury leads to shameful dependence and even a kind of social slavery which corrodes self-esteem, as experienced by Nick and Susy Lansing in *The Glimpses of the Moon*. Wharton's women are often ashamed of their appearance, whether due to fatigue, aging, or simply a lack of beauty, and live a life of invidious comparison, finding other women more attractive, more graceful, more seductive. The desire to be admired is a trap they often fall into, leaving them vulnerable to the shame of being ignored, as Undine experiences in *The Custom of the Country*. In a similar fashion, Wharton's men can be caught in critical assessments of their social inability, their lack of adventurousness, their lack of masculine drive to achieve – think of Vance in *Hudson River Bracketed*, Martin Boyne in *The Children* – and bruising self-contempt in response to any of these situations is guaranteed to produce a further deepening of shame. This oscillation between shame and contempt is a frequent movement throughout Wharton's fiction, men and women feeling the inferiority and exposure of shame, like Lawrence Selden in *The House of Mirth*, Vance Weston in *Hudson River Bracketed*, or Kate Clephane in *The Mother's Recompense*, then sneering at those around them in an effort to restore their balance. Her characters frequently express contempt for themselves or others in response to the shame they find unbearable to experience, but feel trapped by.

Confession rarely produces peace for restless souls in Wharton's oeuvre, but is instead a source of further humiliation; the need to confess is itself experienced with great, and sometimes justified, ambivalence, as for Stephen Glennard in *The Touchstone* and Kate Clephane in *The Mother's Recompense*. All too often, speech is 'impossible' – time after time, characters are unable to share what is inside of them because they dread the shameful exposure. Thus one common need to be held and comforted frequently goes unspoken, however deeply it is felt. Beyond that, her characters long not just for physical comfort, but for reassurance that they are indeed valuable, loved, worthwhile, like Pauline Manford in *Twilight Sleep* and Halo Tarrant in *The Gods Arrive*. The longing invariably goes unanswered, and the good scene of imagined and hoped for reunion turns bad.

Such scenes of shame continue to capture Wharton's artistic imagination because scenes of shame continued to dominate her life, in spite of her success, accomplishments, popularity. Achievement alone can never provide lasting escape from the prison of shame. That can happen only from within, by confronting and eventually assimilating internalized and magnified shame scenes. And this is in part what Wharton is attempting though her art: reworking her own shame in an effort to transcend it. Her characters succeed only insofar as she herself is successful in healing her own shame-wounded self; and her least shame-bound characters are, perhaps predictably, her writers and artists, who can sometimes find relief from the burden of their feelings.

The dramatic scenes of shame that consistently appear throughout Wharton's novels, novellas and short stories point to the very internalized scenes Wharton herself struggled with. We have evidence of how Wharton was treated with contempt in her family, ridiculed about her appearance, the way she spoke, indeed apparently everything about her. Many parents bring up their children believing that such ridicule is appropriate and even necessary to keep their children from becoming arrogant, but the impact of such constant belittling is almost inevitably a shame-based self. And because we learn to treat ourselves as we have been treated by the important figures in our life (parents or others), such patterns of relating become internalized, leading in part to an inner relationship in which contempt is a constant source of inner division. This dynamic appears throughout Wharton's fiction, and she certainly expressed a great deal of contempt and hauteur to others – often defensively, to hide her shame, but not solely for that purpose. The reminiscences of Wharton that point out her humor, her warmth, also describe the ways in which she could look down on others from an immense height. At those moments, it is as if Wharton has become her own mother: critical, aloof, superior, invincibly right, and the terrible distance between this god-like implacable figure and Wharton appears in many forms in her fiction. If the distance is bridged, it is often with one character superior, wiser, in control – consider the tableaux at the end of *The Touchstone, Sanctuary* and *The Gods Arrive*.

Wharton's relationship with Morton Fullerton may have opened her up to the passion her husband could not arouse, and her relationship with Walter Berry may have been a constant source of literary comfort, advice and inspiration – but both men were critical and in their own ways unreachable. Wharton's complaints about Berry's interest in younger women, and her sense of herself as just another dish in Morton Fullerton's ongoing sexual banquet, are profound and enduring disappointments that we see echoed in her fiction. And her fear of being humiliated about her divorce by gossip and press coverage may have roots in her broken engagement and the public notoriety she suffered thereby.

The dramatic scenes of shame in Edith Wharton's fiction can be illuminated through Tomkins' concept of scenes. Shame becomes internalized through imagery. It becomes stored in memory in the form of specific scenes, which comprise visual, auditory and kinesthetic features. These scenes are the internal representations of experienced events. When pervasive, shame scenes come to govern the self, capturing imagination, constricting personality. Wharton's fictional universe became the stage for re-enacting her own scenes of shame, scenes that have until now always been in the shadow because students of Wharton have lacked a perspective that brought them into the light. It is because affect theory and shame theory offer revolutionary insights into human motivation and behavior that they illuminate Wharton's fiction and life in such radical new ways.

Appendix: Discovering Edith Wharton at Pavillon Colombe

Wharton scholarship has seen some remarkable discoveries in the last fifteen years. Cynthia Griffin Wolff unearthed the erotic and incestuous Beatrice Palmato fragment in Wharton's papers at Yale. R.W.B. Lewis learned that Wharton's so-called 'Love Diary' was not about Walter Berry as previous scholars had speculated, but about the bisexual journalist Morton Fullerton. And a few years ago, several hundred letters of Wharton to Morton Fullerton mysteriously appeared in Paris, yielding major new insights into the affair and Wharton herself. As a junior Wharton scholar, then, I never expected to make a dramatic discovery about Wharton, but last summer, in France, that's just what happened to me.

Pavillon Colombe, Wharton's home in St Brice, less than half an hour north of Paris, was not as easy to find as I had thought. People in town kept saying *'Connais pas, m'sieu, Je suis désolé.'* It was stumbling on the Hôtel de Ville that yielded a map and an explanation: her street has only recently been renamed Rue Edith Wharton.

Pavillon Colombe presented an aloof, impersonal front to the street, but opened into a cool dark hall, beyond which, through French doors, stretched an elegant sunny parterre. A shy maid showed me into a salon bristling with beautiful paintings, tables, books and bibelots. A bell rang somewhere, and the maid said *'Madame la princesse vienne'* (the princess is coming). I stood there trying to figure out why the maid had used the subjunctive, feeling that I was already over my head. Waiting, I basked in the elegant simplicity of the rooms opening into one another, and each onto the parterre.

Princess Isabelle von Liechtenstein, the current owner of Pavillon Colombe, chicly dressed in black and grey, her hair in a chignon, came striding up through the garden. In a high piping voice, she was calling out to two bounding white afghans, as she strode past the peacocks. I was painfully aware of how sweaty the search in eighty degree weather had left me. Madame la princesse gave me a brisk but exceedingly gracious tour through both wings of the elegant eighteenth-century home which unfortunately bears no traces of Wharton's presence there. I trailed around with the Perrier she had given me which she said I could put down 'anywhere' – but every tabletop was marble!

'Which bedroom was Wharton's?' I asked, breathless.

I knew, of course, that Wharton wrote in bed, and as a writer, a Wharton scholar, a literary voyeur, I shamelessly wanted to intrude on her intimacy.

323

'She didn't work here,' the princess replied, and then she pointed out of the window before leaving me on my own for a while, after I promised not to take any pictures inside, and after she had relieved me of my Perrier bottle. I didn't understand the meaning of what she said until later, after drifting through the gardens. Though somewhat changed, they reveal Wharton's imprint: a peaceful, inviting progression of orderly spaces, light giving way to shadow, square space to round, grass to fountains. The aged gardener would have earned Mrs Wharton's approval, I think, when he asked me not to take pictures of hedges that were untrimmed.

Rejoining the princess, I asked again about where Wharton had worked, and she took me over. Across the garden immediately behind Pavillon Colombe is a dark and trellis-covered two-story structure – a sort of large brick cottage that I had first taken to be the servants' quarters. It is heavily shaded and even obscured by trees.

Oh no, the Princess assured me, unlocking the door, *this* was definitely where Wharton slept and worked; she had it built for those reasons. Pavillon Colombe was for her guests. But I'd never heard of this little house! The princess said she had absolutely no doubt she was right. When she bought Pavillon Colombe, Wharton's gardener's wife was still alive, and the woman insisted it was so. The princess was in the process of having the little house renovated and wanted to turn it into a memorial for Wharton.

I protested, 'But I've never read about this in any book about Wharton.' Madame la princesse smiled.

The interior was quite dilapidated and the narrow winding staircase a bit dangerous – but through the chaos of ladders, pails, boards and sheets, I made out four rooms, living room below, bedroom and study above. In the first room is a beautifully carved fireplace and mantel – imported from the United States, the princess believes. It looked like a house under construction – or demolition. But from the bedroom, I saw Pavillon Colombe as Wharton must have, elegant, shining, separate.

No one has written about the little house or photographed it, including R.W.B. Lewis. And even his former research assistants who claim that Lewis's prize-winning biography is full of factual errors do not mention the house in Wharton's garden.

The house set me wondering. Was its purpose romantic? Did she have it built so that she could entertain some unknown lover there – or maybe even Walter Berry? Was the little house an effort to save money? Did she live there when there were no guests at Pavillon Colombe because it was easier on her servants? The princess says Wharton's gardener's wife cried when she described Wharton's great kindness to her servants, and how much they loved her. Or did the house fulfill some deeper, and less practical need?

I turned to her fiction for answers. In Wharton's very first novel *The Valley of Decision*, there is a little house, a hunting lodge on the edge of the forest. The house, 'level with the marsh, and so open to noxious exhalations that a night's sojourn there may be fatal' has been used to poison a courtier who was lured there for a romantic escapade in the month of August, 'when the marsh breathes death.'[1] Odo, the future Duke of

Pianura, thinks the lodge looks 'like the abandoned corpse of pleasure.'[2] Here, however, safe from the scheming court of Pianura, the reigning Duchess can warn Odo that he is being carefully watched, and would be safer leaving the Duchy.

There is a little house in *Summer*, where Charity Royall and Lucius Harney meet to have their affair. The 'little old house' is halfway between the orderly and suffocating village of North Dormer, Charity's adoptive home, and the chaos of her birthplace, the Mountain, whose inhabitants live without the structures and restraints of civilization. This house, as Judith Fryer notes, 'seems to promise harmony, fulfillment, possibility.'[3] But the old 'tumble down place of once classical purity in a garden now running wild, with its front door off the hinges, is as vulnerable as Charity's body and as transitory as her youth.'[4]

Most interestingly of all, the first book Wharton wrote at Pavillon Colombe, *The Age of Innocence* has not one, but *two* little houses in it. The first is Ellen Olenska's charming and unusual house in a bohemian quarter of New York. Ellen's touch has turned it into 'something intimate, "foreign," subtly suggestive of old romantic scenes and sentiments.' The house exudes the scent of 'some far-off bazaar, a smell made up of Turkish coffee and ambergris and dried roses.'[5] Responding to Archer's clichéd compliments about her taste, Ellen says with feeling, 'I like the little house. . . the blessedness of its being here. . . and then, of being alone in it.'[6] It is interesting to note Ellen's phrasing, not 'my' little house, or 'this' little house, but 'the little house.'

Ellen's comment calls to mind a passage in *A Backward Glance*, written more than fifteen years later. Wharton describes finding Pavillon Colombe after the war, and her happiness in living there: 'The little house has never failed me since.'[7] Judith Fryer quotes this passage and wonders at that phrase, 'the little house' – by any estimation, Pavillon Colombe itself is not little.[8]

The second house in *The Age of Innocence* is on the van der Luydens' estate in upstate New York. Built in the mid-seventeenth century by the family's ancestor, '[t]he four-roomed stone house' contrasts in its simplicity with the main house, a gloomy ersatz Italian villa.[9] Newland has come here, you will remember, because Ellen fled New York. Entering the little house, his spirits rise 'with an irrational leap': 'The homely little house stood there, its panels and brasses shining in the firelight, as if magically created to receive them.'[10] It is here that Archer has one of his first powerful fantasies of Ellen embracing him, and the truth of his feelings for her almost erupts.

What Wharton's fictional little houses have in common is their being on the periphery, outside, in the middle – Ellen's house is unfashionably situated; van der Luyden's is rarely opened, the hunting-lodge is far from the Ducal palace, Charity's trysting house is half-way up the Mountain. The interactions that take place here are not entirely outside civilization, but they are outside the characters' typical frame of reference – places where sexual passion can be expressed (however dangerously), and the truth can be spoken, even if it is distressing or unsettling. They are outside the order and structure of society – but not so far out that they represent utter chaos. Even the hunting-lodge in *The Valley of Decision*, though primarily seen as negative, offers seclusion and an opportunity for honesty.

In her intriguing feminist meditation on the meaning of space in Edith Wharton's life and fictions, Judith Fryer notes that Wharton 'believed in harmony and proportion in human relationships, in domestic arrangements and in artistic expression.' At The Mount, the progression from room to room, passage to passage gives one 'a sense of "spaciousness and repose,"' each room acting as a small world by itself. The whole harmonious arrangement of rooms, halls, doorways, passages creates the scene of 'a kind of social interaction that is carefully planned, controlled, deliberate.' The gardens were designed with the same ideas in mind, and Fryer reads this house as 'a projection of an idealized self, a retreat, a series of protective enclosures.' Wharton's private quarters, for instance, would be inaccessible, because the stairway to The Mount's upper levels 'is deliberately set off from the public squares of the first floor.'[11]

Biographical reminiscences of Wharton are frequently studded with complaints about her scrupulous order. A typical example is this assessment by Madame Saint-René Taillandier, that Wharton's 'perfection of taste, extending to everything, even to the smallest details of her establishment, the arrangement of the flower-beds, the symmetry of the hedges, the neat ranks of trees in the orchard' was both chilling and intimidating.[12] There is indeed an aspect of Wharton's love of beauty and order that strikes us as more stifling than creative. At times she seems like her own heroine, Rose Sellars in *The Children*, whom she pinned down in this way:

> If Rose Sellars excelled in one special art it was undoubtedly that of preparation. All her life had been a series of adaptations, arrangements, shifting of lights, lowering of veils, pulling about of screens and curtains. No one could arrange a room half so well; and she had arranged herself and her life just as skillfully.[13]

Wharton – in her decorating – was not just a lover of order, but a *perfectionist*. The human toll of such a passion is high. Wharton's perfectionism – which Kaufman describes as 'an attempt to compensate for feeling inherently defective' – was one attempt to overcome her deeply rooted shame.[14] And ironically, she devoted herself to activities that were culturally stereotypic for women – gardening, decorating, being a hostess. When we read about Wharton's cold, aloof mother it is hard not to imagine that, in some ways, Wharton became like her mother, that is, adopted her cool surface as a defense against her own shame. Gilbert and Gubar note the symbolic function of each of her homes, and I think that however much time she spent there, the little house at Pavillon Colombe represents an escape from the world of perfection, the world of surfaces that she had both suffered in and attempted to conquer. What a relief it must have been to retreat across the parterre from the museum-like elegance of Pavillon Colombe to the little house, darker, less formal, more intimate, where she could write, where she could *relax* and enjoy what Ellen Olenska did: the blessedness of being all alone in it, no longer facing a world which she so often greeted stiffly and shyly.

Notes

PREFACE

1. Alfred Bendixen, 'Wharton Studies, 1986–87: A Bibliographic Essay,' *Edith Wharton Newsletter* vol. V, no. 1 (Spring 1988) 5.
2. *Edith Wharton, A Study of Her Fiction*, University of California Press: Berkeley, 1961, 107–8.
3. Annette Zilversmit, *Mothers and Daughters: The Heroines in the Novels of Edith Wharton*. Unpublished Dissertation, NYU 1980, 18.
4. Thomas J. Scheff, 'Shame and Conformity: The Deference-Emotion System,' *American Sociological Review*, 1988, vol. 53, 397.

CHAPTER 1: EDITH WHARTON'S TOUCHSTONE

1. Edith Wharton, *The Touchstone*, in *Madame de Treymes and Others: Four Novelettes* (Scribner's: New York, 1970) 36–37. Parenthetical page references in the chapter will be to this edition.
2. '"The Heart *Is* Insatiable": A Selection from Edith Wharton's Letters to Morton Fullerton, 1907–1915,' *The Library Chronicle of the University of Texas at Austin*, New Series no. 31 (1985) 11.
3. R.W.B. and Nancy Lewis, *The Letters of Edith Wharton* (New York: Scribner's, 1988) 153.
4. *Letters*, 16.
5. *Letters*, 145.
6. Gribben, 18.
7. Margaret McDowell, *Edith Wharton* (Boston: Twayne, 1976) 36; Carol Wershoven, *The Female Intruder in the Novels of Edith Wharton* (Rutherford, NJ: Fairleigh Dickinson University Press, 1982) 144; R.W.B. Lewis, *Edith Wharton, A Biography* (New York: Fromm, 1985) 95; Geoffrey Walton, *Edith Wharton, A Critical Interpretation* 2nd ed., rev'd. (Rutherford, NJ: Fairleigh Dickinson University Press, 1982) 40. My own article, 'Haunted by Shame: Edith Wharton's *The Touchstone*.' *The Journal of Evolutionary Psychology* 9.3.4 (August 1988) 287–296, was the first in-depth critical discussion of this vastly underrated work.
8. Francis J. Broucek, 'Shame and its Relationship to Early Narcissistic Developments,' *International Journal of Psycho-Analysis* 63 (1982) 369.
9. Donald L. Nathanson, 'Shaming Systems in Couples, Families, and Institutions,' in *The Many Faces of Shame*, ed. Donald L. Nathanson (New York: Guilford, 1987) 251.
10. Nathanson, 133.
11. Silvan Tomkins, 'Affect Theory,' in *Emotion in the Human Face*, 2nd. ed., ed. Paul Ekman (Cambridge, England: Cambridge University Press, 1982) 355–56.

12. 'Shame' in *The Many Faces of Shame*, ed. Donald L. Nathanson (New York: Guilford, 1987) 137.
13. Silvan Tomkins, 'Affect Theory,' 355.
14. 'Affect Theory,' 359.
15. *Affect, Imagery, Consciousness: The Negative Affects* (New York: Springer, 1963) vol. II, 118.
16. *Affect, Imagery, Consciousness*, vol. II, 118.
17. 'Affect Theory,' 378.
18. *Affect, Imagery, Consciousness*, vol. II, 156.
19. Afterward to *The Mother's Recompense*, by Edith Wharton (London: Virago, 1986), 389.
20. Gerhart Piers and Milton B. Singer, *Shame and Guilt: A Psychoanalytic and a Cultural Study*, for. Roy R. Grinker (New York: Norton, 1971) 59.
21. *Shame and Guilt: A Psychoanalytic and a Cultural Study*, 68.
22. *Shame and Guilt: A Psychoanalytic and a Cultural Study*, 99–100.
23. *Shame: The Power of Caring*, 2nd. ed. (Cambridge, Mass.: Schenkman, 1985); *The Psychology of Shame: Theory and Treatment of Shame-Based Syndromes* (New York: Springer, 1989).
24. *The Psychology of Shame*, 5.
25. *The Psychology of Shame*, 17–18.
26. *Shame*, 13.
27. *Shame*, 33.
28. *Shame*, 38.
29. *The Psychology of Shame*, 84. See Chapter 3 in that book for a discussion of internalization.
30. *The Psychology of Shame*, 86.
31. *Shame*, 8.
32. *Shame*, 9.
33. *Shame*, 9.
34. *Shame*, 66.
35. *Shame*, 104.
36. Edith Wharton, *The Touchstone*, in *Madame de Treymes and Others: Four Novelettes* (New York: Scribner's, 1970) 3. Parenthetical page references in the chapter are to this edition.
37. *Shame*, 75–6.
38. *Edith Wharton's Argument with America* (Athens: The University of Georgia Press, 1980) 17.
39. *Affect, Imagery, Consciousness*, vol. II, 224.
40. *Shame*, 21.
41. *A Feast of Words: The Triumph of Edith Wharton* (New York: Oxford University Press, 1977) 106.
42. Introduction to *Shame*, xv.
43. *Shame*, 9.
44. Introduction to *Shame*, xv–xvi.
45. *The Psychology of Shame*, 101–2.
46. *Affect, Imagery, Consciousness*, vol. II, 137.
47. *The Psychology of Shame*, 142.
48. *Affect, Imagery, Consciousness*, vol. II, 283.
49. *Affect, Imagery, Consciousness*, vol. II, 289.

50. R.W.B. Lewis, *Edith Wharton: A Biography* (New York: Fromm, 1980) 96.
51. *Affect, Imagery, Consciousness*, vol. II, 277.
52. *Edith Wharton's Argument with America*, 15.
53. Percy Lubbock, *Portrait of Edith Wharton* (New York: Appleton-Century, 1947) 103.
54. Irving Howe, 'Introduction: The Achievement of Edith Wharton,' in *Edith Wharton, A Collection of Critical Essays*, ed. Irving Howe (Englewood Cliffs, NJ: Prentice-Hall, 1962) 18.
55. Edith Wharton, *A Backward Glance* (New York: Scribner's, 1964) 238.
56. *Shame*, 47.
57. *Shame*, 61.
58. *A Backward Glance*, 26.
59. 'Life and I,' Wharton Archives, Beinecke Library, Yale University, New Haven, Conn., 33, 28.
60. *A Backward Glance*, 1.
61. 'Life and I,' 22.
62. 'Life and I,' 43, 5.
63. *A Feast of Words*, 30–31.
64. *A Backward Glance*, 43.
65. *The Psychology of Shame*, 48.
66. 'Life and I,' 12.
67. *A Backward Glance*, 35.
68. *A Feast of Words*, 295.
69. *Shame*, 78–81.
70. 'Life and I,' 5.
71. 'Life and I,' 6.
72. 28.
73. 3.
74. *A Backward Glance*, 20.
75. *A Backward Glance*, 46.
76. 'Life and I,' 24.
77. 'Life and I,' 14, 36, 29.
78. *A Backward Glance*, 68, 69.
79. *A Backward Glance*, 69.
80. *A Backward Glance*, 73.
81. *A Backward Glance*, 73.
82. 'Life and I,' 36.
83. 'Life and I,' 34–5.
84. *A Backward Glance*, 17.
85. *A Backward Glance*, 77.
86. *The Psychology of Shame*, 122–23.
87. 'Script Theory: Differential Magnification of Affect,' in *Nebraska Symposium on Motivation* (Lincoln: University of Nebraska Press, 1979) eds. H.E. Howe and R.A. Dienstbier, vol. 26, 205.
88. *A Backward Glance*, 88.
89. *A Backward Glance*, 78.
90. *The Psychology of Shame*, 40.
91. *A Backward Glance*, 49.

92. Hayley Delane in Wharton's novella 'The Spark' makes some similar negative comments about his family, calling his parents 'martinets on grammar.' See *Old New York*, intro. Marilyn French (London: Virago, 1985) 198.
93. 'Life and I,' 37.
94. *The Psychology of Shame*, 101.
95. *A Feast of Words*, 309. Wolff sees this 'choice' as partly a response to Wharton's overwhelming forbidden love of her father. I read it as a strategy for coping with the intolerable burden of her shame.
96. *Shame*, 24–28.
97. 'Life and I,' 37.
98. *A Backward Glance*, 39.
99. *A Backward Glance*, 121, 122.
100. *A Backward Glance*, 144.
101. *A Backward Glance*, 121.
102. Lewis, 46.
103. *Letters*, 391.
104. *Letters*, 32–3.
105. Lewis, 76.
106. Lewis, 35.
107. *A Backward Glance*, 113.
108. *A Feast of Words*, 48.
109. *The Psychology of Shame*, 24.
110. *A Backward Glance*, 171.
111. Lubbock, 97.
112. Logan Pearsall Smith, *Unforgotten Years* (Boston: Little, Brown, 1939) 264–65.
113. Smith, 266.
114. See Chapter 7 for a discussion of Lily Bart dealing with Percy Gryce's shame.
115. *A Backward Glance*, 104.
116. Gribben, 18.
117. McDowell, 23.
118. *A Backward Glance*, 108.
119. *A Backward Glance*, 114.
120. 'Walter Berry and the Novelists: Proust, James, and Edith Wharton,' *Nineteenth Century Fiction*, vol. 38, no. 4 (March 1984) 526.
121. Lewis, 48.
122. Lewis, 48–50.
123. McDowell, 21.
124. *Letters*, 135.
125. *Letters*, 189.
126. *Letters*, 158.
127. *Letters*, 138.
128. *Letters*, 219.
129. *Letters*, 150.
130. *Letters*, 12.
131. *Letters*, 152.
132. *Letters*, 162.

133. *Letters*, 208.
134. Lewis, 272.
135. Wolff, 226.
136. Wolff, 227.
137. Sandra M. Gilbert and Susan Gubar, *No Man's Land: The Place of the Woman Writer in the Twentieth Century*, vol. I: 'The War of the Words' (New Haven, Conn: Yale University Press, 1988) 191.
138. *Letters*, 216.
139. Introduction to *Shame*, xvi.
140. *A Feast of Words*, 16.
141. William Godwin, *Caleb Williams* (New York: Norton, 1977) ed., intro. David McCracken, 3.
142. Marilyn French, 'Muzzled Women,' *College Literature*, vol. xiv, no. 3 (1987) 229.

CHAPTER 2: FLIGHTS FROM SHAME

1. Cynthia Griffin Wolff, *A Feast of Words* (New York: Oxford University Press, 1976) 422.
2. R.W.B. Lewis, *Edith Wharton: A Biography* (New York: Fromm, 1985) 123.
3. Ibid.
4. *A Feast of Words*, 422.
5. *Edith Wharton's Argument with America* (Athens: University of Georgia Press, 1982) 20–21.
6. '"Sanctuary" – The Strength and Weakness of Edith Wharton's Latest Book,' *Munsey's Magazine*, XXXI (May 1904) 282.
7. Edith Wharton, *Sanctuary* in *Madame de Treymes and Others: Four Novelettes* (New York: Scribner's, 1970) 86. Parenthetical page references are to this edition.
8. *Affect, Imagery, Consciousness: The Negative Affects* (New York: Springer, 1963) vol. II, 224.
9. The male protagonist in *The Reef*, appearing in 1911, shares the same last name. Is there a connection? The earlier Darrow, a loyal friend, is also talented, but poor, and ashamed of his poverty (somewhat reminiscent of Glennard in *The Touchstone*): 'He belonged to no clubs, and wandered out alone for his meals, mysteriously refusing the hospitality which his friends pressed on him' (125). Perhaps what linked these characters for Wharton was the role of shame in their lives, and their lack of fulfillment: Darrow dies in *Sanctuary*, and in *The Reef*, he suffers the death of his pride and his hopes. It is Darrow in *Sanctuary*, however, who wishes that Kate's son didn't care so much for other people's opinions – just the opposite of Darrow in *The Reef*. See Chapter 3.
10. *Shame: The Power of Caring*, 2nd ed. (Cambridge, Mass.: 1985) 76–78.
11. The phrase appears in *The Touchstone*, and later in *The Mother's Recompense* where it becomes thematically central.
12. *Edith Wharton*, 123.

13. *A Backward Glance* (New York: Scribner's, 1985) 24. Wharton writes that this family story was inspiring for a future writer, hinting 'at regions perilous, dark and yet lit with mysterious fires, just outside the world of copy-book axioms, and the old obediences that were in [her] blood. . . .' Indeed, it not only inspired *Sanctuary*, but also *The Old Maid*. See Chapter 4.

14. Wharton herself scorned contemporary reviewers who found the ending positive and thought it 'ought to have ended tragically. *Ought to!*' she wrote in despair to a friend (quoted in Louis Auchincloss, 'Edith Wharton and Her Letters,' *The Hofstra Review*, vol. 2, no. 4 [Winter 1967] 6). Perhaps she was unaware that the novel's last page somewhat confuses the issue of Kate's renunciation. Kate seems to be – like Strether in *The Ambassadors* – determined to have emerged with nothing for herself. We are probably meant to see how meager her little treasure of pride is, but Wharton may not have had sufficient distance from Kate at this crucial point to successfully make clear that the ending *is* tragic, *is* steeped in loss, and is not transcendent. Perhaps we should read it as a cruel irony that Kate's only comfort is such a cold one – and as a number of critics have pointed out, Kate's level of self-awareness is not high.

15. 'Mothers, Daughters, and Incest in the Late Novels of Edith Wharton,' in *The Lost Tradition: Mothers and Daughters in Literature*, eds Cathy N. Davidson and E.M. Broner (New York: Ungar, 1980) 151–52.

16. *Edith Wharton*, 465; *Edith Wharton's Argument with America*, 163; Blake Nevius, *Edith Wharton: A Study of her Fiction* (Berkeley: University of California Press, 1961) 204.

17. Introduction to *The Mother's Recompense*, Edith Wharton (New York: Scribner's, 1986) xii.

18. *A Feast of Words*, 370.

19. Afterword to *The Mother's Recompense*, Edith Wharton (London: Virago, 1986) 349.

20. See *A Feast of Words*, 99–100.

21. French, 347.

22. Edith Wharton, *The Mother's Recompense* (New York: Scribner's, 1986) intro. Louis Auchincloss, 225. Parenthetical references will be to this edition.

23. *Affect, Imagery, Consciousness*, vol. II, 231.

24. The list echoes Wharton's 'strategies' in her correspondence with Fullerton. See Gribben, 18.

25. *The Psychology of Shame: Theory and Treatment of Shame-Based Syndromes* (New York: Springer, 1989) 121–24.

26. *Shame*, 55–60.

27. *Shame*, 101.

28. *Shame*, 38–39, 67–68.

29. See for instance *Edith Wharton's Argument with America*, 163.

30. *Shame*, 17.

31. French, 348.

32. 'Script Theory,' 208.

33. *Shame*, x.

34. Edith Wharton, *The Age of Innocence* (New York: Scribner's 1970) 335.
35. *On Shame and the Search for Identity* (New York: Harcourt, Brace & World, 1958) 249.
36. 'Affect Theory,' 377.
37. *Affect, Imagery, Consciousness*, vol. II, 186.
38. French, 348.
39. Louise K. Barnett, 'American Novelists and the "Portrait of Beatrice Cenci,"' *The New England Quarterly*, 53 (1980) 183.
40. Barnett, 172.
41. Lewis, 233.
42. Barnett, 183.
43. Auchincloss, ix.
44. *The Psychology of Shame*, 180.
45. *Affect, Imagery, Consciousness*, vol. II, 224–25.
46. If the book really *were* emotionally about incest, Wharton would not have made the theme so thunderingly obvious; the book is much more subtle than has previously been recognized. What is central is Kate's shame, and all that she has *hidden* – including this affair, which no one knows about at first. Kate is generally afraid of exposure (since she has so much to hide, both actions and feelings), and this pervasive fear is a response to her shame.
47. 'Affect Theory,' 385. See also *Affect, Imagery, Consciousness*, vol. I, 109, 127.
48. *A Feast of Words*, 372.
49. *Shame*, 76.
50. *Edith Wharton*, 142.
51. *Edith Wharton's Argument with America*, 158, 163.
52. Introduction to *The Mother's Recompense*, xi–xii.
53. *A Feast of Words*, 371–372.
54. Percy Lubbock, *Portrait of Edith Wharton* (New York: Appleton-Century, 1947) 196.

CHAPTER 3: DIVIDED BY SHAME

1. *Edith Wharton's Argument with America* (Athens: University of Georgia Press, 1980) 19.
2. Ammons, 20.
3. Ammons, 20.
4. Janet Goodwyn, *Edith Wharton: Traveller in the Land of Letters* (New York: St Martin's Press, 1990) 12.
5. Goodwyn, 13.
6. Edith Wharton, *A Backward Glance* (New York: Scribner's, 1985) 128.
7. Cynthia Griffin Wolff, *A Feast of Words: The Triumph of Edith Wharton* (New York: Oxford University Press, 1977), 91–2.
8. Carol Wershoven, *The Female Intruder in the Novels of Edith Wharton* (East Brunswick, NJ: Associated University Presses) 39. Parenthetical references in Ch. 3, 54–57, are to Edith Wharton, *The Valley of Decision* (New York: Scribner's, 1902).

9. Wershoven, 34.
10. Wershoven, 35.
11. Wershoven, 38.
12. Wershoven, 40.
13. Cynthia Griffin Wolff, *A Feast of Words: The Triumph of Edith Wharton* (New York: Oxford University Press, 1977) 138.
14. *Edith Wharton* (Minneapolis: University of Minnesota Press, 1961) 17.
15. *Edith Wharton: A Biography* (New York: Fromm, 1985) 164.
16. Edith Wharton, *Madame de Treymes*, in *Madame de Treymes and Others: Four Novelettes* (New York: Scribner's, 1970) 165. Parenthetical page references are to this edition.
17. Thérèse Bentzon, '*Le Monde où l'on s'amuse aux Etats-Unis.*' *La Revue de Deux Mondes*, 1 November 1906, 200, quoted in Robert Morss Lovett, *Edith Wharton* (New York: McBride, 1925) 21.
18. 'Edith Wharton' in *Edith Wharton: A Collection of Critical Essays*, ed. Irving Howe (Englewood Cliffs, NJ: Prentice-Hall, 1962) 65–66.
19. Elizabeth Ammons, 'Fairy-Tale Love and *The Reef*,' in *Edith Wharton*, ed., intro. Harold Bloom (New York: Chelsea, 1986) 39.
20. 'On *The Reef*: A Letter,' in *Edith Wharton, A Collection of Critical Essays*, ed. Irving Howe (Englewood Cliffs, NJ: Prentice-Hall, 1962) 148–150.
21. For various assessments of *The Reef*'s 'Jamesian qualities,' see among others, E.K. Brown, 'Edith Wharton: The Art of the Novel' in Howe; *A Feast of Words*, 208; Lawson 64–65; McDowell 62; *Edith Wharton's Argument with America*, 81.
22. James, 148.
23. Wershoven, 96–97; Ammons, 'Fairy-Tale Love and *The Reef*,' 43; *A Feast of Words*, 219; Henry J. Friedman, 'The Masochistic Character in the Work of Edith Wharton,' *Seminars in Psychiatry*, vol. 5, no. 3 (August 1973), 323–24.
24. Edith Wharton, *The Reef*, intro. Louis Auchincloss (New York: Scribner's, 1970), 3. Parenthetical references will be to this edition.
25. See, for instance, *A Feast of Words*, 209, and Blake Nevius, *Edith Wharton: A Study of Her Fiction* (Berkeley: University of California Press, 1961) 141 for fairly representative views of Darrow at this point.
26. *The Psychology of Shame: Theory and Treatment of Shame-Based Syndromes* (New York: Springer, 1989) 179.
27. *Affect, Imagery, and Consciousness* (New York: Springer, 1963) vol. II 141.
28. Mary Suzanne Schriber, *Gender and the Writer's Imagination: From Cooper to Wharton* (Lexington: The University Press of Kentucky, 1987), agrees with Nevius that Darrow gets off too easily in the book; Elizabeth Ammons, Cynthia Griffin Wolff and Carol Wershoven view Darrow as caddish, hypocritical, peevish, cowardly. These readings simplify Wharton's subtle characterization of Darrow.
29. Richard H. Lawson, *Edith Wharton* (New York: Ungar, 1977) 63.
30. Auchincloss, viii-ix; Mary Suzanne Schriber, 173–75.
31. James W. Gargano, 'Edith Wharton's *The Reef*: The Genteel Woman's Quest for Knowledge,' *Novel* 10 (1976) 43.
32. See, for instance, Geoffrey Walton, *Edith Wharton: A Critical Interpret-*

ation, 2nd. edition, rev'd. (Rutherford, NJ: Fairleigh Dickinson University Press, 1982) 75, and Gargano 42.

33. *Affect, Imagery, Consciousness*, vol. II, 136.
34. *Shame: The Power of Curing*, 2nd ed. (Boston: Schenkman, 1985) 11.
35. Louis Auchincloss, 'Edith Wharton and her New Yorks,' in Howe, 41.
36. *Affect, Imagery, Consciousness*, vol. II, 238.
37. *Shame*, 9.
38. *Affect, Imagery, Consciousness*, vol. II, 145–46.
39. *Shame*, 8.
40. *The Psychology of Shame*, 35.
41. See Ammons, note 4.
42. See for instance Gargano, Moira Maynard, 'Moral Integrity in *The Reef*: Justice to Anna Leath,' *College Literature*, vol. xiv, no. 3, 1987, 285–95, and Lawson 61–62. I find these positive readings ingenious but quite unconvincing, and they seem to exemplify William Dean Howells' remark to Wharton that Americans want a happy ending to their tragedies. One does not have to see Anna 'growing towards greater emotional freedom,' or deepening in *any* way to do her justice.
43. *Shame*, 11.
44. *Affect, Imagery, Consciousness*, vol. II, 283–89.
45. See R.W.B. Lewis, 326 and Walton, 77.
46. *Shame*, 9.
47. *Affect, Imagery, Consciousness*, vol. II, 119.
48. *Edith Wharton*, 325.
49. *A Feast of Words*, 219.
50. See, for instance, the description of Darrow's reflections on 167 (Chapter XVII) in which the phrases 'his pride was humbled,' 'he was ashamed,' and 'humiliating distinctness' quickly follow each other, or part of a scene between Sophy and Darrow in Chapter XX (202–5) where Darrow flushes, Sophy lowers her eyes and blushes twice, and he feels 'a passing pang of shame,' 'more ashamed' and like telling Sophy 'the shame' of his not having thought of her at all, in response to *her* feelings striking him 'down to a lower depth of self-abasement.'
51. See, for one, *A Feast of Words*, 208, for a different view.
52. Walton, 76, *A Feast of Words*, 229.
53. *The Female Intruder in the Novels of Edith Wharton*, 109.
54. 'Henry James's Heiress: The Importance of Edith Wharton,' in Howe, 83; Louis Auchincloss, 'Edith Wharton' (Minneapolis: University of Minnesota Press, 1961), 38; Howe, 13; Nevius 217; *The Novel of Manners in America* (New York: Norton, 1974) 128.
55. Lewis, 484; *Edith Wharton's Argument with America*, 187.
56. Introduction to *The Children* (London: Virago, 1985) v.
57. Introduction to *The Children*, v.
58. *A Feast of Words*, 381.
59. Nevius, 212.
60. *A Feast of Words*, 385.
61. Edith Wharton, *The Children*, intro. Marilyn French (London: Virago, 1985) 270. Parenthetical references are to this edition.
62. *A Feast of Words*, 384.

63. Donald Nathanson, 'The Shame/Pride Axis,' in *The Role of Shame in Symptom Formation*, ed. Helen Block Lewis (Hillsdale, NJ: Erlbaum, 1987) 190.
64. *Edith Wharton* (Boston: Twayne, 1976) 121.
65. *Shame*, 78.
66. Schriber, 166, 169.
67. 'Shame – the "Sleeper" in Psychopathology,' intro. to *The Role of Shame in Symptom Formation*, 4.
68. *An Ideal Husband*, in *Oscar Wilde: Plays*, (London: Penguin, 1971), 194.
69. Introduction to *The Children*, xii.
70. *Edith Wharton's Argument with America*, 174.
71. Wershoven, 115. Cynthia Griffin Wolff somewhat similarly simplifies the relationship between Darrow and Anna Leath when she suggests that 'nothing stands between them' (*A Feast of Words*, 215) when they meet at Givré. As noted in the preface, shame's very ubiquity sometimes makes it hard to recognize.
72. *Affect, Imagery, Consciousness*, vol. II, 138.
73. 'Shaming Systems in Couples, Families and Institutions,' in *The Many Faces of Shame*, ed. Donald L. Nathanson, (New York: Guilford, 1987) 249.
74. *Affect, Imagery, Consciousness*, vol. II, 136.
75. Silvan Tomkins, 'Affect Theory,' in *Emotion in the Human Face*, 2nd ed. (Cambridge: Cambridge University Press, 1982) 385.
76. Judith Sensibar's paper presented at the Edith Wharton Society meeting at The Mount in 1987 asserted that Boyne suffers 'homosexual panic' and that Rose, then Judith and eventually Zinnie act as 'screens' preventing him from acknowledging his true sexuality. Her claim in large part rests on the picnic scene which she completely misreads because of her lack of insight into shame dynamics. Sensibar says that 'Martin's desire for the male face becomes an envious identification with male lust not loss,' but he is not at all envious of Dobree in this scene. Nor does Boyne feel *attracted* to Dobree (and thus to boyish Judith, and in other words, men), but *exposed*, as when he looks into Judith's eyes. Tomkins' Ch. 17 in *Affect, Imagery, Consciousness*, vol. II closely examines the taboo on looking.
77. Nathanson, 'Shaming Systems,' 250.
78. 'Shaming Systems,' 253.
79. *Shame*, 84.
80. The tone recalls Wharton's letters to Fullerton.
81. Wershoven, 119, for one.
82. *A Feast of Words*, 385.
83. Wershoven, 115.
84. *A Feast of Words*, 384. While I do not agree with all its premises, I find Cynthia Griffin Wolff's reading of this novel a wonder of sensitivity and insight.
85. *A Feast of Words*, 387.
86. Walton, 160.
87. *Edith Wharton's Argument with America*, 176–77.
88. *Edith Wharton's Argument with America*, 183.

89. *A Feast of Words*, 384.
90. *Edith Wharton*, 122.
91. *A Feast of Words*, 382.
92. *A Feast of Words*, 384.
93. *A Feast of Words*, 381–82.
94. Howe, 15.

CHAPTER 4: SHAMEFUL RELATIONS

1. Edith Wharton, *Bunner Sisters, Madame de Treymes and Others: Four Novelettes* (New York: Scribner's 1970) 226. Parenthetical references are to this edition.
2. *Edith Wharton's Argument with America* (Athens: University of Georgia Press, 1982) 14.
3. Introduction to *Old New York*, by Edith Wharton (London: Virago, 1985) vii–viii.
4. Edith Wharton, *Old New York* (London: Virago, 1985), intro. Marilyn French, 23.
5. Edith Wharton, *The Old Maid*, in *Old New York* (London: Virago, 1985) 77.
6. *Edith Wharton: A Biography* (New York. Fromm, 1985) 435.
7. Cynthia Griffin Wolff, *A Feast Of Words*, 357.
8. *The Collected Short Stories of Edith Wharton*, ed. R.W.B. Lewis (New York: Scribner's, 1968) vol. II, 620.
9. *The Collected Short Stories of Edith Wharton*, ed. R.W.B. Lewis (New York: Scribner's 1968) vol. II, 807.
10. *Edith Wharton: A Biography*, 75.
11. Margaret McDowell, *Edith Wharton* (Boston: Twayne, 1976) 53.
12. Edith Wharton, *The Fruit of the Tree*, intro. Marilyn French (London: Virago, 1984), 53–4.
13. Vance Weston will suffer similar feelings of social inferiority. See Chapter 6.
14. Susan Brownmiller, *Femininity* (New York: Fawcett Columbine, 1984) 212.
15. *The Female Intruder in the Novels of Edith Wharton* (Rutherford, NJ: Fairleigh Dickinson University Press) 126.
16. Wershoven, 127.
17. *Edith Wharton's Argument With America*, 53.
18. Wershoven, 130.
19. *Edith Wharton: A Biography*, 233.
20. *The Collected Short Stories of Edith Wharton* vol. I, 636.
21. Jenijoy La Belle, *Herself Beheld: The Literature of the Looking Glass* (Ithaca: Cornell University Press, 1988) 59.
22. *The Novel of Manners in America* (New York: Norton, 1972) 128; *Edith Wharton: A Biography*, 445; *Edith Wharton*, 41, 142; *Edith Wharton: A Critical Interpretation* 2nd ed., rev'd. (Rutherford, NJ: Fairleigh Dickinson University Press, 1982) 147; *Edith Wharton: A Study of Her Fiction* (Berkeley: University of California Press, 1961) 196.

23. Cynthia Griffin Wolff, *A Feast of Words: The Triumph of Edith Wharton*, 347.

24. Simon Rosedale's pride in walking with Lily after the *tableaux vivants* is echoed by Strefford's pride in being seen at an art exhibition walking with Susy. The similarity shows Wharton still aware of the importance of shame in social relations, and the powerful desire of social outsiders to appear victorious.

25. Readers of Wharton coming to this novel for the first time will probably be put off by the brittle and unconvincing style of the first chapter, but it is hard to miss that subsequent chapters are written differently. Wharton seems to have wanted to hook her readers in the first chapter, after which she doubtless felt she could write as she pleased – the writing in the rest of the novel is not so weak and 'meretricious,' as Blake Nevius notes, 197. A passage sometimes quoted to indicate the supposed 'decline' of Wharton's writing appears in Chapter XVII, when Susy sees Ursula Gillow in Paris: 'But on the threshold a still more familiar figure met her: that of a lady in exaggerated pearls and sables, descending from an exaggerated motor, like the motors in magazine advertisements, the huge arks in which jewelled beauties and slender youths pause to gaze at snow-peaks from an Alpine summit' (195). In context, this passage is imbued with Susy's disgust for the monotony and predictability of the fashionable world she feels trapped in after Nick has left her. The exaggeration and one-dimensionality are crucially hateful elements of a world that has nothing new to offer her. If she marries Strefford, she knows the 'future by heart' (193). It is one where individuality does not really count.

26. Edith Wharton, *The Glimpses of the Moon* (New York: Appleton, 1922) 15. Parenthetical references are to this edition.

27. Elizabeth Ammons (*Edith Wharton's Argument with America*, 161) says that Nick suddenly develops scruples about what their plan is bringing them, but an understanding of the working of shame in the text yields a more subtle reading of his motives.

28. Edith Wharton, *Old New York* (London: Virago, 1985) 175. Parenthetical references are to this edition.

29. Edith Wharton, *Old New York* (London: Virago Press, 1985) 271. Parenthetical references are to this edition.

30. *The Female Intruder in the Novels of Edith Wharton*, 131.

31. Edith Wharton, *Twilight Sleep* (New York: Appleton, 1927) 49. Parenthetical references are to this edition.

32. In Pauline's schedule, Wyant is always referred to as 'A,' which leads Nona and Jim to call him 'Exhibit A' or 'Exhibit.' Both nicknames are subtly degrading, the first implying that he is evidence of a crime, the second, that he is superannuated. Each one, for all its mocking affection, would keep alive Wyant's grievances against Pauline and the shifting social order that has swept him aside.

33. Wershoven, 135.

34. Wershoven, 135.

35. Wershoven, 135.

36. Wershoven, 134.
37. *Edith Wharton: A Critical Interpretation*, 151.
38. Edith Wharton, *The Age of Innocence* (New York: Scribner's, 1970) 146.
39. Edith Wharton, *The Age of Innocence* (New York: Scribner's, 1970) 39.
40. *Gender and the Writer's Imagination: From Cooper to Wharton* (Lexington: University Press of Kentucky, 1987) 169.
41. *Gender and the Writer's Imagination*, 169.
42. *Edith Wharton: Traveller in the Land of Letters* (New York: St Martin's, 1990) 95.

CHAPTER 5: THE WAR FICTION

1. R.W.B. and Nancy Lewis, *The Letters of Edith Wharton* (New York: Scribner's, 1989) 331.
2. R.W.B. Lewis, *Edith Wharton: A Biography* (New York: Fromm, 1985) 370.
3. Elizabeth Ammons, *Edith Wharton's Argument with America* (Athens: University of Georgia Press, 1980) 170, 128.
4. Lewis, 379–80.
5. Peter Buitenhuis, 'Edith Wharton and The First World War,' *American Quarterly* xviii (Fall 1966) 494.
6. David Clough, 'Edith Wharton's War Novels: A Reappraisal,' *Twentieth Century Literature* xix (1973) 2.
7. *A Feast of Words: The Triumph of Edith Wharton* (New York: Oxford, 1977) 260, 263, 267.
8. *Edith Wharton's Argument with America*, 157.
9. Shari Benstock, *Women of the Left Bank: Paris, 1900–1940* (Austin: University of Texas Press, 1986) 39.
10. Patricia Plante, 'Edith Wharton and the Invading Goths' *Midcontinental American Studies Journal* (Fall 1964) 22.
11. *Edith Wharton* (Minneapolis: University of Minnesota Press, 1961) 26.
12. *French Ways and Their Meanings* (New York: Appleton, 1919) 149.
13. *Letters*, 331.
14. *Edith Wharton*, 27.
15. Frederic Tabor Cooper, 'A Clear-cut Gem of War Fiction,' *The Publishers' Weekly*, 28 Dec. 1918, 2033; 'The Marne,' *Times Literary Supplement*, 19 Dec. 1918, 642; E.F.E., 'The Indomitable Spirit of America,' *Boston Evening Transcript*, 21 Dec. 1918, Pt. 3, 6; 'Mrs Wharton's Story of the Marne,' *The New York Times*, 8 Dec. 1918, sec. VII, 1.
16. *Edith Wharton: Etude Critique* (Paris: Librairie E. Droz, 1935) 65–6.
17. *Edith Wharton: A Study of Her Fiction* (Berkeley: University of California Press, 1961) 163, 165.
18. Buitenhuis, 497.
19. Lewis, 422; Wolff, 295; Ammons, 129.
20. *The Marne*, Edith Wharton (New York: Appleton, 1918) 10. Parenthetical page references in the text are to this edition.
21. Gershen Kaufman, *Shame: The Power of Caring* 2nd. ed. (Cambridge, Schenkman, 1985) 27.

22. *Edith Wharton* (New York: McBride, 1925) 15.
23. Patricia Plante, 23.
24. Margaret McDowell, *Edith Wharton* (Boston: Twayne, 1976) 112.
25. *Shame*, 25.
26. Plante, 21.
27. *Shame*, 9.
28. *Shame*, 9.
29. 'Edith Wharton's War Novels: A Reappraisal,' *Twentieth Century Literature* xix (1973), 4.
30. Plante, 18.
31. Plante, 19.
32. *Edith Wharton: A Biography*, 394.
33. Edith Wharton, 'Coming Home,' *The Collected Short Stories of Edith Wharton*, vol. II, ed., intro. R.W.B. Lewis (New York: Scribner's, 1968) 230. Parenthetical references are to this edition.
34. Edith Wharton, 'Writing a War Story,' *Collected Stories*, vol. II, 360. Parenthetical references are to this edition.
35. Edith Wharton, *A Backward Glance* (New York: Scribner's, 1964) 147.
36. Henry James, 'Broken Wings,' *In The Cage and Other Tales* (New York: Norton, 1969) ed., intro. Morton Dauwen Zabel, 360.
37. *A Backward Glance*, 180–84.
38. Edith Wharton, 'The Refugees,' *Collected Stories*, vol. II, 570. Parenthetical references are to this edition.
39. McDowell, *Edith Wharton*, 109.
40. Edith Wharton, *A Son at the Front* (New York: Scribner's, 1923) 8. Parenthetical references are to this edition.
41. *Letters*, 166.
42. *Edith Wharton*, 110.
43. *Edith Wharton*, 113.
44. Anonymous, 'Mrs Wharton's Novel,' *Springfield Republican* 15 October 1923, 6.
45. 'Edith Wharton's War Novels: A Reappraisal.' 9.
46. *Creative Awakening: The Jewish Presence in Twentieth Century American Literature, 1900–1940s* (New York: Greenwood, 1987) 151.
47. *A Feast of Words*, 436.
48. *Edith Wharton*, 112.
49. *A Backward Glance*, 355.

CHAPTER 6: WRITERS AND ARTISTS

1. Blake Nevius, *Edith Wharton: A Study of Her Fiction* (Berkeley: University of California Press, 1961) 20–22.
2. Nevius, 21.
3. Margaret McDowell, *Edith Wharton* (Boston: Twayne, 1976) 43.
4. Robert Calder notes that Somerset Maugham, even more productive than Wharton, would allow nothing to interfere with a similar schedule he 'followed for all of his adult life.' See his *Willie: The Life Of W. Somerset Maugham* (New York: St Martin's Press, 1989) 65 and

passim. Maugham does not seem to have been criticized for his work habits, as Wharton was.

Her friend Kenneth Clark saw Wharton differently than Nevius: 'It is often said that she never spoke about her work, and almost pretended not to be a writer at all; but this was not my experience. When she came down from her morning's writing – she always wrote in bed till about eleven o'clock – she would talk, as we walked in the garden, about the problems of language and construction that had confronted her that morning, and one realised what a master-craftsman she was. *Another Part of the Wood: A Self-Portrait* (New York: Harper & Row, 1974), 205.

5. Nevius, 21.
6. Penelope Vita-Finzi, *Edith Wharton and the Art of Fiction* (New York: St Martin's, 1990) 101. I received a copy of this fascinating book just as I was finishing my own. Vita-Finzi is one of the few writers on Wharton to discuss Wharton's artists in depth and to acknowledge their significance and success. Her discussion of the role of marriage for artists is especially interesting.
7. Geoffrey Walton, *Edith Wharton: A Critical Interpretation*, 2nd ed., rev. (Rutherford, NJ: Fairleigh Dickinson University Press, 1982) 170.
8. Afterword to *Hudson River Bracketed*, by Edith Wharton (New York: Signet, 1962) 410.
9. Ralph Marvell's writing will be discussed in Chapter 7, Nick Lansing's is discussed in Chapter 4.
10. 'The Bolted Door,' *The Collected Short Stories of Edith Wharton*, vol. II, ed., intro. R.W.B. Lewis (New York: Scribner's, 1968) 5, 10. Parenthetical references are to this edition.
11. *Collected Stories*, vol. II, 102.
12. *Collected Stories*, vol. I, 189.
13. *Collected Stories*, vol. I, 259.
14. *Edith Wharton and the Art of Fiction*, 116.
15. *Collected Stories*, vol. I, 656.
16. *Collected Stories*, vol. II, 306.
17. *Collected Stories*, vol. II, 707.
18. *Collected Stories*, vol. II, 178.
19. *A Feast of Words*, 204.
20. *Collected Stories*, vol. I, 247.
21. *The House of Mirth* (New York: Scribner's, 1969) 55.
22. *Collected Stories*, vol. I, 397.
23. *Collected Stories*, vol. 1, 617.
24. *Collected Stories*, vol. II, 450.
25. *The Age of Innocence* (Scribner's: New York, 1970) intro. R.W.B. Lewis, 200.
26. *The Letters of Edith Wharton*, eds. R.W.B. and Nancy Lewis (New York: Scribner's, 1989) 411.
27. '"The Heart *Is* Insatiable": A Selection from Edith Wharton's Letters to Morton Fullerton, 1907–1915,' *The Library Chronicle of the University of Texas at Austin*, New Series no. 31, 14.
28. *Collected Stories*, vol. II, 118.

29. *A Feast of Words*, 157.
30. *Collected Stories*, vol. I, 29.
31. *Collected Stories*, vol. I, 173.
32. *Collected Stories*, vol. I, 663.
33. Edith Wharton, *The Custom of the Country* (London: Penguin, 1987) intro. Anita Brookner, 112.
34. *Collected Stories*, vol. II, 74.
35. *Collected Stories*, vol. I, 276.
36. *Collected Stories*, vol. I, 440.
37. *Collected Stories*, vol. II, 459.
38. *Collected Stories*, vol. I, 250.
39. *Collected Stories*, vol. II, 209.
40. *Collected Stories*, vol. II, 452.
41. *Collected Stories*, vol. I, 67.
42. *Letters*, 12.
43. *Collected Stories*, vol. I, 106.
44. Afterward to *The Gods Arrive* (London: Virago, 1987) 445.
45. Edith Wharton, *Hudson River Bracketed* (New York: Scribner's, 1985) 104. Parenthetical references are to this edition.
46. *Gender and the Writer's Imagination: From Cooper to Wharton* (Lexington: University Press of Kentucky, 1987) 164.
47. Merle A. Fossum and Marilyn J. Mason, *Facing Shame: Families in Recovery* (New York: Norton, 1989) 144.
48. *Facing Shame*, 145.
49. Afterward to *Hudson River Bracketed*, by Edith Wharton (New York: Signet, 1962) 410.
50. *The Novel of Manners in America* (New York: Norton, 1974) 134.
51. *Edith Wharton: A Biography* (New York: Fromm International, 1985) 491.
52. Edith Wharton, *The Gods Arrive* (London: Virago, 1987) 187.
53. See Wharton's letter to the editor of *The Greater Inclination* in *The Letters of Edith Wharton* (New York: Scribner's, 1988) eds. R.W.B. & Nancy Lewis, 36.
54. Edith Wharton, *The Gods Arrive* (London: Virago, 1987) 349.
55. Afterward to *Hudson River Bracketed*, 413.
56. *The Female Intruder in the Novels of Edith Wharton* (East Brunswick, NJ: Associated University Presses, 1982) 137.
57. Afterward to *Hudson River Bracketed*, 413.
58. *Edith Wharton* (Boston: Twayne, 1976) 132–33.
59. Afterward to *Hudson River Bracketed*, 412–13.
60. *Edith Wharton: A Critical Interpretation* (Rutherford, NJ: Fairleigh Dickinson University Press, 1982) 2nd ed., rev., 176.
61. Edith Wharton, *The Gods Arrive* (London: Virago, 1987) 38. Parenthetical references are to this edition.
62. Margaret McDowell, *Edith Wharton*, 135.
63. The town's name is perfectly chosen. An *oubli* in French is an act of forgetfulness, oversight or omission – such acts will characterize how Vance treats Halo. The name also conjures up the expression *oubli de*

soi, self-effacement or self-negation, which is Halo's painful stance there.

64. *A Feast of Words*, 395; *Edith Wharton: A Biography*, 493.
65. Afterward to *The Gods Arrive*, 452.
66. *Edith Wharton's Argument with America*, (Athens: University of Georgia Press, 1982) 196.
67. Geoffrey Walton, *Edith Wharton: A Critical Interpretation*, 2nd ed., rev'd. (Rutherford, NJ: Fairleigh Dickinson University Press, 1982) 181, 182.
68. *The Novel of Manners in America*, 138–139.
69. *Letters*, 445.
70. *A Feast of Words*, 395.
71. Afterword to *Hudson River Bracketed*, 410.
72. *Hudson River Bracketed*, 239.
73. *Hudson River Bracketed*, 297.
74. *Hudson River Bracketed*, 376–77.
75. *Hudson River Bracketed*, 387, 536.
76. *A Feast of Words*, 105.

CHAPTER 7: WHARTON'S CLASSICS

1. Edith Wharton, *The House of Mirth* (New York: Scribner's, 1969) 15. Parenthetical references are to this edition.
2. *The Psychology of Shame: Theory and Treatment of Shame-Based Syndromes* (New York: Springer, 1989) 103.
3. *Gossip* (New York: Knopf, 1985) 175.
4. *The Psychology of Shame*, 49.
5. *Feminist Dialogics: A Theory of Failed Community* (Albany: State University of New York Press, 1988) 97–8.
6. *The Female Intruder in the Novels of Edith Wharton* (Rutherford, NJ: Fairleigh Dickinson University Press, 1982) 50.
7. *The Psychology of Shame*, 125.
8. In 'Edith Wharton's Challenge to Feminist Criticism,' *Studies in American Fiction*, vol. 16, no. 2, 238, Julie Olin-Ammentorp rather simplistically explains his actions as 'understandable in the context of a social system that views him primarily as a workhorse.' That observation lacks depth, and is utterly inadequate in explaining the violent *intensity* of his feelings.
9. Act II, Scene iv, lines 169–70.
10. Baldesar Castiglione, *The Book of the Courtier*, trans. Charles S. Singleton (New York: Anchor, 1959) 43.
11. *The Female Intruder in the Novels of Edith Wharton*, 58.
12. *Feminist Dialogics*, 108.
13. *Feminist Dialogics*, 100.
14. *A Feast of Words: The Triumph of Edith Wharton* (New York: Oxford University Press, 1976) 230.
15. Margaret McDowell, *Edith Wharton* (Boston: Twayne, 1976) 76.

16. Edith Wharton, *The Custom of the Country* (London: Penguin, 1989) 118. Parenthetical References are to this edition.
17. *The Female Intruder in the Novels of Edith Wharton*, 68.
18. *The Psychology of Shame*, 101.
19. *A Feast of Words*, 247.
20. *Gender and the Writer's Imagination: From Cooper to Wharton* (Lexington: University Press of Kentucky, 1987), 176, 177.
21. *The Psychology of Shame*, 101.
22. *Edith Wharton: A Biography* (New York: Fromm, 1985) 350.
23. *A Feast of Words*, 236.
24. *Edith Wharton: A Biography*, 349.
25. *Edith Wharton: A Biography*, 349.
26. *A Feast of Words*, 238.
27. Edith Wharton, *The House of Mirth* (New York: Scribner's, 1969) 7.
28. Edith Wharton, *Ethan Frome* (New York: Scribner's, 1970) 3. Parenthetical references are to this edition.
29. *The Psychology of Shame*, 200.
30. *Edith Wharton* (New York: Ungar, 1977) 68.
31. *A Feast of Words*, 171.
32. *See* 'Cold Ethan and "Hot Ethan,"' *College Literature* (1987) vol. xiv, no. 3.
33. Kristin Olson Lauer, introduction to *Edith Wharton: An Annotated Secondary Bibliography*, Kristin Olson Lauer and Margaret P. Murray (New York: Garland, 1990) xxii.
34. Edith Wharton, *Summer* (New York: Scribner's, 1966) 7. Parenthetical page references are to this edition.
35. Introduction to *Summer*, by Edith Wharton (New York: Berkeley, 1981) xl.
36. Janet Goodwyn, *Edith Wharton: Traveler in the Land of Letters* (New York: St Martin's Press, 1990) 78.
37. Cynthia Griffin Wolff, *A Feast of Words*, 280.
38. *The Psychology of Shame*, 21.
39. *A Feast of Words*, 275.
40. *Felicitous Space: The Imaginative Structures of Edith Wharton and Willa Cather* (Chapel Hill: The University of North Carolina Press, 1986) 199.
41. *Felicitous Space*, 197.
42. *Edith Wharton*, 70.
43. *Felicitous Space*, 195.
44. Marcia Westkott, *The Feminist Legacy of Karen Horney* (New Haven, Conn.: Yale University Press, 1986) 173.
45. *A Feast of Words*, 305.
46. See 'Is This Indeed "Attractive"?: Another Look at the "Beatrice Palmato" Fragment.' *The Journal of Evolutionary Psychology* 11.1 & 2 (March 1990), 1–8.
47. Edith Wharton, Beatrice Palmanto fragment, Wharton Archives, Beinecke Library, Yale University.
48. D.H. Lawrence, *Studies in Classic American Literature* (New York: Penguin, 1977) 12.
49. *The Female Intruder in the Novels of Edith Wharton*, 77.
50. R.W.B. Lewis, introduction to *The Age of Innocence*, by Edith Wharton (New York: Scribner's, 1970) ix.

51. *The Female Intruder in the Novels of Edith Wharton*, 92.
52. *Novelists in their Youth* (London: Chatto & Windus, 1990) 189.
53. *The Female Intruder in the Novels of Edith Wharton*, 78.
54. *The Female Intruder in the Novels of Edith Wharton*, 91.
55. Carol Wershoven, *The Female Intruder in the Novels of Edith Wharton*, 34.
56. *The Female Intruder in the Novels of Edith Wharton*, 22.
57. Carol Wershoven, *The Female Intruder in the Novels of Edith Wharton*, 90.
58. John Halperin, *Novelists in their Youth*, 165.
59. Preface to *La Récompense d'une Mère* (*The Mother's Recompense*) by Edith Wharton (Paris: Flammarion, 1986), trans. Louis Gillet, 15.

NOTES TO THE APPENDIX

1. Edith Wharton, *The Valley of Decision* (New York: Scribner's, 1902) vol. 1, 266.
2. *The Valley of Decision*, vol. 1, 312.
3. *Felicitous Space: The Imaginative Structures of Edith Wharton and Willa Cather* (Chapel Hill: University of North Carolina Press, 1986), 197.
4. Fryer, 198.
5. Edith Wharton, *The Age of Innocence* (New York: Scribner's, 1970) 71–72.
6. *The Age of Innocence*, 74.
7. Edith Wharton, *A Backward Glance* (New York: Scribner's, 1985) 363.
8. Fryer, 172. One could argue that a pavillion is by definition a little house, but having tramped through Pavillon Colombe, I find it comparable in size (if not in grandeur of setting) to Wharton's home in Lenox, The Mount.
9. *The Age of Innocence*, 131.
10. *The Age of Innocence*, 134.
11. Fryer, 71–4.
12. Cyril Connolly and Jerome Zerbe, *Les Pavillons: French Pavillions of the Eighteenth Century* (New York: Macmillan, 1962) 62.
13. Edith Wharton, *The Children*, intro. Marilyn French (London: Virago, 1985) 38.
14. *The Psychology of Shame: Theory and Treatment of Shame-Based Syndrome* (New York: Springer, 1989), 101.

Selected Secondary
Bibliography

AUCHINCLOSS, Louis *Edith Wharton* (Minneapolis, University of Minnesota Press, 1961).

AUCHINCLOSS, Louis 'Edith Wharton and Her Letters,' *Hofstra Review* 2 (Winter 1967) 1–7.

AMMONS, Elizabeth *Edith Wharton's Argument with America* (Athens: University of Georgia Press, 1980).

AMMONS, Elizabeth 'Fairy-Tale Love and *The Reef*,' *American Literature* 47 (1976) 615–28.

BARNETT, Louise K. 'American Novelists and the "Portrait of Beatrice Cenci,"' *The New England Quarterly*, 53 (1980) 168–83.

BAUER, Dale *Feminist Dialogics: A Theory of Failed Community* (Albany: State University of New York Press, 1988).

BENDIXEN, Alfred 'Wharton Studies, 1986–87: A Bibliographic Essay.' *Edith Wharton Newsletter* 5.1 (Spring 1988) 5.

BENSTOCK, Shari *Women of the Left Bank: Paris, 1900–1940* (Austin: University of Texas Press, 1986).

BROUCEK, Francis J. 'Shame and its Relationship to Early Narcissistic Developments,' *International Journal of Psycho-Analysis* 63 (1982) 369–378.

BROWN, E.K. 'Edith Wharton,' in Irving Howe (ed.) *Edith Wharton: A Collection of Critical Essays* (Englewood Cliffs, NJ: Prentice-Hall, 1962) 62–72.

BROWN, E.K. *Edith Wharton: Etude critique* (Paris: Librairie E. Droz, 1935).

BUITENHUIS, Peter 'Edith Wharton and The First World War,' *American Quarterly* xviii (Fall 1966) 493–505.

CLOUGH, David 'Edith Wharton's War Novels: A Reappraisal,' *Twentieth Century Literature* xix (1973) 1–14.

TABOR COOPER, Frederic 'A Clear-cut Gem of War Fiction,' *The Publishers' Weekly*, 28 Dec. 1918, 2033.

EDEL, Leon 'Walter Berry and the Novelists: Proust, James and Edith Wharton,' *Nineteenth Century Literature* 38.4 (March 1984) 514–528.

FOSSUM, Merle A. and Marilyn J. Mason, *Facing Shame: Families in Recovery* (New York: Norton, 1989).

FRIEDMAN, Henry J. M.D., 'The Masochistic Character in the Work of Edith Wharton,' *Seminars in Psychiatry* 53 (August 1973) 313–329.

FRENCH, Marilyn 'Muzzled Women,' *College Literature* Edith Wharton Issue 14.3 (1987) 219–229.

FRYER, Judith *Felicitous Space: The Imaginative Structures of Edith Wharton and Willa Cather* (Chapel Hill: The University of North Carolina Press, 1986).

GARGANO, James W. 'Edith Wharton's *The Reef*: The Genteel Woman's

Quest for Knowledge,' *Novel: A Forum on Fiction* 10 (1976) 40–48.

GILBERT, Sandra M. and Susan Gubar, *No Man's Land: The Place of the Woman Writer in the Twentieth Century*, vol. I: 'The War of the Words' (New Haven, Conn.: Yale University Press, 1988).

GOODWYN, Janet *Edith Wharton: Traveller in the Land of Letters* (New York: St Martin's Press, 1990).

GRIBBEN, Allen '"The Heart *Is* Insatiable": A Selection from Edith Wharton's Letters to Morton Fullerton, 1907–1915,' *The Library Chronicle of the University of Texas at Austin*, New Series no. 31 (1985) 7–18.

HARAP, Louis J. *Creative Awakening: The Jewish Presence in Twentieth Century American Literature*, 1900–1940s (New York: Greenwood, 1987).

HALPERIN, John *Novelists in their Youth* (London: Chatto and Windus, 1990).

HOWE, Irving 'The Achievement of Edith Wharton,' intro. to Irving Howe (ed.) *Edith Wharton: A Collection of Critical Essays* (Englewood Cliffs, NJ: Prentice-Hall, 1962) 1–18.

KAUFMAN, Gershen *Shame: The Power of Caring*, 2nd ed. (Cambridge, Mass.: Schenkman, 1985).

KAUFMAN, Gershen *The Psychology of Shame: Theory and Treatment of Shame-Based Syndromes* (New York: Springer, 1989).

LA BELLE, Jenijoy *Herself Beheld: The Literature of the Looking Glass* (Ithaca: Cornell University Press, 1988).

OLSON LAUER Kristin and Margaret Murray, *Edith Wharton: An Annotated Secondary Bibliography* (New York: Garland, 1990).

LAWRENCE, D.H. *Studies in Classic American Literature* (New York: Penguin, 1977).

BLOCK LEWIS, Helen 'Shame – the "Sleeper" in Psychopathology,' intro. to Helen Block Lewis (ed.), *The Role of Shame in Symptom Formation* (Hillsdale, NJ: Erlbaum, 1987) 1–28.

LEWIS, R.W.B. and Nancy Lewis, *The Letters of Edith Wharton* (New York: Scribner's, 1989).

LEWIS, R.W.B *Edith Wharton: A Biography* (New York: Fromm, 1985).

MORSS LOVETT, Robert *Edith Wharton* (New York: McBride, 1925).

LUBBOCK, Percy *Portrait of Edith Wharton* (New York: Appleton-Century, 1947).

MERRYL LYND, Helen *On Shame and The Search for Identity* (New York: Harcourt, Brace & World, 1958).

MCDOWELL, Margaret *Edith Wharton* (Boston: Twayne, 1976).

MAYNARD, Moira 'Moral Integrity in *The Reef*: Justice to Anna Leath,' *College Literature*, vol. xiv, no. 3, 1987 285–95.

NATHANSON, Donald 'The Shame/Pride Axis,' in Helen Block Lewis (ed.) *The Role of Shame in Symptom Formation* (Hillsdale, NJ: Erlbaum, 1987) 183–205.

NATHANSON, Donald 'Shaming Systems in Couples, Families and Institutions,' in Donald L. Nathanson (ed.) *The Many Faces of Shame* (New York: Guilford, 1987) 246–270.

NEVIUS, Blake *Edith Wharton: A Study of her Fiction* (Berkeley: University of California Press, 1961).

OLIN-AMMENTORP, Julie 'Edith Wharton's Challenge to Feminist

Criticism,' *Studies in American Fiction* 16.2 (Autumn 1988) 237–244.

PIERS, Gerhart and Milton Singer, *Shame and Guilt: A Psychoanalytic and a Cultural Study*, for. Roy R. Grinker (New York: Norton, 1971).

PLANTE, Patricia 'Edith Wharton and the Invading Goths,' *Midcontinental American Studies Journal* (Fall 1964) 18–23.

SCHEFF, Thomas J. 'Shame and Conformity: The Deference-Emotion System,' *American Sociological Review* 53 (1988) 395–405.

SCHRIBER, Mary Suzanne *Gender and the Writer's Imagination: From Cooper to Wharton* (Lexington: The University Press of Kentucky, 1987).

PEARSALL SMITH, Logan *Unforgotten Years* (Boston: Little, Brown, 1939).

MEYER SPACKS, Patricia *Gossip* (New York: Knopf, 1985).

TINTNER, Adeline 'Mothers, Daughters and Incest in the Late Novels of Edith Wharton,' in Cathy N. Davidson and E.M. Broner (eds), *The Lost Tradition: Mothers and Daughters in Literature* (New York: Ungar, 1980) 147–56.

TOMKINS, Silvan 'Affect Theory,' in Paul Ekman (ed.), *Emotion in the Human Face*, 2nd ed. (Cambridge, England: Cambridge University Press, 1982) 353–395.

TOMKINS, Silvan *Affect, Imagery, Consciousness: The Positive Affects*, Vol. 1 (New York: Springer, 1962).

TOMKINS, Silvan *Affect, Imagery, Consciousness: The Negative Affects*, Vol. 2 (New York: Springer, 1963).

TOMKINS, Silvan 'Script Theory: Differential Magnification of Affect,' in H.E. Howe and R.A. Dienstbier (eds.) *Nebraska Symposium on Motivation* 26 (Lincoln: University of Nebraska Press, 1979) 201–236.

TUTTLETON, James *The Novel of Manners in America* (New York: Norton, 1974).

VITA-FINZI, Penelope *Edith Wharton and the Art of Fiction* (New York: St. Martin's Press, 1990).

WALTON, Geoffrey *Edith Wharton: A Critical Interpretation*, 2nd ed., rev'd. (Rutherford, NJ: Fairleigh Dickinson University Press, 1982).

WERSHOVEN, Carol *The Female Intruder in the Novels of Edith Wharton* (Rutherford, NJ: Fairleigh Dickinson University Press, 1982).

WESTKOTT, Marcia *The Feminist Legacy of Karen Horney* (New Haven, Conn.: Yale University Press)

GRIFFIN WOLFF, Cynthia *A Feast of Words: The Triumph of Edith Wharton* (New York: Oxford University Press, 1977).

GRIFFIN WOLFF, Cynthia 'Cold Ethan and "Hot Ethan,"' *College Literature* Edith Wharton Issue 14.3 (1987) 230–45.

ZILVERSMIT, Annette *Mothers and Daughters: The Heroines in the Novels of Edith Wharton*. Unpublished Dissertation, NYU 1980.

Index